Britten's Musical Language

Blending insights from linguistic and social theories of speech, ritual, and narrative with music-analytic and historical criticism, *Britten's Musical Language* offers fresh perspectives on the composer's fusion of verbal and musical utterance in opera and song. It provides close interpretative studies of the major scores (including *Peter Grimes*, *Billy Budd*, *The Turn of the Screw*, *War Requiem*, *Curlew River*, and *Death in Venice*) and explores Britten's ability to fashion complex and mysterious symbolic dramas from the interplay of texted song and a wordless discourse of motives and themes. Focusing on the performative and social basis of language, rather than on traditional notions of textual "expression" in vocal music, Philip Rupprecht pursues topics such as the role of naming and hate speech in *Peter Grimes*; the disturbance of ritual certainty in the *War Requiem*; and the codes by which childish "innocence" is enacted in *The Turn of the Screw*.

PHILIP RUPPRECHT is Associate Professor of Music at Brooklyn College and the Graduate Center, City University of New York. He has written on twentieth-century music in a number of journals and is a contributor to *The Cambridge Companion to Benjamin Britten* (1999).

Music in the Twentieth Century

GENERAL EDITOR Arnold Whittall

This series offers a wide perspective on music and musical life in the twentieth century. Books included range from historical and biographical studies concentrating particularly on the context and circumstances in which composers were writing, to analytical and critical studies concerned with the nature of musical language and questions of compositional process. The importance given to context will also be reflected in studies dealing with, for example, the patronage, publishing, and promotion of new music, and in accounts of the musical life of particular countries.

Published titles

The Music of John Cage
James Pritchett
0 521 56544 8

The Music of Ruth Crawford Seeger
Joseph Straus
0 521 41646 9

The Music of Conlon Nancarrow
Kyle Gann
0 521 46534 6

The Stravinsky Legacy
Jonathan Cross
0 521 56365 8

Experimental Music: Cage and Beyond
Michael Nyman
0 521 65297 9 (hardback)   0 521 65383 5 (paperback)

The BBC and Ultra-Modern Music, 1922–1936
Jennifer Doctor
0 521 66117 X

The Music of Harrison Birtwistle
Robert Adlington
0 521 63082 7

Four Musical Minimalists: La Monte Young, Terry Riley, Steve Reich, Philip Glass
Keith Potter
0 521 48250 X

Fauré and French Musical Aesthetics
Carlo Caballero
0 521 78107 8

The Music of Tōru Takemitsu
Peter Burt
0 521 78220 1

The Music and Thought of Michael Tippett: Modern Times and Metaphysics
David Clarke
0 521 58292 X

Serial Music, Serial Aesthetics: Compositional Theory in Post-War Europe
M. J. Grant
0 521 80458 2

Britten's Musical Language
Philip Rupprecht
0 521 63154 8

Britten's Musical Language

Philip Rupprecht

CAMBRIDGE
UNIVERSITY PRESS

PUBLISHED BY THE PRESS SYNDICATE OF THE UNIVERSITY OF CAMBRIDGE
The Pitt Building, Trumpington Street, Cambridge, United Kingdom

CAMBRIDGE UNIVERSITY PRESS
The Edinburgh Building, Cambridge CB2 2RU, UK
40 West 20th Street, New York, NY 10011-4211, USA
477 Williamstown Road, Port Melbourne, VIC 3207, Australia
Ruiz de Alarcón 13, 28014 Madrid, Spain
Dock House, The Waterfront, Cape Town 8001, South Africa

http://www.cambridge.org

First published 2001

Printed in the United Kingdom at the University Press, Cambridge

Typeface Adobe Minion 10.5/13.5pt   *System* QuarkXPress™   [SE]

A catalogue record for this book is available from the British Library

Library of Congress Cataloguing in Publication data

Rupprecht, Philip Ernst.
Britten's musical language / Philip Rupprecht.
    p.   cm. – (Music in the 20th century)
Includes bibliographical references (p.) and index.
ISBN 0 521 63154 8
1. Britten, Benjamin, 1913–1976 – Criticism and interpretation. I. Music in the
twentieth century.
ML410.B853 R8 2001
780′.92–dc21   2001035577

ISBN 0 521 63154 8 hardback

To my parents

Contents

Acknowledgments

Ideas for this book grew from conversations with Robert P. Morgan and Allen Forte, and I have been grateful for their continued interest in its progress. For advice on the proposal, and for stimulating responses to each chapter as I wrote, I owe many thanks to Arnold Whittall. For reminding me that *Curlew River* belonged in this study and, more generally, for encouragement over the years, I am indebted to Mervyn Cooke. Several friends were good enough to critique parts of the manuscript: Arved Ashby, Paul Buechler, Tim Gura, Ellie Hisama, Ruth Longobardi, Sandra MacPherson, Jairo Moreno, Caroline Rupprecht, Joe Straus, and Lloyd Whitesell. For many other kindnesses I thank Joe Bartolozzi, Ben Bierman, Vanessa Brown, John Ferri, Mary Francis, Nancy Hager, Harry Haskell, Stephen Hinton, Carol Oja, Janet Schmalfeldt, and Marcel Van Rootselaar. Paul Banks and his successor as Librarian at the Britten-Pears Library, Jenny Doctor, graciously hosted my two visits to Aldeburgh; during the second, Kieron Cooke showed me rare footage of the 1964 *Curlew River*. At all stages of this project, I have benefited from the advice of Penny Souster, my unfailingly patient and helpful editor at Cambridge University Press; for her copy-editing expertise, I thank Ann Lewis. I began this book as a Faculty Fellow of the Wolfe Institute for the Humanities at Brooklyn College in 1997–98, and it was completed during a sabbatical leave in 2000–01. Michael Kinney and David Smey provided splendid assistance with the music examples; the Research Foundation of the City University of New York granted generous financial support. My final thank you is addressed to Cathy Shuman, my most partial critic.

1 Introduction: Britten's musical language

Music, like speech, begins in the moment of utterance. As the cardinal act of performance, utterance is an externalizing of musical ideas in the physicality of vocal or bodily gesture. Utterance is a process of putting forth, emitting – an unbroken flow of sound emanating from a distinct source. Something is revealed, made manifest; utterance, to recall the word's origins, is a bringing "out."[1] For the listener, utterance names an experience of being addressed directly by the performer or (less directly) the composer. By a process both interpersonal and reciprocal, performer and listener make contact. A musical thought moves from "in here" to "out there," so establishing a chain of communication. Both music and speech impinge on the world in the living present of the utterance, whether as independent systems of address, or as paired discourses, acting together in the medium of song. And it is this composite musical utterance – a bringing forth of words and music meaningfully and vividly, as one – that is so clear in all of Benjamin Britten's work.

The phrase "musical language" in my title engages the moment of utterance in two distinct ways. In a first, metaphorical sense, Britten's music is itself a kind of wordless language – a characteristic way of presenting and shaping the interplay of essentially musical ideas (themes, rhythms, motives, or keys) within an unfolding discourse. The sounds of music, on this reading, themselves have properties usually ascribed to speech – expression, eloquence, a rhetorical force. Useful though the familiar metaphor of music as language may be, Britten's music acts as a musical language in a second, more literal sense. In opera and song, music and words encounter one another directly. The fusion of these two media in lyric and dramatic genres, or in sung liturgical ritual, is succinctly expressed in English as a "setting" of words *to* music, and yet the process is by no means a simple one (behind that "to" lies mystery). This musical language is anything but metaphorical, for its powers of communication depend on the material presence of words. At the same time, these words are tied, in their musical setting, to a precisely coordinated role in a composite utterance. My aim throughout this book will be to make the familiar interplay of music and words strange again and to reflect on the intricacies of their fusion in the single moment of utterance.

That the distinctive element in Britten's music is bound up with some quality of utterance (rather than specific details of technique) was a point

Ex. 1.1: Vocal utterance in a lyric setting: "Goddess, excellently bright," *Serenade*

quickly sensed by the composer's early listeners. Henry Boys, writing in 1938, singles out Britten's gift for "sincere lyrical expression of simple moods," a perception echoed by the composer's stated preference for "clear and clean" orchestral textures, and "perfect clarity of expression." Erwin Stein, in 1953, remarks simply that "Britten's way of expression is direct."[2] The music's spontaneity of utterance, Stein feels, is a matter of text setting, in particular the balanced and supple shift between "natural" speech rhythms and a lyric stylization called for by details of poetic imagery. In the Ben Jonson "Hymn" of the *Serenade* (Ex. 1.1), as Stein notes, "the voice announces the words with such lucidity, and the colora-tura on the first syllable of 'ex-cellently' is so 'bright', that the poem appears to enhance the music as much as the music the poem" (1953b: 156). Here is the "sensibility, quick as a fish's fin, to a poetic image" that Edward Sackville-West praises in the *Serenade*, and a clear example of Britten's tendency to place the burden of musical expression in the vocal line itself, not in the accompaniment.[3]

In the early reception of Britten's works, utterance in the texted music is understood largely in terms of what Stein calls "musical diction." Questions of prosody and the "natural" speech rhythms of words – topics on which Britten's music was both praised and damned – remain central for his early critics, as too does his response, through word painting, to the semantic plane of language.[4] But such perspectives, however much they hint at a distinctive tone of musical "speech" – with or without actual words – fall short as a general model of musical utterance. If analyses of Britten's lyric songs tend to dwell, in a recognizably New-Critical vein, on diction and imagery, words on the operatic stage demand a different response. Texted dramatic utterances are *actions* – words and music forged, in the heat of a dramatic situation, into single, "multimedia" events. Hobson's "Peter Grimes!" call (Ex. 1.2) – to cite only the first two sung words of the opera *Peter Grimes* – is mechanical in rhythm and monotone in pitch, yet these features are not based in imagery or prosody but in social relations. This "Peter Grimes!" call is an order, an utterance addressed to Peter with a specifically juridical force in the courtroom, as he is called to give evidence. To recognize that all utterance is, to an extent,

Ex. 1.2: Vocal utterance as dramatic act: hailing the protagonist in *Peter Grimes*

social and interpersonal in nature, is to understand language as political. Utterance engages not only the linguistic ability to describe or signify (though the name "Peter Grimes!" does of course *refer*), but also linguistic powers of coercion. "To *say* something," as J. L. Austin suggests, "is to *do* something" (12; Austin's emphasis). Language, at the moment of utterance itself, is acting as much as signifying.

Returning the emphasis, as I will do throughout this book, to language as act or performance will help define a new set of questions for the role of words *in* music. The discussion raises issues that go beyond the specific case of Britten. If everyday speech can be "doing" as well as saying, does the same hold for words in a musical context? Do acts of song – a category that might include all sung vocal utterance, whether lyric or dramatic – draw on the coercive powers of conventional (i.e. non-musical) acts of speech? Does the social and institutional force of, say, a promise or a prayer function in *musical* promises or prayers, and if so, is this specifically linguistic agency acting independently, or is it supplemented, inflected, or projected by "musical" features of the utterance (melody, harmony, texture, and so on)? If the drama of opera may be said to spring precisely from an intensified enactment of everyday experience, in a more or less heightened vocal utterance, one might well appeal beyond traditional opera-critical concerns – motives, music as a response to "character," genre – to consider operatic drama primarily in terms of individual utterances in specific social situations. Operatic speech, for all its patent artifice, obeys laws familiar from the social world beyond the stage.

Chapter-length readings of four of Britten's operas are central to this book, and my interpretations of musical drama engage various developments in recent opera criticism, not least a renewed concern with codes of narrative and performance, and with representations of the ideological and psychological subject.[5] Little work has appeared, though, towards what might be called a performative understanding of operatic speech –

one that incorporates, say, the insights of linguistic philosophers into spoken utterances.[6] More frequently, utterance in vocal music is still treated largely in terms of textual "expression," locating an originary meaning that is primarily verbal, while downplaying the possibility that music might, as Nicholas Cook puts it, "participate in the construction of that meaning" (1998: 115). Even where music's powers to complement or contest a verbal meaning are acknowledged, Cook adds, discussion is conceptually loose.[7] But there are good reasons, as I will claim, to resist the familiar critical trope that pits words against music as separate media, and it is via the fused and composite notion of the utterance – rather than by an oppositional view of separate strands of the complex single event – that I approach the coexistence of text and music in Britten's case.

The view that linguistic utterance is actional as well as symbolic is common to a range of mid-twentieth-century theoretical positions, from anthropological accounts of ritual performance in tribal societies to J. L. Austin's philosophically tinged theory of the "speech-act" as the foundational unit of verbal exchange and Bakhtin's concept of "speech genres" – forms of discourse peculiar to a given sphere of human activity.[8] The polarity is clear in Saussure's classic distinction between the system of "language" and the event of "speech" as an "individual act of the will and the intelligence" (14). In Saussure's analysis, however, linguistic meaning is sought primarily on the semiotic level of the sign,[9] and Bakhtin, for one, attacks earlier linguists for "weaken[ing] the link between language and life" by excluding language's "addressivity" ("the quality of turning to someone"), and concentrating only on syntax and semantics.[10] The actional, operational view of language, on the other hand, is rooted in the contingency of situation, the primacy of exchange in verbal encounters, and the speaker's ability to accomplish things with utterance.

The first recorded concepts of music encompass a fusion of words and pitches, yet later music history has emphasized only an interplay of "master" and "servant" arts.[11] The tradition is apparent, for instance, in Christoph Bernhard's mid-seventeenth-century distinction between a *stylus theatralis* in which "language is the absolute master of music" and a *stylus gravis* in which the reverse applies (110). Such hierarchical oppositions are called into question by Bernhard himself, in the idea of a style in which "language and music are both masters" – the grandly named *stylus luxurians communis* – and yet Bernhard can be frustratingly brief on the central question of how this sharing of powers might be accomplished: "one should represent speech in the most natural way possible . . . render joyful things joyful, sorrowful things sorrowful, swift things swift, slow things slow" (111). The idea here that musical utterance effects one-to-one representation of some univocal linguistic object (joyful things) seems quaintly mechanical as an account of musical speech, limited as it is to essentially grammatical concepts of subject and predicate.[12] Bernhard comes closer to detailing the moment of utterance itself with the mention of musical settings of "questions," which "according to common usage, are ended a step higher than the penultimate syllable":

> Musical repetition occurs when two successive utterances are similar in subject matter. Musical repetition a step higher occurs in connection with two or more successive questions, when their words correspond in subject matter [*Gleichheit der Worte an der Materie*], and when the last seems to be more forceful than the first. (111)

The passage exceeds the grammatical notion of "subject matter" to consider a discursive category of social exchange (the question), and even a specific context in which the question is reiterated, in conjunction with the musical technique of sequence, to convey the singer's "more forceful" attitude to what is being sung. Later writers, through the doctrine of *Affekt*, increasingly emphasize music's powers to express not only figurative detail but also the speaker's inner state, a matter of emotion and feeling, of which words are only the outer manifestation.[13]

That Britten himself showed more than a passing interest in Baroque models of text setting – notably in the Purcell realizations beginning in the 1940s – need not imply that his concept of musical utterance was bound by the overworked metaphor of music and words as "master" or "servant" arts. One sign of the composer's sense of the utterance as a "fused" event is the prominence, in the texted music, of moments that underline cardinal dramatic points in a single stroke. These gestures of epiphany – one thinks not only of Grimes's "God have mercy!" cry, but equally of Aschenbach's "I love you" and the Spirit's blessing in *Curlew River* – make their effect in ways that are both musically and verbally "new" in a given context. The most telling moments in Britten's work are just that – *moments*, single utterances whose uncanny reverberating force springs from a careful "staging" in relation to larger dramatic unfoldings, as well as on the distinctive profile of local gesture. Examining these moments, throughout this study, I elaborate a view of Britten's musical language as something all of a piece, a single mode of verbal-musical utterance. This foundational intuition is eloquently summed up in a comment of Myfanwy Piper's, on her experience of collaborating with Britten on opera libretti:

> Every word is set to be heard for its part in the unfolding of the story and for its quality as part of the human instrument. Speech articulated in sorrow or joy, in pain or ordinary conversational exchange is as much part of the music

of the voice as the note itself: the word and the note is one thing, not two.
(Piper 1989: 8)

Utterance, in all Britten's texted vocal music, is this "one thing," a point to be elaborated from a number of angles in the ensuing chapters.

In order to explore further the conceptual field I am considering here under the heading of "utterance," the remainder of this opening chapter offers three case studies of works in contrasting genres from different phases of Britten's career. Turning first to Britten's 1936 "symphonic cycle," *Our Hunting Fathers*, I consider the identity of utterance and its functioning in the speech situation. A second study explores the possibilities of utterance in a purely instrumental work, *Lachrymae* for viola and piano (1950), whose unfolding is rich in discursive shifts suggestive of the change of speaker implicit in acts of quotation. To close, I turn to *Noye's Fludde* (1957–58), a staged dramatic spectacle in which the inherently social and interpersonal character of musical utterance is especially vivid.

1. Utterance as speech event in *Our Hunting Fathers*

The term "utterance" refers, in common parlance, to an unfolding process of vocal enunciation (the verb, "to utter") and to the discrete units of vocally realized thought or expression ("utterances") that result. For linguists, the utterance is a minimal unit of speech ("any stretch of talk, by one person, before and after which there is silence on the part of the person"),[14] a usage whose applicability to a musical event such as the soloist's entrance in "Rats away!", the second song of *Our Hunting Fathers* (Ex. 1.3), seems uncontroversial. As in speech, the silences around the edges of a musical utterance are a matter of tolerance, and boundaries here are simply those of the onset and cessation of vocal sounds (excluding, for the present, orchestral contributions to the texture). Identifying the utterance as one stretch of singing says nothing about its formal structure. Musical utterances may or may not correspond to recognized musical phrase types (just as spoken utterances do not necessarily form grammatical sentences, clauses, or single words). The vocal utterance of Example 1.3 expires without conventional melodic closure, curtailed by an instrumental interruption, and its text (one word: "rats!") is grammatically inconclusive. Even so, one hears an utterance, for this is a continuous speech event of defined extent.

To call the vocal utterances in "Rats away!" speech events is to understand them first and foremost as actions performed with language. The fusion of words and music in the song, I will suggest, makes its points less

Ex. 1.3: The first vocal utterance in "Rats away!"

[instrumental interruption]

by projecting the semantic content of individual words, than through a bold interplay of distinct speech events – vividly contrasted utterances that constitute specific actions on the part of the singer. Highlighting a proximity of extreme contrasts in the character of each utterance, moreover, the song builds up a strong tone of parody – setting a mood that Peter Pears aptly dubbed "spiky, exact and not at all cosy" (63). The opening setting of "rats!" is a case in point, far surpassing in sheer exuberance any spoken intonation of the word one might imagine. In Britten's score, the word becomes a quivering series of breathless gasps, a stream of vowel sound that effaces its characteristic phonetic articulations. As a way of introducing the solo voice into the orchestral texture, this near-*vocalise* is a daring ploy on Britten's part (one that lies outside the main text as Auden has devised it). The "rats!" exclamation is a shriek, albeit a highly stylized one, comprising numerous rapid scalar runs that build to a penetrating high-register finish.

In the body of the song, the singer settles down to more conventional forms of syllabic text setting (Ex. 1.4), each quite distinctive in texture: a rapid, monotone chant ("I command all the rats") leads to more tuneful melodic contours ("the holy man"), then the voice drops, finally, to a kind of stage whisper ("Dominus, Deus"), at the lower end of the soprano range.[15] The chant, backed by the hurdy-gurdy sound of open strings (in solo viola), is a litany of holy and saintly names recited with a very distinct purpose. The song, a listener soon realizes, is a prayer of exorcism: "God grant in grace / That no rats dwell in this place." The chant is as mechanical, in its repeating melodic revolutions, as the opening cry was wild, and it is the sharpness of this contrast at the level of utterance within the song that generates its bizarre climax. At this moment, the pious chant and the near-hysteric shriek come together within the soloist's vocal part (Ex. 1.5). As the prayer shifts from English to Latin words for its formal Doxology ("Et in nomine . . ."), the singer reverts to chant, now against an orchestral backdrop more animated than before. But at the same time, as Britten's own 1936 program note puts it, we hear rats "creeping into the soloist's part",[16] scampering between phrases and words – even at one point finding their way *inside* words ("et Sanc – (Rats!) – ti Spiriti"). The voice part fragments, its attempts at formal delivery of the prayer undercut by the high-pitched "rats!" shrieks.

Has the exorcism failed, or are these "rats!" cries a sign of rodents leaving in droves?[17] One is not exactly sure, yet Britten's attitude to setting the text enacts the drama of the situation. The scene comes vividly to life in an experimental overlay of sharply distinct registers of utterance – a prayer, a cry of fright – to comic effect. The technique bears a resemblance, as an act of montage, to the inter-cutting of text and utterance types Britten was employing in his contemporary work on documentary sound film.[18] In its parodic caricature of ecclesiastic chant, moreover, the song looks ahead to the play with sacred and secular musical genres that informs several later operatic scores.[19] Capturing the song's vein of parody almost requires that one make utterance a central term of the analysis; foregrounding utterance, one attends closely to questions of enunciation and delivery – an exaggeration of some recognizable *way* of speaking – while downplaying the more familiar perspective on texted song that seeks only musical translations of meanings grounded in figurative verbal imagery. An utterance-based analysis need not ignore details of illustrative "expression," but it will direct attention to dimensions of the musico-verbal performance that lead beyond the local sphere of a word's semantic reference, and out into its function within the social world. "Rats Away!," as musical utterance, works above all by caricature, and – in a recognizably

Ex. 1.4: Three utterance types in "Rats away!": (a) chant; (b) tunes; (c) stage whisper

(a)

(b)

(c)

Ex. 1.5: Montage of chant and "Rats!" shrieks

Audenish touch – by subverting the expected solemnity of a familiar speech genre, the act of prayer.

Our Hunting Fathers places a vocal soloist within the environment of a full orchestra, so prompting questions on the relation of vocal utterance to a surrounding instrumental texture. If utterance connotes a psychological presence – a sounding of intent, rather than merely a noise – then vocal utterances are not simply happenings, but actions.[20] The vocal soloist in "Rats away!", I noted, casts out evil spirits with her ceremonial speech, but can the same be said for the song's orchestral component? Everything the vocalist sings is an utterance of some definable type (cry, chant, whisper), but do the instruments too have a "voice"? Glancing back to the interplay of voice and orchestra in Example 1.3, one might regard the orchestra as a kind of second, wordless speaker, capable of interrupting the singer. Britten's 1936 program note mentions "an emphatic protest from the wood-wind" here,[21] and this "protest" interrupts with a theme heard previously (also in the orchestra) at the climax of the first song of the cycle. The orchestra, like the singer, would appear capable of a form of speech governed by more than the local exigencies of a verbal text.

To suggest that wordless instrumental gestures, like texted vocal music, are a form of utterance might seem too broad a claim. But explicitly appropriating a general linguistic category in this way foregrounds the role of verbal language in Britten's music at levels beyond that of conventional text "setting." The language in Britten's music, as I will argue throughout this book, resides not simply in the fusion of words and music in texted vocal utterance, but also in a rhetoric of exchange *between* vocal and instrumental utterances, over the entire span of a work. An interplay of texted and "mute" utterance is familiar in the Wagnerian concept of orchestral leitmotive as a melodic or harmonic reference with a precise semantic dimension, and in related concepts of orchestral "narration" as a supplement to the scenic events on the operatic stage (to cite topics addressed in depth in Chapters 2 and 3 below). Returning to *Our Hunting Fathers*, this interplay between voice and instruments is particularly vivid in the second song, "Messalina," which closes with passionate cries of lamentation, first in the voice itself, and then in an extended sequence of instrumental gestures (Ex. 1.6).

The words here – "Fie, fie" – are weak in semantic potential; like the extraordinary "rats!" cry of the first song, their meaning depends on their place in a larger scene:

> Ay me, alas, heigh ho, heigh ho!
> Thus doth Messalina go
> Up and down the house a-crying,
> For her monkey lies a-dying.
> Death, thou art too cruel
> To bereave her of her jewel;
> Or to make a seizure
> Of her only treasure.
> If her monkey die
> She will sit and cry:
> Fie, fie, fie, fie fie!

The poetic speaker begins by reporting Messalina's grief-stricken wanderings, but ends more passionately. The opening line ("Ay me, alas, heigh ho!") retains the sense of sympathetic comment on Messalina's plight, but at the poem's climax, the singer slips into direct discourse, speaking *as* Messalina.[22] In Britten's setting, the force of this utterance goes beyond the detail of its stylized "sobbing" third-figures. As with the earlier "rats!" cry, the moment stands projected by the thematic return of the motto-theme familiar earlier in the cycle, shared now between both voice and orchestra (in Ex. 1.3, the motto "protest" is solely orchestral). From this climactic transcendence of actual voice, the song recedes into an orchestral epilogue. "Lamenting" woodwind solos – flute, oboe, clarinet, finally the saxophone – imitate the voice, drawing out the sobbing into a somber death march. Utterance, in this Mahlerian "Nachtmusik," passes from human sobbing to the wordless speech of the animal world (most notably in the flute's bird-like calls).[23]

Ex. 1.6: "Messalina," vocal and instrumental "lamenting"

Both voice and instruments seem to carry Messalina's lament, but the utterance encompasses a transformational rhetoric, as sung words give way to "mute" pitched articulations. The haunting epilogue of "Messalina" looks ahead to Britten's large-scale operatic dramaturgy, not least to those points where a decisive vocal utterance provides the basis for later, word-less instrumental developments (one thinks, for example, of Claggart's "I accuse you," in *Billy Budd*). The distinction between actual sung words and the wordless speech of instrumental utterance, at such points, is less a shift in the identity of what is communicated (the "message," as it were), than a change in the way performer and hearer maintain *contact*. Voices and instruments may utter versions of one musical message, but they do so through different channels. To restrict the song's utterance only to those passages that set actual words is to polarize artificially the distance between "words" and "music" as Britten construes it. Messalina's laments, instead, suggest that musical utterance is actually a category broader than traditional concepts of "text setting" or "musical diction."

With the idea of "contact" as basic to any speech, and recalling the perception – noted earlier in the case of both "rats!" and "fie, fie" cries – that verbal language need not always assert an explicitly semantic reference – discussion returns to the basic insight that language works as much by action as by signification. Nor is spoken utterance – the simple "stretch of talk" – limited conceptually by the basic need for contact between speakers or the possibility of verbal reference to some non-verbal context. As Roman Jakobson argued in a classic 1958 formulation, the speech event engages a multi-faceted system of interlocking factors:[24]

CONTEXT

ADDRESSER ___MESSAGE___ ADDRESSEE
        C O N T A C T

CODE

The speech event balances relations among an addresser, an addressee, and a message; for communication requires physical *contact* linking addresser and addressee, and a shared *code* (English, for example). The act of speech will invariably engage an outside *context* for a message. Jakobson's influential scheme is a revisionary response to those earlier linguists who would restrict analysis of verbal language to a purely referential function – the position exemplified in Sapir's claim that "ideation reigns supreme in language" while "volition and emotion come in as distinctly secondary factors" (38).

Considering musical utterance as a Jakobsonian speech event, it is possible to go beyond arguments (familiar in Wagner's *Opera and Drama*) that pit the referential precision of verbal language against music's lack of semantic potential. Analyzing Britten's music as a form of utterance, I aim not to overturn the argument outright – by denying the role of verbal signification, or by ignoring music's potential for "emotional" significance – but instead to reframe the discussion in terms that do not isolate questions of semantic reference from the other factors that make up the speech event. The extraordinary prominence, in *Our Hunting Fathers*, of words that seem, at first blush, devoid of reference – an interest continued in the violent "whurret!" roulades of the third song, "Dance of Death"[25] – is a reminder that the meaning of speech is always more than mere reference to the non-verbal "world," and that musical utterance, like its spoken counterpart, resists the separation of a verbally based meaning from the conditions of its sounding passage.

2. Beyond the voice: the song quotations in *Lachrymae*

Musical utterance, in *Our Hunting Fathers*, is neither exclusively vocal nor instrumental, but poised instead on a range of interactions between voice and orchestra. Each speech event echoes and supplements the others, so that the piece as a whole amounts to a composite utterance, made up of many single enunciations – themes and gestures – shared among solo and ensemble, verbal and "mute" (i.e. wordless) performers. In this kind of unfolding discourse, palpable shifts of speaking presence are easily heard. The cyclic returns, in *Our Hunting Fathers*, of the "protest" motto generate one such shift, a chain of instrumental themes binding the songs together, adding expressive depth at strategic moments in the texted song. In a comparable way, the leitmotives that thread their way through Britten's operas articulate a musical discourse operating in the gaps between actual singing. The very familiarity, within post-Wagnerian opera, of leitmotives as an articulate though non-verbal presence almost allows one to forget just how often plot events come to music by a move *beyond* the voice itself as the main channel of utterance (as, for instance, with the mysterious *Grimes* passacaglia, and the returning "interview" chords late in *Billy Budd*).[26] Understanding the continuity of wordless thematic utterance – whether in a "symphonic" or scenic context – requires that one link aural awareness of *what* is stated always to *how* it is performed. The analysis needs to move beyond the cliché that speaks only of a theme's being "given out" at a particular point in a work, as if all thematic "statements" were equally prominent, and identically scored. Music's surfaces are never so absolutely flat, but marked by the distinct unevennesses of an argument – the wrinkled patterns, in other words, of discourse.

How discourse arises as musical utterance unfolds is the main focus of my second case study, of *Lachrymae: reflections on a song of Dowland*, for viola and piano (1950). "Discourse" here denotes the form in which a narrative is articulated, rather than its basic substance (often termed "story"). In a musical sense, discourse arises when a given utterance (a theme, say) is set off from surrounding utterances by discernible articulations or shifts (in mood, topic, or stylistic register, for example). Discourse forges a link between a given event and the circumstances of its enunciation.[27] In *Lachrymae*, as Britten's title already suggests, the most aurally vivid shift is that of quotation, the appearance of a speaking utterance – John Dowland's – foreign to the immediate context. The shift to direct quotation, moreover, is audible stylistically as a traversing of historical distance: musical speech moves from the here-and-now of Britten's mid-twentieth-century idiom to the relatively archaic realm of Dowland's late Elizabethan soundworld. The quotations in *Lachrymae* are discursive shifts in a different, more problematic sense: they are all fragments of *song*, their even, flowing melodies a stylistic marker of a vocal utterance set off from more self-evidently instrumental textures. This purely instrumental vocalism – in the viola-piano medium there can be no actual singing voice – constitutes the work's central expressive mystery. An aspiration towards voice as the truest physical manifestation of human presence haunts *Lachrymae*.[28]

The discourse of quotation in *Lachrymae* is far from being a simple binary opposition of direct and indirect speech, however. The work as a whole suggests rather a sequence of moves along a continuum between Dowland's unmediated voice, directly quoted at one moment only, and the ten variations or – staying with Britten's unusual title – "Reflections" that form the main body of the piece. A complication arises, for while the main variation sequence is addressed towards the closing revelation of its source, Dowland's song "If my complaints," Reflection 6 mysteriously and poetically interrupts the scheme with its fragmentary quotation of a second song, the famous *Lachrymae* of the title. Conceived visually (as in Fig. 1.1), the argument of *Lachrymae* shifts between the direct quotation, in which Dowland's voice asserts autonomy from its context, and indirect discourse, in which it is assimilated, to varying degrees, into Britten's "reflections."

The discourse of literary quotation, the linguist Vološinov observes, is one of dynamic and reciprocal exchange of a reporting voice and a quoted speech – the two "exist, function, and take shape only in their interrelation" (119). At a first glance, the schematic right-to-left shifts visualized in Figure 1.1 for *Lachrymae* suggest a musical analogy for this interactive

Fig. 1.1: Discursive shifts within *Lachrymae*

direct discourse (song quotation)   indirect discourse (instrumental variation)
thematic autonomy ....thematic assimilation
Dowland   Britten

Lento: Dowland, "If my complaints," Phrase 1 …
occluded by Britten's harmonies

Reflections 1-5: Alpha motive (from Phrase
1), variations

Reflection 6: Dowland "Lachrymae" melody, fragment (viola)
with Alpha accompaniment (piano)

Reflections 7-9: Alpha motive, variations
Reflection 10: piano/viola Alpha ostinato
Phrase 1 extensions, viola (m. 16–)
Phrase 1, piano joins (m. 24–)

… Dowland, "If my complaints," Phrases 2-3,
original harmonies (m. 34-end)

process. The move from utterance originating in the *hic et nunc* of the present to utterance drawn from "beyond" is evident, for instance, in the separation of Reflection 6, with its direct Dowland quotation, from neighboring movements that treat Dowland's materials more obliquely as source material for the ongoing "reflection" process. The chart encapsulates too the music's aural drama of dawning presence. Thus the work opens in a tentative and ambiguous manner, poised between exposing Dowland's voice intact, and obscuring its intonation in a setting that is recognizably Britten's. The ensuing Reflections cluster to the right of Figure 1.1, as utterances that assimilate Dowland's voice to Britten's discourse. The mounting intensity of Reflection 10, finally, is that of progressive motion to the left, "towards" utterance that is recognizably Dowland's alone. The lack, in instrumental music, of *literary* marks of indirect discourse – tense and mood shifts, deictic pronouns, reporting verbs – situates any comparison of "quotational" discourses between distinct media at the level of analogy. That said, a closer perusal of the discursive shifts summarized in Figure 1.1 suggests just how far the analogy between media can be pushed. Doing so will reveal a rhetoric of quotation in Britten's music with its own highly developed harmonic, textural, and motivic forms.[29]

In the opening Lento (Ex. 1.7), as I noted, Dowland's melodic "voice" speaks only obliquely, for the melody line of the song "If my complaints" is exposed only in a shadowy and fragmentary form. The two balancing phrases (1a, 1b) of Dowland's first strain appear in the bass at measure 9,

Ex. 1.7: *Lachrymae*, Lento: introducing Dowland's song, "If my complaints"

yet the song peters out without cadence halfway through a repeat. This inauspicious, faltering thematic exposition is itself prefaced by a prologue (mm. 1–8) that gestures towards the song in obsessive meditation on its rising-sixth head-motive. The viola transposes the <C–E♭–A♭> Alpha-cell via an open-string fifth cycle <C, G, D, A, E>; in the piano, a similar pattern governs statements of the <C–D–F> Beta incipit of the consequent phrase 1b. Every pitch in the first eight measures is thematic, yet by conflating the Alpha and Beta cells into dense clusters, the music hides their identity. From its opening measures, the work's thematic rhetoric is intensely motivic, yet veiled in its workings. The stability of Dowland's C-minor home tonic is equally shrouded – notably, by the prominent distortions of Alpha to an augmented triad (mm. 3–4). Here, as elsewhere in *Lachrymae*, it is tempting to trace Britten's quotation technique, in both overall atmosphere and specific detail, to the model of the Bach chorale quotation in Berg's Violin Concerto.[30]

Britten's quotation – unlike Berg's – is fragmentary, both in the sense of stating a single phrase only of its source, and in stripping the melody of its original harmonies. Textural opposition between the bass line's clear C minor and Britten's anachronistic upper-voice triads implies an "interference" of utterance, or else a discourse in which the boundary between Dowland's theme and the mediating context Britten creates is less than clear-cut.[31] Delivery of the song-theme ("legato ma distinto") is shrouded in this opening movement by the indistinctness of tremolando and *luthé* figuration, and by the persistence of instrumental muting, both *sordini* and *una corda*. The harmonic opacities of Reflection 1 – the result of pervasive modal ambiguity, with passing bitonal allusion (m. 4) to a B tonic – compromise the C-minor home tonic (Ex. 1.8), only deepening the atmosphere of speech just slightly out of earshot.[32]

Reflection 6, by vivid stylistic and textural shifts, announces a more direct mode of address (see Ex. 1.9). Abandoning the antiphonal frictions of Reflection 5 with a euphonious mutual accommodation between melody and accompaniment, the music gives internal cues to the listener of a change of speaker. The actual "Lachrymae" quotation here – from Dowland's song, "Flow my tears" – is signaled to performers by the literary quotation marks (" ") surrounding the viola melody in the score.[33] For listeners, the viola's discovery of a singing voice is audible in the emergence of a smooth diatonic line after the chromatic (and markedly instrumental) quadruple stopping of Reflection 5. This quotation, though, stops short of direct, unmediated address; it is fragmentary and infiltrated by hints of a commenting speaker. While the viola melody is apparently "utterance belonging to *someone else*" (Vološinov 116), its actual identity is hidden:

Ex. 1.8: Ambiguities of tonal presence in Reflection 1

Dowland's famous "Lachrymae" tune, starting *in medias res* with its second strain, is disguised. The piano accompaniment, meanwhile, is historically "wrong" and tonally subversive (phrase endings return to the earlier C/B tonic ambiguity). As this momentary reflection of song recedes from view, subsequent musical images – the Valse and Marcia topics in Reflections 8–9 – speak a language more modern than Elizabethan.

Direct quotation, a breaking-through of a voice to direct utterance, emerges in *Lachrymae* (as in the Berg Concerto) by a concluding epiphany.[34] In this boldest of discursive shifts, Dowland's previously hidden song, "If my complaints," is discovered during Reflection 10 and finally allowed to complete itself in tonal cadences long withheld. The approach is gradual, however, starting with a searching motion in the viola (from m. 16 onwards, Ex. 1.10), joined by the piano (m. 24), finally reaching Dowland's original melody and parts, to conclude the song. By a process of unbroken metamorphosis, relatively dissonant modern chordal sonorities transform themselves into a voice-leading that is, for the first time in the work, unequivocally Dowland's.

In this final recovery of the work's source-song after so much oblique "reflection," tense motivic developments give way to broad-limbed melodic utterance. Powers of voice are unblocked. Viola and piano, I have claimed, in their movement between indirect reflection and direct quotation, speak a

Ex. 1.9: Cues for "Lachrymae" quotation, Reflections 5–6

discourse. This discourse, though, is without the crucial linguistic possibility of self-designation – instruments cannot name an "I" or a "we" – and yet, in the end, listeners are compelled to accept the viola as a quasi-vocal presence.[35] For much of the reflection process, I have suggested, Britten's *Lachrymae* conflates speaking presences in a scenario with connotations of utterance occluded or held back, if not of outright struggle among speakers. (In purely instrumental terms, the work prefigures those unsettling convergences of vocal and instrumental utterance so crucial to the interplay of human and numinous presences in Britten's staged works of the early 1950s.[36])

Articulating a purely instrumental claim to voice, *Lachrymae* returns discussion of utterance in Britten's music to Jakobsonian concepts of contact as the channel through which communication flows. The encounter, in every performance, is with an instrumental discourse mysteriously troubled by sustained meditation on the power of song, realized in a yearning for vocal expression – an almost Beethovenian celebration of "songfulness" as a property of instrumental lines.[37] Britten's *Lachrymae* defamiliarizes song, yet it is worth recalling that it does so in a strategy of quotation, arrangement, and glossing that would have been entirely familiar to Dowland himself.[38] Only the estrangement of a distant past, and the mysterious historical reversal by which the predecessor (Dowland) emerges as the *imitation* of its descendent (Britten), reveal a more modern sensibility.[39] Composed around a yearning for what is absent, *Lachrymae* dramatizes the gulf – central to Britten's art – between instrumental utterance that is complete in itself and an articulate utterance, grounded more directly in the expressive capabilities of verbal language.

3. The social utterance: divine speech and ritual in *Noye's Fludde*

> Noye, Noye, heare I behette thee a heste,
> That man, woman, fowle, ney beste,
> With watter, while this worlde shall leste,
> I will no more spill.
>   God's promise, *Noye's Fludde*

Looking briefly at the concluding moments of the children's opera *Noye's Fludde* (1957– 58), I want to end this preliminary sketch of the domain of the utterance in Britten's music with a turn towards the inherently social functions of all speech.[40] Musical speech, in both *Our Hunting Fathers* and in *Lachrymae*, for all the sophistication of its discursive makeup, tends towards a kind of soliloquy, texted or inarticulate, in which a single more or less clearly defined speaker addresses the listener. In *Noye*, on the other

Ex. 1.10: Dowland's "If my complaints," thematic epiphany

[*cf.* "If my complaints," Phrase 1]

[piano harmonies join]

hand, the encounter with utterance is emphatically social, for speech here takes place between distinct persons in an explicitly dramatic setting. God's promise at Ararat – "Noye, heare I behette thee a heste" – never to bring another flood is one of those defining moments in Britten's musical dramas when utterance, by its inherently fused nature (word and note as "one thing, not two"), generates an event of forcefully overdetermined significance, encapsulating the whole action in one shattering musico-linguistic gesture. This promise music (Ex. 1.11) is a kind of acoustic miracle

Ex. 1.10 (*cont.*)

wrought by the appearance in Britten's score of handbells. The brilliant
metallic shock of their peal here mollifies the voice of an angry, destroying
God who earlier speaks only in thundering tones (and drum rolls). But the
promise is more than a local sonic revelation; it is the catalyzing event for a
collective musical response, one that moves the closing moments of *Noye*
from dramatic representation to ritualized enactment. Ending with a
familiar hymn tune, *Noye* unites the costumed performers on stage with the
witnessing congregation in a shared act of song. The progression from

Ex. 1.11: *Noye's Fludde*, God's promise to Noye

mythic promise to general rejoicing is achieved, I will argue, in musical gestures that enact a social contract between speakers. Understanding the persuasive force of Britten's musical language, then, requires that one acknowledge fully its basis in speech as an inherently social phenomenon.

To elaborate a theory of the utterance as a social phenomenon is to recognize that all speech contributes, as Bakhtin evocatively puts it, to a "chain of speech communion."[41] The utterance, he goes on to note, cannot be understood as a discrete linguistic unit (like the sentence), for speech is at root an act of dialogue and communication. Utterance reaches beyond the internal features of individual sentences (units of merely grammatical significance) to invoke relations between speakers – question/answer, assertion/rejoinder, assertion/objection, et cetera. Speech is always "oriented toward the response of the other." An act of speech – unlike a sentence – correlates "directly or personally with the extraverbal context of reality." Such formulations find parallels in other recent theories of linguistic exchange. Thus Bakhtin's emphasis on the "situation" of speech recalls Jakobson's view of the speech event as multi-dimensional, far exceeding the merely semantic sphere of a word's potential for objective reference. Similarly, in J. L. Austin's well-known discussion of so-called performative utterance – where "the issuing of the utterance is the performing of an action" (not "just saying something") – one moves towards an analysis of speech grounded in social ceremony and culture-specific custom.[42] The promise ending *Noye* is such a speech act; a closer look at its place in the closing moments of the opera reveals ways in which the interpersonal dynamics of social speech take sounding form in Britten's music.

Ex. 1.12: Communal speech: rejoicing at the rainbow

The dramatic force of God's promise in *Noye* comes about in its musical union with the congregation's response. Promise and hymn of rejoicing achieve a miraculous fusion as the first verse steals in (see Ex.1.12a). The thrill of this moment, surely, springs from the tingling interplay of separate tonal claims (with the F♮'s of the bell clusters rubbing up against F♯'s in the hymn tune).[43] These distinctive tonal viewpoints span the overall scene. The higher brightnesses of the bell overtones correspond to the

Ex. 1.12 (*cont.*)

Ex. 1.12 (*cont.*)

(string parts omitted)

rainbow itself, appearing on stage as God speaks; Addison's hymn, meanwhile, forms the sounding earthbound contemplation of the "spacious fir-
mament" in which the rainbow shines. The music's delicate resistance to
conventional tonal unity (to diatonic G major, in other words) is only
further inflected in later verses (Ex. 1.12b), particularly by shifts in the bass
line (from an initial dominant pedal to a B drone-pedal). Only in a fifth
verse, sung by the congregation, are the magical bell sounds suspended,
making way for a stolid, earthly G major. The loss of the rainbow's sounding aura of overtones is brief, however; handbells return in the final verse,
combined with recorder fanfaring and loyal bugle calls (Ex. 1.12c). The
complete texture is suggestive, in its stratified layers, and above all in its
tone colors, of Britten's first-hand encounters with Balinese gamelan
orchestras while touring Asia in 1956.

As this final verse of Addison's hymn begins to revolve inexorably through an eight-part canon, its daring tonal stasis – constantly renewing the presence of a G-major tonic triad – forms the earthly foundation for a celestial canopy of glittering percussion. The diatonic warmth of praise is inflected still by pitches from the modally independent promise (B♭'s and F♮'s), and by bugle fanfares associated previously with the entrance of animals into the ark before the flood, and returning here as they leave the stage. In its textural and harmonic synthesis, the complete musical texture matches the expansiveness of the scenic moment. At the end of Britten's *Noye*, the contract between God and man – visible on stage in the symbol of the rainbow – becomes something to *hear*.

The music drama combines the sounds of God's promise with those of mankind's rejoicing. At this moment in the performance, a threshold is crossed. When those watching join in Tallis's ancient hymn tune, echoing Noye's family and all the animals, they pass from silent witnesses to inhabitants of the symbolic world visible before them. With its collective hymn, the music of *Noye* enters the sphere of ritual, its fixed rhythms and unison melody bringing about the coordination of a group into one per-forming body.[44] Each singer takes a place in a miraculous and exotic sounding totality – the music's contrapuntal strictness (canon) is a sounding confirmation of the one as a constituent atomic part of an all. Salient to the experience of ritual, in this case, is the music's negation of historical distance. Britten's score makes a discursive, quotational shift, "back" to Tallis's sixteenth-century tune, thereby subsuming everyday modernity into the unchanging continuity of tradition.[45] In this transcendence of the historic present, a "connect[ing of] the moment to the eternal," the music of *Noye* engages a fundamental quality of all ritual.[46] The thrill of the hymn comes, too, in an act of defamiliarization, as a recognizably European vocal texture is transposed into a new and exotic context. Tippett's observation, that Britten's music works always "in relation to some tradition," is apt.[47] But in *Noye* that tradition is itself defined by an encounter with its other. Mankind's place in the cosmos, as it were, is figured in the bold juxtaposition of European polyphony with a geographically remote musical tradition. With its trilling recorders and revolving metallophone patterns, *Noye* incorporates Tallis's hymn into a gamelan of praise, and it is with specifically Asiatic musical gestures – notably, a heterophony of pentatonic lines – that Britten's score marks God's final blessing and the story's end.

Noye's Fludde places a staged drama within the ritualizing frame of com-munal song, so reflecting an intuitive concern, in all of Britten's work, with the social force of musical utterance.[48] The ending of *Noye* memorably coordinates an entire community in a single act of celebration. But in its

Ex. 1.13: First-person utterance in "A Poison Tree"

evocations of tradition – through the genre of hymnody – *Noye* shares with numerous other scores an ability to work stylistic codes with precise and telling effects in a given dramatic context. One agrees, then, with Arnold Whittall's observation that Britten uses "social" genres (such as the hymn or the folksong) as stylistically coded references within art-music settings, for projecting "dialogue between collective and individual impulses," and with Christopher Palmer's positing of a link between hymnic reference and the composer's preoccupation with the cultural symbolism of childhood.[49] As a kind of footnote to my own capsule reading of *Noye*'s recessional hymn, let me end these introductory remarks on Britten's attention to musical utterance with one brief closing example, from the 1965 *Songs and Proverbs of William Blake*, of the kind of inflection the hymn topos can lend a text setting.

Arresting, in the central setting of "A Poison Tree" (Ex. 1.13), is the song's organum-like support (in parallel minor-triad verticals) for the speaker's opening maledictions. Here, one might suggest, is a lugubrious, twelve-tone underside of the diatonic hymnody closing *Noye*. Britten's setting of the opening quatrain engages hymnody as the textural obverse of the contrapuntal fantasia depicting the growth process of the tree itself, within the body of the song. Here, at the opening, is a sacred genre twisted into something unholy – hymnody as private necromancy, not collective praise.

> I was angry with my friend:
> I told my wrath, my wrath did end.
> I was angry with my foe:
> I told it not, my wrath did grow.

In the shadows of Blake's disturbing myth of origin, we cannot know for certain who this "I"-speaker is, and in Britten's setting of the poem the allusion to the social genre of hymnody allows the speaker to inhabit a curiously ambiguous register of utterance, poised between the collective, the individual and – most disturbingly – the divine.[50]

In each of the studies in this book, I explore the role of language in Britten's music with particular concern for questions of utterance. Britten's musical uses of language, I will argue, are best understood in the performative terms of speech acting within a given social situation. Adopting such an approach, it is possible to address a central feature of Britten's art – his intuitive ability to find compelling musical realizations for speech in all its diversity – from a new perspective. The conceptual field of utterance, I will claim, is usefully broad, in the first place because it offers the possibility of escaping the limiting terms of the discussion that treats words and music as separate and potentially antagonistic media. Focusing attention instead on the utterance as a fusion of "the word and the note," the analysis broaches questions of interpretation that elude the more traditional vocabulary – that of themes, motives, harmonies, and forms – of musical criticism.

To address Britten's music as the site of a fused musical utterance is to engage a cluster of intersecting theoretical problems. Some of these I have touched on already in the preceding analytic vignettes: the range of strategies for verbal delivery in vocal song, and for the interplay of texted and instrumental utterance; the potential in music's textural and thematic discourse for quotation-like shifts of speaking presence; the ways in which music can articulate the basically social, interpersonal force of all utterance; and, finally, music's ability to confer ritual status on collective acts of song. If there is a common thread to all this, it lies in a resistance to the critical practice that would restrict an account of music's engagement with language only to the matter of "expressing" or "reflecting" a referential meaning originating in single words or phrases. Jakobson's view of the speech event as multi-faceted and relational (a matter of differing emphases rather than a single process) suggests both the underlying theoretic sympathies, and the visible pattern of argument in the five chapters that follow.

Each chapter delves more deeply into specific facets of Britten's musical language from a distinctive theoretic viewpoint, grounded in the symbolic and interpretative dilemmas of a given work. Chapter 2, on *Peter Grimes*, for instance, takes the opera's opening words – Hobson's "Peter Grimes!" call – as the key to the terrifying tragedy that ends with Peter's self-destruction. Placing enormous musical energies on a single class of speech act – that of naming – the opera frames questions of the protagonist's identity in the specifically social form of his musico-dramatic interactions with the collective voice of the chorus. My analysis of Grimes's exchanges with the chorus draws on Austin's foundational concept of the speech act, and its extensions in Judith Butler's notion of hate speech – language as an instrument of aggression.

Chapters 3 and 4 focus, in very different ways, on the intricate workings of thematic utterance in Britten's musical dramas. Chapter 3, on *Billy Budd*, centers on the operatic leitmotive as an agent of narrative, attending particularly to the opera's manipulations of point of view in the Act 2 trial scene. At issue here is the applicability of literary categories (narrator, viewpoint) to an operatic discourse of staged singing and orchestral commentary. Chapter 4, on *The Turn of the Screw*, continues the exploration of thematic utterance within a dramatic setting, this time examining a score in which thematic "viewpoint" is problematically conflated. The sharing of returning themes – all born of the ubiquitous "Screw theme" – between the Governess and Quint complicates the moral identity of adult characters engaged in a predatory struggle for access to a childish innocence located in the figures of Miles and Flora. The cultural category "innocence," in this case, finds musical articulation in the children's operatic nursery songs, performances whose bright surfaces serve as an opaque barrier, concealing a childish psychological interior from adult surveillance.

Chapters 5 and 6 take the inquiry about linguistic utterance in Britten's music in two opposite directions. Chapter 5 considers music's ability to engage language in its outer, culturally defined role as an element of social ritual. Examining the English/Latin linguistic tropes of the *War Requiem* as a disruption of the fixity of ritual, I draw particular attention to the work's juxtaposition of antithetical speech genres – lyric poetry, liturgical prayer – as the basis for a discursive friction from which musical tensions emanate. The ritual in *Curlew River*, on the other hand, moves away from the strictly linguistic world toward a verbal utterance united with stylized physical gesture, an interplay of word and act that places the notion of utterance in a fresh light.

Chapter 6, finally, moves toward the territory of the subjective interior as a source of operatic utterance. Aschenbach's interactions with the outer world of sensory experience, in Britten's operatic *Death in Venice*, are created in a musical idiom shot-through with signs of subjectivity. A focus on the protagonist's perception, I argue, emerges aurally through dramatically subtle deployment of layered textural spaces, a registral patterning capable, on occasion, of suggesting a blurring or loss of perceptual definition. In this, the most psychologically detailed of Britten's operatic dramas, music's powers of utterance are inextricably linked to the revelation of a subjectivity in terms that exceed the purely verbal.

2 *Peter Grimes*: the force of operatic utterance

Peter Grimes begins with a repeated calling of the protagonist's name, and already in these opening measures, as Peter steps forward in response to Hobson's cry, the gist of the drama to come – in Hans Keller's pithy gloss, "the story of the man who couldn't fit in" (1983: 105) – is revealed to an audience. One senses Peter's isolation, at this early moment, without reading a plot summary or remembering Britten's poetic source; that he is alone is something one *knows* because the music says so. The two words of hailing – "Peter Grimes!" – do more than announce the identity of the witness in a courtroom. Set to the music of this opening (Ex. 2.1), the delivery of Peter's name interrupts the slightly pompous woodwind tune with a sudden harmonic and rhythmic swerve. As the curtain rises, chromatic pitches pull the music flatwards, landing the phrase rather abruptly on Hobson's "Grimes!" calls. These cut across the previous duple meter, and their intonation is colored by an alien sounding D-minor triad, superseding the bare octaves of the wind tune with somber conflation of chromatic pitches above (D♯ in the flute) and below (the sustained G♯ in the bass). A form of the opening theme returns now in the flute, but its sound is spectral and distorted. From its opening moments, the opera imbues the name "Peter Grimes" alone with unsettling disruptive force.

The tragedy of *Peter Grimes* turns on acts of naming, and my reading of the drama grows, like the opera's Prologue, from an act of speech with both an everyday function and more far-reaching significance as a sign of social identity. Naming provides the mechanism by which Grimes the individual is defined, publicly, within the opera and the means by which he is isolated by the collective. The *Grimes* drama is pervaded by moments when the simple utterance of Peter's name assumes a remarkable power to coerce, to wound and – finally – to destroy. To focus on operatic speech in concrete social situations is to consider individual utterances as "actions," and saying something as a "doing," a performance. Emphasizing the performative dimension of speech in opera will not negate other verbal functions – the referential sense of words as signs or images – but it will (as I argued in Chapter 1) favor an analysis in which musical speech is treated as a powerful fusion of verbal and musical utterance. What is said (sung), in other words, will not easily be separated from the precise form (melodic, harmonic, leitmotivic) of its enunciation.

Ex. 2.1: *Peter Grimes*, Prologue, Peter responds to Hobson's naming call

To elaborate on what (in my title) is termed the "force" of operatic utterance, I will borrow from the linguistic philosopher J. L. Austin the concept of conventional *illocutionary* forces (promises or threats, for example) that govern how speakers interpret one another in a social setting. Naming in *Peter Grimes*, I will argue, is conditioned by the flow of such forces among speakers, so that it is possible for the chorus to attack Peter in a discourse of "hate speech" founded on his own name, and dominated musically by a theme he himself introduces.

Pursuing an analysis of *Grimes* as a kind of social allegory, of course, is hardly a new idea, as the work's reception confirms. Britten, while composing, joked that the opera might prove "so topical [as] to be unbearable in spots!,"[1] a suspicion borne out by a "cloud of sociological, political, even ethical bickering" one observer remarked prior to its much-publicized première (Goddard 217–18). For post-war listeners, *Grimes* was inevitably an emblematic drama dealing – in Edmund Wilson's words – with "an impulse to persecute and to kill which has become an obsessive compulsion."[2] Such a reaction is tinged, one notes, with a pathologizing language, applying to both the opera's protagonist and the society that destroys him. Other listeners, picking up on Britten's own memories of the "tremendous tension" he and Peter Pears experienced as wartime conscientious objectors, have heard a coded reference to the couple's identity as homosexuals, and have sensed in *Peter Grimes* a drama of fairly precise symbolism.[3]

The alluring specificity of such readings does not, I suspect, account for the opera's continuing hold over audiences, nor (as Philip Brett has argued in detail) does the opera in its final form really support a narrowly psychological or sexual account. Britten's sketches, as Brett well documents, reveal a steady movement *away* from any too-precise symbolism:

> all homoerotic overtones, as well as other aspects of Peter's background, were slowly but surely expunged as the opera grew. . . . [Britten] had to desexualize Grimes, and furthermore rid him of his father-figure with all its attendant Freudian implications, in order that the work should not be misinterpreted as a "pathological" study.[4]

For Brett, the opera is a study in "the social experience of oppression" (1983: 192) and the drama hinges on Peter's internalization of feelings of shame and guilt.

One puzzle of the internalization narrative concerns the opera's dramaturgy, in particular the paucity of direct scenes of confrontation between Grimes and the Borough. "The action develops," Peter Garvie says, "from what Peter does, and the way the Borough interprets his acts"; as an early review states: "the chief character is Public Opinion and the protagonist who plays it is the chorus."[5] Grimes and the chorus in fact share the stage only twice – during the opening inquest scene, and then in the Act 1 pub scene. The remainder of the opera is a pattern of non-encounters. The hostile tensions of the two greatest crowd scenes – the Act 2 posse and the Act 3 manhunt – ultimately disperse, as each trails off without either group discovering its quarry. The Borough's only face-to-face conflicts, in fact, are with Ellen in Acts 1 and 2. How then does the opera represent the mechanisms by which Grimes is oppressed?

The beginnings of an answer to the question of operatic representation might be located, as Eric Walter White (79) first pointed out, at the level of musical themes. The prominent role, in particular, of melodic inversion in the opera, according to Brett – elaborating on an example of White's (Ex. 2.2) – may be read "not merely as a sign of Grimes's alienation but as a

Ex. 2.2: Peter's inversion of the Prologue's "gossip" motive (after White 79 and Brett 1983: 186)

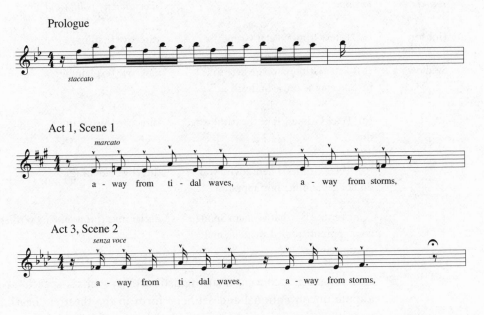

musical clue to his perverse relationship with the Borough through the inverting and turning inwards of the outward forces of oppression" (1983: 186).[6] Returning to the gossips' motive in his Act 1 "Harbour" aria, Peter in effect shows an audience how closely he has been listening to the choral voices on stage. The example is suggestive not simply for what it may reveal of Peter's state – and I will return to the topic of inversion later on – but, more generally, as a case of the power such thematic links have, throughout the opera, in binding together parties whose physical interactions are quite rare.

There is a line of inquiry to be followed here, one that traces in the score's thematic argument a series of relays linking Peter and the Borough. But while I retain, in this chapter, a fairly conventional view of the opera's thematics of plot, my central concern, in what follows, will be to attend more closely than do earlier *Grimes* critics to what might be termed the "mechanics" of oppression. Tracing the operations of a social force that is to some degree abstract and invisible will entail a close account of how operatic exchanges work at the level of individual utterances. Oppression in *Grimes*, in effect, is legible in acts of speech, and yet it resists any straightforward transposition of categories from linguistic philosophy onto the operatic stage. It is one thing to ascribe political force to everyday speech, quite another to transpose that force to the world of opera, where

Fig. 2.1: Utterances of Peter's name in the Prologue

speaker	locution	illocutionary point (and force)
Hobson	(a) "Peter Grimes! Peter Grimes!"	directive (hailing)
Swallow	(b) "Peter Grimes, we are here to investigate the cause of death …"	assertive (explaining)
	(c) "Peter Grimes! Take the oath! After me! …"	directive (instructing)
	(d) "Peter Grimes, I here advise you – do not get another boy apprentice …"	directive (advising)
	"Our verdict is – that William Spode, your apprentice, died in accidental circumstances."	declarative (pronouncing verdict)

speech is song. A conventional linguistic activity such as "speech" assumes a quite unconventional and artificial form in the theatre; "hearing," in opera, is no less complicated as a field of signification involving the mediation of both a singer's and an audience's perceptions by an orchestral "channel" in a three-way process (a situation further enhanced in scenes with off-stage sounds). Yet both activities, as I will show, play their part in dramatizing a single group of speech acts – those that center on naming – that constitutes the most powerful form of utterance in *Peter Grimes*.

1. Naming Grimes: speech as action in the Prologue

Peter's name, I suggested at the outset, serves as a musical intrusion on the scene in the opera's opening moments, and in this gesture is encapsulated much of the tension that will generate the drama to come. Lest such a claim be dismissed as hyperbole, I want to examine more closely the role Peter's name plays in the Prologue as a whole, and beyond that, to suggest some features of the scene's dialogue, as realized in operatic recitative. The Prologue lays out very clearly Peter's "difference" from the Borough. As a first stage in understanding the social tensions that generate the main plot, the analysis can start by considering in more detail the notion of speech as action.

On four separate occasions in the Prologue, Peter is addressed directly by name. In the first case, as already noted, the name "Peter Grimes" is the sole verbal content of the locution; in the other three instances, Peter's name is associated with a distinctive *kind* of utterance (see Fig 2.1).

Each utterance in Figure 2.1 has a precise force: for both speaker and addressee, it "counts" in a particular way. Hobson's "Peter Grimes!" call (a) acts as a *directive*, an order whose authority derives from the power of a court to call witnesses; (b) is *assertive* in function: Swallow tells Peter and the assembled crowd why they are here; (c) is again a *directive*, as Peter is required to take the oath; Swallow's words to Peter at (d) fall into two distinct locutions, the first a directive explicitly identified as such by the speaker ("I here advise you"), the second a more formal locution – a *declarative* – in which Swallow, in his official capacity as coroner at an inquest, pronounces a verdict on the death of Peter's apprentice.

Directives, assertives, and declaratives are distinct speech acts, or, in J. L. Austin's parlance, they are speech acts with distinct "illocutionary force." Illocution, Austin states, is the "performance of an act *in* saying something," a concept he distinguishes from the more basic category of locution, the "performance of an act *of* saying something."[7] (Thus Hobson's locution is "Peter Grimes"; but *in saying* it, he performs an order, an act of illocution.) Language, for Austin, invariably has a performative force, so that "the uttering of the sentence is . . . the doing of an action" (5).[8] The numerous illocutionary forces of speech, John Searle notes, can be divided into five main types of act:

> we tell people how things are [assertives], we try to get them to do things [directives], we commit ourselves to doing things [commissives], we express our feelings and attitudes [expressives] and we bring about changes through our utterances [declarations]. Often we do more than one of these at once in the same utterance.[9]

The phrases listed in Figure 2.1 reveal how different locutions can function with roughly the same illocutionary point (a, c, and d are all directives). Conversely, it is equally clear that a single locution may, in different contexts, assume widely divergent illocutionary forces. The name "Peter Grimes" alone is capable, at (a), of functioning as a directive; at (b), (c), and (d), it is restated as part of other speech acts. Already, in the Prologue, that is, we hear utterances of Peter's name repeated in the formal context of various legal obligations. In Swallow's explanation of the Court's business (at b), Peter's name is a more or less neutral identifying reference; but in every other case, its utterance is associated with some force of legal authority. The Prologue marks the start of a process by which Peter will be judged by the community. This judgment, operatically, is enacted most palpably by acts of naming.

An early draft for a *Grimes* scenario already includes Britten's conception of the Prologue as a "Court – [deleted] Magistrate scene," in which

"P.G. having 'done away with' boy, is let off with a warning."[10] An alternate scenario ("Version II") follows the first until Act 3, where a *second* "terrific" court scene is planned: "P.G. forbidden ever to have boy again. P.G. is dismissed in disgrace. *Epilogue.* P.G. on marshes, goes mad & dies." Already at this early stage, it is clear, Britten was attracted to the inherent theatricality of the courtroom as a way to situate Grimes, in a highly ritualized and formal manner, as an outsider before the community. A notable absence in Version II is the manhunt; the court's public dismissal is humiliation enough to precipitate Peter's madness and death. The drama of a court scene is – even more than in the spoken drama – one of words alone. Apart from the physical entrance and exit of participants, action boils down to a series of dialogues between lawyers, defendants, witnesses, and a judge. Given the centrality of the court scene to Britten's earliest conceptions of the plot, it is no surprise to find in the Prologue of the final score a remarkably fluent tracing of power relations among speakers.[11]

Having introduced the concept of illocutionary force as a guide to the precise effect of a given utterance among speakers, I return once more to the intrusive effect of Peter's name on the opening, attending more closely to details of local harmonic progression. (It is by a virtuoso and entirely "audible" management of harmonic tensions that Britten's operas reveal their dramatic oppositions to listeners.) The singling-out of Peter that begins with Hobson's calling of his name comes about, as I hinted previously, by harmonic means – the abandonment of the court's home tonic (B♭ major) with a swerve by tritone to E and thence (by fifth-motion) to A, Hobson's reciting pitch.[12] Viewed in the context of the scene as far as Peter's first testimony (see Ex. 2.3), this opening swerve initiates an evasion of the court's B♭-major tonic extending all the way through Peter's swearing-in. Only once Peter has finally taken the stand is the unfinished diatonic business of the opening measures – specifically, leading an upper-voice D, as $\hat{3}$, downwards to closure on B♭, $\hat{1}$ – concluded with a rather heavy-handed cadence.[13]

The swearing-in (Ex. 2.4), as any listener will recall, pits Swallow's impatient and mechanical reading of the oath against Peter's more solemn, aloof repetition of the words, a character opposition apparent in the contrast of the lawyer's hectoring chordal punctuation to Peter's halo of sustained strings. It is not simply that Peter's setting of the oath-pitch, C, is more euphoniously spaced (a dominant-seventh on D) than Swallow's chord (whose bass note, G, clashes with the close-position A♭-major triad above: letter *e*, Ex. 2.3), or that the rapid alternation of the two chords suggests a quasi-filmic cutting between close-ups of the two men. More basic, in this case, is the simple *stasis* of Peter's sustained chord. Here, in his first

Ex. 2.3: Tonal disruptions in the Prologue as far as Peter's first testimony

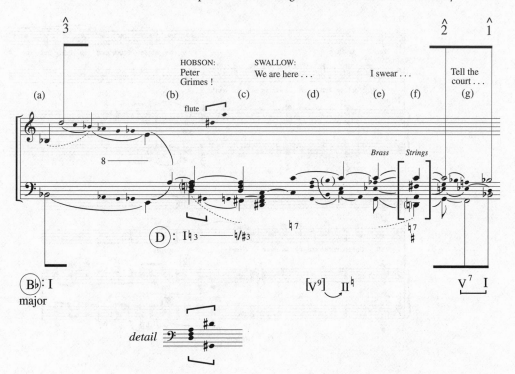

words of the opera ("I swear by almighty God": *f*), his warm D[7] chord mollifies the gruffness of the earlier D-minor music that had set his name. The earlier D minor was troubled first by tritonal satellite pitches D♯ and G♯ (*b* in Ex. 2.3), and further complicated by the modal contradictions of Swallow's reading of the court's mission (an F♯/F♮ pitch discrepancy: *c*). Peter's static pedal-chord, on the other hand, simply rests, a local release from the wayward frenzy of the court's opening music, from Swallow's obsequious-sounding turn to C major as he motions Peter to the witness box (*d*), and from Swallow's oath-chord itself (chord *e*). When, at the end of the passage, Swallow rudely cuts in on Peter's oath by awkwardly imposing a return to the court's erstwhile tonic, B♭ ("Tell the court the story," at *g*), Peter's string chord hangs in the air, unresolved and mysterious.[14]

The Aristotelian view that character is revealed through a more basic category, action, is worth recalling in considering the dialogic exchanges of the Prologue.[15] The formality of the courtroom setting works to heighten a sense of individual utterances as "events" and as speech acts of distinctive illocutionary force. In these first moments of the opera, each singer's recitative exposes character through the to and fro of actional verbal exchange

Ex. 2.4: Peter repeats the oath after Swallow

(rather than in the more stylized "state of mind" expositions of a solo aria, say). Thus Peter is distanced from Swallow, in dialogue, we have already seen, by harmonic inflection (and, of course, by contrasts in their speed of delivery).[16] Installed on the witness stand, where he is questioned about how his young apprentice died, Peter's early calm is superseded, as he relives the awful memories, by music of greater harmonic complexity. Swallow's questions are unaccompanied, but Peter's replies are inflected by a roving triadic motion: asked, in B♭ major, how long he was at sea, his D-minor response ("three days") is a shock, abruptly negating the court's home key with a return to the tonal swerve prompted at the opening by the calls of his name.[17] With its carefully constructed tonal conflicts, the Prologue articulates the "semantic reversals" that animate a dialogue between two speakers,[18] and in doing so, the music exposes character as a function of actional speech.

Even when Peter's speech seems to concentrate on the factual matter of how the apprentice died – what Austin would call "constative," truth-centered utterance – the music's tonal discourse betrays other motivations lurking behind the words.[19] Thus his tonal independence might be heard to enact a subtle resistance to the authority vested in the court's B♭-major home tonic, an interpretation that seems increasingly obvious as the scene develops, and especially, in the way it ends.

The shifts of local tonic that mark semantic reversal throughout Peter's testimony intensify as emotions rise. The contrast between his cooperative response to Swallow's question about the Borough landlady's presence (whom Peter calls "Auntie") and his insulting reference to Mrs. Sedley ("I don't like interferers") rests musically on a stylized raising of the voice: Peter, in the first case, replies with Swallow's reciting tone (D), but in the second case underlines his illocutionary point (insult) by chromatic ascent (taking D up to E♭, "inter*ferers*"), setting off the chorus of gossips in the process. Swallow gets his own chance for *ad hominem* attack, a few moments later, when he calls Grimes "callous, brutal, and coarse" (taking Peter's E♭ a step further, up to E♮). Such moments rely on relatively local harmonic articulation to communicate a speaker's illocutionary point; a far more powerful illocutionary effect, though, comes about as Peter protests the court's final verdict, in a musical (and scenic) argument manifest in both harmonic and thematic challenges.

The authority of Swallow's utterance of the verdict is at once thematic, tonal, and (if one hears a vestigial sonata plan to the scene) formal. Recapitulating the court's opening theme, in its B♭-major home tonic, Swallow returns for the last time in the scene to explicit naming address: "Peter Grimes, I here advise you" ends the scene's proceedings in a display of closure, linking the verdict announcement to a tonal and thematic return. (Even the "accidental circumstances" verdict, locally on an A♭-major tonic, is a kind of return – to the harmony of the oath – as if Swallow's mind was made up from the start.) That all is *not* yet over is evident in Peter's response (see Ex. 2.5). His protests negate the court's tonic by turning it into the implied dominant of a new tonic, E♭, that arrives as Peter throws Swallow's words ("'stand down,' you say") and his theme ("the case goes on in people's minds") back at him. Peter's most directly confrontational utterance – "Let me stand trial" – shifts the tonal ground once more, but is quelled by the brute assertion of *fiat*, in the unprepared resumption of the court's B♭ tonic. The crowd disperses to one last return of the court's theme, but no less thematic, in these closing moments, are Hobson's vocal cries to "Clear the court!" for they recall his opening "Peter Grimes!" calls. The scene ends, then, with a final gesture towards Peter's identity as it appears to the watching Borough – an identity inextricably linked, already, to the force of legal authority.

Grimes's speech establishes what Aristotle calls "character" through a kind of verbal action. We know Peter through an operatically re-created version of the illocutions governing everyday speech. But Grimes's place in

Ex. 2.5: Peter's thematic and harmonic protest at the end of the Prologue

the drama, I will be arguing, is much closer to more modern notions of the "subject" as an ideological entity, one whose actions are at least in part the result of a relationship to an authoritative societal voice. The word "subject," Louis Althusser says, has two distinct senses: "(1) a free subjectivity, a centre of initiatives, author of and responsible for its actions; (2) a subjected being, who submits to a higher authority, and is therefore stripped of all freedom except that of freely accepting his submission" (136). Peter's forced "submission" to the authority of Swallow's court, in the Prologue, establishes a pattern for the plot to follow. In tracing that pattern, I turn now to consider the opera's clearest representative of "higher authority," the collective voice of the chorus.

2. "The Borough is afraid": choric utterance in Act 1

> It is getting more and more an opera about the community, whose life is 'illuminated' for this moment by the tragedy of the murders. Ellen is growing in importance, & there are fine minor characters, such as the Parson, pub-keeper, 'quack'-apothecary, & doctor.
>
> Britten, letter to Elizabeth Mayer, 4 May 1942 (Mitchell–Reed 1991: 1037)

W. H. Auden once claimed that "the chorus can play two roles in opera and two only, that of the mob and that of the faithful, sorrowing or rejoicing community" (1989: 471), and his words are a reminder of the humanist triumph of the solo voice in opera, a post-Renaissance artform grounded in the complexity of the individual psychological state, as transmitted in vocal monody or aria. As a model for human subjectivity, the solo voice will compel more than the crowd's hectoring babble.[20] Auden's mob designation would seem, at first, to apply very well to the choric actors of *Grimes*, above all in Act 2, when they are stirred to form an illegal posse and to march on Peter's hut, and in Act 3, when Mrs. Sedley's "murder" charges yield a full-scale lynching mob. Even so, the operatic chorus is a more complicated animal than Auden allows, if only because it shows far more sophisticated powers of self-expression – in polyphonic musical settings – than its counterpart in spoken drama, where crowds cannot be heard intelligibly as a group.[21] Auden's limited view of the operatic chorus is undercut, moreover, by the highly sophisticated choral writing of his own Group Theatre productions with Isherwood.[22]

In *Peter Grimes*, audiences must contend also with Auden's second group, the "faithful community." Britten's *Grimes* congregation, though, is something of a twist on this idea, for its Act 2 worship is off stage, coming to an audience less as a ceremony in its own right than as a pious and threatening undertow to Peter's argument with Ellen, precipitating his violent ending of their friendship. The indirectness of the choric voice in the Sunday Morning scene is characteristic, and its purely sonic relation to Peter's actual stage presence is crucial to the drama of the Act 2 hut scene (where we hear Hobson's approaching drum), and, most powerfully, in the Act 3 mad scene, founded on their off-stage voices calling Peter's name. The role of the chorus is always indirect, yet powerfully coercive; it is their proximity to Peter's hut that prompts the boy's fatal cliffside escape, after all (and I will return in detail to their role in the mad scene). To understand the chorus's role in the drama, then, its voice must be recognized as something other than that of a mindless rabble. The crowd's collective utterance will, in later scenes, assume a vicious cruelty, but its powers to injure Peter rest as much on the range and distinctiveness of its utterances, as on its sheer material force.

Examining here a moment in Act 1, the point at which Ellen persuades the chorus and Hobson to fetch Peter's new apprentice boy, it may be possible to catch something of Britten's meaning when he spoke of *Grimes* as "an opera about the community." In context, the remark seems to refer to a group that is the sum of several minor characters, rather than to some anonymous collective, and Ellen's confrontation – see the summary, Figure 2.2 – is with both an individual (Hobson, whose cooperation she gains) and a group (the Borough, who disapprove of his acting as "Grimes' messenger"). But the scene is as much about Grimes as it is about those physically present, for he is central to their thoughts and actions.

Looking at the exchange as a whole, the chorus's alarmingly rapid progression from smug commentary to direct attack on Ellen is evident in a

Fig. 2.2: Ellen confronts the chorus, Act 1, Scene 1

1. Hobsons's A theme   E pedal
Hobson: (1) I have to go from pub to pub …
               (2) My journey back is late at night
               (3) Mister, find some other way to bring your boy back.
Chorus: *(1a) "He's right! …"*
Hobson: (3) Mister, find some other —
2. interruption   D♭ major 7th
Ellen: (4) Carter! I'll mind your passenger
Chorus: *(4a) What! and be Grimes' messenger?*
Ellen: Whatever you say, I'm not ashamed
Chorus: *You'll be Grimes' messenger? You!*
3. Hobson's theme, repeated
Ellen: (1) The carter goes from pub to pub …   F pedal
               (2) The boy needs comfort late at night
               (x) I'll mind your passenger
   plus a new cadence figure
Ned Keene: (5) Mrs Orford is talking sense   F: V-I

4. Chorus: *(1, ostinato) Ellen, you're leading us a dance,*   F ^{7}
               fetching boys for Peter Grimes
               because the Borough is afraid
               you who help will share the blame!
5. Ellen: Whatever you say …
   Ellen's B theme
               Let her among you without fault
               cast the first stone   D tonic

stylized choric voice whose varied intonation is produced by a number of textural shifts. Supporting Hobson's demurral in stage 1 (of Fig. 2.2), the chorus proceed by imitative single parts (basses, altos) then duets, finally reaching tutti ("Dirty jobs! He's right!" in the music shown at Ex. 2.6). Four-part homophonic declamation arrives only in the singers' stunned reaction to Ellen's intervention ("What . . .?" Ex. 2.6), and after this strangely luminous moment, their collective voice coarsens into the three-voice writing of the scene's ostinato-driven stage 4 ("Ellen, you're leading us a dance", Ex. 2.6). Text declamation is homorhythmic throughout, suggesting a chorus that thinks and reacts without imagination as one (though this unanimity serves the practical function of projecting intelligible words).

Even within the constraints of its single-voiced declamation, the Borough expresses its changing attitude to the evolving situation in rhythmic and textural ways. Clipped, metrically regular fragments confirm a self-righteous seconding of Hobson's initial refusal, but this response (and Hobson's own repeating phrase) is frozen by Ellen's interruption. Only after her repeat of Hobson's theme does the chorus regain composure enough to issue a measured warning, spelled out over the churning orchestral ostinato in simple, even rhythms: "you – who – help – will – share – the – blame!" Ellen, undeterred, picks up the crowd's high F and, a second time, stops the group in mid-phrase. This particular semantic reversal (as so often in Britten) requires an opposition of rising and falling melodic contours between the choric warning (ascent) and the challenge of Ellen's new descending theme.[23]

Perhaps the most prominent discursive move in the passage comes, as in the Prologue, by interruptive gestures. Hobson's two-fold reiteration (at "Mister, find some other way") of the so- called deceptive or "interrupted" cadence – a V–VI progression in functional chordal terms – is a gratingly predictable harmonic circuit from which Ellen's interjection ("Carter!") provides welcome release. Ellen herself is *interrupting* melodically by curtailing Hobson's phrase, and harmonically, her D♭-major seventh chord is a non-sequitur. Hobson's E-major chord (functionally, a V) is simply abandoned, and we know that the chorus is now focused intently on Ellen, because it responds within her new harmony. Ellen's final dismissal of the chorus is a second interruption, this time silencing a whole group, rather than one singer.

As in the Prologue, the chorus tends to react to soloistic action, rather than to behave independently. When (at 4), it does adopt an original stance – warning Ellen – the chorus builds on an extension of Hobson's theme already in play. The warning phrase, I noted, is declaimed in an even, thematically neutral monotone; its "referent" (Hobson) is identified thematically by the ostinato itself; his vocal phrase has become a bass line. The taking-up of a theme already in play into the quasi-mechanical turnings of an orchestral ostinato is a strategy that will assume vastly more destructive implications for Peter himself in Act 2 (and Britten's sketches document the search, in Act 1, for dramatically apt choral music).[24] Yet the scene presents a rhetorical chorus – its members are genuine participants in the opera's cut-and-thrust exchange, rather than mere lyric witnesses to the actions of soloists. Their contribution to the drama is legible in illocutionary terms as a sequence of quite distinct speech acts:

Hobson: *refuses* (to fetch the boy for Keene);
Ellen: *offers* (to go with Hobson for the boy);
    Chorus: *expresses* dismay (reaction to Ellen); then fear (of Grimes's activities); *declares* a warning (Ellen will share the blame for helping Grimes);
Ellen: *dismisses* (the chorus as hypocritical).

Ex. 2.6: Stages in Ellen's exchange with the chorus, Act 1, Scene 1

Ex. 2.6 (*cont.*)

Db$^{\natural 7}$ *non sequitur*

(1): ostinato

3. "God have mercy upon me": Peter's self-sentencing

> Infants at play, when they perceiv'd him, ran,
> Warning each other – 'That's the wicked Man:'
> He growl'd an oath, and in an angry tone
> Curs'd the whole Place and wish'd to be alone.
>
> Crabbe, *The Borough*,
> Letter XXII, lines 213–16

The force of operatic utterance, I have suggested, draws on the illocutionary forces operating between speakers in everyday linguistic exchange. Orders, oaths, promises, and other speech acts, do linguistic work on the operatic stage much as they do in non-staged settings.[25] The big difference in opera, of course, is that the precise illocutionary force of the words is signaled by primarily musical means. What an utterance counts as is determined by musical signs (rhythms, themes, harmonies, timbres, textures), supplementing or supplanting familiar cues of everyday, non-operatic speech – factors such as mood, tone of voice, cadence, emphasis, adverbial inflection, physical gestural accompaniments (shrugging, pointing, and so on).[26] That the force of everyday words in opera is liable, as Erwin Stein observes, "to increase both [in] strength and subtlety of dramatic expression" in a musical delivery (1953a: 110) is vividly apparent in the *Grimes* Prologue. Here, as I began by noting, what might seem to be a relatively simple, functional speech act – hailing Peter by name – assumes a disturbing force when associated with sudden harmonic swerves away from the plain diatonic vocabulary of Swallow's and the Borough's utterances. Ellen's encounter with the chorus in Act 1, Scene 1 furthers this operatic discourse of naming address, giving a clear view of a collective hostility voiced against Peter even in his absence from the scene. Illocutionary forces are again signaled by harmonic shifts, but the scene depends equally on dramatically revealing thematic appropriations. Thus Hobson's theme, I noted, is taken over by Ellen but then shifts to the orchestral bass, as an ostinato backdrop for the chorus. Turning now to the opera's pivotal crisis point, the moment in Act 2, Scene 1 when Peter quarrels with Ellen, finally striking out at her in defiant rejection, I pursue further the question of how operatic speech asserts illocutionary force. Grimes's monumental words here – "So be it, and God have mercy upon me!" (Ex. 2.7) – have very far-reaching implications for the dramatic action that follows, and yet their speech-act identity, as I will show, is far from clear-cut. However problematic the identity of Grimes's speech act, though, its rhetorical force springs from the introduction of what is essentially a "new" theme, underlining a dramatic turning point.[27] Peter's prayer, as I will call it, is at

Ex. 2.7: Peter's "prayer," Act 2, Scene 1

once the culmination of one event (the quarrel) and – as taken up by the eavesdropping chorus after his exit – the catalyst of an entirely fresh chain of actions. The prayer, as Erwin Stein accurately observed, is a "fateful cadence" (1953a: 113), an event whose momentous delivery at once closes Peter off from the past, and prefigures the remainder of his operatic existence.

Peter's rejection of Ellen is violent, but it is the sung "God have mercy" prayer itself (rather than his first inarticulate cry, or his actual blow) that exerts dramatic power in the scene. This prayer is actional speech – it effects an instant and irreversible shift in the drama. As an utterance that can't be taken back, the prayer marks the beginning of Peter's own end. The origins of the moment, perhaps, lie in the "growl'd . . . oath" Crabbe mentions in his "Grimes" poem, and the operatic prayer shares those forces of utterance made explicit in the verse: an angry "curse" on the Borough, and the wish simply "to be alone." The operatic prayer has too the commissive force of an oath, in Auden's words, "an individual's commitment to his individual future" (1950:141). Nor do these several meanings – rejection of Ellen, curse on the Borough, plea for solitude, oath on the future – exhaust the significance of the words. Taken together, these various "prayers" amount to an expression of despair. Grasping the prayer in all its attitudes, one senses the full extent of what Austin terms the "total speech act" ("the total situation in which the utterance is issued" [52]), and the truth of Searle's observation that the single utterance may "do" many things at once.

I refer to Peter's words as a prayer first to acknowledge the way in which direct address of "God" (on the high B♭) rings out an octave above the personal pronoun "me" in the phrase's pitch contour. Peter's words are prayer-like also as a plea to be forgiven the sin he has just committed – striking Ellen. This plea is prefaced, moreover, by another phrase ("So be it") with ceremonial implications – at once an affirmative reply to Ellen's grim conclusion moments earlier ("Peter! We've failed!") and Peter's version of the congregational "Amen" impinging on the main scene from the worship off stage. Wrestling with the obvious force of Peter's prayer, more than one critic has emphasized its value as an operatic display of subjectivity.[28] For Philip Brett, the prayer is a moment of "self-oppression," the personal assumption, voiced in a liturgical formula, of the Borough's aggression towards him: when "Peter literally take[s] his note and words from out of the mouths of his oppressors . . . [he] not only succumbs to them but also in his own mind becomes the monster he perceives they think him to be" (1983: 76). Clifford Hindley reads the prayer more optimistically, as the "self-affirmation" of a Grimes he sees as a coded represen-

tation of the homosexual outcast: "Grimes is not abasing himself before
the Borough, but is defiantly affirming his right to go his own way."[29] A
problem with such readings, though – aside from their seeming incompat-
ibility – lies in their very specificity; to put too fine a point on Peter's utterance is to risk misrepresenting the raw force of the moment.[30] The
rhetorical power of the prayer, I would argue, is bound up with its *multiplicity* of illocutionary forces and its resistance to any one significance,
whether as the public, voluntary proclamation of an identity (Hindley's
"self-affirmation") or as the outer, verbal manifestation of a social process
operating at less conscious levels, linking the individual speaker to power
circuits within the collective ("self-oppression"). The prayer, welling up in
response to the pressures of a volatile situation, is forceful precisely in its
overdetermination.

All interpretations of the prayer share one thing – an awareness that
Grimes, in this momentous rhetorical utterance, declares himself before
the Borough in a way the audience doesn't see after the courtroom
Prologue. His "big" lyric moments in Act 1 – "Picture what that day was
like," "What harbour" – are voiced in the absence of the chorus, or else dismissed by the Borough as signs of his threat to the community ("Now the
Great Bear" is followed by "he's mad or drunk"). The prayer's claims to
function as a speech act reside, I have said, in its articulation of many distinct illocutionary forces. More than this: taken together, the various illocutionary forces encapsulated in this single moment confer on it the
weight of a quasi-ceremonial utterance. Observing that Peter's "so be it"
echoes the liturgical "Amen," signaling his internalization of a collective
will, Brett draws attention to the relative formality of the prayer's wording.
The point might be extended, in this case moving away from the immediate context of the Sunday morning worship to Grimes's earliest dramatic
appearance, as the principal witness in the biased courtroom of the opera's
Prologue. In the Act 2 quarrel, the moments leading up to the prayer itself
center on Peter's awareness of his own moral guilt, and his insistent references to the justice of an allotted punishment: "Wrong to plan! Wrong to
try! Wrong to live! Right to die!" he tells Ellen. It is this negative litany,
counterpointed by her gentler question phrase ("Were we mistaken?"),
that the full orchestra hammers out repeatedly as Peter's violent self
erupts, knocking Ellen's basket to the floor (see Ex. 2.7, second and third
measures). This prayer, the scene implies, is a *self-sentencing*, a belated act
of self-judgment that fulfills Peter's ill-advised desire in the Prologue –
"Let me stand trial!" – and predicts the opera's ultimate progress toward
his physical self-destruction. "God have mercy upon me," one notes,
is suggestively close to the solemn formula uttered by judges in the

pronouncement of a death sentence: "May God Almighty have mercy upon your soul!"[31]

The effects of operatic moments of such exceptional urgency are rarely bound to the local scene. Britten's Act 2 sketches (as Brett has revealed) document great care in crafting Peter's prayer as a major thematic articulation. The idea of dialogic exchange with the off-stage Borough congregation far preceded the actual words (only in the full score and published vocal score does the phrase "So be it, And God . . . " appear, clarifying Peter's exchange with the chorus and his rejection of Ellen).[32] Looking at the prayer purely as musico-dramatic gesture – an emphatic perfect cadence, ending an extended dominant pedal in a *tierce de picardie* tonic – one senses a second "prayer-cadence" early in Act 3. When, in Scene 1, Ellen finds the dead boy's embroidered jersey, so confirming the fact of his death, all hope for Peter is lost. Beyond the shared tonal rhetoric of the two scenes, it is the presence of Peter's Prayer theme at the crucial moment of long-awaited cadence (see Fig. 2.3) that secures an overarching dramatic link. By a return that is both leitmotivic and gestural, the opera links Peter's Act 2 self-sentencing to the point at which Ellen and Balstrode affirm the inevitability of his physical destruction, in a kind of benignly administered death sentence ("We shall be there with him. Nothing to do but wait, since the solution is beyond life").[33] If the Act 2 prayer, as Brett claims, voices Peter's internalizing of societal contempt, its Act 3 return presents the workings of those same oppressive forces through individuals. What is disturbing, in the Act 3 scene, is the ease with which Ellen and Balstrode – Peter's allies, and even now, figures dissociated from the collective aggression of the manhunt – by uttering his Prayer theme, affirm an active role in his destruction.

4. The chorus and hate speech

The musico-dramatic events of the remainder of Act 2, Scene 1 – the congregation's transformation into a vicious mob, the dispatching of a chanting posse to Peter's hut, and the vast orchestral passacaglia that ends the scene – are fashioned quite directly from the Prayer theme he has introduced. The hostility that erupts in the crowd after Peter's departure – my focus in what follows – is thus the work of his own theme, a reiterated motivic entity that begins, as it were, to work against its originator. The scene's choral action, I will claim, presents an operatic version of the social process jurists define as hate speech, a political discourse of subordination by which words come to "wound" the addressee. The juxtaposition of linguistic and physical vocabularies implicit in such a concept of injurious

Fig. 2.3: Climactic Prayer theme statements as the agent of a dramatic parallelism

(a) Act 2, Scene 1

                                                                          PRAYER

Chorus: I believe …   … Amen

        Ellen: Peter, tell me one thing   We've failed

            … Were we mistaken?

                                           Peter: So be it, and God
have mercy upon me!

        (overlaid prolongations:

            ♭VI, IV)

F pedal ————————————————————————————

B♭ minor: V —   — I♮

                                                 [Perfect Cadence]

(b) Act 3, Scene 1

                                                                          PRAYER

Ellen: Is the boat in?   Embroidery in childhood …   *Ellen, Balstrode:*

                                      Balstrode: We shall be there

                                      We'll find him   with him

F♯ pedal ——————— I   F♯ pedal ——

B minor: V —   — I♯

                                                 [Perfect Cadence]

speech, as Judith Butler notes, raises more fundamental problems surrounding the social formation of the subject, and the extent to which language can "act" against its addressee, topics of compelling interest to the musico-dramatic representation of a society that is *Peter Grimes*.[34] The "force" of operatic utterance mentioned in my chapter title is increasingly evident, as Act 2 progresses, in a hostility voiced by the chorus against Peter, using the Prayer theme. Its leitmotivic returns drive the opera to its end not by distanced comment (a role orchestral leitmotives can play, as Chapter 3 will argue, in *Billy Budd*) but through the musical enactment of Peter's destruction at the hands of a society that rejects his existence. With the single exception of the Act 3 mad scene (where Peter shouts back at his pursuers), each leitmotivic return of the Prayer theme functions as hate speech, directed at Peter himself.

Peter storms off stage after issuing his Prayer, and so does not witness the Borough's response to his break with Ellen. The Prayer theme is passed around the chorus from voice to voice, the crowd's increasingly hostile reactions forming a chain of verbal substitutions on the incessantly repeated theme (the scene follows Britten's first notations: "ostinato with interjections from soloists" [Brett 1983: 64]). Even in a purely verbal summary, the choral reaction to Peter's prayer is clear – what Swallow pretentiously terms a rise in "popular feeling" is really a shift from relatively mild insults to words with far harsher significances for Peter:

		illocutionary force
1: B♭ tonic		
God have mercy upon me (Peter)		*"prayer"*
Fool to let it come to this!... (Auntie)		*insult*
Grimes is at his exercise ... (trio: Keene, Auntie, Boles)		*condemnation*
Now the church parade begins ...		
Each one's at his exercise ...		
2: C tonic		
What do you suppose? ... (trio)		
Grimes is at his exercise ... (chorus)		
3: D tonic		
Whoever's guilty! ... (chorus)		*accusation*
The Borough keeps its standards up! ...		
Where's the Parson in his black? ... (Boles)		
Speak out in the name of the Lord! ... (chorus)		
Who lets us down must take the rap ...		*threat of punishment*
The Borough keeps its standards up! ...		
[A minor "We planned ..." Ellen]		
4: A tonic		
[Murder!]		*accusation*
Now we will find out the worst ...		*prejudiced comment*

Every quoted phrase – except Ellen's words, and the one-word cry of "Murder!" – is set to the Prayer theme. The scene's rising motion, as Peter Evans (114) notes, is made literal in "blatantly crude" stepwise tonal ascent – from Peter's original B♭ tonic to C as the chorus gets involved, then to the shrill D of Boles's tub-thumping. Each key change is an obvious lurch,[35] while the thematic texture is more or less fixed by the ostinato Prayer shape. Auntie's opening gambit is to bathetically replace Peter's "God" with "Fool," seemingly in reference to Ellen (for "wasting pity"), yet it is the next phrase, attacking Peter himself ("Grimes is at his exercise"), that quickly becomes the scene's rallying cry. Pleased with its ring, the trio (Auntie, Boles, and Keene) apply it to mock the pomposity of the emerging church parade. Tensions build more sharply with the participation of the full chorus (stages 2 and 3 in the above chart). Here the verbal attack moves from the loosely derogatory "exercise" refrain to a criminalizing vocabulary ("whoever's guilty"), then to openly voiced threats of punishment ("who lets us down must take the rap").

The angry crowd solidifies a group identity by self-naming – "The Borough keeps its standards up" – an utterance in vivid opposition to the barrage of repetitions of the name "Grimes" that dominates the verbal texture of their wrath. Hostile calling of names, once again, stands at the center of the opera's chaotic eruption. The 'excercise' taunt that goes with Peter's name throughout the scene is among the few direct borrowings in Slater's libretto from Crabbe's poem:

> None put the question, – '*Peter*, dost thou give
> The Boy his Food? – What, Man! The Lad must live:
> Consider, *Peter*, let the Child have Bread,
> He'll serve thee better if he's strok'd and fed.'
> None reason'd thus – and some, on hearing Cries,
> Said calmly, '*Grimes* is at his Exercise.'[36]

Already in Crabbe the key phrase stands out as direct speech, and for its sudden switch from kindly first-name address ("Peter") to the less respectful third-person, "Grimes." This is the poem's only use of the name "Grimes," in fact; whereas in the opera – as now emerges – emphasis on the name is ever stronger, its accrued significances ever more damning.[37]

Butler's analysis of hate speech applies with remarkable precision to the choral aggression of *Peter Grimes*. As a form of illocutionary utterance, hate speech performs an action on its addressee-victim – an insult, derogation, a verbal injury – in the moment of its saying. Hate speech, like the Austinian speech act, depends for its injurious force on the fixed, conventional nature of the utterance itself. Repeating that which has been uttered on countless earlier occasions, hate speech functions within "a sphere of operation that is not restricted to the moment of the utterance itself" (Butler 1997a: 3). The single act of speech assumes a position within a chain of similar utterances. The verbal logic of homophobia provides an example not irrelevant to the symbolic trappings of the *Grimes* plot. As Butler writes,

> "Queer" derives its force precisely through the repeated invocation by which it has become linked to accusation, pathologization, insult ... [and] by which a social bond among homophobic communities is formed through time. The interpellation echoes past interpellations, and binds the speakers, as if they spoke in unison across time. In this sense it is always an imaginary chorus that taunts "queer!"   (1993: 226)

The force of the insult, Jonathan Culler comments, derives "not [from] the repetition itself but the fact that it is recognized as conforming to a model, a norm, and is linked to a history of exclusion" (1997: 106). In *Grimes*, however, a specific agenda of political exclusion is never made explicit at the verbal level of attack; the crowd's "unappeasable hostility to Grimes," as Hindley (1992a: 143) notes, is never very satisfactorily given specific cause. The "murder" cries of Act 2, for instance, tell an audience less about the crowd's belief in Peter's guilt, than about its ability to mimic Boles's hyperbolic talk about "plain murder" of apprentices. The mimicry confirms Butler's main point: that hate speech is borrowed utterance. But the chorus's lack of a real grudge against Peter is the opera's most chilling touch: group hate speech is less an attack on his actions than on his very being. Invoking Louis Althusser's term *interpellation*, Butler aligns hate speech with the societal "calling" by which the ideological subject is formed.[38] Such scenes of hailing, in the opera *Peter Grimes*, are anything but metaphorical, and Peter's "subjected" status is vividly apparent at every point in which he is hailed by the crowd in the intimate terms of his personal name.

The aggression of Act 2 is founded on reiterated verbal attacks linked to Peter's name. In this way, the Act 2 crowd scene continues and intensifies the hostile naming discourse set in motion with the more formal courtroom hailings of the Prologue. Further, as the "ostinato" treatment of the Prayer theme makes clear, the chorus's attacks on Peter are not confined to the verbal material of everyday speech – the more or less unpitched intonation of shouting – but shaped by the opera's melodic argument of returning themes. The power of the chorus's hate speech – the group's ability to injure Peter in song – is bound up, as I began by noting, with appropriation of a theme he himself brings to utterance.

Hate speech in *Grimes* is ultimately more than a discourse of attack on a subject constituted prior to the moment of address. In many contemporary accounts, Butler notes, hate speech "is understood not only to *act upon* its listener . . . but to contribute to the social constitution of the one addressed. . . . such speech reinvokes and reinscribes a structural relation of domination." Hate speech, on such a model, does not "describe an injury or produce one as a consequence; it is . . . the performance of the injury itself, where the injury is understood as social subordination" (1997a: 18). When the opera shows an audience hate speech linked explicitly to Peter's name – "Grimes is at his exercise!" – the illocutionary force of speech cannot be conveniently separated from the protagonist's socially constituted identity. One might go further and claim that Peter's operatic identity is less a matter of "sadistic" or "poetic" qualities revealed in solo arioso,[39] than of a linguistically construed subject position.

Grimes – more precisely, "Grimes!" – is the referent of a series of operatic acts of hailing.

It is the *repetition* of an insult, Butler observes, that ensures its social force as hate speech, and with this analysis in mind, I turn in more detail to the scene's ostinato treatment of the Prayer. An obvious effect of such monothematic obstinacy is to draw listening awareness away from the unchanging melodic content and toward changes in the enunciation process. Thus one hears in the scene an increasingly "raw" choral declamation, largely eschewing the timbral warmth of chordal harmony (the trio's hushed words – "Parson, lawyer, all at prayers!" – are a sneering, parodic exception). Self-evidently crude octave and unison doublings prevail (see Ex. 2.8), and as the crowd's chanting rises in pitch, so too does the effect of hoarseness. The tensions of the scene build equally by a controlled racking-up of tempo (as when the orchestra bursts in, Ex. 2.8c), Bachian crowding-in of imitative entries ("Whoever's guilty!" Ex. 2.8d), and wild lurches between vocal registers, as at "*She* help'd him!" (Ex. 2.8e), where Ellen's name too is reduced to a tag for brazen accusation.

The scene's terrifying effect requires that thematic repetition sound like a threat. Ostinato, in this case, is a relatively uncontrived way of charting a process of mounting collective animation ("the most suitable dramatic form," as Britten himself said of the choice of a round for the Act 1 pub scene).[40] Auntie learns the Prayer from Peter himself, then teaches it to an eager gathering chorus, that parrots it throughout stage 2 of the scene. The ostinato is a constant background presence (Ex. 2.8b), something "in the air" (in the orchestral accompaniment) that the chorus easily picks up. The prayer, by this point, is becoming a mechanical pattern, endlessly revolving in a trivializing thematic argument, the counterpart to the scene's verbal obsession with the name "Grimes" (heard twenty-one times in stages 1–2!).[41]

Peter's Prayer theme is subject to inversion early in the scene – at the trio's stage 2 question, "what do you suppose?" – in a thematic mirroring that quickly invades the manic orchestral texture (Ex. 2.8c), moving to more salient vocal declamation as the chorus pronounce Peter "guilty" (Ex. 2.8d). These choral inversions distort a theme that was, at least originally, "Peter's," but the fact that they are uttered by the Borough in his absence only emphasizes the degree to which his alienation is as much a socially imposed condition as an inherent product of "character." While *Peter's* inversion (or augmentation) of ideas may signal his "maladjustment" (Eric Walter White),[42] or (as Brett claims), "the inverting and turning inwards of the outward forces of oppression" (1983: 186), the *choral* inversions of Act 2 embody a thematic symbolism less one-sided

Ex. 2.8: Forms of the Prayer motive in the choral hate speech, Act 2, Scene 2

PRAYER: ostinato

Ex. 2.8 (*cont.*)

(c)

Keene tries to prevent Boles from addressing the crowd from the Moot Hall steps.

PRAYER: mirror inversion

(d)

Ex. 2.8 (*cont.*)

than either White or Brett recognize. Inversion originates as much *with the Borough* as with Peter, and is reiterated in the opera's thematic argument by reciprocal exchange – inversion cannot be understood in opposition to a melodic "prime" identified solely with either collective or individual.[43] The interplay is clearest, perhaps, in the following hut scene, after the passacaglia. When Peter angrily reproaches the boy ("you sit there watching me") to the inverted Prayer theme, the opera is tracing out a motivic path that links him and the Borough as directly as the one leading the approaching posse up the hill to his hut. Peter takes the inverted shape from the accompaniment (at "you've been talking"); he "hears" its orchestral presence, and then incorporates it into his own singing.[44]

That the monumental Prayer theme – first heard at Peter's moment of crisis – can be adopted, repeated, and so quickly turned against him by a hostile crowd, underlines the fragile nature of the link between speaker and utterance. If Peter's prayer has "performative" force as "an individual and historic act" of speech (Benveniste 236), what then does one make of the Borough's ostinato reiterations of its musical contents? When the Borough turns what was solemn and unique into an endlessly repeated slogan, the effect is both trivializing and threatening. Deprived of its specific illocutionary significance (as I argued above, a cluster of forces), and of its original text, Grimes's Prayer shape becomes the vehicle for Borough prejudices. Prayer is transformed into insult, accusation, and threats of vengeance. The continuity in this chain of verbal substitutions is assured by ostinato repetition, but Peter's original illocutionary point – his *intention*, uttering the prayer – is severed from the musical material (the Prayer theme) no sooner than the words leave his mouth.

The choric hate speech of Act 2 arises through an intersection of melodic and verbal repetitions. Staging the Borough's attacks on Peter in a scene of thematic ostinato, the opera at once finds a structural metaphor for crowd behavior, and lays the groundwork for a discourse of leitmotivic returns that will, by opera's end, accompany Peter to his death. That all this is founded on a theme that is first heard on Peter's lips only highlights what Butler terms the "open temporality" of any and all speech acts (1997a: 15) – their potential reiteration beyond a local context, and their susceptibility to ironic reversal and resignification. Speech, in Butler's view, is always "out of our control" (1997a: 15) – a point that bears amplifying before I turn discussion to Peter's final, demented moments on stage in Act 3. Butler's analysis of hate speech can be understood as a corrective to the Austinian emphasis on speech acts as single moments allied to the motivations of individual speakers. Peter's prayer, for example, is identifiable as prayer precisely in its reiteration of an earlier model (the formula "God have mercy"). But to acknowledge this "quotation" is also to recognize a threat to the idea of a sovereign intention behind its utterance. Peter's intention, at the moment of the prayer, can never be fully transparent. The speaker's intention, as Jacques Derrida writes, "will not disappear . . . but it will no longer be able to govern the entire scene. . . . the intention which animates utterance will never be completely present in itself and its content" (1982: 326).[45] The value of such far-reaching claims will emerge most forcefully in the Act 3 mad scene, for it is here that the opera's staging of a linguistic interplay of

Peter and the chorus – a scenic representation of tensions between "subject" and "society" – finds its starkest and most haunting expression.

5. "Melancholy and incipient Madness": Peter's last scene

> We'll make the murd'rer pay for his crime.
> Peter Grimes! Grimes!
> > Chorus, Act 3, Scene 1, curtain

> Do you hear them all shouting my name?
> > Peter, Act 3, Scene 2

> Good name in man and woman, dear my lord,
> Is the immediate jewel of their souls
> > Iago, *Othello*, Act 3, Scene 3

Crabbe's figure of the mad Peter Grimes – "A lost, lone Man, so harass'd and undone" – returns in Britten's opera for the famous mad scene, though in changed circumstances. In Crabbe, Peter is tormented, like Macbeth, by the spirits of those he wronged: his father, and the boy apprentices he kills by maltreatment. His deathbed speech – "part Confession and the rest Defence, / A Madman's Tale, with gleams of waking Sense" – recounts the daily visitations of "three unbodied Forms," bidding him drown himself, and the "visionary Terrors" of water turned fiery and bloody, "A place of Horrors – ... Where the Flood open'd."[46] Britten's Peter is a different character. He is no murderer, of course, and the composer jettisoned Slater's hints of patriarchal neurosis in redrafting the libretto as he set the Act 2 hut scene.[47] Guilt over two accidental deaths – "the first one died, just died," he sings – is cause enough to tear Peter apart in the opera's closing mad scene. Perhaps the strongest remaining link between Crabbe's deathbed vision and Britten's opera scene is the siren-like calling of voices. In Crabbe, readers hear directly from the spirits, who intone a call to suicide: "And 'Come,' they said, with weak, sad voices, 'come'" (line 324). Britten too allows audiences to hear voices, those of the Borough engaged in a manhunt, but the calling here is of Peter's own name. In Crabbe, the killer is undone by ethereal spirits; Britten's Peter is driven to take his own life by the Borough, who hunt him as a prey.

In the mad scene – and in the "Vengeance Song" and orchestral interlude that precede it – the opera draws its oppressive net in around Peter. Britten's finale centers on the theatrical spectacle, vocal histrionics, and emotional excess so familiar in the operatic mad scene tradition, but the result is no mere set piece. The climax of the opera's naming discourse arrives here; in the mad scene is concentrated a force of operatic utterance that has been accruing throughout the preceding acts. The scene, I will argue, is a struggle for an identity, for a social self – "subject" as such to the collective callings of a society. These claims might remain only at the level of interpretative allegory, were it not for their immediate realization as operatic gesture in highly charged utterances of a single lexical item, Peter's own name.

The chorus who will hunt Peter as murderer comes before the audience in music of unprecedented fury (Ex. 2.9). Their vicious outburst surpasses even the animosities of the Act 2 chorus. The Borough knows now that a second boy is dead; taking Peter for "the murd'rer," they are out to settle a blood grudge. Their "vengeance song" (Britten's own term) is shocking in its own right, but I want to consider here its role in laying the thematic and harmonic groundwork for the mad scene to come. A first point is essentially acoustic and dynamic: the on-stage chorus becomes the presence against which audiences measure the "distant" off-stage cries in the mad scene itself. When the softer cries of the mad scene are heard, we hear them in a way that Peter himself does not, for we have witnessed their ferocity close-up, and dramatic irony takes a directly sonic form.[48]

The choral-orchestral build-up of the "Vengeance song" return to an ostinato-driven frenzy reminiscent of Act 2, Scene 1. There, the animation focused on Borough appropriation of Peter's Prayer shape, and then a dismissal (in overlaid Verdian *parlante*) of Ellen's attempt to defend him. The drama is carried as much by orchestral repetition of themes, as by the voices themselves: in Example 2.10a, Swallow repeats Ellen's first idea (marked a), while her cadence-phrase (the falling fifth at "regular meals") becomes a lower-string ostinato (b) with its own power to undercut her pleas by incessant reiteration. Moments later, the ostinato phrase is modally and rhythmically transformed (see Ex. 2.10b), just as the full chorus overwhelms Ellen with a return to the Prayer theme. Comparable thematic machinations drive on the Act 3 vengeance song, now in a bizarre atmosphere in which all is slightly out of step. After the frivolity of the Borough's social music – a sedate Barn dance, boozy Ländler, and polite "Goodnights" – a more frenzied Galop takes over. Mrs Sedley's "Murder" theme ascends in the main orchestra, initially in chaotic montage with the off-stage dance band, then taken up more urgently by the full chorus ("Our curse shall fall"). Desperate tonal rovings come to a head finally (see Ex. 2.9) in a jarring diatonic arrival (to F♭, evading the A♭-major tonic). The return of the earlier Ländler here, grotesquely magnified and distorted, sets the Borough's chilling laughter in counterpoint with the chromatic Murder theme.[49]

Ex. 2.9: The Act 3 "Grimes" cries: thematic allusion and harmonic detail

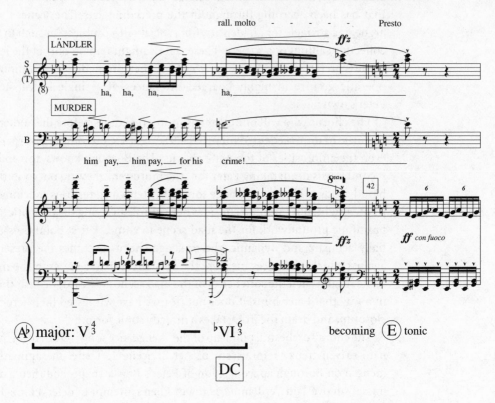

Ex. 2.9 (*cont.*)

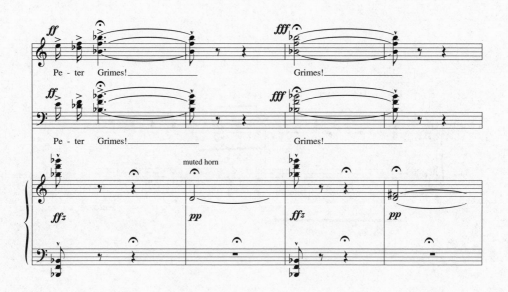

Ex. 2.10: Act 2, Scene 1: Ellen's vocal phrase mocked, overturned in orchestral imitation

(a)

(b)

Peter's name is the sole focus of the Borough's violent choral peroration (see Ex. 2.9, second system), another of Britten's "Dances of Death."[50] These violent hailings confirm what was evident in the Act 2 crowd scene: that Peter's name is not a thing (it is not "his"). A name is a sign performed by a community, conferred in acts of speech. Central to the naming discourse in *Grimes* (as I noted before) is the fact that Peter and the chorus never meet face to face after Act 1, and his name is thus never uttered in direct address. Instead, its utterances exceed mere identifying reference, coming to embody a sense of their own, and to assume an illocutionary force. The proper name "Peter Grimes" now belongs to the abject individual referred to moments earlier ("him who despises us we'll destroy"), and singled out at the climax by the Murder theme ("We'll make him pay for his crime"). Peter's name now means "outlaw" – its utterance alone, in the collective voice of the Borough, becomes an injurious act.

As the vengeance song reaches its ferocious climax, tritonal harmonic disruptions familiar from much earlier in the opera come to the fore. Thus the vexed E bass presence of the 'Grimes!' cries gives way to a B♭ counterpole – shades of the Prologue's opening swerve – while melodically, the voices reiterate Peter's name to a form of the Act 1 Storm-trichord, and even to a pitch-specific hint of the Act 2 Prayer (sopranos, end of Ex. 2.9). Arrival on B♭ establishes the tonal plateau that will mark the climax of the mad scene to come, but is itself undermined as eerie muted horns creep in (with a disruptive F♯). With "Grimes!" still ringing around the theatre, the lynching chorus scatters.

The memories of earlier harmonic tensions here – an F♯ disruption of B♭ recalls the pitch clashes arising with the Act 2 church bells[51] – further the synoptic collation of thematic flashbacks that dominates the so-called "mad interlude" prefacing Peter's actual emergence in Scene 2. Prefiguring the fragmented (but not chaotic) technique of the mad scene itself, the orchestral interlude begins a process by which the protagonist will cease to exist, physically and musically. The interlude evokes human utterance distanced and distorted, with Peter's voice mysteriously articulated in wordless orchestral timbres. Woodwind solos recall Peter's words, leading from Act 1 to the climactic Act 2 prayer (flute: "listen to money"; oboe: "who can turn?"; clarinets: "wrong to plan"). Other themes are subject to extreme registral distortions that set them in a numinous past tense: the Act 1 pub song becomes a strained solo for high violins, Ellen's "were we mistaken?" question a lugubrious bass line.[52] The Interlude offers a retreat from the previous scene's aggression, moving from the collective social world of the "Grimes" calls to the interior desperation of the subject they seek to address. As if to affirm the possibility of some residual subjectivity beyond a social identity, the Interlude builds to a restatement of Peter's Prayer theme. This reprise escapes the mechanical rhythms of the Act 2 crowd, but it quickly expires. Unable to complete itself, the theme lacks its last note, and is liquidated, finally becoming the two-note wail of a foghorn – more than a sound, but less than an utterance.

The mad interlude, like the huge passacaglia at the opera's center, speaks for a moment in an epic, orchestral voice distanced from the passions of the surrounding action. As the tragedy nears its end, the opera temporarily suspends the socially determined illocutionary forces that have been accruing to thematic utterance throughout the drama. In the authoritative address of an orchestral interlude – a wordless communication *ad spectatores* – thematic utterance is *deprived* of any social function as speech. If themes in *Peter Grimes*, as I argue throughout this chapter, are typically vehicles of exchange between society as a whole and the individual subject, the "silent" speech of the mad interlude assumes its own dark eloquence. Drained of a social and linguistic force rooted in words, these themes foretell Peter's coming annihilation.

The "Grimes" cries familiar from the earlier lynching chorus are the first sounds of the mad scene itself, preceding even the appearance of a "weary and demented" Peter. The disembodied voices are much softer now – gentle, even – a spectral backdrop to Peter's solo voice, yet there is no mistaking their force. In the repeated hailings of the mad scene are focused the opera's entire history of namings, from the Prologue all the way to the lynching chorus, where cries of Peter's name bear all the weight of a vow to "tame his arrogance." The force of choric utterance in the mad scene is that of hate speech, bound up with a historic backdrop of hailings – this is the apotheosis of the opera's naming discourse. In contrast with the earlier scenes of crowd aggression – conducted in Peter's absence – the mad scene approaches the form of a dialogue, albeit one possible only in the realm of opera, where chorus and Grimes coexist within a musical soundscape but remain out of physical range.

The scene's madness, musically speaking, is an effect of fragmentary verbal and melodic quotations, continuing the pattern of wordless leitmotivic returns in Interlude VI (and, more distantly, the "dreams" of the Act 2 hut scene). Driving this apparently random surface, though, is a very clear mood progression, defined by a schematic succession of tonal pedal points, introduced always by the choric "Grimes" cries to which Peter's thoughts are responses.

Choric "Grimes" calls: focal pitches, voice ranges	*Peter's response*
1 {D,F♯,C} SA	Steady! There you are! nearly home! . . . The first one died, just died. The other slipped, and died, and the third will . . . "Accidental circumstances"
2 {B,F♯} TB	Peter Grimes! Here you are! Here I am! . . . Now is gossip put on trial . . . "Turn the skies back . . ." "Old Joe has gone fishing . . ."
3 {E♭,G,B♭} S, SA	Ellen! Give me your hand . . . my hope is held by you . . . Take away your hand! The argument's finished! . . . To hell with all your mercy! To hell with your revenge, And God have mercy upon you!
4 E♭,TB {C,E,G} SA	Do you hear them all shouting my name? Old Davy Jones shall answer: Come home!
5 {B♭,F} SATB	Peter Grimes!
	[*Ellen*: Peter, we've come to take you home]
6 {E♭,B♭} TB / {B♭,F} SA	What harbour shelters peace . . .

Peter's thoughts grow at first directly from the foghorn's two-pitch moan, as if its sound reminds him of the "evil day" of the first boy's death. With the off-stage voices mainly in pairs, the dialogue reaches a first peak of excitement at (3) as Peter relives the Act 2 crisis with Ellen, but a more violent crisis follows (at 5) with the first outburst of the full choir. The earlier moment is full of defiance, as Peter, "revoicing" his Act 2 Prayer, curses the shouters. "To hell with all your mercy" (Ex. 2.11) might refer sarcastically to Ellen's imagined presence, or to Peter's own "God have mercy" prayer; repeating to slightly different words ("To hell with *your revenge*"), the theme more explicitly addresses the off-stage Chorus.[53] Their calls prolong an E♭-major tonic, while Peter's rebuke tonicizes G♭ before finally adopting their E♭. His tonal resistance continues as the chanting grows more insistent and rhythmic (Ex. 2.11b), building to the chorus's triumphant return (at stage 5 above) to the B♭ tonic ending the vengeance song, a moment when (the score instructs) the voices must sound "close at hand and very distinct."[54] Peter "roars back," but now it is his own name that he returns. Accepting the identity conferred in choric

Ex. 2.11: Tension among focal pitches as Peter rebukes the Chorus to the Prayer theme

hailings, he nears his own end. His nonsensical "Grimes" repetitions trail off into a single melismatic howl, as if to announce – by phonetic dissolution – his imminent physical departure.

"Semantic reversal" in both verbal and musical spheres promotes a dialogic interplay of speakers, but the scene's underlying progression involves Peter's diminishing grasp of the situation, and the collapse of his independent viewpoint. His early confusion of pronoun deixes – "*his . . . my* sorrows . . . Here *you* are! Here *I* am!"[55] – complicates the issue of who he is addressing. One of only two questions he asks in the scene would appear to be directed, as in soliloquy, at the theatre audience rather than the Chorus: "Do *you* hear them all shouting *my* name?" (were he merely talking to himself, he would say "shouting *your* name"). By the time of Ellen's physical appearance, Peter is oblivious to her presence; calling "Ellen" by name earlier in the scene, he speaks to an imaginary figure. Calling his own name, finally, as Ellen *does* appear on stage, Peter himself speaks from a point at which physical being and linguistic identity are subject to a confused doubling.

The substantial revisions Britten made to Slater's libretto while composing the mad scene allowed the composer, as Brett notes, to increase Peter's isolation. In Slater's original text (the one he published independently of the opera in 1946), Peter's awareness of his own name as something distinct from his physical person is clearer at several points:

> You shouters there – I've made it right. . . .
> You hear them shouting? I'm alone. . . .
> You hear them call my name, the sky
> Hears it, so do the stars, the sea.
> (Slater 1946a: 53–54)

The first line directly addresses the "shouters"; the other two are addressed to Ellen, who appears earlier on in Slater's scene, and with whom Peter speaks more or less lucidly, asking "Was it you who called?" to which she replies, "The cries you hear are in your mind" (53–54).[56] These words do not appear in Britten's final mad scene libretto, but the sense of Peter's growing distraction from the physical world is, in the opera, all too clear. His obsessional emphasis on single words (a traditional feature of the mad scene genre) comes to rest on the semantic cluster surrounding "harbour" and "home," keywords prominent much earlier in the opera. "Home," as Hans Keller suggested, embodies now a kind of "mental retrogression" (1983: 119) in the longing for the oblivion of death by water ("Old Davy Jones shall answer: Come home!").[57] When Peter equates Ellen's breast with a sheltering harbor, moreover, his distraction approaches a fantasy of rebirth, an implication borne out by the final transformation of the fierce "Grimes" cries into a lullaby.[58] The choric voices rock soothingly back and forth in a tonally indeterminate superposition of fifths: Peter himself is now a sleepless child (the fifth intervals a residue of "his" Prayer). It is an eerie moment of calm – beyond fighting the chorus, he goes to his death at their bidding, and with Ellen's help ("Peter, we've come to take you home"). His longing for home finds expression in the repeated melodic falling motion of the last flashback quotation, "What harbour shelters peace...?"

The mad scene situates naming utterance in a remarkable soundscape. The moaning tuba/foghorn, an icon of the solitary, is poised ambiguously between natural and cultural worlds, and between sound and utterance. The orchestral tuba realistically imitates a sound of the marine environment, albeit one designed by humans (utterance of a sort). For Peter, though, the sonic distance of the off-stage foghorn, like that of the Borough manhunt, is a signal of how far beyond society he has come. Peter, as Ellen says – in a line absent in Britten's libretto but printed in Slater's 1945 plot summary – has "walked out of the human world."[59] Characteristic of Britten's operatic dramaturgy is the enactment of a central plot motif in terms of the protagonist's on-stage "hearing."[60]

Earlier in this chapter, I remarked on the striking resemblance of the choric hate speech in *Peter Grimes* to Althusser's image of the ideological subject's formation "along the lines of the most commonplace everyday police (or other) hailing: 'Hey, you there!'" (Althusser 131). Having explored the mad scene's dialogic form, it may be worth stressing some implications of the Althusserian scene of interpellation for an understanding of the opera as a work of allegorical significance. Althusser's model posits both an authoritarian hailing voice, and a subject who turns in response.[61] In this turning motion, though (as theorists of ideology have often noted), is the site of a problematic circularity: how, Terry Eagleton asks, does the individual "recognize and respond to the 'hailing' which makes it a subject if it is not a subject already? Are not response, recognition, understanding, subjective faculties . . .?" (143). For Butler, this theoretic circularity is endemic to an analysis of power acting not only *upon* the subject (by the force of hailing utterance) but also *through* it (in the agency of the turn itself): "there can be no subject prior to a submission" (1997b: 117). The more salient question in Althusser's scene, she argues, is *why* the subject might feel compelled to turn, accepting the terms of its hailing. The psychic disposition of the one who turns, Butler claims, is tied to an acknowledgment of guilt, and a vulnerability to laws – human or divine – whose authority is reiterated by the calling voice.[62]

The forces of utterance in Britten's *Grimes* partake of an Althusserian circularity, one situated in the reiteration of leitmotivic themes shared between Peter and the chorus. Precisely because Peter and the chorus never meet face to face after Act 1, the opera constructs their relationship in solely thematic terms. Each party depends for its operatic being on an interplay of thematic utterance freighted with the illocutionary force of speech (even the purely orchestral passacaglia and "Mad" interludes resound with remembered words). An audience cannot think Peter's identity independently of the choric hate speech of the Borough (who, conversely, have little operatic presence independent of their aggression). This reciprocally formed operatic subjecthood is legible in the score's concentration on one central theme as the relay between individual and society. All of Peter's frustrations and instabilities well up in the announcement of the Prayer theme, and it bears all the weight of the Borough's hatred and calls for vengeance. Later in Act 2, and in the Act 3 mad scene, Peter himself – as if caught up in the dangerously mechanical Prayer repetitions of the choric hate speech and passacaglia – voices resistance to the Borough's calls by resorting to the very theme with which his subordination is enacted.

But the prolonged scene of hailing that is *Peter Grimes* differs from Althusser's in one important respect – its focus on the proper name. The opera's play with the illocutionary force of speech is aligned early on – as early as possible – with hailings of Peter by name. It is the very opacity and emptiness of the proper name, ultimately, that makes it so malleable a figure for identity, and so sinister a vehicle for an allegory of social relations at their most vicious. By naming, the opera enacts a range of speech acts from the calling of a witness to the calling of a death threat, Peter's own capitulation to the chorus and, finally, a lullaby. Proper names, as Searle points out, are a verbal shorthand: they work "not as descriptions, but as pegs on which to hang descriptions" (1969: 172). In the mad scene, acts of naming ultimately return us to an allegorical reading of Peter's tragedy, but one in which the familiar abstractions – individual, society – have stage presence and sounding form in the music's most basic exchanges. Naming, in all its social forces, is what rings in our ears after the applause has died down.

Naming, I have argued, is never an innocent gesture; speech acts, as moments of human contact in language, are inevitably political acts. Peter in the Prologue warns Ellen, "you'll share the name of outlaw too!" and she reassures him – naïvely, it turns out – "Peter, we shall restore your name."[63] The tragic distance traversed in the opera is that between the human contact still possible with Ellen in the love duet – "a hand that you can feel," the sound of a voice that says: "Here is a friend" – and Peter's situation at the end, when he can no longer feel Ellen's hand or hear her voice. The opera manages its isolation of the protagonist in a display of intersecting legal and linguistic forces, matching "the name of outlaw" to the name Peter Grimes.

3 Motive and narrative in *Billy Budd*

Musical motives in *Peter Grimes* are utterances, in the sense that they appear first as musical vehicles for the texted vocalizing of stage characters. Characteristic melodic shapes set sung text, as speech acts, and continue, by their returns, to exert an illocutionary force that is precise, if not entirely fixed. It is only when the orchestra abandons an accompanimental role for a more autonomous thematic "voice" of its own, that motives assume a force of utterance largely independent of the singers. Such wordless moments deepen the semantic charge of a melodic shape, imbuing it with a mysterious presence, an identity of its own. When the orchestral passacaglia magnifies Peter's Prayer motive by obsessive repetition, the prayer comes to stand outside the action, at a remove that opens up a discursive space within which musical drama can operate on a level independent of text-bound expression of a local situation.

Motive, in *Billy Budd*, is a more diverse, intricate, and problematic concept than in *Grimes*. It is less directly associated with vocal utterance, and more often an agent of abstract conceptual, even metaphysical reference. It is by musical motive that the threat of Mutiny weaves its way into the operatic score as a distinct presence; equally, in Act 2, the innately elusive Mist – an image only glimpsed in the novel – looms larger in the opera by its motivic identity.[1] A family of motivic shapes is in play, and there is a greater interaction among them. Further, the opera exploits a basic overdetermination of reference between Vere and Claggart, such that their musical identities converge during the Act 2 trial scene.

This chapter focuses on motives as keepers of the mysteries and secrets so central to Melville's novel. Secrecy requires a concealing motion: a presence is made known, but its precise significance (its "nature," Melville would say) remains obscure. In the book, the thread of secrecy is spun mostly by a third-person narrator, occasionally revealing a character's mental state, but often admitting (via first-person interjections) an inability to grasp hidden truths in words. In the opera, a comparable discourse evolves in the orchestra, via a pattern of motivic returns. I do not claim, however, that this orchestral contribution is directly comparable to the narrator function in literature. Rather, in exploring parallels of discursive construction between literary source and operatic adaptation, my aim is to uncover something of the opera's distinctive reinterpretation of Melville's self-styled "inside narrative." Adapting *Billy* for the stage, Britten and Forster find technical solutions that retain the novella's much-debated ambiguities of tone while, if anything, deepening – through musical translation – those qualities of the mysterious, the ineffable, that frame Melville's parable.

Discussion begins with Vere's situation in the Prologue, as articulated by an introductory unfolding of leitmotives of shrouded significance; turning to Act 1, I explore the function of motives as identifying references, with particular attention to the harmonic and gestural underpinnings of Claggart's musical presence, and the identity of the deceiving operatic mask he presents to the innocent Billy. Moving to the Act 2 trial scene and its aftermath, the dramatic import of motivic return takes on an uncanny dimension with the orchestral manifestation of Claggart's presence following his actual death. Vere at this point is silenced, and so Billy's fate is sealed. In detailing the quasi-narratorial orchestral discourse of Act 2, I take as a starting point the obvious contrasts of pace between the dizzying events surrounding Billy's accusation, and their distanced recounting in the subsequent trial scene. The audience, in effect, experiences events twice, a sequence mediated and controlled by the orchestral play of thematic returns. In the imposing grandeur of the "interview" chords, finally, gestures of return move the wordless orchestral drama beyond the level of directly thematic or motivic utterance.

1. Motive as mystery in the Prologue

(a) Thematic confusion

> Oh what have I done? Confusion, so much is confusion.
>
> Vere, in Britten's Prologue

The intriguing harmonic dichotomy opening the Prologue to Britten's *Billy Budd* has long fascinated operatic listeners as a discourse of musical uncertainty setting the tone for the moral ambiguities of the drama to follow.[2] As the figure of Edward Fairfax Vere appears on stage, now an old man, he struggles to recall the exact circumstances of the action about to commence. These distant memories, and the emotional unease they provoke, are evident in the sounds drifting up from the orchestra, particularly in the music's delicate hesitancy of tonal definition, organized around the focal pitch discrepancy of two tonics (a lower B♭, an upper B♮:

Ex. 3.1a). The Bb/B♮ pitch opposition is evident at first in a bold registral division of tonal strata; as the Prologue unfolds, the same tension is marked out by four cadences, the outer pair prolonging Bb, the inner two pointing to its subversive B♮ challenger. Cadence 1, coinciding with Vere's stage entrance (Ex. 3.1b) breaks the stratified confusion in a moment of local registral coherence.[3] Arriving on the diatonic V_3^4 of Bb major, the cadence offers a momentary sense of tonal resolution and of mental clarity, an impression enhanced by the announcement of new thematic ideas (bracketed on the example). Such provisional calm, though, is brief, and Vere's "confusion," with its vocal line suspended ambiguously between Bb and B♮ (see Ex. 3.1c) provides the central climax point of the Prologue. Throughout these opening moments of the drama, textural fragmentation and tonal dualism produce a fissured musical syntax matching that "quality of conflict in Vere's mind" that had first drawn Britten to the idea of writing an operatic *Billy Budd*.[4]

The harmonic uncertainty of pitch dualism raises questions, in wordless musical terms, over which tonic is in control. Yet "uncertainty" in the sense of an absence of direct reference is equally, in this opera, a thematic phenomenon. There are six distinct themes in the Prologue (nos. 1–6, Ex. 3.2). Each one is projected clearly enough as a melodic shape, but what, in fact, do they stand for? Themes appear to correspond to specific events or concepts in Vere's monologue, by way of musical illustration, yet the precise nature of the reference in each case remains vague. Occasionally, his vocal line abandons amorphous recitative, itself assuming thematic shape, as when announcing theme 5, to Forster's near-direct quotation from Melville: "so that the Devil still has something to do with ev'ry human consignment to this planet of earth." Vere's reflection, typically, is on an unspecified and abstract moral problem ("*something* to do with"), and it precipitates the tonally vagrant climax observed already (Ex. 3.1c). His animation subsides with the return of the soft opening music, but his final cadence and closing question – "who saved me?" – leaves an audience puzzled by what they have just witnessed.[5] Themes 1–6 refer not to stage actions – besides Vere's appearance, there are none – but to tantalizingly vague moments within Vere's text.

The Prologue's musical image of an intricate tangle of memories is built up in a network of shared intervallic contours, linking ideas distinct in other respects. Layout (a) in Example 3.2 displays the intervallic similarity of themes 2, 4, and 6 – each rising a minor sixth – in contrast to the rocking-third and falling-fourth patterns of 1, 3b, and 5. The analysis documents certain readily audible facets of the thematic argument – theme 2's

Ex. 3.1: (a) The focal B♭/B♮ pitch discrepancy at the opening of the Prologue; (b) Cadence 1 and Vere's stage entrance; (c) Vere's "confusion"

(a)

(b)

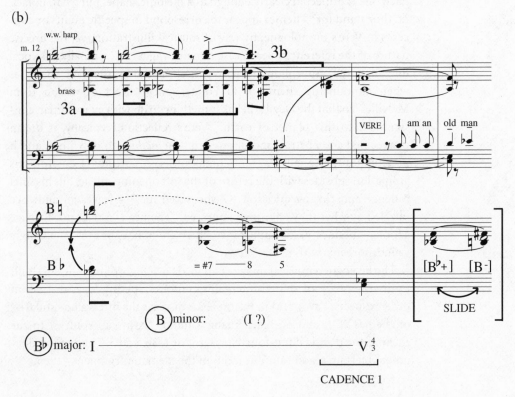

Ex. 3.1 (*cont.*)

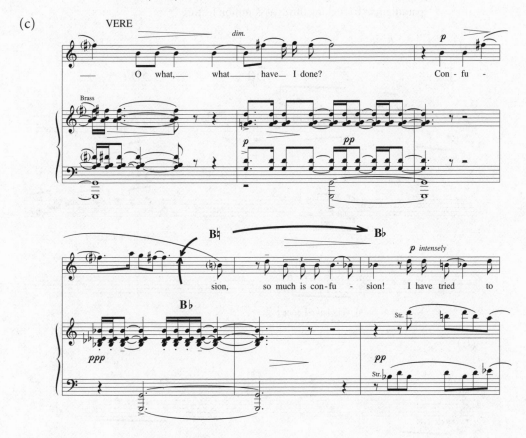

"newness" (a departure from the thirds in 1), and the disruptive quality of
3a–b, an incursion of brass octaves (and martial rhythms) on the gently
rocking string phrases. But one need not discount the presence of a disguised similarity uniting otherwise disparate musical ideas, both as icons
of Vere's confusion, and as a force of underlying motivic purpose. To
propose a second hearing (see layout b) is to draw attention to alternative
paradigms of resemblance. Here, themes 2 and 4 are heard as deriving
from the initial rocking thirds (theme 4, i.e., is identified by rising thirds,
not by its boundary-sixth). This interpretation has dramatic consequences, for theme 4 now embodies a manic acceleration and distortion of
the gently rocking thirds of 1 and 2; or (retrospectively) theme 1 harbors
the seeds of theme 4, as if all Vere's troubled thoughts spiral out from the
deceptively calm lullaby of the opening thirds. Theme 6, in this hearing,
stands apart on the basis of its forthright ascending fifth.

Ex. 3.2: Two hearings of the motivic network of the Prologue: (a) intervallic paradigms; (b) rocking thirds as common feature

Vere's thoughts at times acquire glimpses of precision in the expressive detail of word painting,[6] yet these single-word correspondences are tantalizing exceptions, and the images in his mind are shared with the audience less by specific verbal articulation than through the individuality of the musical gestures that intersperse the monologue. Thus while themes 1 and 2 circulate more or less continuously, 3a and 3b usually precipitate a cadence. Themes 4, 5, and 6 are single statements of gestural and textural individuality: the "stammer" Vere mentions as theme 4 appears is enacted by a rising wave of jerky melodic bursts over a pedal-point trill; theme 5 quells this by Vere's solo vocal outburst, as "the Devil" is named; the desperate question at theme 6, finally ("O what have I done?"), is supported by a momentous bass pedal, a startling event in music otherwise clustering in the high treble end of the registral gamut.

Musically and verbally, the Prologue is suffused with a Wagnerian *Ahnung* – a "foreshadowing" – of themes that will return later on in more clear-cut dramatic contexts. Equally pertinent, in the case of the Prologue, is the novelistic tradition of an "enigmatic introit," where a narrator is initially distant from a character, but later draws the reader into knowledge of motivations and viewpoint.[7] The mystery of Vere's "confusion" comes to audiences in the tension between his verbal abstraction and the music's gestural refinement. Shared thematic contours are not necessarily consciously evident in performance, precisely because each theme is so starkly individual in its rhythmic and timbral features. The Prologue calls into question the truism that pits verbal powers of denotation against music's inability to particularize; here, it is Vere's words that fail to approach the precision and immediacy of the musical themes.

Problematizing musico-verbal alliances, the Prologue establishes a fascination with possibilities of reference, both linguistic and musical. The situation in the Prologue is prophetic, for Vere in Act 1 is relatively undefined, in thematic terms, while his antagonist John Claggart asserts a powerful and subversive presence by thematic forms of disguise (a point I will return to). With this dramatically skewed thematic rhetoric, Britten in the Prologue and Act 1 prepares the ground for the most significant dramaturgical coups of Act 2 – Claggart's uncanny musical reappearance, after his physical death, and the thematically void orchestral "interview," whose effect, ultimately, is achieved by a *withholding* of reference. Before investigating these claims, though, my discussion will lay some vital theoretic groundwork by taking a closer look at the possibilities of so-called "leitmotives," themes that return, and in doing so, point beyond themselves to some precise referent.

(b) Problems of leitmotivic reference

Precision of semantic reference is integral to the leitmotive concept as announced in Wagner's musico-dramatic theory:

> Music cannot think: but it can materialize thoughts [*Gedanken verwirklichen*], i.e., it can give forth their emotional-contents as no longer merely recollected, but made present. This it can only do, however, when its own manifestment is conditioned by a poetic aim, and when this latter, again, reveals itself as no mere thing of thought, but a thing expounded in the first place by the organ of the understanding, namely word-speech. A musical motive [*Motiv*] can produce a definite impression on the feeling, inciting it to a function akin to thought, only when the emotion uttered in that motive has been definitely conditioned by a definite object, and proclaimed by a definite individual before our very eyes.[8]

A musical motive makes a "definite impression" only via association with specifics – a verbal text, a physical object, an individual singer. By this association, the returning motive can "materialize" for an audience its emotional-dramatic "contents." In more modern semiotic terms, music and words act as components of a fused signifier, evoking a signified: dramatic and emotional contents (Fig. 3.1).[9]

Fig. 3.1: The leitmotive as operatic sign at its moment of definition

$$\left.\begin{cases} \text{music} \\ \text{libretto words} \qquad\qquad\qquad\qquad\quad \textit{fused signifier (S)} \\ \\ \text{dramatic/emotional concept} \qquad\qquad \textit{signified (s)} \end{cases}\right\} \text{SIGN}$$

Thus far, the operatic leitmotive conforms broadly to Saussure's model of the linguistic sign. In the perceiving mind, a sign comprises reciprocal motions between motive/signifier and "content"/signified. In performance for attentive listeners, leitmotives ensure a continuous stream of referential musical gestures. But the *Billy Budd* Prologue already departs from this model by its verbal eschewal of specifics; Britten, I claimed, subverts Wagner's model to Melvillean ends, by invoking referents that are self-evidently vague. A second, more general complication arises if one considers ways in which leitmotives typically return: while the signifier at the moment of definition is, according to Wagner, a fused alliance of music and words, later recurrences are frequently untexted and purely orchestral (to say nothing here of associations with new verbal texts). An adequate account of the operatic leitmotive must pay careful attention to the interaction of musical and verbal signifiers.

Leitmotives acquire semantic trappings much as a child learns words: by association. A leitmotive can function as a discrete lexical item – an arbitrary or conventional sound image with a fixed conceptual referent. A leitmotive may retain a root meaning while undergoing transformations that refine a local meaning. In the right context, a motive can move beyond simple ostensive reference to a character's thought or action, to make what amounts to a proposition (in *Die Walküre*, a carefully placed orchestral intervention tells an audience that Wotan is Siegmund's father).[10] Wagner's emphasis on definite reference echoes the mid-nineteenth-century view that music after Beethoven was evolving from abstract tone-play to ever more distinct semantic contents.[11]

When words impinge on music, as they do when a leitmotive is announced, "meanings" – in the form of referential gestures – arise via a chain of verbal-musical relays. But there is a potential slippage here, for while the original words that define a leitmotive may be extensive initially, in later appearances they are truncated, replaced, or absent. A listener at this point may still hear the motive in relation to an earlier verbal signifier – a name for the leitmotive – yet that name must now be accommodated to some fresh context. The problem here, as Thomas Grey points out, is in reducing motives to "fixed musical-semantic tags, static signifiers" (1996: 188) – the Stammer-motive, say – a practice that belies the shifting referents that accrue during a music drama. Yet the naming of musical motives, however suspect, seems unavoidable for the listener following opera's word-saturated drama; as Carl Dahlhaus puts it, "the name that half-misses the object is nevertheless the only way to get at it" (1979: 61).

In the theatre, the listener's desire to know – *why* this theme? – is basic to the psychology of operatic listening (a point Wagner well understood).[12] The question shifts quickly to referents: who or what does this motive stand for? But this "standing for" inevitably falls short, somehow (in Novalis's phrase, "we leave the identical in order to represent it").[13] Once draped over something, names themselves become objects: "To name," Heidegger says, "is to call and clothe something with a word. What is so called is then at the call of the word" (1968: 120). Giving a name (N) to a leitmotive (L) promotes a fiction of musico-verbal equivalence (N ≡ L), a relation conveyed in a whole roster of representation-words, from the plain copula, to numerous verbs – refer, evoke, call to mind, denote – with more or less pronounced physical or mental connotations. But naming also drives a wedge between a pre-linguistic musical hearing and the linguistic part of a listener's perception, for musical themes now possess a linguistic burden always somehow extraneous to their content as non-verbal sounds.[14]

A leitmotive stands out from the ongoing flow of post-Wagnerian orchestral music as something marked. That sense of setting-into-relief that accompanies the announcement or return of a leitmotive is an instant discursive shift, isolating the motive itself from what frames it. By what Erving Goffman calls *keying*, listening moves from a primary framework to one in which the leitmotive "counts" as a referential gesture.[15] Hearing theme 4 in the Prologue, the words first associated with it – ending with a "stammer in the angelic song" – form the basis of a name (Stammer motive) more readily recalled than a complete verbal phrase. (In this case, keying is ensured by an instant shift, beginning with the trumpet's C♯–D trill, to new thematic materials.) The word *refers*, but lacks descriptive "detail"; music, once reference is active, fills out that detail: words refer to a "stammer," but it is by the precise form of the musical gesture – theme 4's coiled energy and unpredictable melodic bursts – that we *experience* the stammer as what Wagner calls an "act of music."

The Stammer–motive – as I will term theme 4 in its role as a returning theme with defined semantic reference – juxtaposes an arbitrary verbal sign with a musical signifier that is "motivated" by a form of resemblance to the referent.[16] The music itself realizes, by onomatopoeic gesture, the action of stammering, while Vere's words point up a metaphysical retinue ("imperfection in the divine image," among other phrases). The concept of "stammer" comes into focus, operatically, through two channels, as arbitrary linguistic signs are coordinated with motivated musical symbols. By the time Billy himself appears in Act 1, Scene 1, the prosaic fact noted by the officers as the motive returns ("he stammers, that's a pity") is already a sign with more abstract reference. The leitmotivic chain is functioning: Billy's stage appearance confirms the Stammer-motive's role in the main plot and "explains," retrospectively, its presence in the Prologue. The two Stammer motives are mutually significant, and it is typical of Britten's operatic technique that "voiced inarticulacies" of Melville's original should assume a directly thematic form in the score.[17]

Whether the musical signifier is motivated or arbitrary, the operatic definition of a leitmotive will arise through some three-way coalescing of words, music, and signified content, as well as evoking higher-order significations depending, for instance, on a wider dramatic context. One could treat the Stammer-motive as a nested hierarchy of signs (following work of Roland Barthes). In model (a) of Figure 3.2, a first-order sign (the lower stage on the diagram) arises from the purely verbal connection of the phrase "some defect" to the notion of a metaphysical flaw; a second-order sign follows when this signifier/signified pair itself functions as signified for theme 4. Yet a higher order of signification places this Stammer–motive

Fig. 3.2: The Stammer motive as a hierarchy of musical and verbal signs (after Barthes 90)

(a)

S: S T A M M E R LEITMOTIVE			**s:** ORIGIN OF VERE'S CONFUSION
S: *Theme 4* [symbol]	**s:** Stammer		
	S: "some defect"	**s:** metaphysical flaw	

(b)

	Theme 4 **S:** .... "some defect"	metaphysical **s:**　flaw

sign in its dramatic context, as a new signifier, something akin to the "origin of Vere's confusion." Model (b) in Fig. 3.2 conflates the lower two levels in model (a) into one sign with music and text "fused" as equal first-order signifiers (a view that accords with the near-simultaneity of presentation of words and music in the *Billy Budd* Prologue).[18] The Barthesian model is something of an ideal, though, for *Billy Budd* is an opera dominated, as Barry Emslie remarks, by "strategies of evasion" (44), a point worth elaborating with reference to a single leitmotive.

(c) The "Mutiny" cluster and motivic return

Discussing the Stammer–motive, I considered reference primarily as the result of an "announcement" – the moment when a motive acquires nameable associations. Attention moves now to forms of reference arising when a motive *returns*, for return is central to motivic identity, no matter how forceful the semantic trappings of an initial appearance. The object of study here is Vere's "confusion" theme, number 6 in the Prologue (Ex. 3.1c above), a theme that gradually accrues, by numerous returns, a commanding presence in the opera's musical fabric and a pivotal role in its plot sequence. It is tempting to identify this theme, as do recent commentators, via a cluster of ideas – "repression, rebellion and mutiny," for instance (Cooke–Reed 1) – depicted or directly mentioned in the libretto at its appearances. Such semantic interpretations posit the motivic workings of an overarching network of associations accumulating throughout the musico-dramatic structure. In Wagner's terms, this "binding alliance" of prominent "melodic moments"[19] might encompass both "*Gefühls-*" or "*Erscheinungsmotive*" (motives embodying feelings, or motives that merely show some physical part of the visible scene).[20] Comparable concepts, including the so-called *tema cardine* – a recurring theme "about which the entire drama is made to hinge"[21] – govern Verdian operatic thought, but it remains to be seen whether such models are relevant to Britten's practice.

Numerous later recurrences of the Prologue's motive 6 (on the lips of all three of the main characters, and heard from the chorus too) cut across any simple division between, for example, abstract "feelings" and concrete "objects": the theme does not stand for any single mood or physical thing, nor is it the property of one character or group. What begins in the Prologue as the theme of Vere's "confusion" returns as the choral worksong of Act 1, Scene 1, only acquiring its direct link to the threat of mutiny – a "confusion" of naval order – in the following scene, when the officers misinterpret Billy's farewell to his old ship. By the time the Novice tempts Billy with guineas (Act 1, Scene 3), this "confusion-worksong-mutiny" theme is familiar enough to serve as a basis for variations. In Claggart's hands, theme 6 is subject to motivic disguise – diminutions in Example 3.3a do not disturb a basic rising-fifth-to-sixth shape. That the leitmotive goes underground as the opera proceeds is itself a sign of Claggart's cunning. In Vere's rebuke to Claggart's Act 2 accusations (Ex. 3.3b), the Mutiny theme's function as an orchestral comment on Vere's situation depends on a discursive contrast between his prominent vocal line and the more subtle thematic presence in the orchestral bass. Initially an untexted adjunct to Vere's vocal line and the upper-register triads, this subversive challenge soon "belongs" to Claggart (whose "Ah, pleasant looks" comment doubles the orchestral theme). Vere's words are heard to confront a theme with a long history, and the result is a leitmotivic reminder that Vere will underestimate Claggart.

Tracing the "mutually explanatory" returns of the Mutiny theme in greater detail, one might dwell on the role other facets of the musical argument – pitch level, for instance – play in assuring aural recognition of each motivic return, or in elaborating the unrest attending the core concept of Mutiny.[22] Such an inquiry reflects the truth of Dahlhaus's basic reminder that motives make their effect not at "the first impact of immediacy, but at the second stage, when immediacy has combined with reflection" (1979: 61). Relatively simple meanings ("Mutiny," "Stammer," and so on) are just a core from which later meanings radiate over operatic time. In *Billy Budd*, an evolving chain of events unfolds, each link "tagged" by a Mutiny

Ex 3.3: (a) Disguised Mutiny shapes in Claggart's music; (b) the Mutiny shape as an orchestral comment on Vere's rebuke.

(a)

(b)

Fig. 3.3: "Mutiny"-tagged plot events as a cluster referring to a central abstract concept

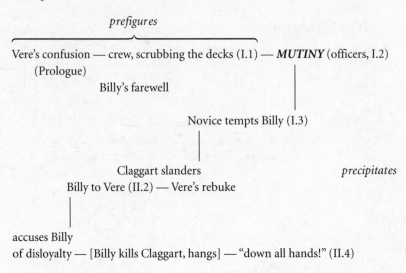

motive, and the result is a distinctive configuration – a plot – rather than a mere sequence of actions. Leitmotives, then, are crucial to the possibility of narrative in opera.

The opera's main plot events are grouped in Figure 3.3 around a single, defining statement (Act 1, Scene 2) of Mutiny as a threat to the world of Vere's ship. The confusion of Vere's Prologue loosely prefigures explicit announcement of a mutiny threat in Act 1, Scene 2; subsequent events are consequences of that threat. Returns of this Mutiny theme trace a path from the Novice's attempted deception, to Claggart's false witness, Vere's rebuke aria, and Claggart's direct accusations of Billy. With the relatively explicit definition of a conceptual abstraction ("mutiny") in Act 1, Scene 2 – where the officers speak of the recent Nore mutiny – other melodic moments apparently function as exemplary instances of a single concept.[23] Despite this centrality, though, it is simplistic to speak of theme 6 personifying "mutiny" as a God might embody an abstract force in Greek tragedy. For audience members, leitmotivic listening requires that we reconcile the semantic certainty of abstract monologic reference with the local semantic flexibility of disparate plot events (Vere's confusion, Billy's farewell, the officer's fears, *et al.*) that happen to share one leitmotive.

Wagner's idea that motives produce "a definite impression on the feeling"[24] captures an interplay of perceptual and emotional responses inherent to leitmotivic discourse. Leitmotives are "mental, not . . . physical image[s]," signs of a character's unspoken attitude to others, to objects, or to situations (Cone 113). They appeal to a listener's memory of earlier dramatic situations; to hear a leitmotivic reference is to recall an experience, rather than simply to retrieve information. The discussion entails not one, but two experiencing subjects – the on-stage character, and the witnessing listener – so that motive 6 in *Budd* signifies not mutiny *tout court*, but attitudes to the threat of mutiny in the minds of certain characters at specific moments in the opera. To draw this distinction is not to throw out the concept of a paraphrasable referent, but to sense its inflection at each appearance, both for those on stage and for those listening.

Talk of mental attitudes raises the possibility of a semiotic model of the leitmotive that embraces the consciousness apprehending signifier and signified. C. S. Peirce's well-known formulation – "A sign, or *representamen*, is something which stands *to somebody* for something in some respect or capacity"[25] – applies quite directly to the workings of the Mutiny motive:

musical/verbal signifier	*signified*	*"to somebody … in some respect"*
"what have I done?"	confusion	Vere, Prologue
"oh heave"	forced labor	Chorus, I.1
theme 6 "farewell, old *Rights o' Man*"	farewell to comrades	Billy, I.1
"the floating republic"	mutiny	Vere, officers, I.2

In each situation, one signifier (theme 6) produces a new signified. In the final case, the abstract category "mutiny" acts as a type of which the preceding signifieds (confusion, forced labor) are understood retrospectively to be tokens.

A Peircean view of leitmotivic semiosis is a reminder that an audience's reception of a given motive may be mediated by a character's on-stage relation to musical ideas and that vocal and orchestral motive statements may address different listeners. When a character on stage *sings* a motive, for instance, its signified might well be understood by others on stage (and only secondarily by a listening audience). Vocal presentation of leitmotives helps dramatize at the thematic level the interpersonal, dialogic exchanges among those on stage (a central concern, I have argued, in the case of motives in *Peter Grimes*). Vocal motives may also promote a sense of phenomenological on-stage "hearing." When, in Act 1, Scene 2, the officers recall Billy's "*Rights o' Man*" cry of the scene before, the return of motive 6 is for them a sign of mutinous intent, but it also mimics the cry they *heard* for themselves. (Billy's use of motive 6, though, cannot easily be understood as proof that he himself heard the chorus's worksong, which had subsided well before his entrance; in this case, one senses the presence of a narrative viewpoint within the opera's thematic discourse, distinct from the utterances of those on stage.[26])

The distinction between vocal and orchestral statements of semantically charged leitmotives helps to differentiate cases of on-stage "hearing" – where the character is (in Peirce's term) the *interpretant* of the sign – from situations where the character is "deaf" to themes presented by the orchestra (while the audience is the interpretant).[27] Vocal statements of motives inflect actual speech among characters; orchestral statements tend toward more epic utterance. Among motives discussed so far, the Stammer motive is initially an orchestral phenomenon with a fairly fixed referential charge, while the Mutiny motive appears more often in the vocal lines, to diverse texts and in superficially disparate situations. But the opera's play of thematic reference is never mechanical, and (as I argue below) much of the leitmotivic argument in Act 2 turns on details of "voice placement" – the precise timbral relations between voices and instruments in a texture at a given moment.

Before making any argument about Act 2, though, discussion must first consider those instabilities of reference attendant on the musical presence of Claggart in Act 1. The Master-at-Arms is remarkable, thematically (as I have already hinted), for his powers of disguise, and it is to this facet of his stage persona – specifically, to the crucial place, within his motivic identity, of certain *harmonic* fingerprints – that I now turn. Claggart's Act 1 musical persona confirms that the operatic *Billy Budd* is (in all senses) a drama of motives. Yet the complexity of his musical being implies further that motives may "refer" in a way that is ultimately mysterious, never fully within our grasp.

2. Claggart's Act 1 presence

> The point of the present story turning on the hidden nature of the master-at-arms . . .   *Billy Budd*, chapter 11

Forster compared Melville's *Billy Budd* to a Greek myth – something "so basic and so fertile that it can be retold or dramatized in various ways" (1951: 4) – and my discussion here will consider the question of retelling in terms of a translation between literary and operatic media. In particular, I am interested in how the elusiveness of the literary Claggart – of whom Melville can say only "To pass from a normal nature to him one must cross 'the deadly space between'" (74; Ch. 11) – finds expression in the shifting harmonic and tonal maneuvers that animate the Master-at-Arms's operatic presence. Britten's Claggart, like Melville's, is a figure of deceit, one who traps the innocent Billy by concealing his true "nature"; in the opera, though, this kind of subterfuge must be communicated to audiences by mechanisms other than the intervention of a literary narrator's voice. *Billy Budd*, as Barbara Johnson has argued, is a tale about Billy's failure to "read" Claggart correctly,[28] and so it is crucial to the opera that an audience witness – that it *hear* – the distance between Claggart as he seems to Billy and Claggart as he really is.

The dichotomous harmonic tensions of the opera's Prologue are (as I hinted earlier) a sign of Vere's "confusion," but they are too a sign of a larger conflation of the operatic figure of Vere himself with that of his petty officer, Claggart. The dramaturgical point is audible at a thematic, as well as a harmonic, level: the severe-sounding fanfare that prompts Vere's entrance in the Prologue (see the brass line bracketed in Ex. 3.1b above) returns to announce Claggart's entrance in Act 1, Scene 1 (Ex. 3.4). Retrospectively, an audience is made aware that it was Claggart who was central to Vere's cloudy memories at the opera's opening, or else simply that Vere's and Claggart's shared thematic affiliation is of some dramatic import. The thematic link, actually, is only *partial* – only motive 3b, the descending-fourth swing, returns, rather than the complete gesture of the Prologue. The contrast has rhetorical and dramatic force. In the Prologue, the brass theme "intrudes," a salient but undefined challenge to the rocking string music shrouding Vere's phrases; in Act 1, Scene 1, though, the theme is plainly announced vocally (Claggart: "Your honour, I am at your disposal") as music defining the singer on stage. Meanwhile, this theme's textural garb – stern octave doublings – moves to the bass register as the bedrock of Claggart's questions (Ex. 3.4, at "Your name?").[29]

Britten's score is already establishing contrasts between orchestral and vocal presentations of leitmotive references, complicating our listening awareness of dramatic presence. But a confusion or conflation of identity between Vere and Claggart is not confined to thematic and textural resemblances. The two entrance musics share a harmonic parallel. The Prologue's B♭-major/B-minor triadic opposition recurs transposed to G♯ minor/G major in Example 3.4. In each case, a major triad moves, by a chromatic voice-leading motion I will call SLIDE, to the minor triad rooted a semitone higher, or vice versa (Ex. 3.4 has both ascending and descending forms).[30] In the SLIDE progression, voices trace parallel chromatic motion in the root and fifth degrees of the two triads, about a common mediant pitch. The B♭-major triad (B♭+) SLIDES to a B-minor triad (B−) in Example 3.1b, G+ to G♯− in Example 3.4.[31] The SLIDE progression deserves a moment's analytic scrutiny, not simply as a harmonic link

Ex. 3.4: Claggart's first stage entrance, Act 1, Scene 1: Thematic and harmonic makeup

between Vere and Claggart, but also as the syntactic basis for Claggart's Act 1 deceit of Billy, and his Act 2 challenge to Vere himself. By an intricate harmonic means, Britten's opera constructs a triangular network of attractions linking the three men.

Claggart's Act 1 "impressing" of new recruits indicates the centrality of close-position triads in Britten's score, albeit within a highly distinctive idiom of restless chromatic strain. Claggart interrogates the first traumatized recruit (Ex. 3.4, "first man forward!"), to an unflinching B tonic, the brute force against which upper-register triads (G+, A−) strain without functional harmonic purpose, subsiding at the pause to the ambiguous, SLIDE-affiliated [F♯,G♯,D♯] trichord (see the analytic gloss). The discovery of Billy's stammer, meanwhile (Ex. 3.5a), is defined by FLICKER harmonies, related to SLIDE as chromatic inflections of a close-position triad, and to

Ex. 3.5: Triadic idioms in *Billy Budd* (a) the Stammer; (b) Claggart's chorale of deceit; (c) Claggart approaches Vere in Act 2

(a)

(b)
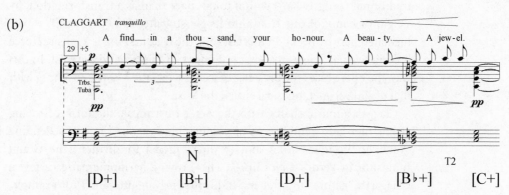

(c)

later forms of Claggart's triadic artfulness. When Claggart lauds Billy's physical beauty to the First Lieutenant, for instance – and whenever Billy himself is within earshot – triadically formed tensions are replaced by euphonious triadic consonance (Ex. 3.5b). The initial move from D+ to B+ here shares with FLICKER the tendency to complete-neighbor oscillations, and the following progression (D+, B♭+, then C+) moves by SLIDE-like semitonal voice-leading initially (D+ to B♭+), but in contrary, rather than parallel motion (followed by an unrelated T2 move from B+ to C+).

When Claggart approaches Vere in Act 2 (Ex. 3.5c), his triads are more consistently minor-mode, more uniformly in close-position voicings (giving a memorable snarl when scored for low brass), and more stable vehicles of a local tonic than are Vere's. Claggart's initial E♯−/F♯− move (Ex. 3.5c) gently "places," rather than subverts, the F♯ bass pedal; Vere's responding phrase, on the other hand, wanders from A+ up to B−, B♭− and finally C+ ("up" here being a literal registral ascent as he gazes at the sky). The A+/B♭− SLIDE itself, as Claggart is announced, works less as a traditional "progression" within tonal space than as a transformation, by sleight of hand, of one triad into its ghostly alter ego (the A+/B♭− pair mediated here by B♮−). In this last case, the triadic SLIDE is a musical force linking two challenges to Vere's judgment – Claggart and the mist. In this way, the opera fuses the presence of a character (the Master-at-Arms) with that of a quasi-metaphysical entity, the Mist.

Claggart's music shares with the Act 2 Mist music the form of roving chains of triads, reminiscent of comparable "vagrant" motions defining Wotan in Wagner's *Ring*, and (a direct model for Britten) the Grand Inquisitor in Verdi's *Don Carlo*.[32] These roving harmonic patterns reveal Claggart's "nature" to listeners. In his first private utterance, for example, Claggart's music SLIDES directly between triadic harmonies, making overt what was more concealed in his earlier entrance music. In the passage summarized in Example 3.6, Claggart's closing F-minor triad – tonicized by conventional cadence – is the dark answer to the bright E major of Billy's preceding "King of the birds" aria and his exuberant "Farewell" to his old comrades. Claggart's arioso is framed by a SLIDE from E+ to F−, in a snarling passage beginning "I heard, your honour." Claggart's closing vocal phrases reiterate in melodic form the E+/F− dichotomy that bounds the lower dyads in the bass stratum.[33] This moment in the scene – the first time Claggart voices his deeply ambivalent feelings about Billy – is remarkable for its tonal and dramatic fluidity. The proto-cinematic "dissolve" as Billy's bright E-major "Farewell" is overlain by the officers' tonally aggressive order ("Clear the decks!" on an A♯) and shipboard whistle sounds (the high F♮/G♮ flutes) effects a rapid change of dramatic perspective, from the naive Billy's

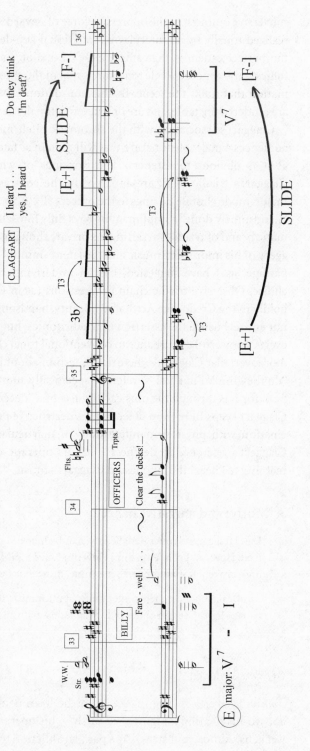

Ex. 3.6: Claggart's response to Billy's "Farewell" cry, Act 1, Scene 1: tonal and melodic detail

subversive outburst to the oppressive force of naval discipline. The drama is realized tonally by an interplay of traditional key-defining mechanisms – the perfect cadences that affirm Billy's E-major and Claggart's F-minor tonics – and a more mobile tonal force, that of the chromatic SLIDE transformation that stalks the scene. By this non-diatonic move, local tonic triads are rendered unstable, and are drawn into a tonally destructive pairing.

Claggart's association with the chromatic pitch-motion SLIDE reveals to audiences a malevolent nature that will remain as fatally hidden from Billy as it is obvious to listeners. The workings of what might be termed Claggart's triadic mask are apparent in the contrast between the warm major-mode chorale he sings to the officers (Ex. 3.5b, reworked later, in the "handsomely done" compliment he pays Billy himself) and the more chromatic brand of triadicism setting his private thoughts. The purposeful savagery of his impressing music and the later F-minor "I heard your honour" passage, as I have suggested, has an underlying systematicity of pitch choice. Obsessive triadic chain progressions (as in Ex. 3.6, and still more boldly in the Credo-like Act 1 aria, "Beauty, handsomeness, goodness") do not entirely usurp the assertion of triadic tonics, but their sequential drive exerts a powerful disturbance to conventional tonal claims. It is significant, moreover, that Claggart's rhetorical question about his superior officers – "do they think I'm deaf?" – refers to specifically auditory powers of cognition, for it is through the musical disguise of a "deceitful" tonal idiom that Claggart keeps Billy from detecting his destructive purpose. Melville's fascination with physical manifestations of inarticulacy – Billy's stammer, Claggart's reference to deafness – has its operatic counterpart in Billy's inability to "hear" the falseness in Claggart's music.[34]

3. Motive and narrative in Act 2

> I see all the mists concealed. Beauty, handsomeness, goodness coming to trial. How can I condemn him? How can I save him? My heart's broken, my life's broken. It is not his trial, it is mine, mine. It is I whom the Devil awaits.
>
> . . . . Beauty, handsomeness, goodness, it is for me to destroy you. I, Edward Fairfax Vere, Captain of the *Indomitable*, lost with all hands on the infinite sea.   Vere, Act 2, Scene 2

(a) Vere's silence

As events overtake Vere in Act 2 – as he loses control of good and evil aboard his floating "fragment of earth" – his operatic voice splinters and weakens. Almost as if struck by a parallel affliction to Billy's stammer, Vere himself is unable to speak. In the trial, this is literally so in Vere's own refusal to speak for Billy and, later, to guide his officers in their verdict (a major departure, this, from his legalistic eloquence in the book).[35] But Vere loses his voice in a sense other than by voluntary silence. When he does speak, he speaks no longer as Vere, but in the words of others. At the moment of Claggart's death, Vere himself adopts Claggart's Act 1 apostrophe to Billy ("Beauty, handsomeness, goodness"; see the epigraph to this section). His other words at this point ("my heart's broken, . . .") are those of the flogged boy Novice in Act 1. And Vere closes the scene, moments before he goes to communicate the sentence to Billy, by returning to these two ventriloquisms. Again Vere sings Claggart's apostrophe to Billy, followed now by words voiced previously in Act 1 by the Novice and the chorus – specifically, the image of being "lost forever on the endless sea" (one that will return in the Epilogue, too). To these strange verbal returns may be added a parallel between Vere's witness-like self-presentation ("I, Edward Fairfax Vere") in Act 2 and that of Claggart's Act 1 "Credo" aria; in Act 2, these confusions of voice are a force drawing Claggart and Vere together into a single, composite speaking presence. This "convergence" (first discussed as such by Donald Mitchell[36]) is a major reinterpretation by Britten, Forster, and Crozier, of Melville's plot, and it raises important questions of agency and narrative point of view. I will return to such questions presently, in a close reading of the trial scene. For the moment, though, I will suggest that the collapse of Vere as an autonomous character (in the traditional sense) develops an idea latent, though never fully revealed, in Melville's text.

Vere's convergence with Claggart is manifest in the return of key phrases in the libretto. But the actual realization of Vere's doubled speaking presence in Act 2 is predominantly a musical affair: Claggart's words are recognized as such because they coincide with salient *musical* returns, both in Vere's vocal part, and in its orchestral context. One might even claim that the finished opera gives us Britten's view of the story, rather than Forster's or Crozier's. Forster had actively pursued a goal of "rescuing" Vere from his creator: the long speeches Vere gives his officers, in Melville's trial scene, on the necessity of a strict martial-law trial for Billy, are replaced in the opera by conspicuous silences. But it is precisely these moments, when the Commander is vocally inactive, that allow Britten to, in effect, short-circuit the unambiguous interpretative rescue of Vere Forster sought. The orchestral commentary that replaces Vere's spoken presence in the trial scene only complicates and compromises his role in Billy's sentencing, by furthering his musical association with the dead Master-at-Arms.[37]

Leaving aside questions of relative authorial influence in the composite medium of opera, one finds, in turning directly to Melville's text, that while the Master-at-Arms's death decisively marks his exit from the novel's action, there are hints that the unexpected event has affected Vere's state of mind. Via the narrator's none-too-subtle intrusions, and in the guise of reported speech among other characters, the book calls the probity of Vere's actions into question. In one such digression, the surgeon examining Claggart's corpse speculates on Vere's own state:

> Was Captain Vere suddenly affected in his mind, or was it but a transient excitement, brought about by so strange and extraordinary a tragedy? As to the drumhead court, it struck the surgeon as impolitic, if nothing more. . . . He recalled the unwonted agitation of Captain Vere and his excited exclamations, so at variance with his normal manner. Was he unhinged?
> (101–02; ch. 20)

That the officers share the surgeon's view – "Like him too, they seemed to think that such a matter [Claggart's death] should be referred to the admiral" (102) – only strengthens the case against Vere, one the narrator continues to bring at the start of the lengthy trial scene of Chapter 21:

> Who in the rainbow can draw the line where the violet tint ends and the orange tint begins? Distinctly we see the difference of the colors, but where exactly does the one first blendingly enter into the other? So with sanity and insanity . . . .
>   Whether Captain Vere, as the surgeon professionally and privately surmised, was really the sudden victim of any degree of aberration, every one must determine for himself by such light as this narrative might afford.
> (102; ch. 21)

In the opera, questions about Vere's state of mind after Claggart's death – questions that ultimately become the crux of the drama in its operatic form – must be pursued by an examination of the Captain's music in Act 2 with particular attention, as I will argue, to purely orchestral forms of utterance. It is through Vere's silence in the trial scene that the opera makes room for instrumental episodes that are eloquent in their exploration of leitmotivic returns. By taking up once more the leitmotivic focus of earlier discussions of Act 1, then, it will be possible to inquire into the narrative possibilities of a purely orchestral "voice."

(b) From summary to scene: narration, action and the flow of operatic time

> Emplotment is the operation that draws a configuration out of a simple succession.   Ricoeur (1984: 65)

> In their suggestive, their ever-warranted return . . . these chief-motives of the dramatic action – having become distinguishable melodic moments which fully materialise their content – now mould themselves into a continuous

artistic form, which stretches not merely over narrower fragments of the
drama, but over the whole drama's self.   Wagner, *Opera and Drama* III.vi[38]

The whole concept of narration in opera needs careful definition. Even
accepting the claim that opera's affinities with the novel are stronger than
its ties to spoken drama, a critic convinced that opera "narrates" must
demonstrate the workings of a narrative function without oversimplifying
the range of such a concept in literary works, and with due attention to the
distinctive technical resources of a non-literary medium.[39] Operatic narration may approximate the effect of literary models, but it cannot dupli-
cate them. To recognize an orchestral "voice" distinct from those of the
singers themselves, capable of *telling* an audience something about the
stage actions they are witnessing, is to acknowledge a narrator-like presence, but one whose function will only loosely resemble some literary
counterpart. My analysis begins with the familiar Wagnerian argument
that the configuring force of coherence in spoken drama and in literary
narrative (what Ricoeur calls "emplotment") has an operatic analogue in
the large-scale thematic continuity wrought by leitmotivic return. But the
claim is a large one, and probing its basis, I will start by emphasizing just
how great the distance between literary and operatic drama really is.

Consider, for example, Melville's description of the pivotal moment of
the *Billy Budd* plot, Claggart's accusation of Billy before Vere:

> With the measured step and calm collected air of an asylum physician
> approaching in the public hall some patient beginning to show indications of
> a coming paroxysm, Claggart deliberately advanced within short range of
> Billy and, mesmerically looking him in the eye, briefly recapitulated the
> accusation.   (98; ch. 19)

Several features of this literary narrative can find no direct translation in
the music of an operatic adaptation: a distinction between present and
preterit tenses; a grammatical delineation of person; precise powers of reference; descriptive specificity. Transposed to the stage, as in Britten's operatic version of this scene (see Ex. 3.7), Claggart's entrance is immediately a
fact of the unscrolling present (the music says "advances" not "advanced").
As he advances, moreover, one cannot be sure of the orchestra's discursive
relation to the singer on stage; instrumental music, unaided by a text,
cannot distinguish between first and third persons: is it "I" or "he" who
advances in the orchestra? Formulating a slightly different question – Does
the orchestra advance *with* Claggart or *as* Claggart? – one confronts
another aspect of literary narrative, the notion of "distance," that cannot
be reproduced in any simple way in the operatic theater.

Even so, music's lack of grammatical markers may not be deemed a
problem here, for the orchestral pit-music arguably has a precise referential

Ex. 3.7: "Claggart deliberately advanced within short range of Billy and . . . recapitulated the accusation": the narrated action realized in Britten's Act 2, Scene 2

link to one live stage action. We don't need a grammatically defined person, tense, or deictic markers of context (such as "now" or "here") to understand this as music that goes with Claggart's "measured step"; the physical actions unfolding before our eyes confer a basic dramatic meaning on the score. We may even catch Claggart's "mesmeric" fixing of Billy in a good production (or a good seat). But a theatre audience will never, by wordless musical prompting, compare Claggart at this moment to an asylum physician, or Billy to his patient. No amount of orchestral music can stand in for the precision of these verbal images. The music will lose the attendant connotations of an institutionalized control – echoing earlier talk of an "unhinged" Vere – that lurk in Melville's phrases. Absent too is the reference to a "coming paroxysm," a danger clear to the reader who recalls Billy's stammer-defect, but not to Vere. Opera, lacking verbal powers of reference, must reinvent the episode on its own, original terms. Some of these are clear in Ex. 3.7: the restless harmonic argument, the textural, timbral, and rhythmic choices, and the thematic shapes, both as local musical agents marked by obsessive repetition, and as familiar leitmotivic shapes, forging links to other moments in the opera (Claggart's reworking here of the Mutiny motive).

But operatic drama is lacking only if the yardstick is a literary original; as drama, this passage is "bigger" than anything in the original, because Melville's narrative report of speech becomes direct speech on stage. The moment of accusation itself is transformed from a compact reporting phrase ("Claggart . . . recapitulated the accusation") into the vocal music of Example 3.7. Direct speech here assumes all the force of Claggart's accumulated aggression. Claggart continually repeats Billy's name and the harsh formal charge "William Budd, I accuse you," while the mounting threat is inadvertently prolonged by Vere's own order, "William Budd, answer!" (see Ex. 3.11 below).[40] Where Melville's narration confers the import of this moment by imagery, Britten's score heightens tensions by expressive details. Even within the "actional" amalgam of recitation and arioso, operatic song colors every moment of direct speech: details such as the somber hue of the orchestral doublings of the voice, and the steadily rising tessitura of the passage, offer a precision of musical inflection comparable in function (though otherwise unrelated) to the descriptive asylum imagery of Melville's narrative.

Moving from the book's *summary* mode ("Claggart deliberately advanced") to an operatic *scene*, one hears Claggart's every word directly, inflected in subtle ways by full-orchestral underlay. A similar shift occurs in translating Melville's one-sentence summary of Vere's testimony, later on, in the trial – "Concisely he narrated all that had led up to the catastrophe,

Ex. 3.8: (a) The operatic scene of Billy's trial; (b) the moment of Claggart's death

(a)

Ex. 3.8 (*cont.*)

(b)

omitting nothing in Claggart's accusation and deposing as to the manner in which the prisoner had received it" (105; ch. 21) – to the operatic stage (Ex. 3.8). The shift, in both cases, has temporal implications. The change from book to stage transforms both the duration of single events, and the speed at which they pass within a narrative chain.

The scene/summary distinction helps delineate how operatic representation departs from a literary source, but it is also familiar in purely literary narration. As Gérard Genette's classic analysis of Proust's style shows, a writer's control of pace is definable as the ratio established between the "story time" of events depicted (a minute, a year) and the "narrative time" taken to recount this period in words (a sentence, a chapter). Scenes in novels give story and narrative-time more or less equivalent duration (as in sections of direct dialogue, for example); summary, on the other hand, compresses the length of story time to some shorter narrative time. In the realist novel, Genette notes, scene and summary alternate as intermediaries between extremes of temporal movement, in a spectrum from a complete pause in the action (for description of some detail), to ellipsis (where omitted events have "zero" textual duration).

Opera, in its focus on a literally "scenic" unfolding of events, lacks the novel's summary mode of depiction. But opera, like the novel, creates a temporal flow; indeed, music can control time more precisely than can a verbal narrative (where actual reading speeds vary). In opera, the pace of the scene is in a very direct sense, a product of tempo;[41] but control of time is also more than a matter of long or short beats or the number of measures allotted a stage action; music that feels "fast" to audiences may convey the impression via non-rhythmic details (e.g., sudden or unpredictable changes in harmony or texture). More importantly, the flow of operatic time shares with novelistic narration the possibility of shifts between a present and one or more pasts. Shifts in the order of unfolding story events may occur by flashbacks or flash-forwards. In Britten's operas, the flow of narrative time, in each case, is achieved with a discourse of leitmotivic return. With this in mind, I turn in more detail to Vere's trial-scene testimony (Ex. 3.8).

The passage at (a) in Example 3.8 differs from Claggart's original accusation in the complexity of its temporal scheme. Where Claggart's earlier music (Ex. 3.7) conveys a continuously unfolding present scene, Vere's recollection of it is shattered by the conflation of several different temporal references. The unfolding "present," the time of the main narrative here, is established by the First Lieutenant's monotone repeating of the charge, in syllabic recitation with minimal orchestral backing. Vere's testimony, following, is immediately more complex. The scenic present continues as he speaks, but beyond this we hear leitmotivic returns of four distinct "past" moments. While Vere recounts the sequence leading up to Claggart's death vocally, the orchestra interrupts his narration with flashbacks. Chief among these, because most pervasively emphasized by recurrence, is the actual moment of Claggart's death (high-register woodwind trichords, marked on the score as "4"). The other three orchestral flashbacks involve the moment of the accusation itself (2), heard in the cello figure introducing and closing Vere's testimony; Billy's stammer (3); and Claggart's Act 1 hymn to Billy (1).

Time is flowing here, but things are out of step: while Vere's verbal narration follows a chronological sequence (accusation, stammer, death), the orchestral accompaniment is taken up most prominently with the single moment of Claggart's death. The ongoing flow of Vere's testimony is at odds with the sudden and fragmentary interruptions of the orchestral flashbacks. As if suggesting Vere's dazed mental state, the *order* of musical events as Vere sings is disturbed: reading orchestral leitmotivic returns, numbered as they occur in the plot sequence, from the beginning of the excerpt, we find the following:

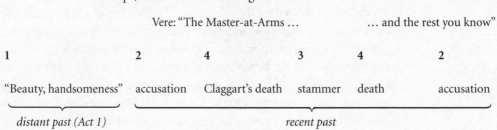

Claggart's death precedes Billy's stammer, reversing the logic of cause and effect. That stammer, in fact, is the only thematic event in the passage that directly illustrates Vere's words ("he stammered") at the moment he utters them. The accusation music, meanwhile, has a ritornello-like function, framing the entire speech. Theme (1), on the other hand – "beauty, handsomeness" – has little to do with the events of Claggart's death. Its local purpose is to accompany Billy's stage entrance, moments before. But one notes here the temporal disruption implicit in this choice of entrance-music: Britten's orchestra reaches back all the way to Claggart's Act 1 "Credo"[42] (as if to underline his role in bringing Billy to this moment). By leitmotivic return, a recent and a distant past coexist as Vere testifies.

Events are disrupted in duration, too. The compact moment-of-death music ('4' in Ex. 3.8a) is "stretched" by its interpolated return amid other fragmentary recollections. If the orchestra may be understood as providing access to Vere's consciousness,[43] then it is clear that he cannot get the moment of Claggart's death out of his mind as he sings.

The temporal unfolding of Vere's speech would appear to be inseparable from the referential charge of its leitmotivic returns. It is not just the fact of these returns that alters one's listening perception of how time passes; variations in the musical presentation of familiar themes influence how one interprets their return. Thus, one easily recognizes Claggart's death music by its contour, bright scoring, and trichordal texture; but one notices, too, that when Vere recalls Claggart's confrontation with Billy, the return is fragmented (compare the original passage, Ex. 3.8b). Glittering death-chords punctuate each vocal phrase, as if the immediacy of Vere's memory inhibits his getting out the words: "The Master-at-Arms [*chord*] . . . denounced the prisoner to me [*chords*] . . . for spreading disaffection [*chords*] . . ." Claggart's Act 1 aria, too – the "earliest" leitmotivic return – is also a fragment. Finally, the actual flow of these various "presents" is a matter of harmonic rhythm: the jagged death-chords occupy a relatively quick eighth-note stratum, while the bass-register trichords move more sluggishly.

The leitmotives identified so far do not exhaust the resonances of this passage. Hearing further, more subtle returns, one senses that Vere's narration is not in the present tense as it is experienced by the First Lieutenant and the audience, but weighed down by the crowding-in of past memories (in this, he resembles the Vere of the Prologue and Epilogue). Heavy bass-register pedals here allude to the recent past of Claggart's accusation music, but in conjunction with the jerky upper-register trichords of the death music, the complete texture reaches back much further, to Claggart's fearsome Act 1 impressing aria (see Ex. 3.4). In the trial, already, Vere is dogged by Claggart's musical presence in ways that go beyond the memory of his recent death.

Vere's testimony at this point in the action complicates the scenic present. By leitmotivic references, by their significant reorderings or varied repetitions, and by the interplay of the orchestra with the vocal line, Vere's words to the court interweave various pasts within the ongoing present. The simultaneity of temporal levels is particularly idiomatic to operatic resources. A counterpoint of vocal and orchestral themes allows for a musical unfolding of activities that is not bound by the needs of a strictly sequential presentation, or limited to a single, "present-tense" unfolding.[44]

4. Operatic "point of view": from Claggart's accusation to Billy's trial

(a) Narrative discourse in Act 2

Comparison of Claggart's accusations of Billy with Vere's trial testimony reveals how the chronology of a story may be transformed by reorderings or interpolations in the succession of its events. In both accusation and trial scenes, I have shown, such discursive work is carried out by a number of thematic returns in the orchestra, mediating the flow of operatic time established by purely vocal and verbal enunciation. A comparable strategy governs much larger spans in Act 2, and the question of narrative can be examined briefly as the result of coordinated processes of tonal and temporal patterning. Narrative *discourse* (as noted in Chapter 1) refers to the familiar distinction between the tale and its telling, and embraces all aspects of the expression of a content (or *story*) in some patterned configuration (or plot).[45] In Act 2, the most significant discursive shift is the event of Claggart's death. It forms the pivot around which the entire sequence, from his false witness to Vere (end of Scene 1) as far as the unseen "Interview" in which Vere communicates the death sentence to Billy, revolves.

Figure 3.4 summarizes musical and dramatic landmarks from Claggart's accusations to the end of the following scene. His death marks the gist of the moral "problem" of Melville's narrative – at this moment, the book's narrator remarks, "innocence and guilt personified in Claggart and Budd in effect changed places" (103; ch. 21). In the opera, the movement of the story from action to retrospection acquires comparable discursive emphasis through a long-range pattern of key and tempo relations.

Fig. 3.4: Claggart's death as the pivotal event in the narrative discourse of Act 2, Scenes 1–2

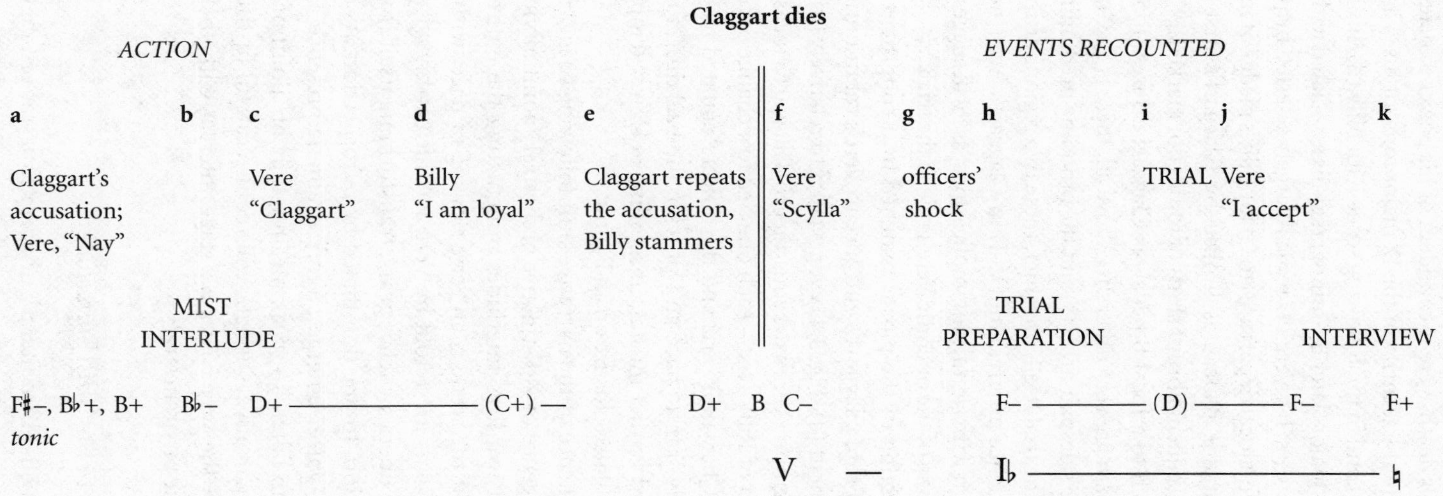

ACTION   *EVENTS RECOUNTED*

Claggart dies

a   b   c   d   e   f   g   h   i   j   k

          Vere   Billy   Claggart repeats   Vere   officers'   TRIAL Vere
          "Claggart" "I am loyal" the accusation, "Scylla" shock   "I accept"
                                 Billy stammers

Claggart's
accusation;
Vere, "Nay"

          MIST   TRIAL   INTERVIEW
          INTERLUDE   PREPARATION

F♯–, B♭+, B+ B♭– D+ ——— (C+) ———   D+   B   C–   F–   ————   F– (D)   F+
tonic

                   V ———   I♭

Before Claggart's death, Vere is confident of his power to defend Billy, an attitude apparent in the security of the D-major tonic of his "Claggart" aria (letter (c), Fig. 3.4) and in the following scene with Billy (d), his home tonic vanquishes the B♭-major (later B♭-minor) regions associated with Claggart's charges and the mist (a, b). Vere's D tonic is largely asserted by pedal point, with only the briefest local departure (to C) for Billy's pledge of loyalty to his captain. This D-major plateau is broken by Claggart's first accusation (section e), by subsequent abrupt shifts of tonic (not marked),[46] and finally, by a powerful lurch to a focal B pedal, as Claggart expires. Tonal motions after Claggart's death are very different. Above all, there is the "new" region of C minor in Vere's despair aria (f), and the brooding predominance of an F-minor tonic in the trial itself. Together, these two regions articulate a vast middleground cadence progression (V–I) in Claggart's Act 1 home key (F minor), a tonal shift with significant implications, as I will suggest presently, for an understanding of the operatic Vere's role in the trial.

This tonal directing of the plot is matched by a congruent scheme of tempo relations. From Claggart's entrance to Vere's cabin until his death, for example (segment (e), Fig. 3.4) events fall into relatively brief passages of three distinct tempi – Vere's nervous allegro, Claggart's measured lento, and the più mosso of Billy's fist – each one tied to a change of tonic. Vere's brief "Scylla and Charybdis" aria and the officers' agitated reactions continue the generally frantic pace and provide the backdrop for the more measured trial and verdict musics, unscrolling at slower tempi, and with more clearly articulated closure on an F tonic.[47]

A main consequence of the narrative shift following Claggart's physical death is the emergence of a distinctive orchestral "point of view," articulated in extended wordless interludes punctuating the entire sequence. Another feature of the scene is an eerie slowing of pace, within the trial itself, as earlier events are retold by Vere as "sole earthly witness." After Claggart dies, the opera switches gears, transforming itself from a narrative driven by action, to one dominated by retrospection. As an autonomous orchestral "voice" emerges, Vere's dramatic presence as a singing character begins to falter. To speak meaningfully of "point of view," as a facet of operatic narrative, though, will require careful justification and close attention to the way voices on stage interact with their wordless counterparts in the pit orchestra.

(b) Point of view in the "mist" interlude

Point of view, as a quality of literary or operatic narratives, may be understood as a response to questions such as "who sees?" and "who speaks?" As a "perceptual or conceptual position in terms of which the narrated situations and events are presented" (Prince 73), point of view is the mediating screen (in novels, a narrator) in a communication system between an author and the primary units (people, events) of a text. In Melville's *Moby-Dick*, for example, a named first-person narrator ("Call me Ishmael") conveys all information about characters and events that I, as a reader, glean from the book. Information is regulated, as Genette notes, not in an even process, but "according to the capacities of knowledge of one or another participant in the story" (162): in *Moby-Dick*, Ishmael narrates the story "from within" since he himself appears as a minor character.[48] The narrator's position in a literary system of communication may be summarized visually (see level (a)):

(a) literary communication

ideal author	(narrator)	characters		(narratee)	ideal reader
S3	S2	S1/R1	S1/R1	R2	R3
Melville	Ishmael	Ishmael, Queequeg, *et al.*		"you, reader"	reader

(b) dramatic communication

playwright	[ ]	actors		[ ]	audience

Level (b) in the chart compares the arrangement of senders and receivers in dramatic texts to that of literary narrative. Stage plays, as Manfred Pfister (1988: 4) notes, often lack the mediating system S2–R2. Plays can do without a narrator (S2) – no one need address an audience (R2) directly. Relevant information will be exposed incidentally, so that audiences follow the drama without any direct "filling-in" to break the illusion of watching a stage world.[49] Still, dramatic narratives very often do include mediating or "epic" structures in the S2 position (as with the Greek tragic chorus, the allegorical characters in medieval drama, and para-texts such as prologues and epilogues). As Hilda Meldrum Brown argues, theorists of stage drama too readily subordinate the role of epic, perspectival structures to a focus on the dialogue as the most distinctive "dramatic" feature (1–22). A polarization of purely "mimetic" drama and strictly "diegetic" narrative will collapse in any case where an authorial perspective is apparent. In drama with a highly organized image network, or in the summarizing utterances of a witnessing chorus, audiences are reminded of a "steering process" outside the scenic action itself.

Transposed to the operatic stage, narrative point of view might find an obvious manifestation in the orchestral music accompanying the staged action. "On the stage," Cone claims, "the singer does not portray a dramatic character directly but represents a character in a narrative" (13). The problem with this view, as Abbate has shown, lies in music's typically mimetic qualities as a temporal art that "traps the listener in present experience and the beat of passing time" (1991: 53). Music will only rarely be capable of asserting the distance narrative creates – of signaling a telling process separate from the tale. And music, she argues, typically lacks the most familiar mark of that distance – it "seems not to 'have a past tense'"; only rarely can musical works "present themselves as the voice of the teller" (1991: 52, 56). Without some force of disjunction from the singer on stage, how sure can a listener be that the orchestra accompanying Cone's singer is not simply enacting that singer's role? How clearly might one ever *hear* narrative "distance"?

Narrative distance is asserted in Wagner's music, Abbate claims, by the ongoing thematic discourse of the orchestra, interweaving past, present and future events by leitmotivic reference.[50] Cone, too, hears Wagner's orchestra creating narrative viewpoint by the sheer continuity of its activity; whereas in number-opera, cadences ending arias fragment the drama and maintain the illusion of characters, an unbroken orchestral contribution to the drama offers "an all-inclusive persona surveying the entire action from a single point of view" (29). Michael Halliwell has modified Cone's position, arguing that while operatic characters *are* products of a primarily orchestral narration, they periodically "break out" of the narrative process to assert their independence, as stage performers, from the sounds in the pit (148). The key to an operatic point of view would appear to lie in the "distance" – if any – perceptible to an audience between a singing character who is verbally articulate and a wordless orchestral utterance more or less freighted with leitmotivic references pertaining to actions on the stage.

The physical situation of opera raises a further question, this time concerning the naively optical connotations inherent in the term "point of view." Whichever analysis of literary point of view one adopts,[51] one deals with a word-based narrative version of how the world *looks*. Point of view in novels implies "seeing with" a given character or characters, whether or not the narrator is identical with that character, or has direct "access to consciousness" in the form of feelings and thoughts.[52] The varieties of literary point of view – from partial "focalization" around a single character's restricted viewpoint to so-called "omniscient narration" with zero focalization – cannot be reproduced in opera, for the theater is a physical environment in which an audience watches in a literal, optical sense. The watching, moreover, is unrestricted: it covers the whole stage (framed only by the proscenium arch), rather than what a narrator chooses to "show" us in a given paragraph. "Seeing with" is replaced by "looking at." An optically restricted point of view is as alien in theatrical mise-en-scène as truly panoramic tableau is in novels.[53]

Without access to the optical restriction possible in literature, operatic point of view, where apparent, might be defined in the terms suggested by the phrase "access to consciousness" as a sounding-forth of the mental and emotional basis of what is occurring on stage. The psychological emphasis is clear in Genette's distinction between *internal focalization* where the "narrator says only what a given character knows" and *external* focalization, where "the hero performs in front of us without our ever being allowed to know his thoughts or feelings" (189, 190). Point of view, in the first case, is as much an "experiential horizon" (Gebauer–Wulf 242) as a physical positioning. Whether or not the music speaks to an audience with privileged access to a stage character's "experience," though, its ability to do so – in ways that are distinct from direct mimetic enactment – will engage some form of disjunction between singer and orchestra. Without some articulated "distance" between the stage action and the narrator's discourse, claims for operatic point of view collapse. Pursuing the point-of-view construct in opera could be imagined as an attempt to *hear* what Genette terms narrative "voice" – one listens, that is, for aural traces of the enunciating instance itself.

The Act 2 "Mist" interlude offers an alluring case of untexted orchestral music imbued with an eloquence based in reference to familiar thematic shapes. Two themes – Vere's chorale-like prayer for "Light" (first heard in his Act 1 cabin scene), and the "Mist" theme (introduced early in Act 2) – interweave in an orchestral interlude, elaborating very directly on the "confusion without and within" that Vere himself refers to verbally. As the curtain falls, the interlude itself presents these twin threats to Vere's judgment in a dialogue-like alternation (see Ex. 3.9), and, ominously, in a harmonic progression – a SLIDE from A+ to Bb− – that signals Claggart's role in the drama's approaching crisis. The clouding of Vere's judgment would appear to take a very precise musical form, one in which the initial major-mode warmth of the Light theme (Ex. 3.9, at a) is lost by transformation into a wordless and harmonically barren orchestral voice (c), while the Mist theme itself (b) retains a form of local triadic definition. "Confusion," in the case of the Mist theme, is tonal: a kind of narrow path the music treads between recognizable harmonic patterning and entropy – each chordal chain is bounded by a single "tonic" triad (Bb minor, at (b) in

Ex. 3.9 A-major Light and B♭-minor Mist themes as a symbolic and harmonic contradiction

Ex. 3.9), and one catches each triad before it vanishes into the cumulative wash of chromatic pitches spanning every register.

From this initial chaotic searching, the interlude moves through a complicating imitative crisis (Ex. 3.10a) to blazing, major-mode triumph. The Mist theme is remade as a single, Lydian-tinged D-major arpeggiation (Ex. 3.10b), heralding the return, at its former A-major pitch level, of Vere's Light prayer (Ex. 3.10c). All traces of the orchestra's Bb-minor starting key are effaced in this fanfare-peroration. As the curtain rises, and Vere himself steps forward alone to warn Claggart ("beware! I'm not so easily deceived"), the orchestra retreats from commenting speaker to a conventional accompanying role.

However schematic the content of the purely orchestral progression – from darkness to light – its dramaturgy prompts questions of interpretation. Are the orchestral themes of the interlude a form of speech (a comment outside actual plot events), or do they instead present an unwitnessed action? As the curtain falls, Vere is confused by the Mist, and prays for Light; as the curtain rises, he returns, finding that "the mists are vanishing." There is an obvious contrast between the two ariosi – in which the orchestra supports the singer's verbal revelation of thoughts (confusion, defiance) – and the intervening interlude, with its wordless working-out of the Mist/Light confusion. The interlude, one might claim, is less directly a depiction of a mental process than a consideration, by an *independent* orchestral voice, of the forces in play. Its sounding narrative is focalized "around" Vere, but this is not that same thing as offering a direct revelation of his state. Reporting the crisis he faces in the form of a struggle among referential themes, the interlude exploits to the full an orchestra's potential for contrapuntal simultaneity (the first Light-theme entrance (at c in Ex. 3.9) overlaps with, and is itself dovetailed with, Mist-chains). The result is something beyond the sequentiality of verbal description, and independent of the outer plot (which does not advance while the curtain is down). The Mist interlude – an utterance of metaphysical significance – speaks of Vere's situation, but in a manner clearly separate from his own on-stage singing.

Restating themes announced vocally, the orchestra marks a distance – sonic and discursive – between vocal and instrumental "voice." Timbrally, too, the orchestra moves to a supra-individual plane of utterance by instrumental doublings.[54] In an orchestral environment dominated by blended hues, the solo trumpet fanfare heralding Vere's return to the stage (Ex. 3.10b) is an icon of individual triumph over massed opposition. This emergence of soloistic utterance at the interlude's climax heightens the retrospective, quotational ambience of the final "Oh, for the Light" statement, in woodwind octaves. Present triumph is set against the earlier

Ex. 3.10: "Mist" interlude: central crisis and closing peroration

(a)

(b)

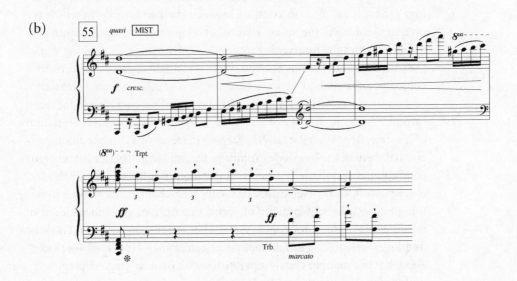

(c)

prayer – a fleeting timbral detail, but one that marks the spiritual distance traversed during the interlude.

A further sign of the orchestral interlude's narrative autonomy from Vere himself is simple contrast of mood – this orchestral music is unlike any of Vere's music elsewhere in the opera. Its brooding dialogue is an obvious contrast to the passionate, major-mode advocacy of his lyric outbursts ("Nay, you're mistaken" and "Claggart"). The orchestra's role here is comparable to the lyric interpolations of a Greek chorus, a commenting witness on the main action, one whose speech stands outside the headlong flow of dramatic time, building links by specific musico-thematic means to other areas of the opera. The bustling diatonicism of the closing "Light" quotation (Ex. 3.10c) recalls Billy's Act 1 "King of the birds" aria; the triad-chains of the Mist prefigure the more extended orchestral triad-chains still to come in the Act 2 Interview. While a protagonist's concern is limited to events of the moment, a chorus escapes the telos of plot motion to function at a metaphoric level, pointing analogies and making connections.[55] Its real dramatic force transcends local actional concerns; the orchestra's thematic argument is an expansive discourse, impressing upon familiar materials a significance beyond the scene at hand. At such moments, the opera orchestra intervenes with the authority and distinctive voice of a narrator.

(c) Voice placement and the intimacy of focalized narrative

The numerous discriminations of literary narrative – in Genette's classic analysis, factors such as the scene/summary opposition, the temporal reordering of story events, the interplay of speech- and event-centered narration, and the degree to which distanced interventions are overt or subtle[56] – offer a range of vocal modes comparable, I have claimed, to operatic modes of story telling. Hearing unambiguous signs of narrative "distance" in opera, though, is tricky; claims that the orchestra narrates are more convincingly sustained when the stage is empty (as in the Mist interlude) than when a listener's attention is trained on the material vocality of singing actors. Yet it would be wrong to conclude that the voice/orchestra relationship is a simple matter of supporting backdrop (Wagner attacked Rossini for using the orchestra only as "a huge guitar for accompanying the Aria")[57] or, conversely, to consider those on stage as mere illustrative figures supplementing a primarily orchestral action. Voice–instrumental relations are nothing if not supple (and literary narratives, Genette [191] notes, can shift mode with great speed). Listening for a range of voice/orchestra relations, one might dispense with the static textural model implicit in loose terms such as *accompaniment*. Polyphonic texture is more than a strict hierarchic display of principal and secondary voices,[58] and by recognizing Britten's subtle control of what I shall term *voice placement* – the textural disposition of singers and orchestra at given dramatic moments – the analysis can document a relative degree of intimacy among vocal and instrumental "speakers" and a basic operatic means of controlling enunciation.

Figure 3.5 summarizes voice/orchestra relations at several points in the drama from the Mist interlude to Claggart's death. Shifting voice placements appear as motion across a horizontal spectrum of possible textures. In the vertical plane meanwhile, temporal flow registers most strongly as a dramatic progression when articulated by changes of textural state. The sequence here begins with a shift that sets off Vere's prayer for "light" from its immediate context, and continues with a second shift (after the purely orchestral Mist interlude) to the obbligato textures of his "Claggart" aria. Further shifts of voice placement are audible once Billy enters, as when Vere's *ad spectatores* asides ("and this is the man . . .") are voiced with a warm upper-string doubling, "placing" his thoughts at a timbral distance from Billy's obbligato horn support. The closing moment of the passage, Billy's stammer (Ex. 3.11), illustrates opera's potential for scenic complexity born of an interplay of mimetic actional dialogue and slightly distanced orchestral contributions. Against the Stammer trill itself, Vere's order to "answer!" is advanced with bright trumpet support, while string octaves draw out rising-fifth intervals as echoes of the direct accusations Claggart has just made (cf. Ex. 3.7 above). These string gestures coexist with the serpentine woodwind flickers that mimic the stammer itself, suggesting Billy's own stunned attempts to absorb the mutiny charge – in Melville, his "amazement at such an accusation" (98; ch. 19) – even as Vere presses him verbally ("defend yourself!"). By simultaneity of viewpoint, the orchestra encompasses the situation of the three men at this supremely tense moment. The orchestral gestures seem poised between simple enactment of Billy's and Vere's attitudes (the Stammer trill, "Vere's" trumpets, "his" D major as the local tonic) and utterance that is more distanced (the string fifths, as echoes of Claggart's accusations).

The conflation of multiple perspectives at the moment of Billy's last stammer complicates the question of voice/orchestral intimacy: it is difficult, in this ensemble situation, to determine where direct orchestral enactment of the characters' situation leaves off and where commentary begins. The scene goes to the heart of Melville's allegory, for it is precisely at the moment when Billy's verbal speech fails him that wordless orchestral utterance looms largest, as a possibly distanced commenting voice. The scene is a reminder that voice-orchestral placement in opera may, like

Fig. 3.5: "Voice placement" in Act 2, Scene 2 as far as Claggart's death

voice placement

| not doubled | homophonic/ chordal | obbligato partner | heterophony | solo instrument | DOUBLINGS (unison or octave) | |
					choir (one timbre)	mixed
	Vere: Oh for the light			*Vere:* Confusion without		
MIST INTERLUDE		*Vere:* Claggart ... you shall fail				
		Billy: You wanted to see me			*Vere:* And this is the man	*Billy:* Wish we'd got that Frenchie
				Billy: Let me be your coxswain!		
					Vere: Claggart!	
					Remember both of you	
					Claggart: William Budd, I accuse you	
Billy: a ... [stammer] ... devil!						

Ex. 3.11: The stammer before Claggart's death

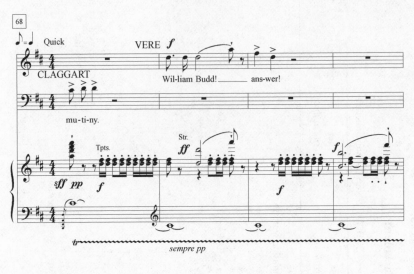

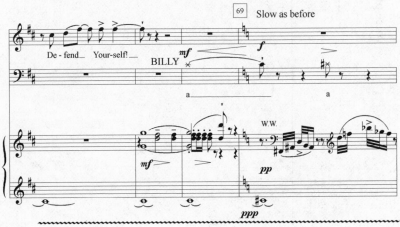

many literary narratives, retain an essential indeterminacy between action and narration. In literature also, so-called free indirect discourse dispenses with the identifying marks of narrative presence ("he said that" and similar tag clauses), blurring the distinction between first- and third-person grammatical subject, and the narrator's and character's habits of speech. The result is a dual-voiced discourse, and a subtly ironic tone common to writers such as Henry James and Thomas Mann (writers to whose work Britten was drawn as an operatic dramatist). The intimacy of voices and orchestra in a score like *Billy Budd* fluctuates in a comparable way, resulting in a constant play of verbalized actional song and commenting orchestral utterance. The fundamental and conventional artifice of all opera – the patent "difference" of voices and instruments – supports moments of proto-novelistic narration from below the stage; only in unaccompanied vocalizing could orchestral distance be deemed entirely absent from sung drama.

Still, music's lack of clearly defined semantic referents – as Abbate rightly notes – will always limit its claims to an immanent, rather than a derived, narrativity. Only when there is a precise referent can we begin to assert that music is really telling us *something*, rather than merely voicing a kind of empty narrative. Questions of semantics bring discussion squarely back to the issue with which this chapter began – operatic leitmotive.

(d) Doubling of speaking presence: the orchestral voice in the trial scene

Vere's role in the opera's trial scene is passive; his silence, I noted earlier, betrays a second, authorial silencing – Forster's attempts to shake off Melville's overt challenges to the captain's sanity and judgment. Listening more closely to Britten's musical setting of the libretto, though, one might go further, questioning the relevance at this point in the drama of "Vere" as a coherent figure – a univocal speaking (singing) presence. Listening for Vere in the trial, one invariably hears another voice, that of the orchestra, and in the orchestra one hears Claggart. The disjunction between Vere's stage presence and Claggart's orchestral presence complicates the plain question, Who speaks? Understanding this departure from Melville's telling of the story brings together both strands of the argument so far – the semantic charge of leitmotivic reference and the possibility of an orchestral narration. In the opera's boldest reinterpretation of its literary source, Vere's culpability as the strict disciplinarian of the trial scene is linked to the uncanny prominence of Claggart's musical voice.

Searching to account for Vere's loss of speaking presence, one might look beyond the layered, psychological atmosphere typical of Britten's operas, or the drama of consciousness in *Billy Budd* (in which the young commander is a figure of memory conjured up by the older Vere of the Prologue–Epilogue frame), to consider "character" itself as a volatile category. Genette's gnomic observation (of novelistic presentations of character) that "absence is absolute, but presence has degrees" (245) serves as a reminder that the separation of literary voices in a text – the division between character and narrator – may at times be less than pristine. In theatrical drama too, classical "character" traits such as a proper name and continuity of physical and moral nature have been questioned when the performing "self" appears divided, or when an actor's physical presence is only the accessible form of an essentially symbolic figure.[59] Such mimetic departures are illuminating in the case of the *Billy Budd* trial scene, for it is here that Vere's operatic character recedes, for a while, into a strange insubstantiality.

Far from rescuing Vere, the operatic trial and its aftermath seem to sharpen an audience's instinct for blame – surely, Vere *could* have saved Billy, even using "the laws of earth"? Britten's and Forster's libretto eliminates Vere's lengthy direct-speech haranguing of the court in Melville's chapter 21.[60] In place of a lecture on the need to try Billy under martial law, Vere in the opera gives only brief testimony, refusing to elaborate despite his officers' pleas for guidance. But this silence during the drumhead court contrasts blatantly with the moral awareness he evinces immediately after the trial in the "verdict" aria. Vere's trial-scene passivity, moreover, is a retreat from his operatic behavior elsewhere in the act. Each of his solo arias dovetails into the following action, providing a continuous viewpoint from which an audience understands events. Thus Billy's affirmations of loyalty (prior to Claggart's death) are counterpointed by Vere's echoing "Claggart" asides, while the officers' shocked discovery of Billy's fatal violence against the Master-at-Arms is juxtaposed with Vere's prediction of the verdict ("struck by an angel, an angel of God, yet the angel must hang"), echoing the book-narrator's damning reference to Vere's "prejudgment" (108; ch. 21). After the trial, finally, the Interview flows directly on from Vere's self-perception as "messenger of death," and his realization that he himself is being judged.

Vere's trial testimony (cf. Ex. 3.8 above), I showed earlier, is saturated with a form of leitmotivic return that makes very precise references to past events. Revisiting the trial, now considered in its entirety, the role of orchestral utterance can be understood in terms that move beyond leitmotives with relatively well-articulated connotations (the Accusation or Stammer themes, for example). One notes very quickly, for example, that Vere's voice is inflected throughout the scene by a series of orders delivered in a curt monotone (see Ex. 3.12). Confined in the trial to such sennet-like utterances (familiar from the on-deck scenes of Act 1 as an extension of "realistic" naval signals),[61] Vere's voice comes to stand for the force of unswerving naval discipline. It is the instantaneity of this change of tone (in relation to the more impassioned voice evident earlier in Act 2) that is most disturbing, as if Britten had responded in operatic terms to the quasi-supernatural transformation in Vere described in Melville:

> Slowly he uncovered his face; and the effect was as if the moon emerging
> from eclipse should reappear with quite another aspect than that which had

Ex. 3.12: (a) Vere's "official tone" during the trial; (b) during the "verdict" aria

(a)

gone into hiding. The father in him, manifested towards Billy thus far in the scene, was replaced by the military disciplinarian. In his official tone he bade the foretopman retire ...   (99–100; ch. 19)

Behind Vere's clipped "official tone" one hears a stifled human sympathy for the unfortunate Billy. At Example 3.12a, the opposition between Vere's awareness of military duty and his private inclination is blatant: barking out preparations for the forthcoming trial process, his delivery softens at the phrase "sole earthly witness," a change of voice brought in the orchestral move from bare octaves to chordal warmth and from brass doublings to solo cello. The wedge-like voice-leading gesture (with pitches building outwards from the trumpets' C octaves) returns as Vere urges the court not to press him for advice on a verdict ("No, do not ask me").[62] But these hints of Vere's personal engagement in Billy's tragedy are brief exceptions, serving only to set the martial voice of the disciplinarian into deeper relief. In his final vocal utterance of the scene, the "verdict" aria, this sennet topic develops into a Schoenbergian "motive of the accompaniment," a persistent reminder of the trial just ended (and of Vere's role in it). Vere reverts to a more lyrical melodic voice in this aria, but his song is now haunted by an orchestral voice, and in the closing witness-like declaration, "I, Edward Fairfax Vere" (Ex. 3.12b), he returns to static monotones and the ineluctable force of martial law. The entire aria places the singer in a curiously powerless position by a metric non-alignment of vocal and orchestral phrases (a contrast to the voice's assertive control of phrase rhythm earlier in "Claggart!").

The dark side of Vere's muteness is his apparent assumption of Claggart's music after the Master-at-Arms's death. The convergence is most evident in "Scylla and Charybdis," as Vere realizes he has failed to protect Billy: at the moment of Claggart's death, Vere himself *sings* with Claggart's words, and with his music too. As Donald Mitchell has observed, the moments at which the two characters' identities directly converge – far more directly than do Quint and the Governess as "doubles" in the *Screw* – pose an interpretative challenge:

> [A]re we to assume an ironic intervention here on the part of the composer, his drawing to our attention the tragic spectacle of the virtuous Vere completing Claggart's task for him, despite – or rather (a further layer of irony) because of – the latter's death? Or . . . are these quotations to be read as an invasion of Vere by Claggart. . . . a manifestation of a disconcerting symbiosis?   (1993: 128)

Each of Mitchell's alternative readings prompts ironic reception of Vere's "character," up-staged at this point either by another figure (Claggart) or by the voice of a narrator (in Mitchell's terms, the implied author "Britten"). But there is more to this than the directly quotational discourse Mitchell cites. The melodic prominence of Claggart-like fourth sequences (see Ex. 3.13), in prime and inverted chains, enact a waning of Vere's musical presence that is more subtle and pervasive. The plot works, in A.-J. Greimas's terms, by conflating two *actors*, Vere and Claggart, into one *actant*, Billy's Destroyer; as in the dream-work, character is over-determined, with two latent identities condensed into one figure of mani-fest presence.[63] This doubling is palpable when Vere speaks of the trial as "mine" using the same chaining of major triads Claggart had in the climac-tic "nothing!" cries of his Act 1 "Credo." The irony is multifaceted: at one level the trial *is* Vere's (not Billy's), but equally it is not Vere's alone.

Doubling of speaking presence again suggests the workings of the opera's dramatic frame, and of the older Vere's memory. As scenes recalled by the old man, the murder and trial might be imagined as playing out from his viewpoint. In Vere's reflective arias, the complication of his voice with Claggart's words and musical voice transcends the more realist trap-pings of the recitative-dominated trial. The drama remakes its mimetic convention to assume the logic of a dream in which one experiences events both *as* oneself, and as if watching oneself from without. Peter Evans's comment here, that Vere *recognizes* "that it is he who has completed Claggart's design" (173) implies a self-consciousness prominent in Vere's text ("I am afraid. . . . it is for me to destroy you"); but the aria possesses something beyond rational formulation, too – a subterranean fusion of speaking presences that is less conscious than a "recognition" made mani-fest in orchestral leitmotivic reference. The speaking presence of the "verdict" aria eschews a one-to-one relation to stage character, for "voice" is a polyphonic fusion of vocal and orchestral utterances. To substantiate this claim entails a closer look at what the orchestra is doing throughout the trial.

With Vere's speech constricted in the trial to that of a witness, the bulk of the verbal exchange comprises the First Lieutenant's questions to Billy, and his responses. The recitative dialogue has near-continuous orchestral underscoring, yet the scene reveals little of the intimacy between orchestra and singer evident earlier in the act. The orchestra, by its very continuity, and by timbral monotony – the predominance of the cellos as melodic voice – asserts distance from those on stage. In the trial, the orchestra itself is a kind of unofficial witness. Throughout, it spins a thread of commen-tary. Only when Billy himself speaks does intimacy return (a reprise of the earlier horn-obbligato aria). Britten's score, having silenced Vere himself, refashions the scene to the accompaniment of a single orchestral voice

Ex. 3.13: Claggart's motivic presence in Vere's Act 2 "Scylla and Charybdis" aria

whose identity is beyond the strictly "possible," yet strongly articulated by thematic and timbral identity.

There is a plausible case to be made for hearing the powerful voice in the orchestra during the trial scene as Claggart's, though it will be important, first, to explicate further what it means to speak of a "voice" *in* the orchestra. In narrative terms, Claggart's orchestral voice provides the clearest evidence in the operatic *Billy Budd* of a wordless, instrumental agent distanced from the singers. If in the "Scylla" and "Verdict" arias, Claggart's voice colors Vere's sung utterances, in the trial itself, it seems to stand apart from the silent Commander, and from Billy and the court. The trial proceeds as if observed by a single presence. Its progress is underlaid with continuous orchestral reminders of the scene it retells: Billy's accusation by Claggart. Claggart seems to "speak" in the trial from beyond the tangible body of his prone corpse through the sounding body of massed orchestral timbre. We hear him as clearly as we do Billy and the First Lieutenant, but we cannot see him. Like the astral body described by theosophists, he floats as an invisible presence sensible to those left on stage after the physical event of his death. His presence is sensed only in the wordless "tone-speech" of orchestral music with recognizable leitmotivic content.

To the listening and watching audience, Claggart is that "uncanny" presence that forces the subject to hesitate between a natural or metaphysical interpretation of everyday experience. Where earlier in the opera it was possible to understand the orchestral accompaniment as intimate with those on stage, the trial presents a new feeling of utterance detached from the action of the vocalists. In the weighty opening orchestral ritornello (see Ex. 3.14), this detachment is a matter of thematic discourse. The melodic and chordal strata assimilate Claggart's Act 1 "Credo" chords – the characteristic fifthless F-minor tonic triad with which the ritornello opens – to his Act 2 Accusation theme; further leitmotivic returns reach back with wordless instrumental returns of each of his Act 1 themes (see motives a1, a2, b, c and d, respectively, in Ex. 3.14). The melodic fragments are strung together in a fluid, developing line of uniform cello timbre. The effect is panoramic, a return of numerous earlier instances of Claggart's vocal contributions to the action. Our awareness of the recent events tells us this *cannot* be Claggart; at the same time, the orchestral voice is repeatedly identified as his alone.

This precision of orchestral viewpoint depends on leitmotivic reference and timbral detail. Thus the Accusation motive (a1) returns in massed lower strings, precisely the instrumental shading in Claggart's direct-speech accusations of Billy. Other vocal motives join the long line, but always in this instrumental hue, as if Claggart's Act 1 statements ("A find in

Ex. 3.14: Claggart's motivic presence in the opening ritornello of the Act 2 trial scene

Ex. 3.14 (*cont.*)

a thousand," at (c) in Ex. 3.14) are revealed retrospectively as leading up to the moment of the Accusation itself. This evident timbral connection alerts listeners to Claggart's speaking voice, and it is reinforced by the scene's characteristic pitch level, with F minor as the controlling tonal frame.

Billy's powerlessness within the trial tells its own story about Claggart's enduring influence and Vere's passivity, and the telling – not surprisingly, in an opera – is inflected by bold and schematic harmonic motions. The scene's tonal journey is circular, bounded by an F-minor home tonic. Billy's D-major responses, in this setting, appear as islands of local toni-cization, quickly negated as the cross-examination reaches the moment of the stammer itself and cast aside by the return of the home dominant as Vere refuses to intercede. Billy's vulnerability here (like Grimes's in *his* court scene) is clear from the displacement of his tonally distinctive inter-polation by a ritornello whose force of utterance is legal and institutional as much as individual – Claggart speaks, as it were, through the court's proceedings (Ex. 3.15).[64]

Thematically and harmonically, the three ritornelli framing the trial (Ex. 3.14 and 3.15 show the first two) offer flexible melodic chains that echo the original Accusation music by their restlessly sequential inner patterning, while tracing, over larger spans, schematic departure and return to an immovable F-minor home tonic. In ritornello 1, the expansive cello melody describes a sustained progression from I to V. This harmonically open gesture is complemented, later on, by an emphatic modal V–I resolution spanning Vere's non-response to the First Lieutenant after Billy's testimony

Ex. 3.15: Act 2, scene 2 trial: Billy's D tonic is displaced by an F-minor home tonic as his testimony concludes

("I have no more to say": C minor) and Billy's exit to an inverted restatement, *fortissimo*, of the Accusation motive (ritornello 2, beginning with the F-minor tonic in Ex. 3.15, at fig. 88).

The final orchestral ritornello of the trial partakes of the V–I cadential rhetoric prominent in the first two, even as it begins a dissolution of Claggart's continuous orchestral presence. As the officers salute and leave, Vere, alone on stage, remains to sing his "Verdict" aria. Outer events are matched by a shift in orchestral viewpoint at this moment, made audible via timbral and gestural details. The solo harp is a poignant return to the meditative Vere of the Act 1 cabin scene, its delicate timbral effect coupled with a dulling of the savage double-dotted rhythms of Claggart's Accusation motive (so prominent in the earlier ritornelli). In this way, and by the simple reduction in dynamics, *sempre più piano* (ritornelli 1 and 2 rise to an urgent *fortissimo*), the wordless orchestral narrator registers a distance from the trial scene just past, and Claggart's powers of operatic utterance are heard to recede.

My earlier claim – that the orchestral voice in the first ritornello of the trial scene *is* Claggart's alone – deserves some qualification, though. The ritornello has a directly gestural meaning as music to accompany the specified stage actions written into the score, preparing the cabin and removing Claggart's body. The telescopic medley of Claggart melodies is easily heard as a retrospective orchestral statement concerning the force of the dead man's actions in bringing about the trial now underway. Its synoptic sweep – the sheer rapidity with which themes succeed one another – could signal the speaking presence of an orchestral narrator *recounting* the dead man's exploits. (Vere, though present, cannot necessarily be considered that narrator here; he did not witness any of Claggart's Act 1 deeds, and so could not now be remembering them.) Synchrony is the keynote in the trial-scene ritornelli: the chain of themes is a breathless concatenation of ideas each developed as autonomous melodic statements previously. This new discourse of fragmentation and juxtaposition connotes an ordering agency beyond the viewpoint of any one character on stage. It is a discourse, moreover, to be heard forcefully at one further juncture: the famous interview ending the entire scene.

The interview in which Vere tells Billy he must hang "takes place" off stage, coming to audiences only as a wordless orchestral passage (Ex. 3.16). Vere's last sung words, as he enters Billy's cabin, are questions: "How can he pardon, how receive me?" The orchestral chords that follow assume the position of the interview in the plot sequence, but the audience sees only the scene of Vere's now-empty cabin. One cannot say that the interview-chords enact the scene before the audience, and it is likewise too much to say that they enact the invisible scene off stage. Changing timbres, dynamics, and chords might loosely suggest a kind of wordless dialogue,[65] but the overall effect, devoid of real melody, is of an imposing emptiness of texture and harmony. The music of the interview matches the memorably opaque account of events Melville's narrator gives in chapter 22:

> Beyond the communication of the sentence, what took place at this
> interview was never known. But in view of the character of the twain briefly
> closeted in that stateroom, each radically sharing in the rarer qualities of our
> nature . . . some conjectures may be ventured.[66]   (114–15; ch. 22)

This wordless orchestral interview, then, is not a sounding response to physical revelation but a kind of reporting speech made at the conclusion of the trial scene just played out, and before the theatrical scene change (the curtain falls only as the last chord sounds).[67] The interview, in a sense, stands as the apotheosis of that narrative orchestral viewpoint that governs ritornelli throughout the trial scene. Yet if the interview narrates, it does so only in a kind of degree-zero narration, distinguished from earlier orchestral contributions by an absence of narrative specifics. Two facets of this blank narrative may be singled out briefly: the singular manner in which F major is confirmed as an unambiguous tonic for the interview, and an "emptying-out" of content in the realm of melody.

The distinctive tonal maneuvres of the interview – its rapid passage through thirty-four major and minor triads on thirteen different roots, homing in finally on an F-major tonic – evoke similar "roving" patterns heard earlier in the drama. Claggart's Act 1 deceit of Billy (in chorale-like passages such as Ex. 3.5b), or (a more subtle link) the inexorable piling-up of triads in arpeggiated melodic chains during the Mist interlude (Ex. 3.9) both prepare the way for the gesture and harmonic technique of the interview. But while it is not completely "new" to the opera,[68] the interview makes its bracing effect through a vast expansion of these earlier models. The chosen chorale-like gesture is revealing less in terms of scenic specifics than in what it says about a larger symbolic narrative: what the interview-orchestra "tells" an audience about Vere's final encounter with Billy is – at least gesturally and harmonically – something about the other two central dramatic agencies of the opera, Claggart and the Mist. That these "topics" are raised in a subconscious way – rather than by directly leitmotivic return[69] – says much about the distinctive possibilities of an orchestral narration in which the *lack* of determinate physical reference (and the absence of verbal denotation) enables a form of speech with broad synoptic and metaphorical powers of utterance.

The much-analyzed tonal system of the interview is remarkable, as Whittall (1990b: 156) notes, for an avoidance of common-tone voice-leading, especially at the outset. The point could be elaborated, in the present context, by considering the internal breaks in a sequence (Ex. 3.17) that moves from sharing of a single pc in the opening (chords 1–3: F+, A+, D♭+), to an unbroken run of eight chords lacking any common tones (chords 4–11: C+, D-, A♭+, D+, B♭-, A-, B♭+, A♭+), before settling down, at the close, to the single-common-tone oscillation of an F-major tonic and a C-major dominant.[70] Claggart's Act 1 deceit of Billy, as I showed earlier, was marked by a chordal discourse rich in warm close-position major triads and in single common-tone linkages (see Ex. 3.5b), while his truer destructive impulses were grounded in the chromatic SLIDE transformation (distinct in effect from traditional tonic-dominant functions, and from Riemannian dual-common-tone progressions). The disjunctive element in the chordal syntax of the interview – the tendency "for contrast to challenge continuity" (Whittall 1990b: 156) – can actually be interpreted in more specific terms as a final banishment of Claggartian movement from the score. The return to tonic/dominant security is only one aspect of what happens during the chords' "mysterious cleansing process" (P. Evans 173), and it is the nullification of SLIDE as a subversive challenge to tonic presence that is crucial. The two F♯-minor chords (nos. 14 and 24) are both disruptive,[71] yet they do nothing, within the sequence, to challenge the overall F-major tonic. The final SLIDE progression here (F♯– to F+, chords 24–25) works in context as a mere chromatic-neighbor embellishment to an already secure F-major tonic. Reversing an earlier mirroring SLIDE-challenge to the "verdict" aria's F-*minor* tonic (Ex. 3.18), the last F♯-minor chord of the interview completes a compound SLIDE subsidiary to the larger F-minor-to-major *tierce de picardie* move from verdict to interview.[72]

The neutralization of SLIDE as a chromatic challenge to tonic key presence is further identified as a signal of Claggart's demise through timbral choices. Boldly evident to the ear in this chorale of unblended orchestral choirs is the absence of trombones as an unmixed timbre and the prominence of "Billy's" horns.[73] These timbral emphases act as subliminal character references, furthering the possibility of a narration centering on an unspecified spiritual transaction between Billy and Vere, "saving" the powerless captain from his unwilling actions. Certainly the way in which the chords home in on V/I oscillations in F major is timbrally defined (with initial exceptions: chords 1, 4, 13) as a pairing of Billy's horns to (Vere's?) woodwinds.

The carefully managed triumph of F major over an F-minor tonic so closely affiliated to Claggart's role in the plot bestows on the interview a kind of specificity that is beyond the merely verbal portion of operatic drama. Even without words, the orchestra speaks, as it were, in a chordal language the opera has taught its listeners to read very closely. No such claim seems possible in confronting the absolute vacancy of thematic activity, though. While there *is* an audible melodic continuity – by arpeggio patterns (see Ex. 3.19) – binding Vere's "verdict" aria to the interview itself, and flowing on into Billy's song in the Darbies, it works at an archetypal, "pre-thematic" level removed from the referential leitmotivic discourse so prominent in the earlier drama. The absence of thematic activity, though, is just too striking not to register dramatically. Emptiness itself counts here as a telling gesture, one more voiced inarticulacy in the drama. Britten's wordless interview is a more sincerely affecting experience than

Ex. 3.16: The "interview" chords, Act 2, Scene 2

Ex. 3.17: Contrasting forms of chordal "progression" within the interview sequence

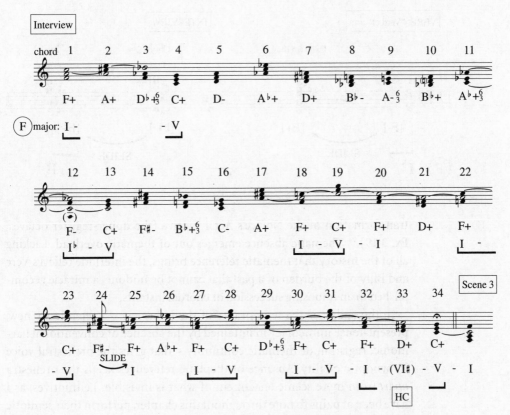

the rather arch liturgical motifs Melville's narrator introduces as "conjectures" to fill the gaping absence of real knowledge of the event itself ("there is no telling the sacrament, seldom if in any case revealed to the gadding world, ... holy oblivion, the sequel to each diviner magnanimity, providentially covers all at last" [115; ch. 22]).

The interview's thematic emptiness *tells* as a release from the almost obsessive leitmotivic undertow of preceding scenes. The trial, I have shown, is one long backward glance, an agonizingly formal recounting, via dense leitmotivic return, of Claggart's accusations and death. And Vere's "verdict" aria is, if anything, denser still: martial brass sennets and a bass-voice recollection of the trial's stepwise ascent (opening of ritornello 1) lead to arresting "Claggart" horn calls, and – in the surging final paragraph – to a new vocal form of the "Hanging" motive, punctuated in the orchestra by a

Ex. 3.18: Washing Claggartian SLIDE progressions away as the F-major tonic of Act 2, Scene 2 is finally secured

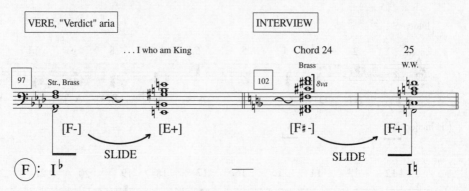

transformation of the Novice's Act 1 motive (the upper-register octaves, Ex. 3.19).[74] Thematic absence emerges out of thematic overload. Lacking all of the history that thematic reference brings, the interlude relieves Vere and Billy of the burden of a past that cannot be undone, a miracle accomplished in an imposing succession of chordal instants.

In the end, it is the temporality of the interview – a relentlessly new, present-tense immediacy maintained by the absence of conventional harmonic, registral, or thematic continuity – that gives the orchestral voice its synoptic quality. Absence of thematic references keeps the orchestra *apart* from mere scenic enactment of what is invisible. Leitmotives, as I have been at pains to note throughout this chapter, perform their semiotic task by a temporal bridging motion, a bringing *back* of that which is already past. Foregoing this possibility, the orchestra, in the interview, finds a voice that manages to engage the drama while maintaining an audible distance.

The trial scene and the interview with which it ends raise, but do not answer, difficult questions concerning the workings of a narrative point of view within opera. How, for example, might those features of the orchestral voice that suggest an anonymous narrating presence – a synoptic interweaving of numerous leitmotivic returns, contrapuntal textures combining several motives simultaneously, exclusively chordal utterance – be reconciled with the specific references that support the possibility of Claggart as a numinous speaker? Examining the trial, discussion confronted the thorny question of whose voice fills the auditorium as Vere stands silent. What might be termed the "uncanniness" of the operatic trial has much to do with music's power to reanimate past events

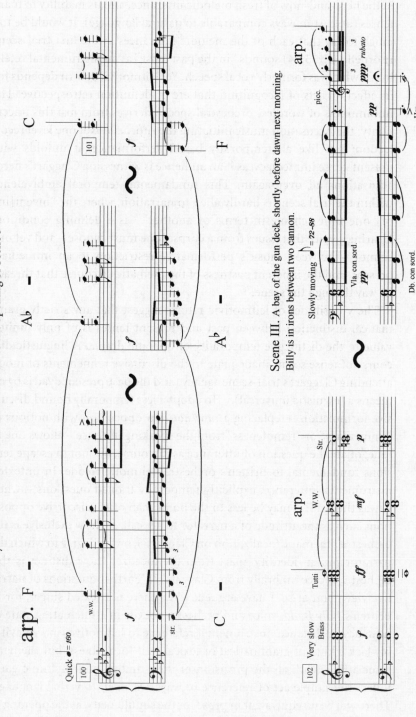

Ex. 3.19: Gestural continuity from the "verdict" aria and interview to the opening of Scene 3

in the here-and-now of fresh melodic utterance, and its inability to mark tenses (at least in ways comparable to natural language). It would be too much to say that each of the melodic utterances in the first trial-scene ritornello (Ex. 3.14) sounds "in the past tense" as an instrumental retelling of what was formerly vocal speech. Yet leitmotivic return depends for its effect on acts of recognition that are by definition retrospective. The uncanniness of wordless orchestral speech derives from just this uncertainty: the Accusation music initiating the ritornello *is* at one level recollection; but like all temporally based performance, it unfolds with present-tense immediacy, as if an audience is witnessing Claggart's fierce accusations all over again. This fundamental temporal ambivalence within the trial scene is hardly alien to narration, where the "invent[ing of] one time scheme in terms of another"[75] is a defining condition. Hearing a voice that issues from a corpse, one must choose – and yet one cannot – between music's performative restriction to an immediate present, and the inherent pastness of the thematic discourse that threads its way through the scene.[76]

The vicissitudes of leitmotivic return suggest that any strictly grammatical distinction between past and present tenses is of only limited value to the distinctive temporality of operatic drama. A linguistic discourse of tense seems inadequate to the discursive refinements of mood attending Claggart's trial-scene agency (and the past/present dyad is by no means a linguistic universal).[77] To adopt a less temporally bound discursive formulation – replacing a *now/not-now* opposition with notions of "immediacy" or "remoteness" from the speaking instance – allows one to renegotiate the question of utterance as discourse, but not to escape tensions fundamental to Britten's orchestral leitmotivic code. In untexted instrumental utterance, explicitly temporally framed questions – when is/was this said? – may be less to the point than other discursive oppositions such as the attitude of a narrator to a focalizer (how exclusive is the orchestra's thematic focalization on Claggart?), or the degree to which the narrator has an identity apart from the focalizer (how distinct is this orchestra's voice timbrally from Claggart's?). Further questions of narrative viewpoint arise, I have argued, when there is a texted singer, for in Britten's *Billy Budd*, voice and orchestra coexist in a fluctuating state of intimacy or distance. Instrumental reference to leitmotives may inevitably lack a kind of grammatical or lexical well-formedness; but thematic associations, with all the precision of their timbral and rhythmic garb, inflect the simple act of reference in ways not open to verbal language. There will be no equivalent in prose for the simultaneity, at the opening of the trial, of thematic gestures separated in the earlier action by more than an hour of performance time, or for the long-range resolution of tonal problems achieved by the interview-chords. At such times, Britten's music *is* a language, and operatic music is indeed a form of speech with a point of view quite distinct from anything to be found by readers of Melville's story.

4 *The Turn of the Screw*: innocent performance

> Thank you for your suggestions of titles. I do not feel we have arrived yet,
> although something to do with Bly is hopeful I think. I am not worrying about
> it until forced to, but I must confess that I have a sneaking horrid feeling that
> the original H. J. title describes the musical plan of the work *exactly*!!
> > Britten, 30 March 1954, letter to Myfanwy Piper[1]

> Lost in my labyrinth, I see no truth. Oh innocence, you have corrupted me,
> which way shall I turn? > The Governess, Act 2, Scene 1

The title of Henry James's novella presents an intriguing image even before
a reader opens the book. What can the figure of a turning screw stand for?
How is the phrase to be read? That the words *do* hold some sort of importance for the story about to begin is intimated early in the unnumbered
opening chapter, a framing prologue in which James's narrator reports the
conversation following an evening of ghost tales, quoting one of those
present, Douglas, directly:

> "I quite agree – in regard to Griffin's ghost, or whatever it was – that its
> appearing first to the little boy, at so tender an age, adds a particular touch.
> But it's not the first occurrence of its charming kind. . . . If the child gives the
> effect another turn of the screw, what do you say to *two* children – ?"
>
> "We say of course," somebody exclaimed, "that two children give two
> turns!"[2]

Douglas's reference to "another turn of the screw" can hardly fail to strike a
reader as a reiteration of James's title, and yet the phrase itself is playfully
vague in its connotations, scarcely more precise in its reference than the
title itself. Only the context of Douglas's remark – the discussion of the
merits of the tale of "Griffin's ghost" (a story not shared with the reader) –
confirms that the turning-screw image refers to some quality of the story's
telling, and that this narrative "effect" relates somehow to the presence of
children.

Is there not something faintly disturbing in Douglas's conflation of
the title image of a screw with the appearance of a ghost to a child?
However mysterious, the turning screw *is* a material, real-world reference, albeit one whose connotations of the mechanical – the industrial,

even – seem oddly out of place in the nursery. And yet this is not the first time in James's fiction that a young child encounters the force of a screw turned by adults. The image crops up a year before *The Turn of the Screw* itself in James's 1897 novel, *What Maisie Knew*, at the moment when Maisie's first Governess, Mrs. Wix, reacts to a threat of dismissal from the girl's mother.

> [H]er feet were firm in the schoolroom. They could only be loosened by force: she would "leave" for the police perhaps, but she wouldn't leave for mere outrage. That would be to play her ladyship's game, and it would take another turn of the screw to make her desert her darling.[3]

James draws together the rules of "her ladyship's game" and the tangible physicality of Mrs. Wix's resistance (her feet can "only be *loosened* by force"). The play of forces is between two adults, but the struggle centers on Maisie herself: "the crisis," the narrator adds, "made the child balance."

The cruel hostility of this power struggle has its roots in a social hierarchy (Mrs. Wix is a servant), a scheme in which Maisie herself, though central, lacks a force of her own. To her divorced parents, she is "the little feathered shuttlecock they could fiercely keep flying between them."[4] Childhood, in James's metaphoric realm, is something fragile caught up in a play of forces far from gentle; the shuttlecock is small and feathered, but it is struck with ferocity. In *The Turn of the Screw*, equally powerful forces – of desire, attraction, compulsion – describe the young Governess's initial dealings with the children's Guardian, "the person to whose pressure I had yielded" (174; ch.3) in the decision to take the appointment at Bly. In *Maisie* and in the *Screw*, the turning-screw image marks the axial center of a game played by adults, with children as passive receptors or – as James's Preface has it – "small victims" (xxi).

Britten himself apparently gave James's title much thought,[5] and the turning-screw image was in fact destined to influence the opera's dramaturgy in quite direct ways. Britten's comment, two weeks into writing the score, that "the original H. J. title describes the musical plan of the work *exactly*!!" is no hyperbole; screw shapes – specific kinds of turning figures or motions – are integral to every level of the opera, from local motivic details to far more long-range harmonic rhythms.

Beyond the implication of force, the turning-screw image suggests a spiraling motion – a turn to some inside, or, as the Governess herself sings, a desperate turning within some "labyrinth."[6] At one level, we will see, the opera's turning is the steady tracing of a pathway, both in the local note-to-note patterns of melodic gesture, and, over wider spans, in the evolving progression from one short scene to the next. My analysis will begin by exploring these fairly prominent turns, but it soon uncovers a level of sinuous motion beyond the foreground of thematic contours. Each turn is also a movement of displacement, and a characteristically Brittenesque atmosphere of uncertainty reflects the volatile harmonic scheme within scenes. In its sudden shifts of mood, the score seems to mimic the often violent twists – the "succession of flights and drops" (158; ch. 1) – recorded in the Governess's tense narrative.

James's screw-image embodies a mysterious force at Bly, a force that presses most urgently on the two children. In the opera, our awareness of their fragile innocence comes about through a sequence of self-contained "phenomenal performances" (to use Carolyn Abbate's term for songs heard as music by those on stage). These nursery songs, overheard by the adults, are a familiar, received emblem of childhood, a subject space made visible (audible, in operatic terms) to adults. But the song performances are opaque, the sounding surface that hides a childish interiority for Miles and Flora, inaccessible to the Governess. It is in this performed innocence that Britten's *Turn of the Screw* most vividly poses the difficult questions of James's text: what do the children know? are they possessed? – are they corrupt?

In the face of these questions, an audience must struggle for bearings within the opera's densely woven thematic network. Building on a reading of the opera's central "Screw theme" as a controlling force, the analysis here explores returning themes as agents influencing, perhaps even controlling, the vocal utterances of characters on stage. Ultimately, I argue, the opera's action shifts the weight of Jamesian literary ambiguity from doubts about the Governess's perceptions to doubts about the children's nature. The questions James fashions by restricting literary point of view[7] are given voice in Britten's score by an overdetermined motivic discourse, one in which the antagonistic figures of the Governess and Quint are, by their sharing of themes, treated as doubles.[8] My account of *The Turn of the Screw* furthers an analysis of Britten's thematic utterance begun in earlier chapters, but here, the question of what is being said (or being withheld) increasingly engages a broader symbolism. In Britten's *Screw*, as in James's, the most disturbing encounters occur on the wider cultural field in which childhood is construed in opposition to adult sexual desire. Acknowledging the opera's *staging* of such archetypes – its presentation of innocence as something revealed, paradoxically, only through a performance – one uncovers, perhaps, a source of its abiding fascination.

1. The sound of the turn

> The Serpent: him fast sleeping soon he found
> In Labyrinth of many a round self-rowld
> > *Paradise Lost* ix, 182–83

(a) The identity of the Screw theme

The motion of a clock might be understood as more or less automatic, but screws do not turn on their own. Even before the appearance of children and ghosts, James's (and Britten's) title poses an unsettling question – by what outside force does the screw move? The repeated article (*the* turn of *the* screw) only heightens a sense of material presence, yet the mystery of who, or what, is acting remains. In the so-called "Screw theme" (Ex. 4.1), first announced in the opera's Prologue (and marked "THEME" in the score), one encounters an archetypal turning mechanism that is all-encompassing. Every other melodic event in the opera betrays its characteristic form. It is a measure of this absolute motivic control that the opera's next distinctive thematic announcement – in the Prologue initially, but then more audibly in Scene 1, as the Governess wonders "why did I come?" – turns out to be the alter ego of the Screw theme, whose ascending pattern is inverted and embellished by scalar passing motions (Ex. 4.2).[9] This "Thread theme" (as I will call it) traces a patterned sequential motion in one direction, like the Screw itself, though its first entry into the drama – in the music for the Governess's journey to Bly (Ex. 4.1, end) – obscures what might otherwise sound as too obvious a link: the Thread theme appears as an inner-voice melody, unwinding beneath a covering pedal point.

The Screw theme, by its announcement in the Prologue, establishes a framing distance from the main action, a distance retained in part by its subsequent treatment as the subject of the orchestral variations (so titled in the score) that precede each of the opera's sixteen scenes. Each variation forms an instrumental prelude, flowing directly into the following scene (Variation 12, in which Quint's *voice* is heard off stage, is an exception). Translated to the operatic stage, the guaranteed unity of the variation form becomes a machine of obsession for an unfolding plot sequence. The claustrophobic effect results not only from an ongoing formal process of variation; within each scene, the Screw is much in evidence. Allowing a single source-theme to dominate both scenes and variations, Britten has created an entity that is apparently inescapable.

Ex. 4.1: Act 1, Prologue: the Screw theme announced and the Thread theme concealed

The turning of the screw, in James, begins with a fairy-tale-like interdiction. The Governess is to have no contact with the Guardian. In the words of the opera's Prologue, "she was to do everything, be responsible for everything – not to worry him at all" (Ex. 4.3). Here, again, the story's plot turns by a motion in which agency is complicated: authority is displaced, John Carlos Rowe notes, from the absent Guardian to the Governess, and it is, fittingly, at this moment in the opera – the point at which the Guardian, as it were, extricates himself from events – that the force of the musical Screw theme is first manifest. The dotted French Overture rhythms and the chain of rising fourths here unmistakably prefigure the Screw theme's fully fledged appearance moments later, at the end of the scene. Yet it remains

Ex. 4.2: The Thread theme as alter ego of the Screw theme

... *inverted*   ... *with passing motions*

difficult to hear in the opera's thematic structure any direct significance for this theme; beyond its self-evident turning principle, that is, the theme does not "stand for" anyone or any thing. The Guardian may set the screw in motion, by sending the Governess to Bly, but he hardly seems responsible for its turning so far as to cause Miles's death.

A first question – *who*, in James's book, is turning the screw – might easily implicate the Governess herself, as unnamed first-person narrator. Especially for readers like Edmund Wilson who question her sanity – an issue I will take up later on – the increased tension of each chapter is the index of a progressive *loosening* of her grip on reality. The Governess, in this reading of James, is hallucinating, and "the story is a neurotic case of sex repression."[10] But Wilson's interpretation works less well for the opera, where the Governess is a singing character, rather than narrating center of consciousness, and where the "Screw" of James's title has an autonomous identity as a recurring theme, voiced primarily in wordless orchestral utterance.

The prominently announced "Theme" in Britten's score was equated by critics, almost immediately, with the opera's title as a "Screw theme,"[11] and this thematic autonomy is itself remarkable for reasons that go beyond an obvious screw-like melodic shape. For one thing, talk of a "Screw theme" asserts verbally a musico-dramatic presence distinct from the named characters on stage. Bluntly put, the Screw theme, whatever it represents, is something independent from the Governess or Quint. But the leitmotivic critical practice that creates a "Screw theme," however useful a way of distinguishing recurring ideas from unmarked local themes, is also a crude one. The opera's "Screw" is never clearly an object (a sword or Tarnhelm) or dramatic principle ("Fate") in the Wagnerian leitmotivic mould, or even the thematic memory of a sung text marking a single dramatic event

Ex. 4.3: Act 1, Prologue: the Screw theme foreshadowed

("renouncing love," say). Aside from its correspondence to the figural connotations of the opera's title, the Screw theme lacks physical or metaphysical referent.[12] To suggest, moreover (as Colin Mason does), that the theme's
appearance in the Act 2 finale confirms it as Quint's,[13] is to ignore the
Governess's behavior towards Miles, and her own vocal adoption of the
theme. I will return to questions of thematic identity in considering
the interaction of the Governess and Quint below. For now, the Screw
theme might be understood as essentially a narrative principle: its function
is not tied to specific elements of plot or character, but to the way in which
these are presented to the audience; the Screw is less a part of the story than
of its telling.[14]

Even so, the Screw remains a disturbing force, if only because we assume
that any theme with so much control of the musical surface *must* have a dis-
coverable function. But Schoenbergian notions of comprehensibility – the
listener's satisfaction in "follow[ing] an idea, its development, and the
reasons for such development" (215) – apply only with qualification, as will
emerge, in an opera in which thematic relations are self-reflexive and circular, rather than "logical." In the semantically freighted world of opera –
especially a James opera – even the venerable function of providing thematic
"unity" appears sinister.[15] Finally, it is hardly insignificant, in the context of
Britten's personal brand of tonal symbolism, that the malign nature of the
Screw should be imagined in musical terms as a twelve-note theme.[16]

Ex. 4.4: The circular progression of tonics, Acts 1 and 2

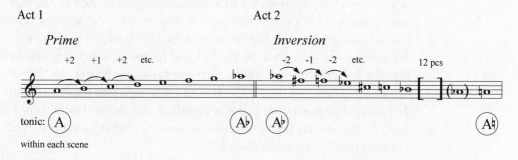

When Britten, on 21 May 1954, wrote to Eric Walter White that "the new piece progresses in a *circular* direction," he was giving a succinct description of the work's tonal architecture.[17] The operatic "Screw," then, is much more than the shape of the Screw theme itself. With typical literal-mindedness, Britten creates a screw-like tonal progression between the successive tonics of each scene in the opera (Ex. 4.4). In the most long-range sense, the opera is a circular journey, departing from an A tonic in Act 1 and ascending by steps to Ab, and falling by the same intervallic sequence in Act 2, returning finally to the A tonic of the opening. The pattern of steps no doubt reflects Britten's own observation that "[James] planned that story . . . so very carefully that if you miss one rung in the ladder you miss your footstep" (Britten 1984: 91). The parallelism between the surface shape of musical themes and the much broader pattern of tonal motion between scenes is among the subliminal means by which the opera makes its characteristic effects of intricacy – of trapping all on stage in some dense web of sound.

While the opera's background rise and fall of key centers is for many listeners something felt rather than consciously perceived, the Screw theme asserts a very prominent framing function by plain melodic statements bounding each act:

ACT 1			ACT 2	
Prologue	Variation 7	Scene 8	Scene 1	Scene 8
(1) "Theme": piano accumulating tutti	(2a) solo horn	(2b) solo horn	(3) Quint, Miss Jessel with doubling	(4) Governess with doubling
[no text]	[no text]	[calling the children]	"Day by day the bars we break"	"Who made you take the letter?"
tonic A	Ab		Ab	A

So the Screw theme is both a "principal theme" (Stein 1955: 6), creating large-scale formal symmetry, and a dramatic presence. Each of the four main statements is a distinctive gesture. The initial "Theme" statement (Ex. 4.1) is a gesture of boldly annunciatory significance,[18] growing timbrally out of the solo piano of the Prologue recitative, which is gradually engulfed by the orchestral environment of the opera proper. As Wilfrid Mellers aptly says: "we start in the 'real' world, from which the inner life of the psyche emerges as the piano is absorbed into the orchestral sonorities."[19] This opening theme-statement is already, dramatically, the start of a turning motion, a motion inward.

The remaining thematic Screw statements each create a different balance between voices and orchestral instruments, exploiting to the full the special potential of a "thin," chamber-orchestral ensemble.[20] Without the familiar sonic imbalance of solo voices against full orchestra, links between vocal and instrumental utterance can be especially telling as dramatic signs. The solo horn Screw theme closing Act 1 (two statements, really) stands apart from the vocal ensemble on stage. At the beginning of Act 2, on the other hand, the ghosts' texted Screw theme has very direct orchestral doubling, while the Governess's concluding Screw theme is doubled only by lower instruments. "Voice placement," in each case, makes a dramatic point. While it may be possible to adopt Wagner's distinction between a theme's "dramatic significance and effect" and its "role within the musical structure [*Satzbau*],"[21] the monothematic intensity of Britten's *Screw* is such that melodic return comes to represent something more than a formal necessity. As in those situations Freud terms "uncanny," the return reveals something "that ought to have remained hidden and secret, and yet comes to light" (1963b: 28). Certainly, for those who follow Wilson in regarding the Governess's ghostly experiences as hallucinatory, the fact of thematic return might assume very direct psychic connotations, with the Screw theme itself embodying that "repetition-compulsion" Freud (later in the "Uncanny" essay) observes as the outer manifestation of a force of repression.

(b) "Flights and drops": the turning screw as melodic impulse

The Screw theme is abstract in character because it is insulated from direct semiotic reference to a person or event. As a melodic icon of the twisting motion signaled in James's title, though, Britten's theme could hardly be more precise or direct. Positioned as it is, immediately following the opera's Prologue, the theme exactly corresponds to the opening phrase of Chapter 1 of the Governess's first-person narrative, a strangely diffuse account of her first impressions of Bly: "I remember the whole beginning as a succession of flights and drops, a little see-saw of the right throbs and the wrong" (158). Readers might well wonder what precisely the Governess is describing at this moment. The "whole beginning" is vague; and are these "flights," "drops" and "throbs" *feelings* or experiences of the outside world? The Governess moves more towards the referential in describing the "bumping swinging coach" of the journey. But James keeps the language playfully dancing in real-world reference: Mrs. Grose, the housekeeper, at the door "dropped me . . . a curtsey"; later, "I had no drop again till the next day" (159). Melodically, at least, the Screw theme follows the mysterious figurative twists of James's language. "Flights and drops" are directly present to the listener in the Screw theme itself as a path of constantly shifting direction, a "see-saw"-like balance between ascent and descent.

The Screw theme adapts a melodic topos familiar from Britten's instrumental music. Its questing sequence of rhythmically taut leaping fourths recalls two other variation themes – those of the op. 21 *Diversions* (a 1940 work Britten revised in 1954) and the Second Quartet's "Chacony." The latter (Ex. 4.5) shares the Screw's roving mobility, while avoiding chromatic saturation: the Chacony uses only seven diatonic pitches (five from the same white-note collection); its directedness towards a concluding C tonic emerges by the introduction of an eighth, B, as leading-tone, and by the repetition of tonic and dominant degrees. Harmonically, the Screw theme's note-to-note unfolding is tonal only in a fleeting sense, each tonicizing "V–I" leap being negated as the Screw turns further.

Analysts typically point to the systematic nature of the Screw pattern: "Reduced to its most compact form of alternating rising fourths and falling minor thirds, [the Screw theme] . . . might theoretically be continued indefinitely in the same direction as the alternation of two rising whole-tone scales a fourth apart."[22] Colin Mason's reduction (summarized as Ex. 4.6a) from actual pitches and rhythms to the more abstract, register-free realm of pitch-class brings out the Screw's intervallic homogeneity and its vertiginous rising character. But the analysis also downplays the variety of pitch contour within the theme: each tetrachordal cell has a unique span (Ex. 4.6b) and occupies a distinct register. The theme's first announcement (Ex. 4.1), with its textural progression from single note to massed chromatic occupation of several octaves, generates a powerful shift of mood, from the drawing-room warmth of the Prologue – a wash of diatonic thirds – to the sharper-edged soundworld of the opera's main action.

The Thread theme, I noted, inverts the Screw theme,[23] but the two share more than this concealed intervallic identity. Both are patterned (and

Ex. 4.5: Quartet No. 2, "Chacony" theme

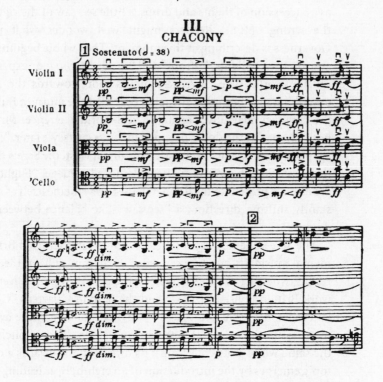

potentially endless) gestures of evasion and displacement. In textural senses, too, the music favors concealing gestures: the weakness of tonal feeling in the Screw theme reflects a constant overlay of new pitches, progressively shrouding the initial A, and saturating the registral space; the Thread is obscured as an inner voice. The iconicity of musical "turning," then, is at once melodic, harmonic, and textural in its detail. It is this roving principle of motion that carries the drama forward for nearly two hours in the theatre. Much of the "ambiguity" of James's narrative is located in the Governess's reporting of her experience. Britten's opera, lacking these extended narrative interludes between plot actions, spins its own ambiguities in the incessant "flights and drops" of the Screw theme.

(c) Non-melodic turns: the mysterious pattern of each scene

Britten's "sneaking horrid feeling" that the opera was taking on a ground plan directly analogous to James's turning screw is true in ways that are entirely independent of the Screw theme itself. Nor am I speaking simply of the shape of the plot, in twenty-four short chapters, one whose clock-

Ex. 4.6: (a) The Screw theme as a pattern of interlocking whole-tone collections; (b) intervallic features: (i) tetrachordal homogeneity; (ii) distinctive contour- and pitch-interval segments

(a)

collection 2

whole-tone collection 1   *(Britten's pitch-class spellings, Act 1 Prologue; Act 2, Sc. 8)*

(b)

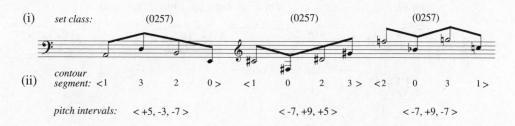

(i)   *set class:*   (0257)   (0257)   (0257)

(ii)   *contour segment:* <1   3   2   0 >   <1   0   2   3 >   <2   0   3   1 >

       pitch intervals: < +5, -3, -7 >   < -7, +9, +5 >   < -7, +9, -7 >

work connotations were not lost in its original serial publication, in twelve installments.[24] The turning motion of the book is a matter of the way circumstances change instantly as a result of specific events. The first such event is the arrival of Miles's dismissal letter; the Governess's sightings of Quint and, later, of Miss Jessel, are equally sudden. In the operatic *Screw*, these turns are especially audible by repetition of a single harmonic gesture – the modal shift from major to minor – throughout the two-act scheme. Without changing tonic, a shift of mode provides an instantaneous shift of perspective within a scene.[25] There is a pattern of such motions in nearly every scene of the opera, one almost as consistent as the opera's thematic pattern of variations, or its rise and fall of tonic notes (though far less commonly discussed). Particularly in Act 1, shifts from major to minor mode – a sort of harmonic "blighting" – generate the unstable atmosphere within scenes.

Two modal shifts, at the moment of the Governess's arrival (Act 1, Scene 2) and the letter of Miles's dismissal from school (Act 1, Scene 3), are especially clear harmonic markers of a dramatic change: these are moments at which audiences feel the screw turn. In the first case (Ex. 4.7),

Ex. 4.7: A rapid modal and textural shift in Act 1, Scene 1

the Governess's entrance to Bly, with her upbeat semi-formal greetings ("I'm so happy to see you ") are undercut by something far more somber: the Thread theme, high above the monotone vocal recitation, a single melodic strand, sinuously upstaging the Governess by its eerie melodic process. The contrast here is as much textural as harmonic; the moment of shift from major to minor third (D♯ to D♮, in relation to a B tonic) coincides with an instant loss of tonal support, and a melodic abandonment to chromatic uncertainty. A very similar textural and harmonic shift occurs at the next appearance of this theme, as the Governess reads of Miles's dismissal (Ex. 4.8). In each case, sudden reduction to the sparsest of recitative textures, with voices on equal footing with solo instrumental colors, gives the odd impression of voices being led (rather than "accompanied") by the Thread theme.[26]

These highly schematic shifts of mode and texture in Scenes 2 and 3 are already the beginnings of a pattern, for they originate in the more ambivalent and complex moment that is the climax of the Governess's Scene 1 journey. The harmonic uncertainties here (see Ex. 4.9) involve both the interplay of G♮ and G♯ discrepancies between voice and accompaniment, and the chromatic tension of a C-major – C♯-minor triadic maneuver (the SLIDE progression familiar from *Billy Budd*). In this way, Britten prolongs a

Ex. 4.8: A comparable "blighting" motion, Act 1, Scene 3

focal discrepancy, centered on the potential leading-tone of the scene's A tonic. The harmonic complications here coincide with revelation of the Thread theme itself (hidden, we saw, in the opening of the Scene). The Governess's doubts cannot completely destroy the scene's background pitch level – an A tonic returns immediately after this moment – but by a tense compound of chromatic detail, the security of that tonic is seriously challenged even before she has arrived at Bly.

The operatic turning begins, then, as early as with the journey to Bly in Scene 1. With blighting major–minor shifts strongly in evidence in Scenes 2 and 3, the first actual ghostly appearance – Quint's in Scene 4 – can

Ex. 4.9: A source of later blighting gestures in Act 1, Scene 1

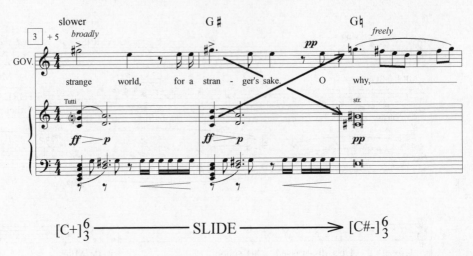

conform to a pattern already well underway. Moving on briefly to later manifestations of this harmonic discourse, I dwell on one facet of the turning mechanism in which the Governess and the children are gradually enmeshed.

The major-to-minor turns of Scenes 4 and 5 – from D and E tonics, respectively – correspond to the split-second shifts of perspective the Governess describes in the book for each encounter with Quint. His appearance on the tower arrests her with "the sense that my imagination had, in a flash, turned real" (175; ch.3); through the window, too, "One step into the room had sufficed; my vision was instantaneous" (184; ch.4). Equally rapid, in the second case, is the "flash of . . . knowledge" that Quint is looking not for her, but for Miles.[27] James, in both cases, gives us a Governess who is in no doubt as to the strangeness of what she sees. Part of the power of James's ghosts is their plain visibility; these first two appearances are in broad daylight; what marks the visitations out as horrific is not any supernatural behavior, but the reactions of the Governess herself.

Quint's first appearance (Ex. 4.10) shatters the "tranquil, serene" summer evening for the Governess by the timbral novelty of the celesta, heard only once before (Scene 3, as Miles's dismissal letter is read), its high register here a translation of his spatial location on the tower. The Governess's lower register ("who is it?") locates her in opposition to him, but it is the harmonic "turn," from the initial D major sonority, and the F♯–D third ("se-rene") to the D–F♮ emphasis of the agitated woodwind figures, that breaks the mood. The next sighting (Ex. 4.11) reworks the modal shift signaled by the key signature in several ways. The last major-mode event is the children's trailing

Ex. 4.10: Quint's first appearance, Act 1, Scene 4

Ex. 4.11: The children's nursery rhyme and Quint's appearance in the window, Act 1, Scene 5

off on a high G♯ (major third of the E tonic); Quint's celesta figures displace the bright final pitch of the nursery rhyme with modally ambiguous chromatic oppositions. The ghostly music here grows naturally out of the children's song – the shake-figure of the accompaniment is simply taken up by the celesta – and the implication is already of a sinister undertow to childish horseplay.[28]

Drawing together these moments by a returning major to minor shift, the opera suggests the presence of a hidden plan underlying even the most glancing of local melodic gestures. The major-to-minor third motion is common to each scene of the opera, in some way, and especially prominent in these first ghostly moments of Act 1.[29] Having sketched out the varied thematic and harmonic forms of the opera's turning motion, I shift attention to those for whom the Screw poses the greatest threat – the children.

2. Innocent ceremony: children's songs and the performance of interiority

(a) Retrieving childhood

"You see, I *am* bad, aren't I?"   Miles, Act 1 curtain

I like Miles['s] last remark because it is clear, bright, and in short phrases, which I think is right for the boy's character and his manner of singing.
Britten, letter to Piper, 31 January 1954,
on the choice of words to end Act I[30]

Once upon a time, there was a prep-school boy. He was called Britten mi., . . . his age was nine, and his locker was number seventeen . . .
Britten, 1955 note to a recording of his *Simple Symphony*

Shortly after the première of *The Turn of the Screw*, Britten wrote, in a letter to Desmond Shawe-Taylor: "I think in many ways you are right about the subject being, as it were, nearest to me of any I have yet chosen, (although what that indicates of my own character I shouldn't like to say!)."[31] The words are cryptic and evasive, yet they say something – by their very lack of specificity – about the dangerous nature of the opera's subject matter. The work's central figures are children threatened by the possibly corrupting influence of adults, a scenario that raises difficult interpretative questions, including those prompted by Britten's private sexual identity. Interpreting the prominence of exotic-sounding, pentatonic sonorities in the James opera – the Moorish cantillation of Quint's

"Miles!" cry,[32] the gamelanesque role of tuned percussion in the Act 1 finale, for instance – Philip Brett has argued that "orientalism is one of the means by which desire unacceptable to or feared by the (Western) Subject can be projected on to the Other" (1994b: 245). Brett claims that Western listeners will associate such sonorities specifically with the erotic undercurrents of the drama, so that "Quint is marked as homosexual and threateningly so by his 'oriental' music" (246–47). The orientalist trope, in the *Screw*, allows Britten symbolic access to a sexual discourse he could not, in 1954, openly address on the operatic stage.

The specific historical context of the opera's genesis, moreover, prompts some listeners to hear the *Screw* as a work of autobiographical significance. The opera may, Brett writes, have mattered to Britten as a means "to exorcise . . . a darker side of his own reality" (1992: 24). Like other mid-twentieth-century homosexual men, Britten could rely on the mechanisms of the "open secret" to ensure no public scrutiny of his private lifestyle,[33] but there remained very real risks emanating from institutions other than the press. That Britten, as a homosexual, himself faced the possibility of prosecution in 1954 is a matter of historical record,[34] and he was well aware of the parallels that might be drawn between his operatic imagination and his private life.[35] The possibility that his affinity for children of all ages might be misunderstood is a subtext of all the testimony Carpenter assembles to document what appears to have been a clear differentiation of parental instincts and reined-in sexual urges on the composer's part.[36] Interpreting *The Turn of the Screw* from the distance of nearly half a century, then, it will be important to move the discussion beyond biographically tinged speculation. The image a text presents of its author can never claim to be more than a textual production (this is true even in the case of autobiography), and I shall not consider Britten's opera as a kind of encoded personal history.[37]

More central to what follows will be an exploration of how the *Screw* depicts childhood as a realm distinct from the adult. The opera continues a long line of Britten works engaged, at one level or another, with childhood as a symbolic category remote from adult experience, and viewed with more or less Romantic nostalgia. That said, a critical response to Britten's musical evocations of childhood must move beyond familiar clichés of an Edenic past, hymned throughout by a composer naively identifying with memories of his own boyhood (a relatively happy and quite extended period, to judge by Carpenter's account). The range of the works themselves discourages any reduction of the childish to some univocal symbol of innocence. To think only of Britten's "boyish" scores is to encompass both the Nativity-scene child, and something more mundane. The frankly sexual vigor of the "happy, dirty, driving boy" in the *Spring Symphony*, is evoked by a treble choir (the text's "schoolboys playing in the stream") and an adult soprano soloist-narrator. But the scene is colored too by the morbid lure of the orchestral tuba which, as Arved Ashby observes, "hints surreptitiously that the pubescent male might not find spring to be all strawberries and cream" (225). The centrality of unbroken boys' voices to Britten's timbral imagination should not cause one to confuse *those* (pubescent) schoolboys with the far-off angelic voices of the *War Requiem*, or the transfigured boy spirit of *Curlew River*.

Writing about imagined children (James's Miles, for instance) risks the dangers attendant on all attempts to retrieve the past: an urge to sentimentalize, identify with, project onto, or reify, in children, aspects of adult experience. Writings about children more often than not betray an adult imagination, in Carolyn Steedman's words, a constellation of "adult beliefs, desires and fantasies that are expressed in the figure of the child" (5). In *The Turn of the Screw*, though, we are primarily faced with the Governess's sense of the children as defenseless dependents – "innocent little precious lives" in her charge (197; ch.6). We confront an adult picture of a childhood defined, I shall suggest, by its inaccessibility, and (as Steedman argues) by its articulation of an interior, psychic space. Since Freud, we have learnt to identify in beliefs, feelings, and memories of childhood, the traces of a remote and irretrievable realm, the unconscious.

Britten himself, it seems clear, *did* idealize childhood, as is confirmed by works like the *Simple Symphony* on juvenilia themes, or ventures such as the publication in 1969, of *Five Walztes* [*sic*] written as a twelve-year-old. In many respects, his view of childhood appears to reflect a Victorian view, wherein children, in the increasingly industrialized landscape of nineteenth-century England (the milieu of James's tale and of other Britten scores), were the "last symbols of purity in a world that was seen as increasingly ugly."[38] But this image and the Wordsworthian sense of childhood as the realm of something valuable yet irrecuperable in later years is balanced, in the James opera, by a tradition of childish demons – beings indistinct, in a specifically moral sense, from their adult guardians. *The Turn of the Screw*, as opera, presents audiences with the intriguing (and quite original) possibility of retrieving childhood through a sophisticated drama with children in prominent singing roles.[39] But it is precisely by treating the children as performers, characters "playing" a role, possibly with the intention of deceiving adult onlookers, that the opera, as I will argue, makes its most disturbing impression.

(b) Performing childhood

> *Miles and Flora*:
> Lavender's blue, diddle diddle,
> Lavender's green,
> When I am King, diddle diddle,
> You shall be Queen.
> *The Governess and Mrs. Grose*:
> . . . Yes! The child is an angel!
>
> Act 1, Scene 3

> "Their more than earthly beauty, their absolutely unnatural goodness. It's a
> game," I went on; "it's a policy and a fraud!"   James, p. 237, ch. 12

Britten's *Screw* brings figures of childhood before us in song. The too-predictable pattern of the Screw theme itself is in a sense, "childish," more unformed tracing-out of a shape than real theme. The Governess's arrival at Bly is a scene in which the "proper" and musically wooden formalities of welcome (Miles's bow, Flora's curtsey) compete with the boisterous sing-song of childish high spirits: Mrs. Grose hushes the children just as the Governess appears, but their bright, major-mode phrases burst in soon after ("we want to show you the house"), drowning out the two adults' reflective arioso duet. And then there are the scenes that transpose play as we recognize it from the non-operatic world – the play of nursery rhymes, singing games, and dolls – to the heart of the score. The traditional "Lavender's Blue" rhyme wafts in to the adults through the window just after the fateful letter of dismissal comes from Miles's school, and as the adults listen, they can only think that Miles is "an angel." One scene later, as the ghostly sounds accompanying Quint's first appearance to the Governess give way to "Tom, Tom, the piper's son," the children ride in on their hobby horse and take turns to "steal a pig." Whatever may have upset the Governess, does not, on the face of it, distract the children from their imaginary world. In its brightly tuneful major-mode lines, and in the inclusion of well-known children's games, the score blends into its self-contained musical world bits of naive oral tradition. Here is a sounding picture of what Erik Erikson calls the "intermediate reality between phantasy and actuality" that is children's play (212).

That the childlike can on occasion infiltrate an operatic world that is primarily adult to devastating effect is something Britten would have known from Berg's *Wozzeck*, where the closing horror of Marie's death is followed by the cruelty of the children's "Ringel, Ringel" rhyme, superimposed on the scene as her orphaned infant plays alone.[40] In *Albert Herring*, Britten's comedy of adolescent rebellion, the freshness of similarly realistic children's music – the bouncing-ball game of Act 1, Scene 2 – is set against the more pompous false-childishness of Miss Wordsworth's "May King" anthem, and the ball-song, in several reprises, comes to symbolize a freedom of spirit that Albert himself is denied by his mother's infantilizing strictures.[41] It is typical of Britten that the "bounce me high" rhyme was one he himself knew from playing with Montagu Slater's young daughter a couple of years before.[42] In some senses, at least, the link between Britten's personal contact with children and his creative imagination of child-like things, could be absolutely direct.

James's tale provides obvious hints for this operatic staging of the childish. To begin with, the narrative sets up a very marked contrast between the noisiness of the children and the absolute silence of each ghostly episode. In the Governess's melodramatic first-person account, Quint's appearance is bound up with a sonic transformation. Strolling in the park amid "all the music of summer," the idyll is shattered moments later by the figure on the tower, as if

> while I took in, what I did take in, all the rest of the scene had been stricken with death. I can hear again, as I write, the intense hush in which the sounds of evening dropped. The rooks stopped cawing in the golden sky and the friendly hour lost for the unspeakable minute all its voice.   (176; ch. 3)

Against this perilous loss of "voice," James packs the book with the sounds of the children as a reassuring sign of distance from the ghostly: "with our small friends' voices in the air, their pressure on one's heart and their fragrant faces against one's cheek, everything fell to the ground but their incapacity and their beauty" (210; ch. 8). For the Governess, the children's physical beauty, and their helplessness, are part of a childhood brought forth in make-believe, her breathless reports of a "cloud of music and affection and success and private theatricals" (219; ch.9) evoking a "normal" childhood devoid of spirits. In Britten's opera, silence is not of course an option for evoking uncanniness; the score must find audible musical alternatives to James's silent ghosts. Creating operatic figures from literary children, Britten imbues a theatrical convention with unusual significance for the story being told. Like James's children, who are always delighting the Governess with theatrical exploits of one kind or another ("They not only popped out at me as tigers and as Romans, but as Shakespeareans, astronomers and navigators"; 219; ch. 9), Britten's and Piper's children are performers. By having them perform *within* the opera itself, their childish nature is manifest to the Governess on terms identical to those an audience witnesses. In the scene of the children singing "Lavender's blue" while a rapt Governess and Mrs. Grose listen in, the opera fashions a figure of childhood that is at once true to what we know from everyday experience and – in its stress on the performance itself – intensely operatic.

The "Lavender's blue" rhyme dispels, or at least displaces, the Governess's worries over Miles's unexplained dismissal from school by its disarming simplicity of utterance. After the ominous machinations of the Thread theme in the dark-hued straining viola, Mrs. Grose and the Governess's consideration of Miles's behavior slithers uncertainly in a chromatic vein, the marked suspension of harmonic direction painting voiced doubts as to what the letter means ("he can be wild but not bad!"). The spell is broken by the song itself: somber oboe/bassoon timbres give way to sweeter harp harmonics, and to the unison of Miles's unbroken voice and Flora's soprano (Ex.4.12). Timbral precision is crucial: Miles's unbroken voice, in context, has a timbral reality, an authenticity, not merely in contrast to adult voices, but as the white, ascetic tone of the boy treble, heard among trained operatic voices.

On stage, the adults hear voices at a slight distance ("the children are seen at the window"), and the song stands apart in every way from its context: by its gentle three-beat lilt, and by its primordial stepwise melody, anchored around a new tonic, G (the scene previously suggested a C tonic). The tune outlines a simple six-note mode, to which the harp adds a natural seventh (F♮) later. The music is "angelic" in the traditional sense of sounding "high": the darker bass register falls silent, while the listening adults add their vocal contributions mostly above the melody, to pitches that jar against its utter simplicity. The traditional tune's repetitive design – something Britten takes over in his invented children's songs elsewhere in the opera – is a foil to the melodic freedoms of the preceding recitative.[43]

Everything points to a vision of childhood's "more than earthly beauty," and the details of mise-en-scène here – with lighting effects ("the window fades") timed with the sonic cross-fade of the voices to the solo harp – confirm a separation of those performing the song and those on stage who attend to its sounds. The adults, we noted, are in a harmonically separate realm from Flora and Miles; their sharp-key interpolations go with the orchestral winds, but strike disconcertingly against the G-modality of the children (with *their* instrument, the harp). Certainly, this is a "phenomenal" performance (to borrow Abbate's term), in that it is heard by those on stage as a performance. But this performance differs from other familiar examples (Carmen's Seguidilla, Cherubino's love-song, Essex's lute song in *Gloriana*), for it is not really addressed to the adults. Indeed, the dividing-off of realms that phenomenal performance creates here functions as a

Ex. 4.12: Performing childhood: the "Lavender's blue" rhyme, Act 1, Scene 3

sign of distance from the surrounding operatic world. In their singing, the children perform their separation from adult surveillance and care. Unlike the self-conscious songs of nineteenth-century operas, the children's rhymes and games in the *Screw* only rarely point outwards to the surrounding world of adult reality. Their songs are not self-reflexive allegories of the surrounding drama; rather, they point inward, to a private world, a world of nonsense rhymes and make-believe.

The nursery-rhyme scene, and the horseplay of the following song, "Tom, Tom, the piper's son" are childish performances in the sense that they embody culturally made universals – the innocent child, the beautiful child. The opera's play with such tropes is to be understood within a broader cultural imagination in which the figure of the child comes to stand, for adults, not simply as the archetype of dependency, powerlessness, and bodily weakness, but as the clearest emblem of a selfhood focused within. If the "Romantic child" of Wordsworth's time came to represent some "lost realm, lost in the individual past, and in the past of the culture," then, as Carolyn Steedman has argued, this myth engages wider narratives of the modern self as a layered interior, an *inside*, "created by the laying down and accretion of our own childhood experiences, our own history" (10, 12). Freud's analyses theorize childhood by another name – the unconscious – discovering in a lost past the basis of individual psychic identity. Similar fascinations with what lies beneath the bodily exterior – the increased awareness, in Kathy Psomiades's words, of "surface that points elsewhere for its meaning" (49) – animate the heavily aestheticizing Victorian discourse of femininity. To gaze on the beautiful face, or to watch the beautiful child, amounts, in the post-Victorian imagination which links James, Britten, and our own era, to the same thing: to observe the opaque surface of a psychic interior. The contents of that interior, however, remain mysterious, and in the opera, the site of that mystery is the children's performances.

For the Governess, this immaculate image of the children must be protected at all costs. The unspecified sexual threat posed the children by their "false friends" drives her fears, and possibly, her madness. It is here that the bright vision at the window fades. Hearing through the Governess's ears, as it were, we begin to suspect, that the "unearthly beauty," the glinting brightness of all the music is, in her words, "a policy and a fraud." As Christopher Palmer observes, the score's focus on percussion-rich orchestral colors (Quint's celesta, Miss Jessel's gong), and the gamelan-like overlay of watery figurations in the ghostly ensembles (notably in the Act 1 finale) offer an exotic alternative to European textural models. The brightness of the children's songs, to pursue Palmer's reading momentarily, harbors an "inverted symbolism" such that the opera's pentatonic charm – even the fourths of the Screw theme itself – offers a "musical incarnation of *im*perfection."[44]

But to speak of an absolute deception is to foreclose on the opera's irreducible ambiguities, which re-create, in distinctly operatic terms, the inbuilt ambiguities of James's literary form. The function of the children's songs is not to enact a corrupt game of deception but to keep the question of their morality (angels or devils) irreducibly open. If the audience is convinced one way or the other – that the children are corrupt, or that the Governess is deluded – the tale loses its bite. The children, in their musical performances, must keep open both possibilities. In the book, of course, the ambiguities must be teased out through the voice of the Governess's first-person account, which a reader may deem reliable or symptomatic of instability. In the opera, as we have noted before, ambiguities of perception move from the visual field described in her narrative to the auditory realm of the score as a whole. Because the opera invites us to hear *with the adults*, the score can, on its own terms, engage the question of perception. A listening audience must decide how to interpret the sounds it hears. In the book, our knowledge of the children is from the Governess's point of view; in the opera, our knowledge of the children is above all musical, and it is here that the possibility of retaining the Jamesian literary ambiguity resides. (I return, below, to the issue of the "reality" of the ghosts in the operatic staging.)

The challenge, musically, is to find a compensating factor for the richly metaphorical discourse by which James's Governess imagines the children's possible corruption. The book's literary imagery – "a small shifty spot on the wrong side of it all," the jerking back of a curtain, a fleeting "view of the back of the tapestry" (211–12, 231; chs. 7, 11) – is absent from the opera libretto, and so there remains a tricky question: what is the musical evidence for the children's corruption?

(c) Sinister scenes of play

The simple "Lavender's Blue" rhyme in the operatic *Screw* is an icon of childhood itself. Set off as found object from the surrounding performance, and itself constituting a performance for adult ears, the nursery rhyme is a figure of childhood interiority, an opaque sounding emblem of that which remains inaccessible to the adult perception. The rhyme, though, is closer to childhood as adults perceive it than it is to childhood as experience. In the oral tradition, nursery rhymes are taught children by adults. As the opera proceeds, though, the Governess and audience sense ever more strongly that the various scenes of childish play have a sinister undertow. The musical evidence of this reverse side to the figure in the tapestry is a series of performances witnessed by the adults, either on stage (making for "phenomenal" performance) or in the audience.

Children's play, in everyday life, may be dismissed as trivial, nonsensical even; the opera, though, presents the children's performances as empty signifiers into which the Governess's worst imaginings can flood (and the reader's or audience's too). That child's-play itself might assume a sinister significance reflects a willingness to entertain psychological interpretations. Play, whether solitary or social, gives the child an imaginary mastery of the environment, and that offers, in the symbolic realm of fantasy, a rectification of some real-life experience of displeasure (as in Freud's allegorizing of an infant's "*fort-da*" game with toys in relation to awareness of his mother's absence and return).[45] Our unrest at the children's games in the *Screw* is grounded in this sense that Miles's and Flora's imaginary activities connote more than the experiences common to all children. These games might well point to private, even secret, thoughts; play, as Erikson notes, may gain "a *unique meaning* to individual children who have lost a person or an animal and therefore endow the game with a particular significance" (219). The losses affecting little Flora and Miles at Bly are all too evident: beyond the immediate loss of their parents, and the absence of the Guardian, they have lost a previous Governess, Miss Jessel, and the Master's servant, Peter Quint. The novella hints that Miss Jessel's disappearance and Quint's unsavory and unexplained death are related (she disgraced as a lady consorting with a servant, possibly to the pitch of vengeful murder and suicide?). Whatever the unknowable facts of the past – ghosts or no – the reality of childish loss, especially for Miles (whom Quint was "free with") and the possibility of more wrenching experiences, offers only too rich a fund of "play material" for the children to dramatize. The return of the ghosts – whether real or imagined by the Governess – recalls this prehistory of the children's present, solitary predicament at Bly. Locked up in the country estate, dismissed from his school (and not returning after the holidays have ended), Miles's craving for boyish companionship ("I want my own kind") is a quite reasonable request. Even if one were to consider the children's former relations with Quint and Miss Jessel as entirely benevolent (a claim not well supported in the text), their sudden deaths alone might provide an obvious source of childish anxiety, an anxiety that could reveal itself in the imaginary realm of play.

That the children's play *is* significant, at some level, seems clear, and the emphasis it receives in the opera, through musically realized performances, only deepens its mystery. "Tom, Tom, the piper's son," in Act 1, Scene 4 is "real" play made sinister – if we choose to listen for that possibility – by the music's overtones of violence, both in the harsh cluster formations, and the brash timbres (pizzicati strings, pointed by a rasping side drum). The sexual overtones of the dialogue between siblings here, and the possibilities open to stage directors in how suggestive or coquettish to make the children's romping around on the horse,[46] should not obscure what are ultimately more directly sinister "facts" of the plot. The opera places this scene immediately after Quint's first appearance to the Governess, and the children's music, by its own Screw-like ascent to the higher register, tails off directly into Quint's new appearance at the window (see Ex. 4.11 above). Those clustering upper-register trichords are revealed musically as identical to Quint's signature celesta-chord (the children's chords on F♯ then G♯, Quint's a step up, on A♯).

The opera's musical plan here works to sinister effect, for the Hobby-Horse game, with its violent cross-accents, is not at first visible. What we experience, instead, is a musical variation (no. 4) that is much fiercer in mood than the three before; the game emerges out of this as a softening of effect (as the nursery tune appears, the surrounding harmonies are less abrasive, though still bristling with cluster-chords). The game, in other words, is heard to spring directly from the turning screw mechanism of the variations.

Supernatural forces are still more directly audible in Flora's doll lullaby (Act 1, Scene 7), and not merely because of her disturbing fixation on the "*Dead* Sea" in response to the Governess's geography quiz ("dead" sung to Quint's E♭). Britten and Piper closely follow James's scene here, by having Miss Jessel's apparition at the lake emerge out of the little girl's solitary lullaby, which sounds as an incantation. The operatic scene, like that in the book, reports the Governess's vision, but keeps open the question of whether Flora actually sees Miss Jessel at this point, as stage directions confirm:

> She goes on rustling and patting the doll . . . she turns round deliberately to face the audience as Miss Jessel appears at the other side of the lake. The Governess looks up from her reading and sees Miss Jessel, who disappears.

Productions that tip the scales and allow Flora to see the ghost disregard the ambiguity of the directions (faithful to James) and their coordination with the musical action here.[47] The steady sinking-whole-step bass line marks Flora's ability to dislodge the scene's G tonic, something Miles does too in the "Malo" song (in Scene 6), reversing the rising-tonic force of Act

1. Still, the music "won't tell" here, either; or rather, it tells us more about the Governess's state of mind than Flora's. Miss Jessel's low gong sonorities are harmonically distinct from both Flora and the Governess (though suggestively derived from the whole-tone orientation of Flora's lullaby), but as the Governess moves off "to find Miles," the return of the jumpy phrases of her Quint-sightings ("who is it?") helps an audience to know only that the Governess sees.

The children's corruption gains its strongest musical depiction in Act 2, again within the frame of a phenomenal performance. The reality-deepening effect of such mis-en-abyme constructions, is, Abbate notes, a "kind of double negative (performance within performance) that becomes a positive, affirming what we see" (1991: 97). The self-reflexivity of the "Benedicite" in Act 2 is different from the autonomy of the Act 1 "Lavender" rhyme. Few listeners can miss the chilling side of the children's ecclesiastical parody in Scene 2 (an authentic gesture, in that folklore recognizes in many childish jingles the "fossil remains," distorted, of liturgical sources.[48] Beyond this, though, the eeriness of effect is a matter of self-reflexivity. The children, that is, are "really" singing a song that the adults hear; but that song, as we in the audience hear, is a miniature version of the Screw theme dominating the variation that introduces the scene. The audience's hearing is different from that of the adults on stage. They hear "a song"; we hear "a song within the performance." It is the reflective doubling of scene and variation – Screw theme and children's song – that forms a kind of perceptual oscillation.[49]

Here, finally, the Governess voices her fears – "they are not playing, they are talking horrors" – and the musical setting gives full rein to such suspicions. Aside from the naughtiness of the children, their disrespectful rewriting of Anglican liturgy, we note their allusion to Quint and his usual haunts in the text ("O ye bells and towers: praise him. O ye paths and woods"). The praise, moreover, is for *him* (Quint?), while the prayer for protection is for *her* ("Mrs. Grose, bless ye the Lord: / May she never be confounded"), as if taunting the Governess, under the guise of addressing the housekeeper.

The more obvious aural forms in the Bells scene – the disconcerting trill pitch (G♮) gnawing at the security of the scene's home tonic (F♯), the clanging of the bells – are only superficial parts of an extraordinary musical uncanny. The bedrock is a pronounced harmonic strangeness. In the brash orchestral tutti that concludes the scene, for instance (Ex. 4.13), are compacted all of its harmonic tensions: the strange mismatch of the diatonic-sounding change-ringing in the bells (*i*) with the ostensibly

Ex. 4.13: Harmonic tensions in the "Bells" scene

simple diatonic harmonies below, and the penetrating descant above (which goes its own way); and the wrenching shift to far more ambiguous chordal agglomerations (*ii*), then clusters betraying Quint (*iii*).

In fashioning children's songs as naive diatonic music that interacts with a far more complex-sounding orchestral backdrop, Britten finds an aural equivalent for the double-sidedness of Jamesian screens, curtains, and tapestries. We hear childhood simplicity, and we hear too a mendacious undertow that speaks of corruption. This combination, I have argued, takes us to the surface of an interior that is unreachable, and the focus on performance as dissimulation takes us far into believing that the ghosts have control of the children. Miles's piano playing, late in Act 2, is perhaps the strongest sign of a childish performance corrupted. But to understand it, we must examine the song that "steers" him through the opera.

(d) Solitary yearning: senses of malo

A child has much to learn before it can pretend.
                              Wittgenstein, *Philosophical Investigations*, p. 229

Malo: I would rather be
Malo: in an apple-tree
Malo: than a naughty boy
Malo: in adversity
          Miles, Act 1, Scene 6

Miles's "Malo" song, by its somber, hesitant musical expression, and its cryptic but unmistakable Edenic allusions, stands apart from the earlier set-piece performances the Governess has heard from the children. If the brightness of the nursery rhymes suggests to the Governess an unreadable "goodness" that may be only a hoax, the "Malo" song sounds at face value as a brooding expression of unhappiness. Like the wistful song of yearning that Goethe gives his orphan-girl Mignon to sing, Miles's "Malo" song seems to encapsulate for adults everything enigmatic and unknowable about the boy (including the crucial question of his own sexual knowledge),[50] yet retaining the power to move the Governess and us to pity and tenderness. But the song's strangeness – "Why, Miles, what a funny song! Did I teach you that?" – also has a disturbing quality, for it shares the restless and mechanical sequence constructions of the Screw and Thread themes. Melodic chains of wandering thirds recall the Screw theme itself, and the pitches of Quint's celesta-trichord (B♭,D♭,E♭) stands at the melody's head. The ambiguity of the harmonic wanderings here (by parallel seventh) conceals a careful placement within the scene: the initial triadic emphasis on E♭ makes the song's opening a "sinking" in relation to the scene's earlier F tonic; and the "real" tonic here (F minor) is another blighting, emerging only at the end of Miles's fourth phrase. Miles's song places him in a musico-dramatic pattern of which he himself may be ignorant.

In its profligate conjuring of verbal meaning, the doggerel of the schoolboy mnemonic could stand for the wider confusions of reference that confound our attempts to interpret the situation of the tale as a whole. If a single Latin word can encapsulate so many competing senses, then what are we to make of the opera's wider ambiguities, whether regarded as duplicities or multiplicity? Miles's rhyme encapsulates present unease ("I would rather be") and anxiety ("in adversity"), and it is also an expression of his shame at having been dismissed from school ("a naughty boy"), an event whose cause remains mysterious to us. The fourth sense of *Malo* here ("in an apple tree"), is a mythic link of the Latin–English mnemonic with a scene of learning.

Miles sings, the score says, "to himself." In thinness of accompaniment, and by the interaction of the vocal line with the wordless English horn obbligato, the song conveys an interior subjectivity that the Governess can take no part in. The solo viola – so often Britten's symbol for small boys[51] – here behaves very differently from its earlier appearance. Where the viola in Act 1, Scene 3 challenges the adults' vocal lines, it acts in "Malo" as the voice's shadow, drawing out the first note of each phrase, echoing and responding as the song winds down. The other instrumental color here, a harp, could almost be a stylized lute (suggesting the self-accompaniment of Essex's lute songs in *Gloriana*), reinforcing the song's "performed" separation from the surrounding music.

The "Malo" song differs from the other childish performances, for it returns at significant points in the later opera. Britten's original idea, of a song for Miles "the tune and echoes of which could steer him through the work,"[52] is apparent immediately as the schoolroom scene fades. Here, the song tune itself forms a smooth melodic link – made smoother still by a timbral cross-fade of English horn to other woodwinds – to Variation 6, thus erasing the previous pattern of "new" variations breaking in at the close of a scene. Strains of "Malo" pervade the variation as inner-texture woodwind lines, and a snatch of the tune returns as Flora mentions Miles to the Governess in Scene 7 itself. The song, or at least its harp timbre, has almost the last word in Act 1, accompanying Miles's coy admissions of disobedience ("You see, I *am* bad") in trichords that are Quint's. Its readily audible appearances in Act 2 – in the bedroom at night, and after Miles steals the Governess's letter to the Guardian (Scenes 4–5), then in Miles's piano playing – establish a direct musical link between Miles and Quint. In the first two scenes, Miles's tune is heard in its original English horn scoring, and both scenes include Quint's unseen vocal contribution (in the first, Quint's presence in a glockenspiel chord is also generalized into his trichords in the harp). Further evidence that Miles's song reflects Quint's influence is more subtle, though no less audible if one listens closely: the song Quint sings in his Colloquy with Miss Jessel as Act 2 opens is new and yet familiar, for its bass line turns out to be a rhythmically disguised and speeded-up form of the earlier "Malo" tune.

> I seek a friend, obedient to follow where I lead,
> Slick as a juggler's mate to catch my thought,
> Proud, curious, agile, he shall feed
> My mounting power.
> Then to his bright subservience I'll expound
> The desp'rate passions of a haunted heart,
> And in that hour "The ceremony of innocence is drowned."

Quint is singing of Miles in terms that suggest not intimacy, but subjugation to a controlling force, and initiation into matters suggestively erotic ("passions of a haunted heart") that will put an end to the child's innocence, and in a rather violent way (drowning).[53] But the "Malo" song cannot be reduced to an emblem of Miles's unwilling subservience to a ghostly male power, for its final return is of course that heard on the Governess's lips. Her adult rendition of the boy's tune, as Joseph Kerman heard, "encapsulates the entire action" by conflating "his tragedy and hers" (1988: 221). In a drama that presents an inaccessible childhood interiority in scenes of vocal performance, this final "Malo" song makes its point in a scene that gradually erases the child's voice from the opera's musical world. Miles's final responses to the Governess move from voiced song to unvoiced shrieks ("Is he there? . . . Peter Quint, you devil!"). Miles's death coincides precisely with the return of his earlier vocal admissions, sung jointly by Quint and the Governess ("Ah, Miles! you are saved / we have failed . . ."). The Governess's closing version of "Malo" begins as a passionate outburst, only to retreat to the realm of verbal and musical uncertainty, as her enigmatic question – "what have we done between us?" – slips in between the last two phrases of the dead boy's tune.

3. Ghostly machines: the drama of themes

> Britten is always aware of the extraordinary adaptability of "obvious" tunes
> . . . . In his music, everything goes with everything else.
>
> Imogen Holst (1962: 162)

(a) Themes as agents

Musical themes, in the operatic *Screw*, unfold a dramatic discourse significantly different from either the forceful speech-act orientation of *Grimes*, or the orchestral commentaries that are ever more detached from moment-by-moment action on stage in *Billy Budd*. The big difference in the *Screw*, as I began by showing, is the omnipresence of a controlling thematic force. The Screw theme dominates each act by its framing appearances, and each scene, by its ubiquitous activity in the intervening variations. Yet it dominates autonomously, without forging direct links to those on stage, live or ghostly. The Governess, the ghosts, and the children are all enveloped by the theme's characteristic shape, but the references are subliminal (often tucked away in speech-rhythm vocal recitative). In such fleeting forms, the Screw theme, in and of itself, is not a menace. Its rising fourths and falling fifths are simply a saturating influence at all points in the drama, as common to the Governess's nervous doubts, her happy arrival, and the serene nature music of Scene 4 as to the first incursions of Quint's ghostly presence (see Ex. 4.14). In each case, traces of the Screw's distinctive turning form are easily audible, whether the pitch order is strict, free, or some feature – such as the whole-step gap between fourths – is abandoned (for halfsteps, as at the phrase "and Miles?"). Intrinsic to the Screw's spiraling design is the potential for synecdoche, one tiny fragment invoking an absent whole.

The opera's thematic discourse resembles the narrative technique of James's book. The Screw theme embodies, in Tzvetan Todorov's phrase, the "absolute and absent cause" that James places so often at the heart of a story. The theme, though absent mostly as a surface feature of the musical argument, frames each act and interleaves each scene. In these instrumental variations, we recognize in it a mysterious "cause." The Screw theme, far more than the ghosts, is the opera's ultimate mystery, and so Todorov's account of the archetypal James plot applies to the thematic rhetoric in Britten's operatic *Screw*:

> [T]he secret in Jamesian narrative is precisely the existence of an essential secret, of something not named, of an absent and superpowerful force which sets the whole present machinery of the narrative in motion. This motion is a double and, in appearance, a contradictory one. . . . On one hand [James] deploys all his forces to attain the hidden essence, to reveal the secret object; on the other, he constantly postpones, protects the revelation – until the story's end, if not beyond.   (1977:145)

In musical terms, this double motion is evident in the questing character of the background thematic rise and fall that spans the entire opera, and resulting circularity of its tonal journey. By opera's end, we have traveled from A to A♭ and back in sixteen discrete rising and falling moves. But the reinstatement of the initial A♮ tonic is not marked rhetorically as an arrival point, nor is that tonic forcefully triumphant during the final scene. The opera concludes, in fact, by retreating entirely from the Screw theme. The Governess's question – "what have we done between us?" – is answered by the "Malo" song, *not* the Screw theme. And though we *do* end up on the Screw's original A tonic, it is only precariously a tonic, and real cadence is lacking. All possibility of a conclusive dramatic revelation is postponed indefinitely.[54]

Local disguise governs the internal workings of the variations, moreover. The accumulating tutti of the opening Screw theme statement connotes "announcement," but in subsequent variations, the theme itself is increasingly less prominent. Thus it becomes a bass line beneath lively

Ex. 4.14: Screw-theme derived vocal utterances

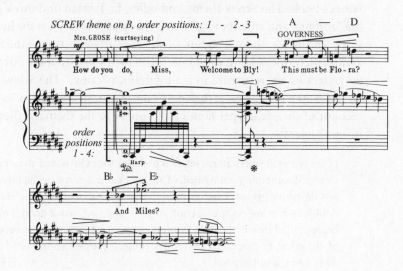

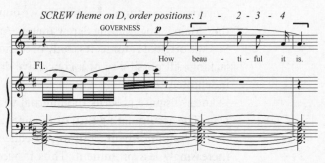

Ex. 4.14 (*cont.*)

upper-register figuration (Variations 1, 2, 4, 6) or its melodic continuity is broken up, as in Variation 3, where the initial oboe–flute presentation is lost by the third phrase in a filigree of harp figuration; Variation 5 treats the theme on F merely as a scaffold for a fugato exposition on a free subject.

Thematic repetition, in opera, is usually significant less as a form-building force (the da capo aria aside) than as a dramatic effect. Listeners sensing a theme's return feel that it returns for a reason – to underline some detail of the situation, or to establish a link between the present moment and some earlier scene. But when thematic repetition becomes automatic, it is rendered strange; literal (rather than varied) musical repetition, as Robert Morgan has noted, is fairly rare (it has even been called "unnatural").[55] In the *Screw*, a quasi-mechanical thematic repetition is built into the work's musical plan, both at the local level of the theme itself, and in the large-scale variation plan. These returns, more or less explicit in their melodic projection, take on a fearsome, uncanny quality – here, surely, is the mechanism that drives action forward.[56]

But the Screw theme's returns, however "mechanical" as formal events, are not uniform in dramatic impact. For one thing, tempo variations regulate the flow of story-time: Variations 1 and 2 are spritely transitions that suggest the arrival of Miles's dismissal letter is soon after the Governess's arrival at Bly;[57] the slow and pastoral Variation 3, on the other hand, conveys a longer passage of time and the allaying of the Governess's "fluttering fears." Further, the framing variations of Act 2 are exceptional, in that they do not flow seamlessly into the following scene (this facet of the other variations only reinforces an interpretation of the opera's action as "caused" by the Screw theme itself). Variations 8 and 15 stand apart from the scenes they preface by obscuring the Screw theme as a melodic force, while introducing dense chordal masses of indeterminate harmonic value.

In both cases, the thematic absence of the Screw is a tactical delay, herald-ing pivotal vocal Screw statements within Scenes 1 and 8 of Act 2, by the ghosts and by the Governess, orchestrally doubled. At these two points only, the singers give direct voice to complete Screw themes, rather than mere fragments.

These two texted statements of the Screw theme delineate a forceful dra-matic conflict by patent contrasts of musical tone, as well as by the obvious opposition of viewpoints expressed in the sung words. The Ghosts' theme, for example, with its throbbing chordal underlay, embodies the Screw's power as a supernatural force against the children; it is at this point, after all, that Piper adds texts that explicate facets of James's tale (where the ghosts are silent):

> Day by day the bars we break,
> Break the love that laps them round,
> Cheat the careful watching eyes.

This is a ghostly credo affirming malicious intent (for listeners who know their Monteverdi, the *stile concitato* rhythms of its accompaniment spell combat). It follows the Screw theme's original dotted rhythms, and its tonal setting derives urgency and power from a quasi-functional triadic surface and the smoothly linear bass. Moreover, it stands entirely apart, in this shift to a motoric rhythmic pattern, from the flowing figuration of surrounding music. The Screw theme is projected here as isolated musical utterance. The Governess's Screw theme, in the final scene, is very differ-ent, and not only because of a more conversational tone ("Who made you take the letter? . . . Only say the name, and he will go for ever") recalling the direct speech in James's scene. This theme is challenged by the superposi-tion of Quint's "Paths" song, and so its tonal revolutions between A tonic repetitions serve as a bass line that has direct harmonic challenge – in Quint's A♭-major reference. Nor is the theme set off from its surround in the way that the Ghosts' statement was: the complete Screw theme here is introduced subtly, as the bass line to Quint's song, and since its turning is drawn out by protracted tonal pedals at the fourth and eighth pitch (E and G♯), the overall motion sounds sporadic and desperate, rather than force-fully questing, as was the ghosts' Screw theme.

Thematic repetition, though, is many things, and the present narrative will, in its own Jamesian fashion, postpone further comment on the Screw theme. We have seen something of the score's translation of Jamesian nar-rative movements into a thematic drama: like narrative agents, themes return in various ways, and in different relations to the named characters on stage. The musical themes resemble Propp's narrative *functions*, in that they do not depend on a single character for their execution as part of a plot (19–21). The Ghosts and the Governess both voice the Screw theme, and (as is clear from Example 4.14) it saturates all characters' scenic speech as well. But the drama of themes includes another significant agent besides the Screw theme itself, one whose role is crucial in articulating the Governess's struggle with Quint.

(b) The Thread theme as problematic utterance

The Thread theme has far greater presence *as a melodic theme* than the Screw theme. As "absent cause," the Screw is heard in framing utterances, as the controlling force of the whole opera, but retreats, in the variations, to a more veiled presence.[58] In this sense, the Screw theme is closer to originary "source" than theme proper; the Thread theme, by contrast, is always a foreground musical agent. Not only do we hear it intact at numerous significant dramatic points; it is also identified very clearly with both the Governess and Quint. This *double* identification, though, works to confuse an audience as to the motivations of the singing characters. Like the thematic conflation of Vere and Claggart in Act 2 of *Billy Budd*, the interpenetration of the Governess and Quint reveals an uncanny thematic discourse operating behind the facade of named characters. If two characters sing one theme at different times, that theme will acquire an identity unrelated to character. This autonomizing effect applies far more clearly to the *Screw*'s Thread theme than it does to Claggart's music in *Billy Budd*. In *Billy Budd*, we can still speak of "Claggart's theme" (even after it takes over Vere's sung utterances in the Trial); in the *Screw*, though, to recognize an equivalent "Governess's theme" is to oversimplify the way the score works.

Just how independent is the Thread theme's activity in Act 1? Answers must weigh its place in a given scene, and the manner of its utterance. In Scenes 1–3, an interplay of instrumental and texted vocal utterance complicates the impression of the theme as "belonging" to the Governess: in Scene 1, with the solo vocal utterance "why did I come?" (cf. Ex. 4.9 above), the theme quite clearly does belong to her. But in Scenes 2–3, the Thread theme's appearances coincide with the fatal "blighting" shift from major to minor mode. Both Thread statements are now instrumental lines that cloud the vocal recitative by an ominous upper-register covering line. As with the Governess's Scene 1 misgivings, these themes halt the preceding animation of the scene; the listener, with the Governess, is brought up short by the incursion of the sinister twisting theme. The switch from vocal to instrumental placement estranges the Governess from the theme, and at both these moments, it is independent enough to lead the vocal line (see Exx. 4.7 and 4.8 above). In Scene 3, the theme's arrival is placed to "reverse" Mrs. Grose's bright C-major singing; far from expressing the Governess's viewpoint, it confronts her as an outside force. The theme here (Ex. 4.8) refers to Miles (the letter's subject), not the Governess, for its characteristic twists are timed as interpolations between the Governess's bewildered questions: "He's dismissed his school . . . little Miles . . . What can it mean – never go back? . . . for that he must be bad . . . an injury to his friends."

A shift from vocal to orchestral speech involves more than the loss of a direct "verbalization" of the melody itself: the Governess's "why did I come?" phrase is just that – one *phrase*, controlled by the length of a singer's breath. We might, in context, dismiss this plangent little moment in Scene 1 as a brief qualm. But in the next two scenes, the instrumental Thread mechanism is spun out by sequential extension, draped as a spiraling sinking form that offsets both recitatives. As instrumental utterance, it is, if anything, more eloquent than as directly vocal statement. For in combination with a separate recitative voice ("he's dismissed his school"), the solo viola can *embody*, locally, the verbal referents, intensifying them by an instrumental objectification, and linking specific words to specific pitches. Thus at the moment of arrival, the Governess's formal introduction to the children ends with Miles's name, on the middle-register E♭ that will be so important to Quint, and Miles's musicalized bow, with its prominent D♯'s acquires a sinister little coda, reiterating once more the scene's D♯-D♮ blight. In scene 2, another E♭ (this one strained high in the viola) is the crucial pitch creating the blight from C major to C minor (see Ex. 4.8, above). Here, the long notes, and the careful placement of the recitative phrases in relation to them, stress certain aspects of the exchange: the keyword "bad," here, becomes a marked term moments later (see Ex. 4.12, above). Mrs. Grose's final word on the matter, "He can be wild, but not bad!" significantly reiterates the E♮–E♭ blighting pattern with which the entire conversation started, and the tension hangs in the air as a chromatic intrusion on the childish G major of the "Lavender's Blue" rhyme that now breaks in. This association of the Thread with James's teasingly unspecific allusions to Miles's "bad"-ness is one way, as we have seen, that the opera frames the childish performances as ciphers for a corrupted innocence. By fixing the theme initially as a vocal utterance, and then by magnifying its melodic prominence in subsequent scenes, the opera establishes an intricate exchange that suggests levels of discursive meaning far beyond any paraphrasable "content" to what is said verbally.

The significance of the Thread theme, then, is so far to be judged in considering whether it is instrumental or vocal in delivery. Thus in Scene 5, its glacial instrumental arrival is again a counterpoint to the Governess's recitative, as she turns over in her mind Mrs. Grose's stories about Quint (who has by now appeared at the window). The Thread here, as instrumental obbligato, forges a motivic link to the imposing new phrase Mrs. Grose uses in identifying Quint ("Dear God, is there no end . . . ?"), and so stands, in context, for his "dreadful ways." In the scene's conclusion, the Governess's brave defiance ("See what I see. . .") involves her taking back the Thread as specifically vocal material. Themes do not stand for any one thing – thus the Governess's defiance is paralleled, again by the Thread on E♭, with her despair, after Miss Jessel's appearance to Flora ("I neither save nor shield them"), a statement that returns later in Act 2 after Flora's collapse at the lake. The Thread theme, as Patricia Howard writes, serves "not to identify and individualize characters but to draw connexions between them."[59] Quint's mysterious calls – emblematic of his unspecified influence over young Miles – are heard for the first time, it is worth emphasizing, in the Act 1 finale, long *after* the Governess's vows of shielding the children. Whether or not he can have "heard" the Governess's utterances is moot; we in the audience, though, have all the benefits of dramatic irony, and cannot forget that he sings a melody she has sung too. The thematic strategy maintains ambiguity, for one either hears in the Governess's statements a prefiguring of supernatural visitations, or else one hears Quint's calls as a projection of an hysterical Governess's imagined fears for her charges' innocence.

The opera's thematic argument never escapes a kind of hermeneutic circularity, for there is no way to hear themes in isolation; in metaphorical resemblances between themes, and on the syntagmatic plane of a recurring chain of thematic returns, themes deflect attention away from the moment towards their affiliation with other moments. The labyrinth effect can only intensify as the plot turns from one short scene to the next, and as Quint and the Governess struggle ever more fiercely for the boy's devotion.

(c) Lost in the labyrinth: the Governess and Quint as doubles

The literary double, in Otto Rank's early Freudian analysis, is linked to the Narcissus myth through the idea of death made visible as a self-image. And while criticism has largely moved beyond the need to psychoanalyze literary figures as if they were flesh-and-blood analysands, Rank, in 1911, is quick to describe a roster of "symptoms" – paranoid feelings of pursuit, fear of sighting the image, a pervasive sense of guilt – that correspond well to the neurotic constellation embodied by James's *fin-de-siècle* Governess. By her actions, moreover, the Governess is frequently a physical double for

Quint, in that she moves to occupy his place. As he appears at the window, she gazes at the ghost through the glass, and he at her. When she "runs out and looks through the window, as Quint had done" (Act 1, Scene 5, stage direction), we are close to Ovid's mythic image of the boy by the pool. Miss Jessel, too, in the schoolroom, is in the Governess's place, an even more obvious doubling (as the previous Governess). Likewise, Rank's character-izing of the double as "unequivocal rival in sexual love" (131) describes one view of the Governess's battle with Quint for possession of Miles's "heart." In Rank's interpretation, the slaying of the double that the Governess undertakes (in attempting to force Miles to exorcise Quint's influence by naming him) is a substitute suicide, "in the painless form of slaying a different ego: an unconscious illusion of the splitting-off of a bad, culpable ego" (128).

Musical evidence of a Quint/Governess doubling is perhaps all too easy to find. For one thing, the musical foreground is saturated with melodic inversions, as if the scene were physically strewn with shards of mirror-fragments. In the first appearance of this music (see Ex. 4.10 above), the upper (B♭,D♭,E♭) trichord seemingly corresponds to Quint's presence on the tower, but it is mirrored by its inversion (D♮,E♮,G), providing pitches for the Governess's words ("Ha! 'Tis he!"). The mirroring interlock of I-related trichords persists throughout the Governess's subsequent ques-tionings ("who is it?"), so sustaining the ghost's musical presence for a noticeably long time after he vanishes. The music might well support an understanding of Quint as a physical object of the Governess's perception, for by registral separation – especially after he vanishes – the distance between her viewing position (below) and his location (above on the tower) is replicated. But if the space between the two is evident registrally, the music in other respects lacks a differentiation. Upper and lower tri-chordal strata replicate one another here, their amalgam a magical chro-maticism, and the motive accompanying Quint's vision quickly becomes a vehicle for the Governess's nervous questions, as much as for the ghost as a distinct entity. This music returns for Quint's appearance at the window (Ex. 4.11 above), but again it outlasts his visible image, and it is the Governess herself, recounting the episode, who appears ghostly to Mrs. Grose ("My dear, you look so white and queer"). Act 1 as a whole will close with the "who is it?" question, drummed out to a Screw-fourth.[60]

The opera is often said to pair the Governess and Quint through the resemblances of her Thread theme utterances and his "Miles" cry, yet the case for their rivalry is still clearer in those three scenes in which the two sing simultaneously on stage. The Governess and Quint, it is true, share the stage in the Act 1 finale (and again in the opera's closing moments), but in the more intimate milieu of the Act 2 Bedroom scene, their twinned threat to the vulnerable Miles, "sitting restlessly on the edge of his bed," is depicted more directly as a sexual threat.[61] Throughout the scene, the Governess appears oblivious to Quint's audible vocal presence ("I am here"), even as her own insistent questions to the boy spring from the same spectral woodwind duet that animates his unseen utterance.[62] The nocturnal timbres of the scene – alto flute, bass clarinet, a bright glockenspiel chiming Quint's distinctive $(B\flat, D\flat, E\flat)$ trichord – precede the Governess's entrance, yet they run on undisturbed once she is on stage, and undisguised melodic forms of the Screw theme guide her singing no less directly than they do Quint's (Ex. 4.15). The other main thematic agent of the scene, Miles's "Malo" song, spells out his unhappy state, but the score will not allow an audience to decide which of his rival adult claimants – the Governess who wants to "help" him, or the ghost who only "waits" – poses the greater threat.

4. The corrupt imagination: on seeing and hearing ghosts

> Ben and I argued about the haunting; had it to be explicit, or could it be the product of the Governess's paranoia – *she* was convinced that something was wrong, but was it really? I insisted on ambivalence, he on the need for the composer to make a decision – and he *had* taken one: that the haunting was real.
>
> George, Earl of Harewood (139)

> We are afraid of something unnamed, of something, perhaps, in ourselves.
>
> Virginia Woolf (Kimbrough 180)

James's *The Turn of the Screw* disturbs its literary readers most by avoiding the particular while adumbrating what James in the New York Preface calls "the depths of the sinister" (xx). Everything depends on maintaining a sense of "suspected and felt trouble . . . the tone of tragic, yet of exquisite, mystification" (xviii). Almost from the start, readers have doubted the Governess's testimony. The ghostly visitants who threaten the children at Bly may be fact – though the children never speak of them – or delusion. The Governess's ghosts, as Edna Kenton, in 1924, observed, may be only "exquisite dramatizations of her little personal mystery, figures for the ebb and flow of troubled thought within her mind."[63] As opera, though, the *Screw* appears to lose some of its obscurities, simply by virtue of the chosen medium. Articulate, singing ghosts seem to settle the whole "two-stories" debate that for so long dominated the book's critical reception – as vocal beings, the ghosts seem as real as the Governess, Mrs. Grose, and the children. (Joseph Kerman makes a similar point from an opposite angle: "the

Ex. 4.15: The Governess and Quint in Act 2, Scene 4 (The Bedroom)

characters are all ghosts" [1988: 225].) From Miles's "vantage point of abjection," Philip Brett argues, ". . . the ambiguities of the tale recede a little as we see the lovable boy caught between a dominating lover and a possessive mother" (1994b: 249). Singing ghosts, Gary Tomlinson has claimed, destroy the "systematic ambiguity" of James's first-person narrative. When Britten decided that "the haunting was real," the very solidity of vocally articulate visitants undermined "the listener's ability to sustain the illusion of ghostliness" (155–56).

But to debate the reality or illusionary nature of the opera's ghosts is surely to miss James's and Britten's point. Literary ghosts, as T. J. Lustig sensibly cautions, are always "irreducibly hypothetical" (xv) – they are textual rather than sensory objects – and James's goblin episodes are never subject to the kind of after-the-fact naturalistic explanation famously spoiling the enigmas in Ann Radcliffe's *The Mysteries of Udolpho*. To debate the narrator's sanity is to mistake one genre – the ghost story – for another – the case history. The origins of the *Screw*, James notes, are firmly with the old-fashioned "heart-shaking" tales of "sacred terror," not the modern "'psychical' case" (xv). Britten's determination that his ghosts should sing – "no nice anonymous, supernatural humming or groaning," Piper remembers (1989: 9) – is hardly reducing the interpretative range of the action, simply by choosing a realistic mimetic convention. "I don't think Ben really took sides" Piper told Patricia Howard:

> That evil exists whether in life or in the mind . . . and is capable of corrupting
> – or perhaps not necessarily corrupting but causing the loss of innocence –
> he was, I think, quite certain. The Governess's good intentions were
> destroyed by her experiences, whether real or imagined, and her love of
> Miles was corrupted, in that it became possessiveness and she was aware of it.
> Hence the last words "What have we done between us?"
>
> (cited Howard 1985: 23)

The ghosts are real enough for the Governess and – the opera seems to indicate – for the children, that we in the audience cannot dismiss their presence with psychoanalytically inflected talk of "paranoia" or hysterical delusion. My argument here will counter claims that the opera, with its singing ghosts, is somehow less ambiguous than James's story.

It is not that Britten and Piper abandon Jamesian ambiguities; rather, that they refocus the ambiguities of the original to center, not on the Governess's state (delusional or "reliable"?) but on the children. James's tale, Piper writes, "is vague only in one thing: in what, if anything, actually happened between the children and the haunting pair" (1989: 9), and it is in the children that the opera's central ambiguities reside. While the score at times supports hints of a hallucinating Governess – by a rapid cut from the ghosts' Act 2 Colloquy to her "labyrinth" aria, for instance[64] – the activities of the children pose a greater mystery. Britten's *Turn of the Screw*, without the book's first-person narrator, is less an opera about seeing and hearing ghosts than about our perceptions of childish interiority. The opera makes this shift of emphasis, I have argued, by performative means. In the nursery rhymes, childish interiority is center-stage. Innocence, that familiar but elusive cultural-metaphysical quantity, is made visible – audible – for us on stage by the dramaturgy of "phenomenal" performance. The songs overheard by the adults – adults on stage and those in the audience – enact either a fragile innocence, or its deceitful simulacrum. The ghosts may be luring the children; but the children's songs too may be a lure for the adults.

That the story's central motif, innocence corrupted, continues to fascinate modern audiences attests to the constancy of certain widely circulating, culturally specific ideas about children. James's Preface speaks of the "values" in the tale as "positively all blanks" (xxii), and so the question of what precisely makes Bly "reek with the air of Evil" has never been (and can never be) satisfactorily answered. Most frequently, of course, the nature of the "corruption" sensed by readers and opera goers has been sexual. In reviewing what the opera tells us about the children, this sexual motif looms large. Guessing at the "injury" Miles caused his school-friends before being dismissed, we assume some kind of sharing of sexual knowledge. Speculating on the "hours they spent together," we interpret Quint's being "free" with Miles in sexual terms. Our tendency to jump to conclusions – one James was counting on – in being compelled to "*think* the evil" for ourselves (xxi) helps explain the hold the opera exerts on audiences, no less immediate, perhaps, than the fascination of the book to late Victorian readers. The opera's power to haunt and disturb stems from bringing children up against hidden and malign forces. Whether or not these forces are supernatural, they must, we fear, be sexual.

Britten's *Turn of the Screw*, I take it, engages the same free-floating cultural models of childhood, adulthood, and their separation, that James's audiences would have recognized. Without diminishing the complexities of the tale's reception, it is easy to find common ground between present-day views of these categories and those of Victorian society. This shared conceptual base helps account for the work's meteoric rise to "classic" status, its mid-century fascination for Britten, and its ongoing popularity in recent cinematic dramatizations.[65] If corruption, in the *Screw*, turns menacingly about the central figure of the child, then it is emphatically the child at risk sexually. Modern-day repugnance for pedophilia, one historian notes, shares with Victorian attitudes the sense that "sexual pleasure and the capacity for sexual pleasure may not be a good" (Mason 1994: 224). The tensions engaged in the *Screw* articulate deeply seated cultural anxieties. A post-Freudian awareness that the child's existence is far from devoid of sexually charged experience clashes directly with equally prevalent models of the child as not-yet sexual. The child, for the Victorians, and for us, is defined to begin with in erotic terms. Children are a "species . . . free of sexual feeling or response"; adults, on the other hand, have "crossed over into sexuality" (Kincaid 6–7). James's elusive "*amusette*" speaks, indirectly, of topics more familiar, but no less difficult, in our own era, with its more marked emphasis on the importance of libidinal fulfillment. The turning *Screw* engages desires, not only of the sexual variety; the *Screw* speaks of the cultural desire to police the boundaries of sexual knowledge.

What is remarkable in Britten's setting is the way hints of innocence corrupted are intertwined with and complicated by competing models of adult sexual desire. The opera, in other words, stages the issue of corruption as a struggle between the Governess's possessive, smothering love for Miles, and Quint's homoerotically tinged interest in the boy. In both cases, the adults' motives are complex enough to rouse our suspicion: of the Governess, whose love of Miles in some sense substitutes for her attraction to the absent Guardian; and of Quint, whose interest in Miles as "a friend" contrasts with his cruel rejection of Miss Jessel ("self-deceiver!").

The homoerotic implications of Quint's threat to young Miles may be stronger these days than they were for Britten's first British audience. It is not simply that we see the opera today aware of the composer's own complex sexual identity, while in 1954, homosexuality caught the public gaze only through the periphrastic mechanisms of the "open secret."[66] Interpreting the operatic Quint's desire to possess Miles as identifiably homoerotic in motivation, then, we must consider the very specific cultural conditions attendant on all interpretations. In the *Screw*, a drama in which the main symbolic values are self-evidently unspecific, meanings are legible above all in the contingent and historically determined codes of social attitudes. Quint's ability to "corrupt" the boy, in other words, need not be understood solely – or even primarily – in terms of an active homoerotic desire. For James's late Victorian readers, the possibility that Quint was a homosexual, or, in this case, a pedophile, was arguably an unnecessary assertion: whatever the precise nature of relations between the older valet and the boy, Miles's "corruption" was assured as a matter of social hierarchy. Quint is a servant, and for an upper-middle-class child, intimacy with a servant was the taboo that would most likely provoke the imagination to scenes of corruption.

The perception of domestic servants as a moral threat was a commonplace in *fin-de-siècle* Europe. Freud, though rejecting a seduction theory of sexual neurosis, could still draw attention to the starkly addressed warning, recounted in a 1903 clinical text on so-called *psychopathia sexualis*: "Parents, if you have children, beware of the morals of your servants."[67] Quint's danger to Miles when they were "perpetually together" might well have been sexual, if not directly in an abusive sense: the boy might have learnt *about* sex from an exposure to the valet's socially illicit affair with the former Governess, Miss Jessel. The Victorian fear of initiating children into a knowledge of sex, after all, was bound up with notions of desire as a social artefact. The boy's sexual feelings had best be left unstimulated by a prema-ture knowledge gleaned from an association with adults.[68] Miles's associa-tion with Quint was "corrupt," from this point of view, whether or not their intimacy had any direct sexual basis. James's novel depicts very starkly the forbidden nature of Quint's romance with Miss Jessel, as voiced by Mrs. Grose: "*She* was a lady ... And he so dreadfully below" (207; ch. 7). As Bruce Robbins notes, the Quint–Jessel relation is a strange inverse of the Governess's own class-transgressive interest in the Guardian (288). In *The Turn of the Screw*, social and sexual transgressions intertwine, eclipsing even the ontological questions of the supernatural plot – references to "the others," Robbins notes, consistently conflate ghosts and servants (286).

A more intent focus to the Quint–Miles relation is one of the more notable shifts of emphasis Britten's opera makes in adapting James. The dead valet and the young boy are associated in the opera not only in those scenes they share in James (on the lawn at night, in the final scene with the Governess), but at many other points. By wordless thematic utterance, and then by off-stage vocal calls, the opera brings Quint's presence to Miles in the bedroom (Act 2, Scene 4) with the Governess. When Britten and Piper stage Miles's taking of the letter (an episode we learn of in the book only retrospectively), Quint's direct off-stage promptings ("take it!") do not seem too crude a display of motivation; by this late point in the opera, the two are so closely associated by a network of musical interactions.

The words the operatic Quint sings may, paradoxically, by their very vagueness and mystery, increase an audience's perceptions of an explicitly homoerotic desire for Miles. This is because the opera replaces the novel's meaning-gap with a bevy of oblique, indeterminate formulations. Singing to Miles of "all things strange and bold," Quint may articulate what Piper herself had tried for – "not so much to show him as evil as to suggest what there could be about him that attracted so inexperienced and innocent a child" (1989: 12). But as the periphrases tumble out – "I am the smooth world's double face ... deceit. The brittle blandishment of counterfeit ... the hidden life. ... The unknown gesture" (Act 1, Scene 8) – it is equally possible to sense preteritive utterance – allusions to that which cannot be mentioned. The prominent secrets in James's fiction, Eve Sedgwick has argued, offer a fullness of meaning redolent of the verbal discourse sur-rounding closeted homosexual experience. Quint's resort to the "quasi-nominative, quasi-obliterative" – "In me secrets, half-formed desires meet" – sounds like nothing so much as Lord Alfred Douglas's utterance, of the Wilde trial: "I am the Love that dare not speak its name."[69] Miss Jessel's relation to Flora, by contrast, though ghostly, can still claim the socially legitimate form of a professional governess.

The opera's ambiguities, I have said, transcend the mimetic question of whether the ghosts are "real" – whatever that means in literary and operatic worlds – leading us to the complications of the children in their musical, performative being, and to the complexities of an "innocence" closely defined in opposition to adult sexual desire. But all debates about reality, corruption, and innocence circle inevitably back to the Screw theme itself, the opera's most potent and inescapable force, the most ambiguous and, in James's phrase, "positively blank" of all its dramatic agencies. Tomlinson's claim that singing ghosts lose their supernatural aura neglects the Screw theme's own presence. The ambiguity function of the Governess's narrative is taken over, in the opera, by a thematic system at whose center stands the Screw theme. As I earlier argued, the Screw theme constitutes a secret, all-powerful force encircling events at Bly. By its melodic sinuosity, and by the mechanical patterning of its shifts of key, the action takes an unstoppable screw-like movement.

Reflecting on the controlling force exerted by the Screw theme, it is easy to forget the determining role of the large-scale variation scheme in shaping the plot's larger narrative rhythms (as well as the local melodic and harmonic soundscape). Britten's own memories of planning the *Screw* are revealing:

> . . . you have to be prepared to adjust, and that particularly in opera when, as E. M. Forster says, the characters take over. . . . the first drafts for *The Turn of the Screw* were in . . . three-act form, and even I think the libretto was written in that shape. And I realized there was something wrong . . . we had omitted some of James's own episodes, and put others together, and he planned that story . . . so very carefully that if you miss one rung in the ladder you miss your footstep . . . I then discovered that what we were really planning was something in a certain number of scenes which must follow very closely. And I was then looking for an idea which could be varied through these scenes . . . . Because really the story could be rather fancifully described as a theme with variations.
>
> (1984: 91)

It is not just that Britten reimagines James's literary structure as an extended variation process. Most striking in these comments is Britten's wish to illustrate Forster's point about letting operatic characters "take over." The Screw theme – the opera's variation subject – is for Britten itself a *character* whose force he cannot, finally, ignore.

The variety of thematic functions the Screw theme can assume, and the range of its manifestations – from direct "declaration" to subtly disguised harmonic forms – marks it out, as I showed earlier, as a discrete agent of the drama, far more than a background principle of construction. For the listener who feels the Screw theme at all these levels, the opera can only seem more saturated with the supernatural. When, in the opening variation of Act 2, the theme takes the form of dense harmonic clouds, interspersed with flashback-memories of the bewildering nighttime scene ending the first Act – memories of Quint's "Miles" call, and of his songs – one wonders who is present, who speaks? Similarly, in the final variation, after Flora's breakdown, when her "can't see anything" shrieks return at the outer extremes of the orchestral register, whose presence does the music reflect? It is in these moments of wordless instrumental utterance – when there is an argument but no speaker, a gesture of recollection without anyone being present – that the opera comes closest to evoking the ghostly as a numinous realm at the bounds of the conscious, if not of the articulable.[70]

Britten's idea for the shape of the operatic *Screw* – for many short scenes linked by orchestral passages – works, Piper felt, because it allows the composer to place the stage voices, ghostly or living, within a complete "fabric of sound and of echoes and memories of sound." As time passes, listeners sense a build-up in the "weight of musical experience" comparable in effect to James's accumulation of "evidence and fantasy" (1989: 8). It is the force of this mysterious, untexted thematic principle that presses so fatally on the musical interiority of the children. The central expressive coup, in Britten's *Turn of the Screw*, was to make the Screw theme more ghostly than either Quint or Miss Jessel; to establish, in its incessant turning, a wordless supernatural force, controlling, threatening and finally overpowering the operatic performance of innocence.

5 Rituals: the *War Requiem* and *Curlew River*

That the commission, planning, and composition of the 1961 *War Requiem* interrupts the much longer gestation of the church parable *Curlew River* (completed in 1964) is one sign of their shared engagement with musical performance as an event of ritual significance. Britten comes close to defining his own concept of ritual in the notion of "occasional music" central to the Aspen Award speech given shortly after the première of *Curlew River*. Referring to music's ability to "utter the sentiments of a whole community," and to the essentially unrepeatable quality in any individual performance of a single work – the "magic [that] comes only with the sounding of the music"[1] – Britten (in a rare moment of public self-analysis) articulates features central to a range of theoretical formulations of ritual as a recognized cultural activity. Beyond its direct reference to music's ceremonial and religious functions, the speech stresses the precise conditions of any performance, and of the concert experience itself, characterized as an act of listening that "demands . . . a journey to a special place" (20). In each case, Britten's concept of "occasion" bears obvious affinities with anthropological notions of rituals as "named and marked out enactments. . . . different from 'ordinary,' everyday events," and as performances that mediate between fixed, canonical forms and the inherently "indexical" variations introduced in any single physical gesture, however stereotypical.[2] Britten's reference to the "holy triangle of composer, performer and listener" (20), likewise, defines the musical event in the specifically communal terms inherent to ritual in its varying forms. A collective event is inscribed in the texture of the *Requiem* and *Curlew River*, not simply in the size of the forces required, but more precisely, in the calculation of every gesture for performance in a church acoustic. In *Curlew River*, moreover, the Abbot's direct address to the assembled congregation announces the communal event about to take place – "Good souls, I would have you know / The Brothers have come today / To show you a mystery" – as something symbolic in form but purposive in nature.

The word *liturgy* comes from the Greek term for a "public work" (Rappaport 177), and a central concern in my discussion of ritual in the *War Requiem* will be the way in which a fixed and known liturgy – the Latin Mass for the Dead – has been troped with a voice that is jarring not only in its intrusion on a prior sequence of words, but also in its swerve away from the collective, toward the essentially subjective experience of lyric poetry. Ritual itself is a term referring to "the thing done" (the Greek *dromenon*); in turning to *Curlew River*, my discussion will shift focus, initially, to questions of gesture, a category the first Church Parable radically redefines in emulation of the hieratic stylization of Japanese *Nō* theatre, by its strict coordination of vocal and instrumental utterance with physical movement. But the argument will return, ultimately, to notions of liturgy as the formalized expression of an encounter with the numinous, above all in attempting to account for the force of the mystery enacted at the work's conclusion.

The paired genesis of *Curlew River* and the *Requiem* begins at least with Britten's reported interest in Japanese *Nō* theatre in the early 1950s, though the *Requiem* idea has roots in still-earlier plans, in the later 1940s, for an oratorio on a pacifist subject.[3] The composer's interest in *Nō* was certainly piqued in 1955, when his friend and collaborator William Plomer suggested he see a live performance in his upcoming tour of Asia.[4] Soon after his return from the tour, in May 1956, Britten asked Plomer specifically about the play *Sumidagawa*, enquiring, a year later, about English translations. By July 1958, Britten told Plomer that the play was "boiling up inside me," and later that year the poet finally began a draft libretto based closely on an authorized English translation.[5] Typically for Britten, this two-and-a-half year gestation period was filled with other big projects: the ballet *The Prince of the Pagodas*, finished July 1956; *Noye's Fludde*, composed in autumn 1957, and the *Nocturne* song cycle, in summer 1958. It was at just this moment in mid-1958, with the *Sumidagawa* libretto at last underway, that a formal liturgical project intervened. On 7 October 1958, Britten accepted an invitation from the Coventry Cathedral Festival Committee to write a work for the 1962 rededication of the new Cathedral, built on the remains of the fourteenth-century structure destroyed in 1940 by bombs during World War II. He visited the cathedral site in August 1959, and, around this time, plans for a 1960 première of the *Nō* opera were postponed. Much of 1960 was taken up with *A Midsummer Night's Dream*, and the composition of the *Requiem* itself followed in 1961. Work on the *Curlew River* libretto resumed over Christmas 1961, though it was only in July 1963 that the libretto was finalized, with the composer settling down to create the score early in 1964.

What is most striking about this creative schedule (beyond its sheer industry) is the intermingling of sacred and secular spheres, not merely in the alternation of overtly liturgical projects – the 1959 *Missa Brevis*, the 1961 *Jubilate Deo* canticle, both written for use in Anglican services – with concert and operatic works, but also in the synthesis of the two realms of experience within a single work. *Noye's Fludde*, the English mystery play, offers a sacred story dramatized in relatively secular terms, with costumes, spectacle, and comic business. The secular, though, is itself framed – as I argued in Chapter 1 above – by the ritual utterance of religious ceremony. Incorporating Anglican hymnody into the score's musical argument, *Noye* brings its audience directly into the performance at each dramatic crux. Against this sacred backdrop, the predominance of child performers – the procession of "animals" entering the ark – on stage and in the orchestra links the entire event to its common institutional setting, that of a school, and *Noye* shares with the school-opera genre of the 1930s the didactic enactment of a story with a message. But where a work like Copland's *The Second Hurricane* (which Britten knew well) makes its point in directly social terms – the individual's need to act for the common good – the "lesson" in *Noye* is revealed by an encounter with the divine.[6] The Covenant of the Rainbow, in its scenic representation of a miracle, prefigures the ending of the "church parable" *Curlew River*, and both works end with a blessing. Each performance engages in distinct ways with ritual as a larger social category, even as it challenges any clear conceptual division of sacred and secular.

A similar generic ambivalence governs the ritual of the *War Requiem*. The dramatic properties of its musical setting – its rapid shifts of mood, speaker, and "location" – spring from the inherent plot-motion of the Mass itself (as the commemoration of the life of Christ, for example).[7] But though usually performed in the consecrated setting of a cathedral, the *War Requiem* remains a "concert-mass," for there is no actual celebrant. The intermingling of "sacred" liturgical and "secular" theatrical realms in *Noye* is symptomatic too of its composer's ambivalent attitude to Christianity, a significant point in considering the powerfully disruptive troping of the liturgical text in the *War Requiem* libretto. Here, and in that earlier Requiem, the 1940 *Sinfonia da Requiem*, Britten's allusion to an ancient Christian liturgy hardly connotes the unquestioning expression of devout faith.[8] The Latin movement titles – "Lacrymosa, "Dies irae," "Requiem aeternam" – in the purely orchestral *Sinfonia* define both a private act of mourning (in a work dedicated to the memory of Britten's parents) and a more public "statement" against the European war that had erupted shortly before the commission was finalized.[9] The liturgical titles, in this case, contribute one layer to a work whose complex symbolism owes as much to extra-liturgical musical topoi – the violent "dance of death" rhythms that reverberate in Britten's music of the later 1930s, say – as to a specific devotional program.[10] Equally, in the late fifties, the paired genesis of *Curlew River* and the *War Requiem* underscores the intricate and mutually complementary balance struck, in each work, between an extant ritual and some outside force of symbolism. Thus the Buddhist Nō play becomes a "Christian" work almost at the same moment as the Coventry Mass is transformed, by the interpolation of English texts, into a composite symbol, far more skeptical in tone than the sacred liturgy embedded within.

In considering such a self-reflexive juxtaposition of sacred and secular within each work's "ritual," chronological details are again revealing. Although both Britten and Plomer would later stress their desire to cultivate distance from the Nō source,[11] Curlew River began as a direct reworking of the play Sumidagawa. Plomer's 1958 libretto draft, Cooke observes, lacks the liturgical frame of processional chant and Abbot's address, and retains all Buddhist references and Japanese names (1998: 139). The original ending lacks the promise that "the dead shall rise again" to meet "in Heaven." Britten's dramatic decision to transform "the Noh play" into "a Christian work" (letter to Plomer, 15 April 1959, cited Cooke 1998: 142–43) is telling, coming so soon after first contacts with Coventry over a new Mass setting. (Equally revealing is the decision to write a Missa Brevis for the boys' voices at Westminster Cathedral in May 1959.) The revised conception of the "Noh play" was prompted, it would seem, by more than the practical details of mounting performances in a local church;[12] Curlew River, as an operatic drama framed and concluded by specifically liturgical ceremony, first emerges in recognizable form, around the time of Britten's renewed contemplation of Christian liturgy. Meanwhile, plans for the Coventry Cathedral commission formed, perhaps as early as December 1958, around a large-scale choral-orchestral score, religious in nature, but not designed as an actual Mass setting for liturgical use.[13] The precise symbolism of the "Owen-Mass" (Britten to Plomer, August 1961) is bound up, indeed, with something antithetical to religious conventions – a bold invasion of the Latin text by English words on the subject of war. Even so, the manner in which these two starkly contrasting texts coexist can itself be traced to a liturgical precedent.

My analysis of the War Requiem centers on the function of Owen's words as a subversive trope, surrounding the Latin text by a commentary depicting in direct, even graphic, terms the horrors of modern warfare. The Requiem issues its powerful symbolic statement against the backdrop of formal liturgy, though its vein of ambivalence cannot be reduced to a simple "critique" of the Mass. Rather, its success as a quasi-universal pacifist statement – its claims to "utter the sentiments of a whole community" – is grounded in a complex act of resistance to the inherited communal symbols of ritual.

1. Liturgy and trope in the *War Requiem*

The expressive force of the *War Requiem* inheres in what Plomer described as Britten's "power to connect the seemingly unconnected."[14] The interpolation of nine poems by Wilfred Owen into the Latin liturgy is rightly viewed as the work's most original stroke. By the tension of this ground-plan the work may be said to speak in authentically modernist tone, and yet, as I will argue, the entire strategy of linking alien textual voices – the Mass liturgy and the Owen poems – can itself be traced to a familiar ecclesiastic practice of "troping," by which extant biblical texts are surrounded by other, non-biblical texts, creating a composite result for liturgical use. The resulting composite utterance – a "heteroglossia" of speaking voices, as the literary critic Mikhail Bahktin might say – had long fascinated Britten.[15] One might ascribe this interest in competing levels of textual discourse, along with Britten's catholic poetic tastes, to Auden's mentorship, yet the composer had experimented with such textual juxtapositions well before he met the poet.

In the 1932 choral variations, *A Boy Was Born*, each word of Rossetti's "In the bleak mid-winter" (Variation 5) is drawn out as a long-held pedal point, effacing semantic identity, and radically stretching the duration of each sentence. This music for women's voices becomes the background against which boy trebles intone a quicker lullaby on anonymous fifteenth-century words. Timbral contrast between older and younger "high" voices defines the opposition of speakers and linguistic registers – while the women paint a landscape without figures ("snow on snow"), the boys sing of a child borne away by a falcon.[16] If dense layerings of multiple texts in *A Boy Was Born* (the Finale has no less than four) and the focus on repeating single words prefigure the cumulative effects of the much later *War Requiem*, Britten's ability to match shifts of speaking presence within a text is a still more significant technical precedent. The very early *Hymn to the Virgin* (1930) builds its antiphonal scheme by a regular alternation of English and Latin lines. *Our Hunting Fathers* (as seen in Chapter 1) throws great gestural weight behind the single word "Rats!" a distinctive utterance that returns to disrupt the chanting of the first song's closing Latin doxology: "Et in Nomine (Rats!) Patris et (Rats!) Filii. . . . " Nor is the identity of voices within a text limited necessarily to everyday speaking conventions: God's voice in *Abraham and Isaac* is rendered by a shift from solo vocal delivery to an alto–tenor duet; the tenor switches, in *Still Falls the Rain*, to *sprechgesang* at the anachronistic Marlowe quotation in Sitwell's poem, and the same work registers a divine voice in the chastened simplicity of its closing two-part counterpoint (tenor against the obbligato horn): "Then

sounds the voice of One / who like the heart of man / Was once a child."
With these examples in mind, it is not surprising to find that the *War
Requiem*, as a purely verbal textual composition marked by shifts of
speaker, mood, and contrasting speech genres (lyric poem and liturgical
formula), first took shape in a distinct phase of sketching that far preceded
the actual "notes."[17]

Britten himself describes the work's textual scheme as one of the Latin
words interspersed with Owen's English poems as "a kind of commentary
on the Mass" (1961 letter to Dietrich Fischer-Dieskau, cited Carpenter
404–05). At the same time, this large-scale English textual trope did not –
as analysis below of the score's final form will confirm – obscure awareness
of inherent dramatic contrasts within the *Missa pro defunctis* itself. While
prayers for "rest" and "light" are prominent themes in the Introit, they are
overtaken in later sections by the more desperate tone of a plea for deliver-
ance and mercy. The "Dies irae" poem is full of brazen first-person pleas
for mercy ("Salva me"; "Oro supplex et acclinis"), and is thus in itself an
intrusion on the atmosphere established in the Introit. (The poem is a
Sequence, preceding the Gradual, and adopted into the Requiem Mass
only in the fourteenth century, and its vivid account of the Day of
Judgment blends more than one biblical source.)[18] The "Offertorium", in
praying for the release of the souls of the faithful, leaves few of "hell's tor-
tures" to the imagination: graphic images of "the bottomless pit" and the
"mouth of the lion" precede the promise of salvation and a return "into
holy light"; not until the "Agnus Dei" does the prayer again speak of rest.
The calmest meditations on rest and light come in the Responsory of
Absolution, "Libera me" (to coincide with the ritual aspersing and censing
of the catafalque), rather than in the Mass itself. At the burial, this mood
continues in the "In paradisum."

The drama of the *Missa* text, even before Britten's troped additions,
encompasses a range of moods and speakers. Thus the Introit begins with
restrained, reverential prayer *for* the dead ("Requiem aeternam dona *eis*"),
but moves to a more urgent call by the speaker to be heard ("exaudi orationem *meam*"). The keynote of the "Dies irae" text is the speaker's fear of
judgment, while the "Offertorium" moves back to pray for "souls of the
faithful." Further shifts of speaker occur in the Absolution and burial texts:
"Libera me" is I-centered; "In paradisum" switches to a prayer for the
departed soul, addressed in the second person. In tracing how Owen's
poems impinge on the *Missa*, one must recognize inherent tensions within
the liturgy itself, as they are projected and intensified in the choices of
Britten's settings; only then can one fully gauge the effect of the English
tropes.

Documentary evidence suggests tracing the *War Requiem* strategy not merely to Britten's desire to project an extant drama of textual utterance, but to his specific awareness of liturgical troping as a practice defined by a dialogue-like interplay of speakers. Thus his well-known and active interest in medieval liturgical drama, as he prepared *Noye* and contemplated adapting *Sumidagawa*,[19] stands directly behind the idea of fusing Owen's voice with that of a liturgical text. The result of this fusion, as the earliest medieval examples suggest, is a dramatic exchange. The famous "Quem queritis" trope to the Introit for the Mass of Easter, for example, is a dialogue between "Christians" and "Angels" at Christ's tomb:

> *Int[errogatio]*: Quem quęritis in sepulchro, Christicolę?
> *R[esponsio]*: Iesum Nazarenum crucifixum, o caelicolae.
> Non est hic, surrexit sicut predixerat; ite, nuntiate quia surrexit de sepulchro.
> *Resurrexi, et adhuc tecum sum . . .*[20]

The angelic announcement of the Resurrection (line 3) and the call to proclaim this news prefaces the actual words of the Introit ("*Resurrexi . . .*"), which are Christ's own, and in the first person.

Tropes, in the medieval repertory, are above all dramatic mechanisms, a kind of liturgical stagecraft. The language of introit tropes, as Bruno Stäblein points out, is replete with specifically musical references: "again and again, one is made conscious that there is singing here."[21] Trope texts refer frequently to the actual performers, leading directly into the liturgical texts (in "Eia, canendo sonos supplici modulamine dulces *Gaudeamus*," a gerundive construction precedes the chant itself, which starts on the last word; Stäblein 87), even referring to specific vocal groupings ("concentu dicant supplici *omnes atque singuli*"; 88). Biblical persons depicted in the chants themselves are presented by direct references to their "voices," sounding alongside the singer's own: "old and new are equated; both are of the present."[22]

Stäblein's analysis of the "musically realistic atmosphere" (88) established in medieval chant tropes is suggestive of Britten's strategy for interpolating Owen's English words as a trope to the Latin in the *Requiem*'s opening Introit movement. Here, more than anywhere else in the work, the linkage of the *Missa* to the English poem centers on textual evocations of sound. The Latin Introit moves quickly from the visual images of eternal light and rest to the sounding activity of worship: the text's early reference to "songs of praise" ("Te decet hymnus") could, in Britten's setting for the boys'-choir, be construed as the sound of angelic voices, though it is followed quickly by reference to the earthly realm, in the utterer's plea to be heard: ("exaudi orationem meam"; hear my prayer).

Owen's English poem is itself saturated with a vibrant aural imagery, beginning with the darkly ironic title, "Anthem for doomed youth." One might speculate that Owen's titular allusion to liturgical song prompted Britten to adopt the poem as the *Requiem*'s opening trope. The speaker's anger is expressed, throughout the first stanza, by a comparison of the solemn but mechanical sounds of formal mourning ("hasty orisons") to the violent noises of battle:

> What passing-bells for these who die as cattle?
>   Only the monstrous anger of the guns.
>   Only the stuttering rifles' rapid rattle
> Can patter out their hasty orisons.
> No mockeries for them from prayers or bells,
>   Nor any voice of mourning save the choirs, –
> The shrill, demented choirs of wailing shells;
>   And bugles calling for them from sad shires.[23]

The incongruity of the juxtaposed scenarios is harshest at the close of the stanza, where the reiterated key-word, "choirs," names first the participants in a liturgy, and then, in heavily qualified form ("shrill, demented choirs"), invests the sound of artillery-fire with metaphoric voice.

The poem's sonic preoccupations are sharply audible in Britten's musical setting, both in the onomatopoeic timbral effects of the chamber orchestra, where high, falling woodwinds mimic the "wailing" descending artillery shot in the air over the distant rumbling of the bass drum, and by the strict hold of edgy march rhythms (Ex. 5.1). As in Owen's poem, the music's sonic realism is focused on the central incongruity of warfare and worship. Thus while "bugles" are literal features of the music's surface, directly before our ears as the words are sung, talk of "choirs" names not merely shells, but also the performers heard earlier in the movement. The "passing-bells," as both poetic referent and sounding presence, provide the common image about which the entire shift from Mass to trope text pivots. The soldier-soloists intrude, that is, on the sound of actual orchestral bells – tolling throughout the earlier movement – which recede and cross-fade into the sound of a harp, the blurring of the transition ensured by the wetness of a cathedral acoustic.[24] The implied scenic location shifts from "in here" (in the church with the choir), to "out there" on the battlefield. The move is both arresting in its abruptness, and – at a deeper level – subversive, for while the soloists establish an aural-acoustic distance from the sounds of liturgy (with the move from full to chamber orchestral

Ex. 5.1: *War Requiem*, "Introit": the cross-fade from Mass to Owen's trope text

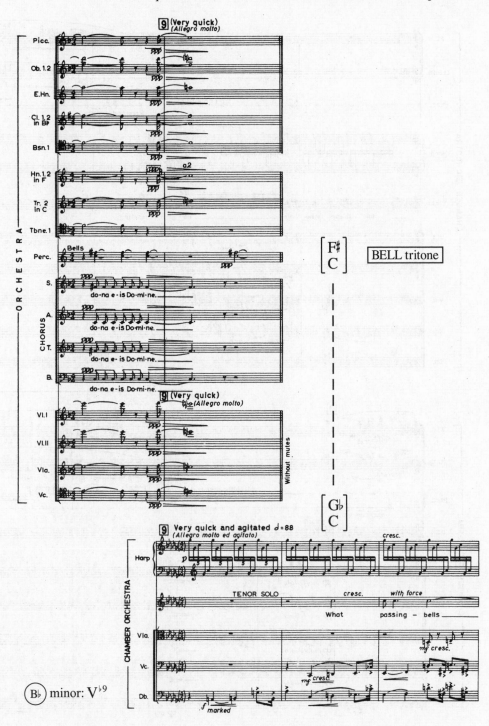

Ex. 5.1 (*cont.*)

sonority), the listener in a church performance remains seated within the sacred location in which the entire work began.

Thematic and tonal mechanisms amplify the tropological shift of scene engineered by the verbal cross-references between trope and host text. Thus the crucial C/G♭ tritone of the Owen scene (in the harp) is a tonal "pun," resetting, within a B♭-minor context, the C/F♯ bell-tritone of the earlier choir music. But while the harp dyad hovers nervously over a dominant pedal (see the F bass pitches entering at "cattle"), the bell-tritone at the opening (Ex. 5.2a) fits less easily into a local tonal context. Here, the layered choir-orchestral texture is riven with internal harmonic tensions. The uneasy counterpoint of a D-minor melody with octatonic dyads is set against the fixity of the remaining percussion activity (the C/F♯ bells, and the low piano A doubling each gong stroke). These percussion pitches fit neither the diatonic nor the octatonic hearing of individual textural layers.[25] The opening supports a synchronicity between a bass-generated gravitational tonality and a weightless, axial tonal environment: the "gong" A, in the first case acts as dominant to the D-minor melody stratum, and in the second, as an axis of pitch-class inversion about which the bell pivots from C to F♯ and back (a symmetrical move, later brought center-stage in the mirror-inversions of the boys' "Te decet hymnus" melody).[26] Later phrases (Ex. 5.2b) reconfigure, but do not dissolve, the stratified tensions. To compare the *Missa* and the Owen settings, then, is to confront two ways of configuring a shared tension, and to hear the distance between a realistic scene of chaos, and a formal plea with its own sense of restlessness and desperation.

2. Liturgy as ritual: theoretic perspectives

> The invariance of a liturgy may be an icon of the seeming changelessness of
> the canonical information that it incorporates.   Rappaport 182

The cultural significances of the *War Requiem* swirl around its engagement with the timelessness and fixity of liturgy as the sequenced textual basis of archetypal, socially symbolic action. It is the presence of an extant liturgical text *within* the *Requiem*'s libretto that sets it apart from other large-scale choral-and-orchestral works of mourning. Where Nono, for example, in *Il canto sospeso* (1956), draws out the force of first-person documentary narratives into a collective, universal voice (dispersing the "I" of the quoted texts among a multitude of singers), Britten's first-hand witnesses, the soldiers reporting from "out there" on the battlefield, retain a forceful individuality. Their proclamations, as "characters," sound against the collective voice of the choir. For both Nono and Britten, the choir

Ex. 5.2: (a)The opening of the "Introit": tonal oppositions among melody and dyad strata; (b) the initial diatonic/octatonic opposition reconfigured in a later phrase (two measures before R3)

(a)

Ex. 5.2 (*cont.*)

(b)

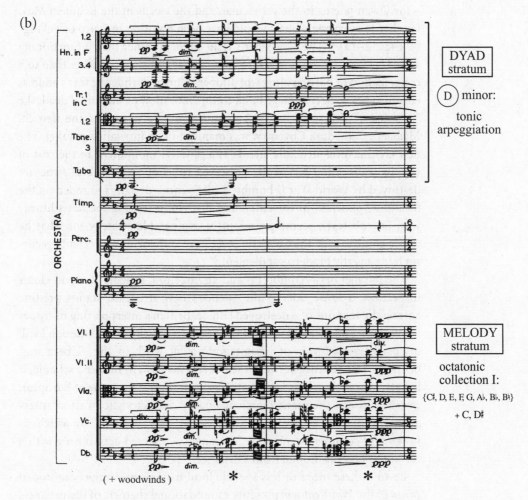

stands for humanity – a collectivity facing the audience, and with whom that audience can identify – but in Britten, choric speech is restricted to the liturgy. The choir sings only in Latin, and its collective prayers are called into question by the nature of the soloists' non-liturgical tropes. Each work voices a collective "protest," but where Nono's account of approaching horrors is documentary in tone ("today they will shoot us"), Britten's graphic images of war appear alongside the events of an ancient eschatology, communicated in standardized form.

Whether or not the *Requiem*'s Latin text is known to individual listeners through first-hand experience of the celebration of a Requiem Mass, its recognizability *as* liturgy is basic to its symbolism. "The text of my *War*

Requiem," Britten himself felt, "was perfectly in place in Coventry Cathedral – the Owen poems in the vernacular, and the words of the Requiem Mass familiar to everyone – but it would have been pointless in Cairo or Peking" (1964a: 12–13).[27] The *Missa*, here, is an emblem rather than a functioning sacred "action"; it is addressed to an audience of listeners, rather than to a congregation of participating worshippers. Further, while the text's address encompasses society at large in its commemoration of unnamed dead, the "occasional" nature of its 1962 première, in the setting of the new St. Michael's Cathedral, Coventry, was manifest in an intriguing parallel. The new architectural structure stands as a physical monument to the cost of war, its walls rising out of the preserved ruins of the medieval structure destroyed by World War II bombs. Basil Spence's design is founded on the idea of a "phoenix" at Coventry, and Britten, in troping the Mass liturgy with Owen's texts, seemingly adopts a comparable strategy for what he would come to call "the Coventry piece" – reconfiguring an ancient precursor by an overtly modern supplement.[28]

The parallel between libretto and architectural scheme is, upon closer inspection, a loose one. While Spence's new structure stands pristine among the remains of a destroyed edifice, Britten's interpolating of tropes leaves the existing verbal form of the *Missa* essentially intact (though I will discuss *musical* forces of "disintegration" at work in the "Libera me" below).[29] The distance between the old and the new, in Britten's scheme, is less structural, than linguistic. Latin, as the traditional tongue of European worship, asserts the marked archaic quality characteristic of ritual utterance. It functions according to that "rule of sacral speech" by which, as Jungmann comments, one may "designate . . . sacred action only with a certain reserve, as though from a distance."[30]

Beyond these more or less specific local historic meanings, the troped *Missa* in the *War Requiem* presents a foundational rhetoric of disturbance. Something intrudes on the canonical. The fixity of the liturgy is violated. This opposition – between a sanctioned and a rogue text – asserts itself as prior to specific questions of textual contents. From the perspective of ritual, all that is important about the *Missa* is that it is fixed; both its inner drama, and the anger in Owen's words are secondary to its invariance as canonical text.

The formality and fixity of liturgy as a mode of ritual action is central in anthropological accounts. In Roy Rappaport's analysis, ritual is a "performance of more or less invariant sequences of formal acts and utterances not encoded by the performers."[31] While levels of formality familiar in daily life vary – in greetings, court cases, public ceremonies – religious liturgies tend towards the invariant; virtually every word and gesture is specified. The performance of religious rite is stylized, repetitive, and stereotypical. The performer's role and the status of the action itself differ significantly from dramatic models. The Mass celebrant is "doing something," in a way that the character actor is not, and the efficacy of the action engages occult rather than patent sources. In the words of the Mass, as in all ritual, "the distinction between ritual as communication and as efficacious action breaks down" (178). With words that "have by definition been spoken . . . before" (179) – prayers, blessings, absolutions, and so on – liturgical utterance is performative in Austin's sense. Ritual utterance, by its fixity, both enacts some meaning (a prayer for the dead, for example) and displays that meaning clearly and explicitly (190).

Pursuing the notion of a global disturbance of the canonical in the *War Requiem* at more local levels, the shift, by troping, from the Latin *Missa* to the English poetry represents an immediate loss of formality. The *Missa* texts abound in archetypal, repeating formulas of supplication and praise: patterned repetition defines the "Kyrie" litany and the "Sanctus" texts; in the "Dies irae," stark end-rhymes heighten the incessant trochaic march of short four-feet lines throughout. Owen's poetry asserts a distance from the liturgical verse less in terms of its rhyme schemes, than in the viewpoint of its speakers. Particularly in the earlier texts Britten has chosen, the emphasis is on personal expressions of anger. The opening trope, for example, begins rudely and dismissively with a question that is a direct challenge to the solemnity of the foregoing liturgy ("What passing-bells . . . ?"); in the second, the tone is markedly colloquial in register, jaunty even ("Out there, we've walked quite friendly up to Death; / Sat down . . .").

Owen's tone is personal and experiential in a way that the Mass's pleas for mercy never can be (based as they are on an *imagined* fate awaiting the soul of the departed). Owen's speaker recalls scenes with the vivid detail that signals first-hand experience ("Bugles sang, saddening the evening air") or reports dream-like visions ("It seemed that out of battle I escaped"). In the closing text, the longest of Britten's tropes, the speaker's extended first-person narrative culminates with the direct speech of an enemy soldier, the words of a ghost ("'I am the enemy you killed, my friend'"). The Mass, as noted earlier, does not lack for first-person expression, but it arises only in brief interjections – in plain performatives ("Oro supplex," I pray, on my knees) or in raw outbursts of fear ("Ingemisco," I sigh) – interrupting more sustained descriptions of imagined scenes of eternal rest or damnation.[32]

Such contrasts of tone raise the issue of the performer's relation to that which is performed. The idea of "authority or directive," Rappaport finds, "is *intrinsic* to liturgical order" (192); to enact a ritual is to conform to a canonical text, and to make an act of acceptance: "by performing a liturgical order the performer accepts, and indicates to himself and to others that he accepts, whatever is encoded in the . . . order in which he is participating" (193). Acceptance is a public act, to be contrasted with belief, an inner subjective state. To take part in the *Missa pro defunctis* is to acknowledge, in the performed act of prayer, the power of a divine authority.

Owen's speaker, though, voices only contempt for received institutions, particularly for the alignment of religious fervor with patriotism. Thus parody is central to Owen's technique in the biblical language of the "Parable of the Old man and the Young" and the lines beginning "Be slowly lifted up, thou long black arm." The obverse of acceptance – outright rejection of the liturgy and its ceremonial garb – underlies the first trope's blunt unanswered questions ("What candles may be held to speed them all?").

Amid all these contrasts between liturgy and trope, there remains one point of contact. The liturgical speech of the *Requiem* Mass is apocalyptic: it predicts and describes a future occurrence that will mark the end of time.[33] Owen's verses, while founded in the real terrors of a poetic present, rather than in the voice of prophecy, play into this non-cyclical, rectilinear tradition. The horrors of war invoke the decadence of men living, as Frank Kermode notes, "in the dregs of time." Both the Mass and Owen herald the End itself (in Revelation, the three-and-a-half-year reign of the Beast which precedes the Last Days). The "Dies irae" (as a late addition to the *Requiem* liturgy) reflects the urgency of medieval speculations as to the identity of the Antichrist; by the 1960s, a comparable apocalyptic urge could appropriate fresh imagery in the real threat of nuclear war.[34] Britten's earliest ideas for a pacifist oratorio came in direct response to the Hiroshima–Nagasaki bombings of 1945, and the later *War Requiem* is very much of a piece with such widely circulating expressions of the fear of Armageddon as Stanley Kubrick's black comedy, *Doctor Strangelove* (1963). One of the Owen tropes – "After the blast of lightning from the East" – offers an Apocalyptic vision, though without the possibility of a dawning new age.

The analysis of utterance, as Mikhail Bakhtin famously argued, inheres not in the linguistic facts of individual sentences in isolation, but in the contingent reality of concrete speech situations. Utterance is always dialogic, an encounter governed by the received forms of existing "speech genres" and ongoing discursive activities – question and answer, assertion and objection, suggestion and acceptance – located at the boundary of the change between speaking subjects.[35] The single utterance, for Bakhtin, only assumes its meaning in relation to a surrounding reality. In the case of the *War Requiem*, a foundational troping strategy heightens the rhetorical force of discursive boundaries – moments at which the speaker, scenario, and action shift instantaneously. In turning now to the work's movements, in individual detail, the analysis can build upon the Bakhtinian insight – closely allied, after all, to the Austinian notion of performance seen in *Grimes* in Chapter 2 – that the meaning and force of an utterance is at root situational. As discrete linguistic formations, the Mass and the Owen texts might be considered autonomous statements. As utterances, though, their meaning is bound up with the context of their pairing. Britten's texts, in this sense, speak within a dialogic field at whose extremes stand the ritual-ized, fixed, and timeless formulae of the liturgy, and the more personal, skeptical, and urgently present-tense voice of the poet.

3. Utterance and stylistic register in the "Dies irae"

Melodic, gestural, and tonal resemblances between Britten's *Requiem* and Verdi's *Messa da Requiem* are at their most pronounced in the "Lacrimosa" (Britten's opening, Ex. 5.3, for instance, shares with Verdi a melody suspended between third and fifth degrees of a clear B♭-minor tonality, with prominent E♮ coloration).[36] Precisely because the stylistic allusions are so obvious for knowledgeable listeners, they prompt questions as to their gestural value in context. What expressive point is made by evoking Verdi so audibly at this point in the "Dies irae"? Answers may be sought less in terms of composerly "intentions,"[37] than from the listener's perspective. The Verdian moments, Malcolm Boyd argues, give a "familiar background against which certain disruptive elements in Owen's verses and in the music's tritonal relationships may stand out more forcefully" (6). Boyd's claim downplays the role of the tritone as a link *between* both musics: note the proximity of B♭s and E♮s in the "Lacrimosa" itself (Ex. 5.3a), a tension to which, as Arnold Whittall suggests, the movement's F-major "Amen" gives "remote resolution" (1963: 202). But the larger point here – that the musical vocabulary shifts to something relatively familiar and thus aurally striking – can be extended. In particular, stylistic shifts can be considered as a mechanism by which the musical discourse articulates reversals, shifts of viewpoint, and other forms of interruptive gesture. Utterance, in the *Requiem*, encompasses both purely verbal juxtapositions between Latin host-text and English trope, and the specifically musical forces by which a juxtaposition (to varying degree) is projected for a listener. Throughout the "Dies irae," but most markedly in the closing "Lacrimosa" verse, shifts of stylistic register are sensed less in terms of specific allusions to an absent Verdian precursor (however recognizable) than as the encounter between the movement's vividly contrasting musical dialects.

Ex. 5.3: "Lacrimosa": interplay of trope- and host-text utterances

(a)

(b)

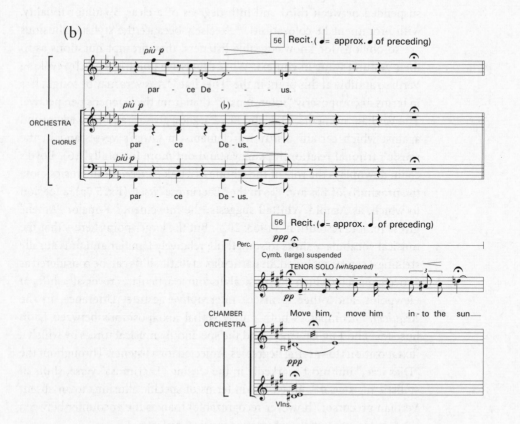

Ex. 5.3 (*cont.*)

Four times in the "Dies irae," Owen's English words interrupt the flow of the Latin stanzas. The first two interruptions offer an odd mood of release from the terrors of the Latin text itself. The rousing fanfares that punctuate the initial "Dies irae" march, for instance, are transformed, in "Bugles sang," into a drowsy sleep-music, the "bugle" motto distantly echoed in warm string chords and a delicate woodwind tracery. A bustling military quick-step returns in the second trope, "Out there, we've walked quite friendly up to Death," yet here too the raw fear of the Latin prayers "Rex tremendae" and "Salva me" is supplanted by a lighter mood. Begging for mercy gives way to defiant bravado in the face of that "old chum," death. With the third trope, though – "Be slowly lifted up" – relationships to the main "Dies irae" narrative become more direct as the boundaries between Latin and English utterances become narrower. Owen's text forces itself upon the listener, abruptly breaking in when the timpani snatch hold of the choir's "confutatis" cry. The poem's final, intense outburst, directed at a giant mortar gun – "May God curse thee, and cut thee from our soul!" – precipitates the main climax of the entire movement, a return to the heavy march of the opening. Because the "Dies irae" poem itself focuses on the vivid imagery of apocalyptic terrors, Owen's scenes here do not work, as the Introit trope does, to puncture the solemnity of the Latin texts. Instead, they assume the role of illustrations – modern instances of horrors described equally vividly in the short, heavy syllables of the Latin.

But the most intimate interplay of musico-verbal utterance emerges only in the closing "Lacrimosa" section. On the face of it, there is a meeting of voices here. The four lines of the "Lacrimosa" verse are sung first by solo soprano and choir, then lines 1–3 are restated one by one as interpolations to the English of Owen's sonnet, "Futility."

> Move him[, move him] into the sun –
> Gently[, gently] its touch awoke him once,
> At home[, at home], whisp[']ring of fields unsown.
> Always it woke him[, woke him], even in France,
> Until this morning and this snow.
> If anything might rouse him[, rouse him] now
> The kind old sun will know.
>
> 1 *Lacrimosa dies illa, . . .*
> Think[, think] how it wakes the seeds, –
> Woke, once, the clays of a cold[, cold] star.
> Are limbs[, limbs], so dear-achieved, are sides,
> Full-nerved – still warm – too hard to stir?
> Was it for this the clay grew tall?

2   *Qua resurget ex favilla, ...*
        [Was it for this(, for this) the clay grew tall?]
3   *Judicandus homo reus. ...*
        – O what[, what] made fatuous[, fatuous] sunbeams toil
        To break earth's sleep at all?
                Pie Jesu Domine,
                Dona eis Requiem. Amen.

Owen's poems, acting previously as autonomous interpolations to the *Missa*, now intermingle lines within a single verse of the host text. Repetition is especially marked in Britten's Owen setting, by the frequent reiteration (shown in brackets) of single words, and in the tenor's poignantly repeated question ("Was it for this the clay grew tall?"). As in "Bugles sang" and "Out there," Owen's words are stretched by such repetitions, dramatizing their speech-like quality, and intensifying the contrasting bluntness of the shorter Latin lines.[38]

Largely for harmonic reasons, this musico-verbal interplay sounds closer to a dovetailing than actual interruption. The terrifying onward tread of the earlier march slows now to a gentle, halting prayer; the shedding of tears is soothing, almost languid. The tenor's first entrance smoothly picks up the soprano's E♮ appoggiatura pitch as a starting tonic ("Move him," Ex. 5.3b). And while the choir's V^7 chord is left unresolved, the tenor solo soon moves into the choir's harmonic orbit: his first "Was it for this?" returns to "their" B♭ tonic (Ex. 5.3c); his second leads by conventional V–I cadence motion to their E-major "Judicandus" (Ex. 5.3d). The all-important tritone motto is *shared* here – in the long-range B♭/E triadic emphases – between trope and host, its "disruptive" potential softened.

The warm diatonic atmosphere fails, though. The tenor's music, having grown closer and closer to fusion with the choir's prayer, suddenly retreats. With the sonnet's despairing final couplet, the bell-tritone of the first movement makes a sobering reappearance, and the movement ends in the provisionality of F major. This, finally, is the real interruption. The choir's text repeat breaks off at line 3. The "Pie Jesu" prayer that intervenes is harmonically inconclusive in relation to the choir's local B♭-minor tonic (a half-cadence to V) and remote from the G-minor tonic with which the whole "Dies irae" sequence began.

The despair of this close goes beyond its harmonic open-endedness. As utterance within a dialogic context, the tenor's return to the C/F♯ tritone in his bleak final question – "What made fatuous sunbeams toil / To break earth's sleep *at all?*" (Ex. 5.4) – abandons gestural engagement with the soprano soloist's drooping sigh-figures in favor of a melodic form that transcends the immediate vicinity. The returning bell-tritone, as a cyclic

Ex. 5.4: "Lacrimosa" and trope: the tenor soloist's imitation, then final abandonment of, the soprano soloist's melodic idiom

link between movements, calls into question the local Verdian warmth of the "Lacrimosa," a warmth without issue, as it were. The choir's final "Pie Jesu" plea for mercy shifts back to the choral voice of the first movement, racked by doubt embodied in the bell-tritone, even though, in the new context of the "Dies irae," we may catch a distant echo of march steps (Ex. 5.5).

Tapping into a deeper vein of despair than the first three "Dies irae" tropes, the closing sonnet abandons a merely scenic perspective on the prospect of judgment. The tenor's restrained utterance leaves behind the drumming and rowdy chorusing of the earlier tropes. The growth of his voice – from the softest recitative to a fully operatic intensity borrowed from the soprano soloist – is, in the end, a melodramatic failure. By its verbal, harmonic, and gestural interplay with the "Lacrimosa" host text, and by its final rhetorical reversal, the trope presents more than a simple "intrusion." The tenor's response to the soprano's Verdian idiom, likewise, takes stylistic allusion as the starting-point for a whole progression of moods, and for a challenge to the hierarchy of voices within the "Lacrimosa." The choir, for instance, are at first a shadowy presence, supporting the more extravagant soprano soloist. She and the choir sing in agreement when they engage in dialogue (as at the first "judicandus"). By the tenor's intervention, however, the soprano's ornamental manner is silenced, and the choir's pleas are revoiced in terms of an earlier humility.

Ex. 5.5: The bell-tritone recontextualized at the end of the "Dies irae"

echoing

One returns, in Hans Werner Henze's phrase, to "a world in which the lyrical is denied."[39] The meditations of the trope – suspended between the warmth of a "kind old sun" and the hard surfaces of winter – end by bringing listeners, in a rather literal sense, down to earth.

4. Tropes and irony: the "Offertorium"

The "Dies irae" tropes, as a complex intrusion on the liturgy, prompt listeners to hear the host text itself from an unfamiliar perspective. Irony arises, but it would be truer to speak here in the plural. The range of ironies active in Britten's troping strategy, from movement to movement, is broad. The "intrusion," for example, of Owen's despairing questions (in the sonnet "Futility") on the "Lacrimosa" is an ironic encounter resistant to *précis*. I advance no single view of the expressive force of the tropes, and verbal epithets – of Owen's poems as "critique" of the liturgy, say – appear suspiciously reductive; as soon as one contends with individual encounters between the Mass and Owen, the scene, in its bristling tensions, suggests something more complex and less dispassionate than a critique. So while it may be true that the clash of viewpoints in the "Offertorium" inscribes ironies in deeper relief than at other points in the Mass, its expressive detail cannot stand as an emblem of the whole piece.

Irony opens up a gap between speaking intention and listening reception. There is an inherent semantic unreliability to all irony, for ironic meaning is the compound of two meanings. As an interplay of surface and depth, irony complicates the face-value statement with the concealed or unspoken. Irony, like allegory, is a mode of utterance that defers meaning slightly. One hears first what is being said, and then what *else* is being said. This subversion of univocal meaning is forceful in Britten's "Offertorium" tropes, but as I will suggest, it extends beyond the obvious dualism of Latin and English texts, and into the shockingly flawed narrative of the English trope itself. The "Offertorium," in effect, gives listeners a trope within a trope.

The rhetorical shifts enabling this multi-layered narrative strategy are palpable already in the opening of the Latin host text. Separate musics define first the distant boys' choir, praying for dead souls to be released from punishment, and then the chorus's vigorously rising phrase, centered verbally on the soul's journey from darkness to light; a lively fugue follows, the reminder of a promise ("as once you promised to Abraham and his seed"). A more detailed rhetorical level is evident, too – the boys' bright, upper-register hailings ("Domine, Jesu Christe") are answered, antiphonally, by low, muted phrases, opening up a registral distance within the utterances of one vocal group. Such rapid shifts of voice within the Latin host text do not in themselves promote ironic perceptions, but their motion between different vocal-instrumental speakers prefigures the technique of the main trope.

Owen's "Parable of the old man and the young" centers on the figure of Abraham himself, named in the Latin verse. Sacrifice, the focal symbolic action of the Mass, is too the defining event in Owen's poetic retelling of the Genesis account of Abraham's sacrifice at Moriah. The old man's obedience to God's strictest command – to sacrifice his first-born son – is replaced by an Abram (the name change is telling) who disobeys God by refusing the "Ram of Pride" and carrying out the dreadful slaying of Isaac. Owen's words closely follow the biblical account until the climactic moment of the Angel's appearance,[40] at which point the "Parable" makes its hideous reversal of the expected ending. Obedient until the Angel's voice is heard, Abram defiantly carries out the deed he has prepared: "But the old man would not so, but slew his son, – / And half the seed of Europe, one by one." The symbolism works at more than one level. The "old man" here invokes the "old men" of Europe – politicians, generals, clerics – by whom, the poem says, "the young" were sacrificed. But the old man is also,

more mysteriously, God the Father, who offers His own son as mortal sacrifice. Situating Christ's passion in this light, equating the Divine with
both the figure of Abram and the voice of the angel, the poem itself refuses
to listen to all religious justifications for war.

Britten's setting of Owen impinges on the Mass by a move from the
remembrance of the biblical figure of Abraham to direct quotation (or so it
would seem initially) of the Genesis story of his sacrifice. As the baritone
begins to narrate

> So Abram rose, and clave the wood, and went,
> And took the fire with him, and a knife.

the accompaniment signals the incursion of a trope by the now-familiar
timbral shift from full- to chamber-orchestral forces. The move in this case
is minimally disruptive, for the choir's fugue subject persists melodically
into what can be called the main trope. Here, as in the Latin host text, the
musical delivery is dramatic in tone, dividing speeches among the tenor
and baritone soloists as characters in the plot (Fig. 5.1).

Listening closely to the main trope, one hears an interplay of singing
voices and narrative levels. A story sequence (numbered 1–5 in Fig. 5.1)
unfolds by shifts from the opening events (1), in which the baritone sings
of the old man, as a narrator, to the moment of Isaac's first words (2), sung
by the tenor, singing directly as Isaac.[41] As the story returns to Abram (3),
we shift away from the biblical account to Owen's version of events, with
Abram building "parapets and trenches." Shifting voices again, we hear
more direct speech (4), this time in a composite angelic voice (baritone
and tenor in close harmony), whose command Abram ignores (5).

The scheme shows a progressive movement "away" from the Mass (left)
and "into" the trope (right). As the analysis suggests, this motion is far
from being a simple binary juxtaposition of Latin Mass and English trope,
for the trope itself harbors its own discursive shifts. The direct speech of
Isaac and the angel (2 and 4) might be assigned a purely local significance.
But it is as Owen rewrites Genesis, introducing the imagery of a modern
war (3 and 5), and finally destroying the original ending, that one senses
the turning away from the biblical account as a kind of "inner trope,"
working from within the English trope itself. More strictly speaking, the
rightmost narrative level is less a trope – the grafting of a new text onto an
extant older text – than an abandonment or reversal of events in the main
Genesis narrative.

Britten's setting ensures that one hears each shift of perspective as a
vivid articulation. Each shift of voice is inscribed in the musical discourse
of the score. As any listener will realize, the shifts to direct speech, and to

Fig. 5.1: Shifts of speaker in the "Offertorium"

Missa
Quam olim Abrahae
promisisti ...
(chorus)

> **Owen: main trope**
> *Genesis narrative*
> 1. So Abram rose, ...
> (baritone)

>> *direct speech*
>> 2. Isaac the first-born spake
>> and said, My Father, ...
>> (tenor)

>>> **inner trope**
>>> *Genesis abandoned*
>>> 3. Then Abram bound the
>>> youth ... (baritone)

>> 4. When lo! an angel called
>> him out of heaven saying,
>> Lay not thy hand upon the lad
>> (tenor and baritone)

>>> 5. But the old man would not
>>> so, but slew his son (baritone)
>>> And half the seed of Europe
>>> (baritone and tenor)

Missa
Hostias et preces ...
(boys)

Owen's sinister distorted narration, are as starkly audible as the initial shift from Mass to trope. Isaac's speech (2) is very clearly set off from its context by a halo of tremolando strings, and by the sudden appearance of a warmly triadic E major. In Abram's response (3), one begins to sense a more profound disturbance to the local thematic context, by the incursion of thematic references to the "Dies irae" and to the battlefield music of the Introit. With the return to direct speech, now that of the Angel (4), comes the sudden appearance of the purest C-major triadicity.[42]

Mapping discursive shifts as an interplay of musically distinct voices exposes the ironic distance between the Abraham of the Mass and the defiant figure of the trope, an irony that only begins to emerge at (3), with the non-canonic actions of trench building, and then with the slaying itself (5). But the most surprising move, and the most violent clash of viewpoints, comes with the conclusion of the main trope. As the slaying of "half the seed of Europe" is announced by the soloists and chamber orchestra, the organ (silent since the movement's opening "Domine" calls) enters in its own slower tempo, with an eerily dissonant ostinato, joined moments later by the distant piping voices of the boys'-choir (Ex. 5.6). Their words here return us to the Mass itself, and specifically to its symbolic sacrifices ("Hostias et preces"). By this direct superposition of forces, ironies are asserted, for the first time in the *Requiem*, in simultaneous juxtaposition rather than in sequence. The "Hostias" music is not troped between sections of the Owen text; rather it goes on *behind* it. Acoustically, and harmonically, two realms come into direct contact, yet without any musical interplay. The eerie chromatic ostinato of the organ eventually finds loose, modally ambivalent definition in relation to the trebles' A-Aeolian mode, but this clashes vividly with the simple E major of the reiterated Owen phrases.

Equating the liturgical sacrifice of the Mass directly with children's voices, the *Requiem* makes an ironic point about the European sacrifice of Owen's trope. The church acoustic functions here (as it will again at the climax of *Curlew River*), as the realm of the numinous, within which unseen voices sound as ethereal, spirit-like emanations. The repeated cutting here – seven times we hear the soloists sing "Half the seed of Europe" – only emphasizes the magnitude of the slaughter described in Owen's words, just as the suspended harmonic motion – an E-major tonic triad subverted by the organ's chromatic cluster – makes for an atmosphere of delirium.[43] One is unsure, at this moment, what is happening. Here, in the climactic, acoustic stroke of the "Offertorium," is the *wrong* sacrifice, the man-made, European one. The aural distance of the boys' voices, their archaic-sounding melody and temporal autonomy, suggest a scene of occult incursion. In the remainder of the movement, a hushed, inverted review of the earlier choral fugue, Britten writes a necessary retreat from the defining crisis closing the trope. Again, the boldest effects are the simplest: the whispered delivery of the second fugue sounds strange, as if the singers themselves no longer know why they are speaking the liturgical words. As the choir sings once again of a divine promise, one realizes that it is precisely this part of the Genesis story – God's blessing on Abraham and the promise to "multiply thy seed as the stars of the heaven" (verse 17) – that is lost in Owen's parable.

Britten's quotation of music from his own *Abraham and Isaac* (Canticle 2, 1952) adds a further, much-noted layer of irony to the "Offertorium."[44] For listeners who know both works, the decision to set the troped biblical episode using music adapted from the earlier score perhaps deepens the

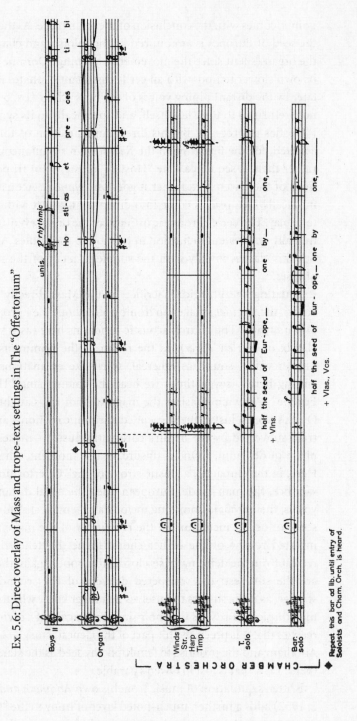

Ex. 5.6: Direct overlay of Mass and trope-text settings in The "Offertorium"

sense of an originary text brought into new surroundings. A break between the Genesis story and Owen's distortions is heightened, moreover, by the musical break, *within* the Canticle quotation. The turn, at "Then Abram bound the youth," from quite close recollection of the earlier piece to a different mode of intertextual reference – the cyclic return of bugle calls from the *Requiem*'s "Dies irae" movement (with touches of percussion noise) – underscores the significance of the self-quotation. As Owen's verbal reference to "parapets and trenches" parts company with the wording of the Genesis story, so the musical quotations go audibly awry, as "outside" contexts proliferate.

But such intertextual ironies remain distinct from those of the main trope strategy, and the "Offertorium" can work its central ironic effects even for listeners who miss Britten's self-quotation. The movement's ironies are first and foremost those inscribed at the verbal level in Owen's Genesis parody, and in Britten's thematic "Dies irae" quotations. The Canticle references are a more private gesture than Owen's blatantly anachronistic departures from the familiar language of the King James Bible (with the mention of "Europe," for instance). Britten's borrowings draw very little attention to an outside source, nor is the process neatly restricted to the music for Owen's English words. Canticle derivations begin much earlier in the movement, with the "quam olim Abrahae" fugue subject, a theme that flows on into the main trope.[45] The *Requiem*'s quotations from *Abraham and Isaac* remain a stealthy intertextual gesture,[46] ancillary to more foundational tensions between Abraham and Abram – the merciful God and the murdering figure of Owen's trope. In the end, it is the defiant attitude to divine authority depicted in Owen's reversal of the Genesis story that resonates most with the larger pattern of *Requiem* tropes – their secular interventions challenge the canonical authority of the sacred.

5. Ritual disintegration

The *War Requiem* concludes with texts from the Absolution and burial ceremonies performed after the close of the Mass itself. The textual echoes of the Mass in the two canticles – "dies illa, dies irae," in the "Libera me," and the return of the Introit prayer, "Requiem aeternam," in the burial antiphon, "In paradisum" – have traditionally prompted musical returns. (Both Mozart and Verdi frame their *Requiem* settings by repeating complete musical segments for these words.) Britten too, in the "Libera me," repeats material, though in more fragmented forms, and to rather different ends. Here, in a text praying for the soul's release from "eternal death,"

Ex. 5.7: Textural "chaos" at the opening of "Libera me"

the repeats articulate a destructive scheme, one in which the formality of the liturgy is progressively obliterated, making way for a climax in words "beyond" the Mass itself – those of Owen's "Strange Meeting." Britten's "Libera me" presents no simple liturgical prayer for absolution and release from eternal death; the intervention of Owen's two dead soldiers, speaking from some desolate, subterranean netherworld, makes for something more complicated and irresolute. By its scheme of thematic returns, and by the interpolation of Owen's vision, the "Libera me" works towards a collapse of the liturgy that prepares the simple and tentative speech of the closing "Amen" prayer.

Addressing the chorus at a rehearsal for the 1963 *War Requiem* recording, Britten described the "Libera me" as "a steady march rhythm underneath your cries of lament . . . [that] gets faster and faster . . . and gradually catches you up." Elsewhere, Britten called the "Libera me" "a kind of recapitulation of the whole Mass."[47] Tempo acceleration in the orchestral plane ultimately overtaking the speed of the choric utterances gives the peculiar chaos of this picture. At the solo soprano's entry ("tremens factus sum"), as Anthony Milner says, "thematic material begins to disintegrate" (344), and as the soloist's line becomes a series of frantic gasps, the choir itself begins to lose urgency and power within the complete texture. The orchestra here (Ex. 5.7) overlays the former measure lengths with a spritely "ghost"-meter, an incessant "dance of death" (redolent of the motoric repetitions of a much earlier pacifist score, the 1939 *Ballad of Heroes*,

Ex. 5.8: Chromatic descent as a figure of lamentation, opening of "Libera me"

though without its firm tonal focus). The march's greater animation and novelty crowds out the thematically plain invocations of the choir, restricted now to monotone utterance, tritones, or thematically "void" arpeggios. Against an endless churning derived from the original march shape, the voices struggle for definition.

In earlier movements, the choral voice was formal, thematically coherent, taut in delivery; here, this clarity of thematic address unravels. For continuity, one can point only to the amorphous falling chromatic line of the initial cries, marked "lamenting" (with an equally chromatic march undertow: Ex. 5.8), and the growing urgency of their recurrence. The plan is of a centripetal narrowing down to the wailing, sounding less like a litaneic refrain, a formal act of contrite supplication, than the voice of sheer desperation.[48]

Libera me, Domine, de morte aeterna, in die illa tremenda:
  Libera me
Quando caeli movendi sunt et terra:
  Libera me, Domine, de morte aeterna
Dum veneris judicare saeculum per ignem.
  Libera me [etc]

By a sort of vast gestural failure, the climax of the choral portion is the thematic and rhythmic return of the "Dies irae" music, marked out as a significant functional arrival on G minor appearing from the tonal waste-lands of earlier tritone-infested chordal agglomerations. "Strange meeting" itself arises from this new tonal level, though the rootedness of G minor is compromised here, just as Britten's excision of Owen's explicitly infernal references – "By his dead smile I knew we stood in Hell" – clouds the question of what realm we encounter at this point. Tonality here is frozen, clogged, the G-minor drone itself made strange by the stabbing string chords, floating around the stability of the last, simple admission: "I am the enemy you killed, my friend." To the recapitulation of the main "Libera me" section, "Strange meeting" will add a further round of return-ing gestures, deprived of their original context.

This final English trope, the longest and most intimate first-person expression of the *War Requiem*, draws authority away from the ritual utter-ance of the preceding Mass. The poem, indeed, though no longer directly infernal in setting, eschews the possibility of simple reconciliation. Owen's later poems, as Douglas Kerr points out, offer no escape from war's land-scape. Amid the sufferers ("Yet also there encumbered sleepers groaned"), there is complete desolation: "war has swallowed the world: there is no world elsewhere" (330).[49] The tenor's benighted assurance – "'Strange friend,' I said, 'here is no cause to mourn.'" – is countered by the disconso-lation of the baritone's long reply, with its promise of the march-like "trek from progress," a "retreating world." Eschewing false comfort, the final trope prepares the ultimate provisionality of Britten's ending – an "In para-disum" that bathes the ear with pentatonic clouds over a D pedal, only to be offset, finally, by one more return of the bell tritones, and the contradictory close of the choir to an F major that is warmly consonant yet remote.

Britten's idea of a "kind of recapitulation" of the whole Mass works by a negative rhetoric. Thematic returns, in the "Libera me," far from rounding out the piece in some splendid gesture of arrival at familiar landmarks, rob the liturgy further of its efficacy as symbolic action. The thematic recapitula-tions of the "Libera me" are grotesquely distorted versions of their earlier selves – as in the shattered crawl of the march, speeding to a desperate, manic dance. The only really new theme here, the repeated "Libera me" cry itself, is a stylized wailing. In this setting, the montage of fragments in "Strange meeting" only confirms the idea, translated into musico-thematic terms, of a landscape peopled with lifeless objects. In the hieratic, stereotypical element of all liturgy comes a ritual focus on the moment – the perfection of the isolated gesture. Thematic return, unless it replicates this perfection, can only be viewed as a lessening of performative force. If a theme, when it sounds "again," lacks an earlier perfection, then its previous force – as a translation, into sounding musical shape, of the action formalized in liturgical speech – may appear compromised. The rapid dynamic decay that follows the climactic "Libera me" cries disturbs us less by any intrinsic thematic or harmonic crisis – the G-minor triad is an unusually plain tonal anchor here – than with the possibility that its liturgical plea is futile.

6. *Curlew River* as ritual

I began this chapter by observing the links between Britten's interest in the "occasion" of musical performance and working anthropological definitions of ritual as something bracketed apart from the world of everyday experience. To move beyond this seminal point, though, in order to account for such easily acknowledged distinctions as that between, for example, theatrical performances and religious rituals, requires local knowledge of the conventional forms of ritual in a particular society. So while the ritual element in both the *War Requiem* and *Curlew River* is loosely recognized in each work's allusion to culturally specific symbols (the Latin Mass, the ancient Japanese *Nō* repertory), a closer understanding of how the performance achieves that allusion raises very specific questions. In the *War Requiem*, I have argued, ritual allusion depends on the presence of a canonical text; in *Curlew River*, the ritual element is primarily a matter of performance. A central concern in my reading will be the quality of single physical movements in the stage action, and their intimate connection to the score's sounding vocal and instrumental gestures.

As the sociologist Erving Goffman has noted, both stage plays and rituals are encounters whose events are pre-formulated. The distinction between the two genres of action turns not simply on what happens in each, but also on the texture of that happening. For Goffman, the distinction between a play and what he terms "ceremonial" performance is above all in the quality of the individual deed in the latter:

> [W]hereas in stage plays ... preformulation allows for a broad simulation of ordinary life, in ceremonials it functions to constrict, allowing one deed, one doing, to be stripped from the usual texture of events and choreographed to fill out a whole occasion. (58)

In Goffman's notion of "ceremonial,"[50] physical deeds or gestures (the "one doing") are the focus of attention. It is this physical, bodily quality – the heightened awareness of the single gesture – within performance that first drew Britten, in the later 1950s, to the Japanese *Nō* theatre as a possible source of artistic renewal within the European musico-dramatic genre of opera. Attending to the question of ritual in *Curlew River*, the focus of discussion shifts, at least initially, away from the liturgical formulation of ritual in the *War Requiem* – ritual as a prescribed verbal sequence – to a staged, costumed performance, where ritual comes before witnesses in the very nature of the performers' musical and physical gestures. The balanced interplay of words and deeds remarked upon in recent anthropological accounts of ritual will be a useful model,[51] in this case, with which to approach the work's intricate and stylized notion of gesture.

Britten's creation of *Curlew River* began with his first-hand experience, in Tokyo, in 1956, of a performance of the *Nō* play *Sumidagawa*. He was moved enough to see the play for a second time a week later during his visit (and to acquire a specially prepared tape recording for later study).[52] Recalling the experience in a 1958 radio broadcast, Britten mentions in particular his admiration for "the deep solemnity and *selflessness* of the acting" in *Nō*.[53] Writing in 1964, after the completion of *Curlew River*, the composer would recall in more detail his first reactions to the unfamiliar performance convention:

> The whole occasion made a tremendous impression upon me, the simple, touching story, the economy of the style, the intense slowness of the action, the marvellous skill and control of the performers, the beautiful costumes, the mixture of chanting, speech, singing, which with the three instruments, made up the strange music – it all offered a totally new 'operatic' experience.
>
> (Britten 1964b)

Britten goes on to sum up what the church parable draws from the Japanese *Nō* tradition in terms of an "intensity and concentration" in the overall transaction going on between stage and audience, and it is these facets of *Curlew River* that most convincingly draw it into the sphere of ritual. My concern, in the following analysis, is less with the work's material allusions to sacred ritual – the monk's-habit costumes, for instance – than with more basic, yet also more elusive qualities of "intensity and concentration" in single musico-dramatic gestures.

The ritual of *Curlew River* takes the directly physical form of staged actions set to music, whereas that in the *War Requiem* grows from the canonic status of a purely verbal textual form. Yet the new genre Britten and Plomer devised, the "parable for church performance," is more than a simple translation, for Western eyes and ears, of gestures specific to the Japanese *Nō* model. *Curlew River* is a fruit of Britten's skill for evading mainstream musical genres,[54] and of a specific inter-cultural cross-pollination. As the composer himself explained, the work is essentially hybrid in origin:

> Surely the Medieval Religious Drama in England would have had a comparable setting [to the *Nō* theatre] – an all-male cast of ecclesiastics – a simple austere staging in a church – a very limited instrumental accompaniment – a moral story? And so we came from *Sumida-gawa* to *Curlew River* and a Church in the Fens, but with the same story and similar characters.[55]

Beyond this explicit reference to the medieval tradition of a liturgical drama presented by clerics, *Curlew River* draws on the model of the "miracle-play" – performed originally on a cart – adapted in *Noye's Fludde*, a score designed explicitly for a church space.[56] Just as *Noye* presents its action "raised on rostra, but not on a stage removed from the congregation,"[57] so *Curlew River* unfolds on a specially constructed wooden stage approached by the performers in a processional through the congregation. In both works, the instrumentalists are clearly on view; in *Curlew River*, in fact, they sit immediately next to the main stage. Other features of the church parable staging are inherited from *Noye* – the restriction to a few simple props, the employment of masks, the adaptation of religious vestments to act as symbolic costumes, and the directional symbolism of movements in a restricted stage space. In these specific ways, as Mervyn Cooke has shown in a documentary study, Britten consciously brought English mystery play and liturgical drama traditions into contact with the *Nō* story.[58]

Hybrid in its origins – poised between the European Christian tradition of liturgical drama on biblical themes, and the Buddhist inflected Japanese *Nō* theatre – *Curlew River* engages with ritual in some fairly obvious ways. The chosen performance space, clearly, imbues the work with (as Plomer wrote) "an atmosphere fitting its religious, legendary nature,"[59] and the sacred tone of the proceedings is reinforced by other details: the cast of "monks" in habits, the framing processional and recessional to a plainsong melody (as in the *Ceremony of Carols*), and the centrality of the organ within the score's timbral palette. But these are scenic factors only, and it is in the unfolding of the action in *Curlew River*, as a series of discrete, formal, and relatively slow physical motions, that one experiences "something unlike ordinary activity" (Goffman 58). Anyone familiar with the Japanese *Nō* theatre will recognize its influence on the performers' movements in Britten's church parable. But such a fusion of stylized physical

acts with verbal or musical utterance is a characteristic of ritual that transcends the specific Japanese source (one need only recall the censing of the
altar during the Introit, and the kissing of the page following the Gospel
reading, in the Roman Mass, to accept this near-universal aspect of the ceremonial).[60] And it is precisely in this fusion of act and utterance, that the
performance of *Curlew River*, at the level of each single gesture, draws near
to a ritual.

7. Ritual gesture

> I feel that with the advent of films, opera may turn its back on realism, and
> develop or return to stylisation – which I think it should.   Britten (1944: 4)

The character written *Nō* refers to "accomplishment" or "exhibition of
talent," and the genre's characteristic subtlety of physical articulation is
encapsulated in the Zen word *yūgen* (rendered by Arthur Waley as "what
lies beneath the surface").[61] Such qualities are readily evident in the gestures of *Curlew River*, but defining them further demands that one consider first what is meant, in fact, by the term "gesture." Gesture, in the
present context, denotes a composite articulation in which bodily motions
on stage and vocal or instrumental utterances occur more or less as one.
The first appearances of the Ferryman and the Traveller (Ex. 5.9), in their
balance of musical and mimetic contributions, typify the gestural idiom in
which the story of *Curlew River* unfolds.

The Ferryman's opening gesture (at *a*), for example, shows a close
fusion of the sung utterance ("I am the ferryman . . .") with an accompanying instrumental flourish, and two bodily actions cued very precisely in the
score. The first of these (numbered "15") is specified in Colin Graham's
production notes as a turn by the Ferryman to face the front, arms out-
stretched in a stance of self-revelation (Figure 5.2 shows both the written
instruction and the illustrative drawing given in the Notes appended to the
published score). This stance is assumed at the onset of a characterizing
musical support with its own distinctive morphology: punctuating low
drum signals, scalar horn phrases (often with a sustained final note), and
subtle string accenting of the horn's melodic framework. The pervasive
heterophony by which parts interact as independent variants of a single,
shared melodic impulse is among the score's direct links to Japanese
models, though heterophony itself is hardly new to Britten's style with
Curlew River.[62]

The Ferryman's first gesture, however straightforward in its dramaturgy
– identity is announced to the audience, with no attempt at "incidental"

Ex. 5.9: (a) *Curlew River*, the Ferryman's entrance; (b) the Traveller's entrance

(a)

(b)

Fig. 5.2: Production note 15: initial stance of the Traveller and illustration

(15) **The Ferryman** turns to face the front (see
    Fig. 15);

Fig. 15

(16)   raises left arm to indicate
                           boat;

(17)   moves left arm forward to
                           indicate river;

exposition – is complex and refined in its details. The horn has a partner-like dialogic relation to the Ferryman's voice, and is louder (*f*) than the other instruments (*mp*: strings; *mf*: drums). All four instrumental lines taper their sound by diminuendo, but the dynamic shadings are subtly disparate, so that each horn phrase falls to *piano*, making way for the *mezzo forte* drum signal, and revealing an "after-impression" in the two strings (*mp*), sustaining beyond the literal duration of either horn or drum articulations. Such details are tailor-made to enhance and project the sonority of this ensemble in a resonant church acoustic: horn notes need to be shorter, if they are not to mask less forceful instruments; drums must taper off rapidly, or their echoes will drown out pitches with noise.

Describing the physical details of staging *Curlew River*, Colin Graham begins by stressing its evasion of direct pastiche: "The style of the first production . . . although suggested by the Japanese *Nō* Theatre, created a convention of movement and presentation of its own" (Production Notes; Graham 1983: 143). Considering musical aspects of this "presentation" (however artificial the isolation of sound and act in this case), one notes that the danger of pastiche is avoided in the greater range of harmonic and textural possibilities afforded in Britten's seven-player instrumental group, by comparison with the *Nō* ensemble of solo flute and drums. In Britten's score, the drums introduce carefully developed ensemble utterances, while the voice and the horn engage in a pitched dialogue, adding a harmonic component lacking from the sparer-textured *Nō* ensemble.[63]

The role of the drums is central to the definition of each gesture. Britten's interplay of drum beats with the voice and instruments recalls the *Nō* exchange of foot stamps and drum beats.[64] What results, in both *Nō* and in *Curlew River*, is a kind of drummed punctuation, emphasizing the formality of discrete gestures within the work's relatively fluid rhythmic continuum. In the Abbot's opening address (Ex. 5.10), drum signals follow the sense and even the grammar of each utterance, while more animated flourishes underline the central theme of his words ("to show you a *mystery*"), and mark the advent of a new physical action (at 4, the monks "bow their heads in acknowledgment"). As an unpitched interruption of pitched vocal-instrumental utterances, the drums "space" each gesture, in a manner not dissimilar to the setting-apart of actions noted by Walter Benjamin in Brecht's work ("the more frequently we interrupt someone in the act of acting, the more gestures result"; 151). In the end, it is this attitude to gesture, in *Curlew River* – more than details of melodic idiom or instrumentation – that is most "authentic" in relation to the Japanese source. In the controlled unfolding of each gesture at relatively widely spaced intervals, and in the intense, economical way that the single bodily act is precisely coordinated with sounding vocal and instrumental utterance, both *Nō* and church parable achieve the linkage of different sensory channels, remarked upon by ethnography, as typifying ritual.[65]

The entrance of the Traveller (*b*, Ex. 5.9) brings a second character-music – appropriately triadic for this figure "from the Westland" – and another, looser form of rhythmic interaction between voice and ensemble. "Trudging" quarter-notes here convey weary footsteps, each one performed in a "heavy (but sustained)" articulation. But this traveller has his own tempo, one notes, and so his vocal recitative, though melodically related to his instrumental partner (the harp), is always set off slightly from the surrounding accompaniment. This gesture reveals something of the score's refined harmonic idiom as it emerges in the relationship between the performer's voice and a surrounding instrumental context. In both the Traveller's and the Abbot's music, one hears clearly how the singer's voice on stage is often inflected by harmonic discrepancy in relation to the accompaniment. The effect is particularly obvious in the case of the Abbot's focal B♭ ("Good souls," Ex. 5.10) in the astringent context of the organ's tingling cluster harmonies, which include an upper B♮.[66] Thus while there is a gestural proximity linking vocal and instrumental phrases,

Ex. 5.10: Drum punctuating the Abbot's opening address

the intimacy of their relation, harmonically speaking, varies widely. At times, the instruments act as plain mirrors, reflecting back some element of the sung gesture (as in the horn's melodic preparation of the Ferryman's bluff opening phrases). At other times the composite image projected by pitched vocal and instrumental utterances appears more complex, or even distorted.

8. Estrangement and presence

> The forms of common "natural" behavior obscure the truth; we compose a role as a system of signs which demonstrate what is behind the mask of common vision: the dialectics of human behavior. At a moment of psychic shock, a moment of terror, of mortal danger or tremendous joy, a man does not behave "naturally." A man in an elevated spiritual state uses rhythmically articulated signs, begins to dance, to sing. A *sign*, not a common gesture, is the elementary integer of expression for us.   Grotowski 17–18

Britten's attraction to "the deep solemnity and *self*lessness" he perceived in *Nō* acting addresses ritual in terms of a performed relationship between an actor and a role. That *Nō* appears free of "self" by comparison with modern European theatrical acting styles only deepens the symbolic value of each gesture, and the formality of the whole. The stock figure of *Nō* theatre (Madwoman, Traveller) is distant from the conventional "round" character of the naturalist theatre. That a single composite gesture might support a separation among its elements – in harmonic tensions between voice and instruments, say, or in some rhythmic way – is a possibility glimpsed already. That such a separation might connote an estrangement of actor and role raises foundational questions of "presence" to which I now turn. Accenting a division between the experiential component of an action (an emotional or psychological charge to a given gesture) and the function of each as a symbol, *Curlew River* defines human performance in ritual terms. A division of the performed "self" relates, on the one hand, directly to the Madwoman – a figure whose sense of self is confused – and the miracle of healing to which the drama moves. But the point can be pursued equally at those moments where the individual actor – and the witness in the congregation – is subsumed, as Rappaport writes, into "something larger than what is ordinarily experienced as the self" (213).

Graham's production notes stress that a distance between naturalistic and ritual action should be visible to audiences as a contrast between the work's frame – Monks' procession, Abbot's address, robing ceremony – and the inner, costumed action proper:

The opening and closing sections of the work should be performed in a fairly naturalistic, although ceremonial style. The action of the story itself should be as formalized as a ritual: unlike naturalistic acting, emotion should never be expressed with the face or eyes but always by a rehearsed ritualistic movement of the hands, head or body . . . To assist with this, and to place the protagonists at a further remove from naturalism, masks should be worn by the Madwoman, the Ferryman, and the Traveller . . .

There should never be any question of female impersonation of the Madwoman's role: one should always be aware that monks are *representing* the characters, just as their movements *represent* and are symbolic of their emotions.   (Graham 1983: 145)

The formality of the gestures – the viewer's constant sense that they mime a state of being without pretense to verisimilitude – is evident (as Graham goes on to point out) in their repetition at key moments: thus the Madwoman falls to the ground weeping twice in the same stylized collapse. Exact repetition reminds an audience of a distance between actor and role, and pathos is avoided. Other gestural details challenge an illusion of naturalism: as the Traveller first hails the Ferryman, for instance, his call and the Ferryman's reply are juxtaposed with the return of a soft choric hymn to the river itself ("Between two kingdoms, O River, flow!"). Graham's direction for this moment foregrounds the artificiality of the montage by suspending the flow of story time:

Abbot and Chorus sway as before ["*very* gently to left and right (one movement per bar), to simulate gentle rocking of stationary boat": note 22] while Ferryman and Traveller hold a suspended conversation, i.e., no time elapses *for them* during the pauses between their lines.   (note 39)

Juxtaposing the characters' conversation with the hymn to the river, Britten's score overlays two orders of time, a narrative contrivance accentuated in Graham's direction to the soloists to remain inanimate when not actually speaking (singing).

This suspending of human time is an early sign of the spiritual realm beyond the here-and-now associated throughout *Curlew River* with the tonally amorphous cluster-chords of the organ's upper register. That the actors are miming, not "acting," is equally clear in events such as the Madwoman's frantic brushing of imaginary grass (as Graham's note 61 directs, "the hand must never touch [the] floor or [the] illusion is destroyed"), or the chorus's instantaneous freezing in place for group utterances. These obviously "prepared" gestures,[67] by the standards of naturalist theatre, are artificial; but naturalism hardly applies to a work so focused on the return of ghosts, and magical reincarnations. States of memory, rather than the living present, are the main concern in Nō drama.[68]

The suspended conversation is the outcome of an interweaving of distinct musics for Ferryman, Traveller, and Chorus. Each appears as a self-contained gesture, in a patterned scheme introducing first the Ferryman, then the Traveller, each time with a choral comment interpolated between two strophes. The conversation itself – as the first encounter *between* two actors, rather than between one actor and audience – concludes this scheme in a musical meeting corresponding to that on stage:

i: Ferryman
    A   "I am the ferryman"
      B   *chorus:* "Between two kingdoms the river flows"
    A'   "Today is an important day"

ii: Traveller
    C   "I come from the Westland"
      C, echo   *chorus:* "Far, far northward he must go"
    C'   "Behind me, under clouds and mist"
    D   "May God preserve wayfaring men!"

iii: their meeting
    A   "Ferryman! have you a place for me?" (Traveller)
          "Very well, sir" (Ferryman)
superposed on
      B   *chorus:* "Between two kingdoms, O River, flow!"

The score evades a too-predictable pattern by giving the Traveller an extra phrase (D), and by allowing the chorus to pick up his melodic material in a brief echo-phrase. The meeting of the two protagonists, finally, is possible as a vertical overlay of the Ferryman's short melodic gestures on the longer flow of the "River" chorus.[69] (Since the Traveller has now reached a halt, the omission of his trudging music [C] from the ensemble is dramatically apt.) Tonally, the entire passage is quite firmly anchored around a D tonic – one reason why events flows on smoothly, despite the frequent change of foreground melodic design. "Interruptions" are felt, to the extent that each music does not so much cadence as break off to make way for another. But interruption, as in the case of the drum signals, is perhaps the wrong word for a musical discourse whose articulations reveal simply the boundaries of individual dramatic gestures. The musical pattern grows from that in the drama; each phrase *acts*.

The dreamlike quality in *Curlew River* is focused around the spiritual state of the central figure, the Madwoman. The madness here is one of

Ex. 5.11: The Madwoman's adoption of the chorus's D tonic

restraint rather than excess. Grief brings her to what one Japanese writer calls a "highly spiritual state accompanied by separation from the self,"[70] a distraction, rather than a raging. Examining her musical presence, one becomes increasingly aware of an obvious ritualized construction in the way her solo calls are answered by choric responses. Behind this apparently schematic arrangement of materials, though, one finds a dense intermingling of melodic shapes, and a blurring of the ties of musical gestures to the physical stage presence of a single actor.[71]

An audience is introduced to the Madwoman by melodic shapes (see Ex. 5.12) more angular and dissonant than either the Ferryman's stolid declarations or the Traveller's weary sequential repetitions; since we hear her voice off before she appears, her madness must be audible. Her music has a topsy-turvy logic of shape: each phrase folds back on its own mirror-image (primes and inversion contours are marked on Ex. 5.13 below), or else takes the form of a stylized lamentation, a gliding motion suggestive of a wail or a more muted sigh. She is freer than the other roles vocally from the instrumental ensemble, her frequent unaccompanied song bringing her close to the expressive vocal delivery of a *Nō* protagonist or *Shite*. The sense of her apartness from the scene, as well as of intrusion, is evident as a harmonic opposition, for while those already on stage continue to anchor their vocal utterance to a D-pedal tonic, the Madwoman's initial cry (the "Curlew"-motive) pivots about a prominent D♯ high in the tenor range. The D♮/D♯ focal-pitch discrepancy – so idiomatic in Britten – persists throughout this first passage, a chromatic tension defining an initial hostility of those present on stage to the Madwoman. Choric comments are held apart from her sphere by harmonic means; conversely, her plea to be allowed to board the boat dissolves the dualism, as she adopts their D tonic (Ex. 5.11)

The harmonic separation of the Madwoman from those around her is only one dimension of her gestural presence, and the complete situation reveals a subtle undercurrent of motivic and rhythmic interactions between all on stage as she reaches the scene (Ex. 5.12 summarizes motivic landmarks). The Ferryman's question (1a) to the Traveller ("What is that strange noise?") is followed by the Madwoman's three distinctive cries (2a, 3a, 4a), a choric comment (5a), and then the composite gesture of the "Clear as a sky" song (6). Though each event comes across as an autonomous gesture, they are also woven together in a network of correspondences. The accompaniment figure to the 4a cry, for instance, in its repeating notes, reveals an affinity to the stutter-like delivery of the 1a question and response (hence the label 1b). Similarly, the choral comment 5a, with its prominent ascending and descending fourth shapes, subtly varies the Madwomen's curlew-cry, 2a. The song itself (6) more audibly synthesizes various active ideas: the flute ostinato (2b) is a diminution of 2a; the viola accompaniment (1c) is a multiplication of the earlier 1b figure to two pitch levels. Finally, the pentatonic "clear as a sky" melody (3b) is an obvious clarification of the earlier nervous gesture, 3a. As if to suggest the song's mesmerizing effect on those listening at the scene, the Madwomen's subsequent questions ("Where is my darling now?") are answered by first the chorus's "wandering" phrase (5a), then by a more animated choric outburst, "Dew on the grass," a musical thought completed by the Madwoman as she strokes the imaginary grass.[72]

Both arrival scenes – the Traveller's and the Madwoman's – are interactions formalized in a procession-like sequence, each moment of solo song answered by the more formulaic choric utterances. The Madwoman's appearance, I noted, precipitates gestural interplay among those on stage, with freer circulation of a small pool of recurring shapes. A previously close link of musical and physical gesture loosens. By exact repetition, a melodic gesture may – as with bodily motions that return unchanged – enhance the audience's awareness of a distance between performer and action. By subtle variation, on the other hand, melodic gestures can advance the action, at the same time imbuing the performer's physical actions with a suddenly enhanced quality of undivided presence. The Madwoman's startling switch to an Asian-sounding pentatonic melody for the "clear as a sky" song (Ex. 5.13) is a case in point – a seemingly new idea whose core-pitches (G♯ and D♯) derive from the earlier Curlew shape. The overall dynamic of the score is true to the process of steady intensification

Ex. 5.12: Gestural continuity in the Madwoman's first lyric

Ex. 5.12 (*cont.*)

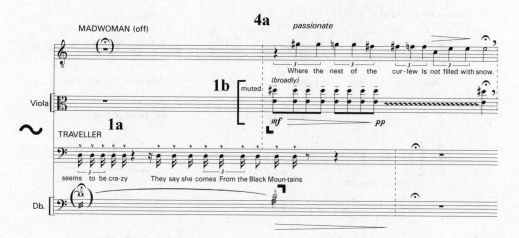

Ex. 5.13: A chromatic-to-pentatonic "clarification" of harmony

idiomatic to *Nō* dramaturgy, and distant from the conflict-ridden progress of more Aristotelian plots.[73] One facet of this, in *Curlew River*, is harmonic – the score is mobile rather than static, but individual moments of tonal arrival lack the rhetorical prominence so familiar in the common-practice gesture of cadence. This "intensification" writ large, in the steady drive toward a single defining moment, counts among the more direct links between the *Nō*-plot of *Curlew River* and archetypal ritual patterns.

My comments on dramatic presence so far draw on specific harmonic and melodic relations among those on stage, but it is worth recalling, too, just how much has been left out of the discussion. *Presence*, encompassing all ways in which actors or singers reveal themselves to an audience, is a hard thing to quantify. Writing of spoken drama, the actor Joseph Chaikin mentions "a quality that makes you feel as though you're standing right next to the actor, no matter where you're sitting in the theatre" (20). Significant here is Chaikin's focus on the physical space of theatre and on presence as a transcending of physical separation (without saying how this is achieved in practice). Presence is less about being in close physical contact, than in *feeling* close. In musical drama, the presence of the individual actor-singer is complicated, or challenged, by forces that divide an audience from the actual stage, and the more elaborate an orchestral component, the more a singer on stage must work to assert a distinctly vocal presence. *Curlew River* abandons such conventions, in the first place by situating its small instrumental group visibly to the side of the stage. Further, as will by now be obvious, the church parable constructs its musico-dramatic presences by a close coordination of vocal and instrumental utterance with physical gesture. But there is another factor here, one arising from the physical and acoustic quality of the prescribed performance space. The church milieu brings audience and performers together not only by the absence of a proscenium arch, framing the acting space. In a stone-walled church, quite brief gestures have an ethereal sonic residue in reverberations sensed equally by all in the space. Presence is something acoustic.

Curlew River continues Britten's interest in creating an ideal of operatic chamber-music with "a subtlety, an intimacy . . . lacking in grander forms" (1961:7). Intimacy is possible, for a solo voice fills the entire space easily, without force. Reverberations keep sounds hanging in the air, allowing for what Robin Holloway evocatively calls a "retuning" of each pitch amid an ever-changing sonic backdrop ("We seem to 'see' the notes in all their relationships from the simplest to the more and more complex . . . even the building seems to change in sympathy"; 218). Added resonance inflects the live utterance; but it can also be a source of estrangement, with disembodied spectral voices shadowing the singer's live speech. Utterances acquire an acoustic afterlife. This presence, of course, is familiar in liturgical chant, and it is with the reflecting of voices against stone walls that *Curlew River* opens. By its material *sound*, the parable returns listeners constantly to liturgical antecedents.[74]

A moment such as the Madwoman's memory of her son's loss (Ex. 5.14) reveals just how the church acoustic shapes the score in performance. Britten's sparse textures match the verbal paradox here – "one day he vanish'd: with silence ev'ry room was full" – in their acoustics. Phrases are brief, each instrument "vanishing" into silence, yet the room is replete with the sounding silence of echoes. The drama of a mother's frantic search is all there in the overlap of ever-new instrumental colors in unpredictable "places" (high and low registers), and by pitch choices (while the voice is fixed to C and D, the instruments fill out a whole-tone backdrop).[75] The forlorn "Loss-motive" is shared by singer and ensemble, so intimately and obsessively that it becomes an extension of her vocalizing. Instrumental and vocal utterance coalesce as proliferating forms of the

Ex. 5.14: Vocal and instrumental presence

same gesture. The Madwoman's presence goes beyond her being there on stage, or those moments at which she sings. In this acoustic, it is not too much to say that her presence fills the air, as does the closing instrumental unison, a shattering incursion of an ensemble "voice" after the freely aligned solo gestures. (As the scene recedes to choral comment, the Loss motive remains before the ear, fleetingly: transmuted in the harp's fragile plucking motion beneath the chorus, its gradual diminuendo is a performed imitation of the sonic decay attending everything in the preceding scene.)

Stage presence, at such points, is not limited to vocal utterance, but elides with its instrumental imitation. Musical shapes, whether originating in vocal or instrumental utterance, appear to hover over all on stage, like the wild birds that transfix the Madwoman. The intense focus on solitary gesture in the Loss motive is not unique. A comparable magnification of a single idea generates the climactic ensemble growing out of the Madwoman's "Birds of the Fenland" riddle. Her vocal presence and that of the flute are "estranged" (harmonically speaking) from one another, and from the harp ostinato that flows eerily below. As the Madwoman circles the stage, watching the birds, all those present watch her, and are lost in their own visions of what the birds suggest (Graham calls the scene a "multiple soliloquy"). Her original solo phrase becomes collective utterance, overwhelming any one voice. In the overall wash of voices and instruments, only the solo flute retains its autonomy climbing to ever-higher registers, rising above the massed sonorities, before vanishing mysteriously.

Blurring of gesture conveys both the Madwoman's distraction – as a kind of aural multiplication of presence – and, in a rather different and profoundly ritualistic way, the merging of individual selves into a collective reality. The "presence" in *Curlew River* is distinctive, no doubt, in its fixed acoustical conditions, but it is no one thing. Part of what sabotages all definitive talk of "presence," surely, is the sheer transience of every gesture in the score, in the present tense of its sounding delivery.

9. "A sign of God's grace": acoustic mystery and the power of prayer

When we arrived [in Venice] . . . I still couldn't quite see the style of it all clearly enough. I was still very drawn towards the Nô, too close for comfort. However, a few days here, although Arctic in temperature, the Gothic beauty & warmth, and above all the occasional Masses one attended, began to make their effect.   Britten, letter to Plomer, 15 February 1964

(cited Cooke 1998: 148)

> So shall my word be that goeth forth out of my mouth: it shall not return
> unto me void, but it shall accomplish that which I please, and it shall prosper
> in the thing whereto I sent it.   Isaiah 55:11

The coordination, in *Curlew River*, of formalized bodily movements with a limited set of returning vocal and instrumental gestures recalls, I have claimed, the formality and stereotypy inherent to ritual as a distinct mode of symbolic action.[76] Musico-dramatic utterance here possesses a refinement and concentration far from naturalist conventions of representation and dramatic character. "Presence" to the audience is bound up with the multi-faceted interplay of voice and instrumental lines, and with an acoustic diffusion of source utterance within the playing space. Even so, *Curlew River*, while hieratic in gestural idiom, enacts a story, and in this sense is less an actual ritual than an opera inflected by ritual experience. Categoric distinctions are further called into question as the drama moves to its climactic ending, where formal aspects of liturgical ritual – above all, the collective singing of plainchant – are directly invoked. The concluding events of the story – the Madwoman's prayer at the tomb of her son, the miracle of his voice heard within, and then the appearance of his Spirit visible without, restoring his mother's sanity in a blessing – are actions of directly ceremonial status (heightened in formality even in relation to the strict gestural world of the parable as a whole). A central facet of sacred ritual, "fruitful exchange between the occult and the human" (Tambiah 1985b: 128) is dramatized in *Curlew River* in acts of prayer answered by a miracle of healing. Part of this scene's power comes in its breaching of generic boundaries. When the story of the Madwoman reaches its climax in the specifically liturgical form of Christian plainchant, the opera's inner action mirrors its liturgical frame. Britten's idea that such a shift of utterance would "somehow tie the whole thing together, & match the entrance & exit chant,"[77] works, then, by enhancing the opera's climactic mystery by musical affirmations linked within European culture to traditional worship and the sanctity of the performance space itself. The representation of prayer will carry greater weight in a church than in the secular setting of the opera house.[78] A look at this closing moment, the drama's focal point, at which the Madwoman is healed in "a sign of God's grace," returns discussion to a notion of liturgy, so helping to situate the ritual engagements of the Church Parable in relation to those of the *War Requiem*.

Curlew River shifts at its end from ritualized performance of an essentially secular story to directly liturgical actions. As the Madwoman and chorus kneel in prayer before the tomb of her dead son, the audience encounters the ritual act of prayer and the magical powers vested in words alone in a ritual setting. Ritual, as commonly defined by anthropology, resists definition solely in terms of nonverbal acts, nor is the simple opposition of "words" and "deeds" adequate to the analysis. Rather, one must acknowledge words as the bearers of thought, and, ultimately, as the locus of power in ritual. Numerous cultures, in ritual acts of contrasting form (blessing, exorcism, spells and prayers) affirm a simple point: that the actual power of a given ritual is "in the 'words'" themselves (Tambiah 1985a: 18). This power, though, can manifest itself only via words "uttered in a very special context of other action."

The scene of healing ending *Curlew River* contrasts vividly to the ending of *Sumidagawa*, where the boy's ghost emerges from the tomb only to fade from sight. As his mother grasps desperately at the vanishing form of his apparition, she is left alone on stage, weeping.[79] For European audiences, Britten's more affirmative ending evokes the Gospel writers' account of the empty tomb near Golgotha, and it was Britten's and Plomer's achievement, as Mervyn Cooke has shown, to rework the Buddhist source text in directly Christian terms. The church opera can be understood, Cooke argues, as a remarkable synthesis of influences from the *Nō* original – the deep bell heard upon reaching the tomb has its origins in the mourning-gong (*shōgo*) of *Sumidagawa* – with elements of European liturgical drama, where there are precedents, for instance, for representing angels by solo boys' voices (1998:145, 163). In the present context, I want to consider the results of this synthesis specifically as ritual acts. In particular, I will focus on perhaps the most salient musical innovation of the opera in relation to its *Nō* source: the agency of plainchant within the scene. Where in *Sumidagawa*, the act of prayer is restricted to the chanting of a brief Buddhist prayer – "Namu Amida" – and the tolling of a gong, *Curlew River* reworks the scene into a far more elaborate musical texture in which plainchant melody is central.

A large bell tolled by an acolyte is the first musical sign, in the scene at the tomb, of a shift to formal worship. Its first stroke is integrated into the action both tonally (the single pitch C is the Ferryman's reciting tone) and by its physical effects: as Graham's Notes direct, "On the first stroke, the Madwoman shoots upright, on her knees, facing front with a convulsive movement, her hands raised . . . on the second stroke she falls on her face" (1983: 157). The prayers offered at the tomb by the Abbot and Pilgrims are prefaced with English words, closely adapted from *Sumidagawa*: "The moon has risen, / The river breeze is blowing, / The Curlew River is flowing to the sea." The actual prayers, though, are offered in Latin, sung to an ancient Gregorian hymn melody, "Custodes Hominum." The shift from the profane language of the journey (English) to the sacred language of ritual is marked musically, by a turn to more metrically regular, syllabic utterance (though the melody remains shadowed in the score's by-now-familiar heterophonic idiom), and by the ascendancy of a modal tonic, D. The singing is "led" tonally by the new brightness of a second, smaller bell, high above the warm low-register voices (Ex. 5.15).

Linguistic and tonal shifts are the foundation for the more fundamental, discursive move by which the dramatic moment is realized: the turn from an immediate stylistic context to the received tradition of liturgical chant. As in *Lachrymae* and *Noye's Fludde* – though without the sung audience participation of the latter – a dramatic climax is defined by a movement to an archaic musical source, in this case to a chant melody similar in style to that of the Parable's framing processional. Whether or not an audience understands the Latin words of the chant, it is significant, from a ritual perspective, that they be in a language distinct from that of ordinary communication. (The distance is marked, too, by the English prayers of the Traveller and Ferryman overlaying the pilgrims' at this point).[80] Ritual language, Tambiah observes, is often designedly ancient: its authority as liturgy depends on perception of a truth transmitted via inherited texts, a speech that "harks back to a period of revelation" (1985a: 26). Britten's decision to quote both the plainsong and the original Latin words – rather than translate them into the English of the main action – fashions the prayer as a directly liturgical event embedded within the opera's action.[81]

If the scene's return to Gregorian chant signals the formality inherent to liturgy, the appearance of the boy's Spirit enacts the incursion of the supernatural through a miracle that is by nature acoustic. As the chanting pilgrims' voices swell to a climax, doubled by the ensemble and by the higher tintinnabulating of the bells, the resonant echoes of each phrase fill the air. Beginning a new verse, much louder, the voices form an acoustic screen from behind which, suddenly, a distant solo treble voice – the boy's Spirit – is heard (Ex. 5.16).

"I thought I heard the voice of my child": what is real for the Madwoman is no less so for the listening audience. Our relation to the action is altered in a single stroke. Suddenly, we listen *with* her. The acoustic nature of the miracle places audience and protagonist on the same plane. Her words call aural attention to something hidden in the swirling chant-tutti. We too catch at the delicate sound of the boy's voice, piping out in repeats of the chant phrases that mingle with the echoes swirling round the church. The climactic revelation depends on a uniquely close linkage of the action with the physical attributes of the performance space. The boy's voice is an acoustic revelation, an epiphany in sound.

Ex. 5.15: The chant "Custodes hominum" appears

Ex. 5.16: The acoustic miracle of the Spirit's voice

The disembodied voice of the Spirit is too a "purifying" harmonic gesture, returning the texture to the modal clarity of the chant itself. Earlier on in the scene, the tonally disruptive voices "from the river" – the flute, in an excited fantasy on the earlier Curlew-motive – overlay the chant as the Madwoman gazes into the distance (at birds she imagines as "souls abandoned"). His off-stage voice, shrouded in the unearthly sound of an organ cluster, is separate from his Spirit's visual appearance, a distinction clear to those on stage ("Hear his voice! See, there is his shape!"). As the

Ex. 5.16 (*cont.*)

Spirit circles above the tomb and then around his Mother, the voice is silent, replaced by a second acoustic miracle. The Curlew-flute "becomes" the piccolo, and the Madwoman's jagged-fourths call is softened into a familiar pentatonic shape, at the very moment her mind is wordlessly healed.[82]

The larger shock here is one of tense – a shift from the earlier drama of memory (the Madwoman's of her son, the Ferryman's story of the boy during the voyage) to the present miracle of the Spirit's appearance. The action in *Nō* drama, "does not take place before our eyes," as Waley puts it, "but is lived through again in mimic and recital by the ghost of one of the participants in it . . . a vision of life indeed, but painted with the colours of memory, longing or regret" (53). *Curlew River*, from this perspective, makes its greatest departure from *Sumidagawa* in the concluding miracle. Replacing the somber image of the weeping Madwoman with the miracle of a Mother restored to her right mind,[83] it also turns the entire drama into a rite of passage not evident in the original, the Madwoman's initial separation from society, her liminoid transformation period (the river journey) concluded, finally, by a return to the community (the miracle of blessing and restored sanity).[84] The transformed ending, I have suggested, is heavily dependent in this on the allusion to specific musical elements of Christian ritual. The "sign of God's grace" here is conjured up in an act of collective worship. In its stylistic distance from the musical idiom of the main action, this chant establishes a link between the inner performance and the outer ritual frame of the Monks' procession and recession. The Latin words of the prayer-scene chant, finally, assume a very ancient function, as creative agents – the linguistic revelation of the mystical and supernatural force to which all sacred ritual ultimately speaks.

Curlew River fashions its drama into an optimistic, life-affirming message, yet its ritual engagements, I have argued, are as vivid as those of the more somber *War Requiem*, the score with whose genesis the church parable is so closely linked during the later 1950s. But while the two works apparently share the newly ascetic quality of utterance that would inform much of Britten's work of the 1960s and beyond, their "ritual" identities are quite distinct. The *Requiem*, as an extant liturgy invaded by a modern linguistic trope, presents a very different project from the Church Parable, where an essentially dramatic plot is set within the frame of liturgical worship. Ritual, in the *Requiem*, is invoked by a confrontation of two speech genres – liturgical prayer and lyric poetry – whose points of contact generate a discursive friction, calling into question the canonic status of the older text. *Curlew River*, on the other hand, alludes to liturgical practice, while establishing its ties to ritual at the physical level of stage gesture. Yet the climax of the drama, in its return to Latin plainchant, tends, like the *War Requiem*, towards the representation, for a witnessing community, of a known liturgy. Invoking ritual as an order of ideal reality bracketed off from the everyday, each work asserts, in a very different way, that interplay of sacred and profane that runs through so much of Britten's music.

6 Subjectivity and perception in *Death in Venice*

> Music is our myth of the inner life.
>
> Suzanne Langer (245)

Britten's opera *Death in Venice* opens, like Thomas Mann's novella, on the scene of Aschenbach's writer's block, his creative composure shattered by an unfamiliar nervous excitement. The psychic disturbance, vividly apparent in the music's pulsating cloud of rhythmic energies, prefigures the drama to follow. As Aschenbach's mind spins unproductively, we sense immediately that Venice itself will be ultimately just a picturesque exterior, the backdrop to a story whose cardinal events belong to a mental world – to what Mann called "reality as an operation of the psyche."[1] In *Death in Venice*, more than in any other Britten opera, the question of utterance points within. What Aschenbach says verbally is always the voicing of a psychological interior, the articulation of a consciousness. It is psychic reality that commands the audience's attention. The opera's characteristic atmospheres and textures are those of the interior domain of the experiencing subject. That other, *external* reality – the world around Aschenbach – has operatic life only as an object of his perception.

In Aschenbach's detachment from everyday reality, and in his ultimately fatal pursuit of perfect beauty, we may recognize the figure of the creative artist, and of the passionate lover, caught here by the depredations of a purely sensual gratification, humiliated by an uncontrollable infatuation, and finally destroyed by the workings of a numinous agency, by "fate." The two figures – artist and lover – are twin subjects within the intricate counterpoint of Mann's tale, the thread running from Aschenbach's aroused state in Munich to his plague-ridden collapse on the Lido beach. The story probes desires that are overtly sexual – where the *Screw*, for instance, was covert – yet it would be a mistake to regard its artistic-philosophical questions as somehow peripheral.[2] Mann's interweaving of aesthetic and erotic discourses, in *Death in Venice*, embodies a recognition that the erotic in Aschenbach's quest is precisely, in Eve Sedgwick's words, "the most physically rooted and the most symbolically infused" side of his being.[3] Returning to Mann's idea of "psychic reality," it is in Aschenbach's perception, in the sensory workings of his consciousness, that the intersection of erotic and aesthetic desires is most immediately apparent. Mann's tale is rich in the minute workings of perception, yet their operations are complicated, subverted even, in its later stages, by the literary force of a narrator's voice, ever more distinct from Aschenbach's own thoughts.[4] Britten's opera, I will suggest, works differently from the book: the full complexity of Aschenbach's self is no less evident in the layered density of orchestral sound, but he is released from the distanced judgment of a literary narrator. The opera goes further than any earlier Britten score in giving utterance to the inner experiences of a single subject.

The prominence of the perceiving self in Britten's *Death in Venice* might not, at first glance, appear so distinctive. Opera as a genre first emerged in temporal proximity to Descartes' formulation of the *cogito*, and throughout its history, its conventions have reflected changing models of the self.[5] Opera was always a public staging of subjectivity. But what is new in *Death in Venice* comes into closer focus if one considers briefly its departure from Britten's earlier operatic practice. Absent, in *Venice*, is the socially formed utterance of *Grimes*. Motives in the opera do not voice a societal presence, but point back to Aschenbach himself, as a creature of feeling and desire. Absent too is the orchestra as narrative force, so powerfully identified in *Billy Budd* with the uncanny presence of the dead Claggart. In *Venice*, a substantial narrating distance rarely opens up between orchestra and singer; with Aschenbach almost always on stage, there are few wordless interludes. The only significant musical agent distinct from Aschenbach himself is that personified in the recurrent "death"-figure (the Traveller, the Fop, and others). Very few musical themes, indeed, are not part of Aschenbach's own presence. The one exception – the "Marvels" shape, increasingly identified with the plague threat – lacks the independent force asserted by the Screw theme in Britten's first James opera. In *Venice*, it seems, the struggle is completely internal. The plague itself is less an external power than an index of something deep within.[6] Aschenbach's physical death in Venice is by Asiatic cholera; his spiritual death comes in the surrender to Dionysus, a loss, in his own phrase, of "self-possession."

The self, as Irving Howe notes, is an elusive abstraction: "No one has ever seen the self. It has no visible shape, nor does it occupy measurable space" (249). In the operatic *Death in Venice*, nonetheless, my central claim is that audiences confront Aschenbach's self most directly by vivid sounding translations of his physical perceptions – in particular the transfixed "sonic gaze" attending his awareness of Tadzio – more directly, even, than by full-orchestral eruptions of what can only be called instinct. Meanwhile, those other moments of literary reflection set by Britten as recitative soliloquy are episodes in Aschenbach's failed self-observation.

The story's tragic tone – and much of its fascination – comes down to this dramatization of a lack of self-knowledge.

1. "My mind beats on": the conscious self in Scene 1

[I]ntoxication has done with reality to such a degree that in the
consciousness of the lover the cause of it is extinguished and something else
seems to have taken its place – a vibration and glittering of all the magic
mirrors of Circe—   Nietzsche, *The Will to Power*, §808

Aschenbach's first sung utterance – "my mind beats on" – reveals the writer in all the quiet, monosyllabic desperation of a creative blockage: "no words come." Everything about the scene suggests that his problems are indeed of the mind, though perhaps not in a way he recognizes, for they are problems of instinct, understood here as the very opposite of an external stimulus. Instinct, in the sense defined by Freud, reveals itself "as a constant force" acting from within (rather than "a momentary impact" from without) against which "no flight can avail."[7] In this case, we at once confront the twentieth-century subject in its most recognizable form, as a body beyond the reach of the Cartesian rational subject, a materiality drastically severed from the psychic agency of consciousness.[8] Aschenbach's mind beats on in authentically Freudian rhythms, for it is controlled at this point by sexual drives of which he is unaware. Before turning to harmonic evidence of a specifically erotic charge in this scene, I will delve more into its world of musical gesture.

There is a taut, constructed quality to the unfolding discourse here (see Ex. 6.1); the music calls attention, as it were, to its own rigor. It is as if the scene's opening minutes are run by some intricate, glass-encased clockwork, its inner mechanisms clearly on display to the audience, though not to Aschenbach himself. In its reverberating ostinato rhythms and accumulation of static, directionless figuration, this operatic opening corresponds closely to Mann's picture of the writer's fatigue:

He was overwrought by a morning of hard, nerve-taxing work, work which
had not ceased to exact his uttermost in the way of sustained concentration,
conscientiousness, and tact; and after the noon meal found himself
powerless to check the onward sweep of the productive mechanism within
him, that *motus animi continuus* in which, according to Cicero, eloquence
resides. (3)[9]

The repeating, rhythmically uncoordinated woodwind ostinati here provide the scene's *motus continuus*, against which vocal phrases edge forward by cramped intervallic steps. No goal or tonal resolution appears,

Ex. 6.1: Aschenbach at the opening of *Death in Venice*

only harp and piano figures, wildly thrashing about, yet locked within pitches already traversed. The three independent tempi of the winds embody "sustained concentration," albeit that of a "productive mechanism" spinning out of control.

The presence of twelve-note pitch aggregates here is as much a structural symbol as a means of local melodic order. Aschenbach's first two vocal paragraphs are two abortive starts, each a row of twelve pitch-classes, the second (at "taxing, tiring") taking up the terminal E♭ of the first, in a strict intervallic inversion returning to the F with which everything began; these melodic exertions, as attempts at tonal progress, are (in Aschenbach's own word) "unproductive." All the familiar traits of Britten's serialism are here: the creeping, deadly force of melodic chromaticism – prominent in the 1965 Blake songs – and the arid, mechanical tone of a mirror inversion so evidently balancing the prime as to connote forced parallelism.[10] As Aschenbach wanders the twilit fields of the Munich suburbs, there is too a sense of chromatic saturation as the sign of magical transformation afoot (a Bavarian analogue to the dusky opening of Britten's *A Midsummer Night's Dream*).[11] The rigor of this particular all-chromatic scheme is the expression of an inner state from which Aschenbach cannot free himself: "I, Aschenbach, famous as a master writer" attempts to change the subject with its proud fanfares and the sudden incursion of E-major triadicism. But this strained appeal to reputation – the façade of a public self – quickly trails off, and the sounds of nervous exhaustion return.

In exclusively negative terms, Aschenbach outlines his artistic philosophy –

> I reject the words called forth by passion
> I suspect the easy judgement of the heart –
> now passion itself has left me

and again, the music smacks of merely cerebral contrivance: the three plain vocal statements are each "stuck" on the same brief idea, and tied still to the minor-seventh boundary interval of the opening phrases (Ex. 6.2). Orchestral support is mechanical, too: a busy contrapuntal duet in which imitative exchange barely conceals an underlying harmonic monotony (in the whole-tone motion of the ascending scale). The voice, meanwhile, shares the E tonic, but states only seven pitch-classes; the other five arrive, fittingly, in a final remark about "fastidious choice."[12]

Returning now to my opening claim, that Aschenbach's unrest is erotic in origin, it is revealing to find the ultra-rational planning of Aschenbach's twelve-tone vocal line concealing the underlying presence of a distinctive "*Tristan*-chord" sonority. The initial chordal pitch classes of Wagner's Prelude (spelled F,A♭,B,E♭) act as guide to Aschenbach's first three vocal

Ex. 6.2: Scene 1: Aschenbach's "fasitidious" pitch choices within the total chromatic collection

complementary **X**: *[D♯, E, F, G♯, B♭, B♮]*
hexachords   **y**: *[C, C♯, D♮, F♯, G♮, A]*

phrases; the chord reappears (a fifth lower) several minutes later as the Traveller bids Aschenbach "travel to the South" (Ex. 6.3).[13] The music's intertextuality, one notes, has a literary prompting in the subtle references in Mann's narrative to a specifically Dionysiac eroticism. Aschenbach's vision, among the gravestones, of a tropical swamp is prefaced by a sudden "consciousness of a widening of inward barriers," and at one point, he sees "the eyes of a crouching tiger" (5, 6). The sudden break with a surrounding naturalism is explained in Mann, with only a single comment: "Desire [*Begierde*] projected itself visually" (5).[14] Britten's *Tristan* references, by their strategic placement, directly link Aschenbach's mood at the opening to the fantasy he experiences at the mortuary, operatically transformed into the Traveller's "Marvels unfold" aria. Not coincidentally, Aschenbach's interpolated lyric expression of "inexplicable longing" here itself outlines the opening *Tristan* pitches (Ex. 6.3, at c). A subtle reference,

Ex. 6.3: *Tristan* chords as omens of "inexplicable longing" in Scene 1

perhaps, but the shrouded utterance is itself true to Aschenbach's own hazy grasp of unfolding events at this point.

The scene's long-range tonal unfolding projects failure – Aschenbach's repeated failure to escape dissonant melodic boundaries, and the inability to define a stable home tonic. The exquisite tensions of the opening reflect an essential lack of significant motion, despite the fussy animation of the foreground twelve-note unfoldings (as preciously erudite as the Ciceronian Latin of Mann's prose). Both the opening prime statement ("my mind") and the inversion-response ("taxing, tiring"), after all, unfold their respective harmonies within the same outer-voice pair, an F/E♭ dyad. Example 6.4 shows the harmonic landmarks: the opening *Tristan* chord moves to a dominant-seventh (at *a*), which, acting as an augmented sixth prepares a brief root-position E major (at *b*); the tonicizing gesture quickly dissolves, though, by creeping regression (at *c*) to the original F/E♭ instability. The remainder of the scene turns on comparable long-range ambivalence; not until Aschenbach himself resolves to travel ("Should I let impulse be my guide?") does real harmonic motion ensue. With the trombone-blast of the boat's horn in Scene 2, announcing a new tonic (F♯), the pregnant instabilities of the first scene are gone.

This first scene in *Death in Venice* establishes Aschenbach's conscious self by the proto-serial workings of an intellectualizing "mind" (the word is constantly repeated in Britten's setting). At the same time, one hears the characteristic yearning of Wagner's *Tristan*, a background harmonic-contrapuntal presence of which Aschenbach seems unaware. The opera's tone, in other words, is marked by a subtle form of dramatic irony; the vocal protagonist cannot know the full nature of what is revealed, by orchestral means, to an audience, particularly where revelations are at the level of the subject's own instinctual drives. Aschenbach senses a

Ex. 6.4: Tonal ambivalence at the opening of Scene 1

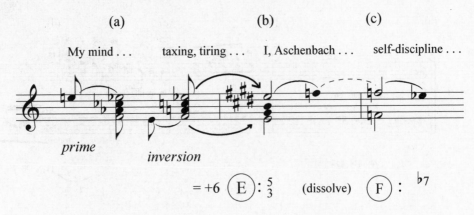

"longing," but to him it remains "inexplicable."[15] The complete musical texture presents a topography of the divided self, a manifest, conscious vocal utterance backed by the latency of an orchestral instinct. Such psychic analogies are of course not new to our hearing of accompanied song,[16] but in Britten's operatic Aschenbach, the metaphor works, surely, in a musical vehicle of rare precision. Still, the scene in Munich, in its subjective intensity, remains vacant, tingling with nervous vibrations, yet devoid of so-called outer reality. As Aschenbach travels to Venice, the opera opens up to a fine-grained realism, and with it, to a greater emphasis on the writer's perceiving experience of the world outside the self.

2. "The traveller's mind": inner and outer experience on the water

> A solitary, unused to speaking of what he sees and feels, has mental experiences which are at once more intense and less articulate than those of a gregarious man. They are sluggish, yet more wayward, and never without a melancholy tinge. Sights and impressions which others brush aside with a glance, a light comment, a smile, occupy him more than their due; they sink silently in, they take on meaning, they become experience, emotion, adventure. Solitude gives birth to the original in us, to beauty unfamiliar and perilous – to poetry. But also, it gives birth to the opposite: to the perverse, the illicit, the absurd. Thus the traveller's mind still dwelt with disquiet on the episodes of his journey hither: on the horrible old fop with his drivel about a mistress, on the outlaw boatman and his lost tip.
>
> Mann, *Death in Venice*, 24

Aschenbach's journey to Venice continues the chain of disquieting events that began in Munich. His subjective experiences here are, if anything, more vivid than when he was alone, for the world of sensory perception surrounding him is full of disturbing details. On the boat, he shudders in horror at the sight of a rouged and vulgar dandy, and already, things are starting to lose "ordinary perspective, beginning to show a distortion that might merge into the grotesque" (19). The gondola-trip to the Lido, rowed by a menacing character physically similar to the Munich Traveller, is no less macabre to the writer: "even if you . . . send me down to the kingdom of Hades, even then you will have rowed me well" (23). In the novella's elaborate narrative observations on Aschenbach's solitary mental experience ("more intense and less articulate than those of a gregarious man") the reader glimpses, by an elegantly turned ordering of phrases, the mingling of Aschenbach's own thoughts with those of a hidden narrator's voice. The opera offers no direct equivalent for such ruminations. No "solitude" aria is needed; rather, everything that unfolds is mediated by Aschenbach's viewpoint, coloring even the most everyday occurrence with a special intensity.

In the opera, the fundamentally strange tinge in Aschenbach's encounters with the fop and the gondolier is revealed by a striking orchestral realism. The subtle distortion Aschenbach feels – the lost "ordinary perspective" – is felt in relation to vividly detailed mimicry of the everyday world. As listeners, we hear *with* Aschenbach. His sensory experience – the noises of the boat engine, the rhythmic swaying of the gondola – is translated into sounds that are iconic in their resemblance to some part of material reality, yet also subtly askew. Events, by their distortion, "take on meaning" (in Mann's phrase). This blurring of Aschenbach's perception is heard, in the opera, at all musical levels: thematic, textural, and harmonic.

More so even than in the *Screw*, where literary ghosts become sonic as well as staged presences, *Venice* is an opera in which an optical discourse – a tale more than usually replete with imposing views and sustained gazes – finds a sonic translation. We hear the environment *as Aschenbach experiences it*; we hear his gaze, as it were. The opera is thus devoid of the kind of quasi-narratorial orchestral comment so central to *Billy Budd*; everything the orchestra plays reveals Aschenbach's sensory perceptions, and there is no independent orchestral voice (exceptions occur only late in Act 2). Aschenbach himself is not without a characteristic detachment: as in Mann's novella, he is the Nietzschian figure of the artist cut off from reality. In the opera, though, this ironic tone is transmuted into a musical scheme for conveying Aschenbach's perceptions at several distinct levels of absorption.

The opera tells Mann's story at three separate levels of action. Aschenbach's ironic, novelistic comments on events are set as recitative, with piano accompaniment, a black-and-white mode of speech; full orchestral colors depict his more public experience of Venice and the Lido. Beyond these two lies the gamelan-like percussion music of Tadzio and the children's beach games.[17] The three operatic planes rework the subtle layering of viewpoint Mann achieves in the novel by free indirect speech. Thus the first recitative, immediately after the "Marvels unfold" aria, conveys Aschenbach's return to his senses: taking out a notebook, he reflects on his need for a break justified by "growing fatigue." These musings are set off, as prose, from the metrical lyrics he sings at the orchestral level.[18] (Britten felt that Aschenbach, in the recitatives, was "reading from his Diary"; in one production, he actually jots thoughts down in the book.)[19] As he puts the book away, orchestral music resumes, and the journey itself begins.[20] Not until after Aschenbach reaches the Hotel (in Scene 4) will he again soliloquize alone. What occurs between these two moments of detachment he can only describe as "odd, unreal, out of normal focus," a perception that deserves closer scrutiny.

(a) Inner and outer worlds on the boat to Venice, Scene 2

Aural effects of distorted perception, in Scene 2, depend on the clear musical separation of Aschenbach's perceiving consciousness and the objects of his attention. At every level, the interplay of markedly disparate "inner" and "outer" perspectives generates the note of unease. The sheer sonic realism of the outer-world sounds here has often drawn comment. As the boat prepares to leave, we hear both its horn-blast (trombones, bells raised, fast diminuendo to suggest prolonged echoes) and incipient engine-whirr (tenor drum, with brushes), the two noises a realistic backdrop to the youths' "Serenissima" calls to those on the shore (Ex. 6.5). Set off from this orchestral mimicry of real-world activity is music without local scenic reference, music we recognize from before as the sound of Aschenbach's longing to travel (Ex. 6.6). The rhythmic non-alignment of the string lines now articulates Aschenbach's drowsy state. Yet even here, his mood is linked to the outer scene, in this case, to the gradual emergence of the Venetian skyline from the haze as the boat nears.

The atmosphere of the scene is suspended between these two points of view. Aschenbach's musical separation from the boat is often sharply etched. The "Serenissima" tune, for instance, has a simple tonic–dominant rocking motion, grounded in the F♯ tonic of the boat horn, and the stylized roughness of the counterpoint – the recurring C♯/F𝄪 tritone at "Se-re-nis-si-ma" – conveys the vagaries of a crowd singing. Aschenbach himself, though, is musically remote from this lullaby: startled to discover the

Ex. 6.5: Outer-world sounds in Scene 2: the youths' "Serenissima" song as the boat departs for Venice

impertinent fop on deck is a fraud, his reaction ("why he's old!" Ex. 6.7) bounds up and away from the register and tonality of the singing. By a sudden orchestral close-up, listening attention moves from the overall scene onboard to the writer's gesture of alarm (Britten's experience writing the 1970 television opera, *Owen Wingrave* should not be discounted, hearing the speed of this proto-filmic "cut"). The musical transformation here is less a shift to new material than a drastic manipulation of ideas already in play: Aschenbach's twelve-tone dyads are an all-chromatic version of the youths' less sophisticated-sounding two-part singing.

As Venice nears, though, the distance between inner and outer realms narrows. Aschenbach's drowsy string lines shimmer more brightly than the youths' singing; the harmonies are richer and more diverse (Ex. 6.6, again, marks chords (|) of a distinctive non-triadic hue).[21] Beyond contrasts of intervallic content, the string scales create a diffuse wash-effect, hazily floating upwards (and "outwards," as the lines spread in registral separation) from the narrow tonal-registral reference point of the boat horn (the third, F♯/A♯). The blurring, I noted, is a mimetic fusion of Aschenbach's dreaming with the Venetian outlines of the larger scene. This is not the first time in the opera, though, that a loss of perceptual focus can be detected, and the watercolor scale patterns of Scene 2 might be compared to other sounding discourses (textural, thematic, tonal), each with its own graduated range of definition. Blurring of a different kind, for example, shrouds the opening *Tristan* chord: a registral scattering of Wagner's constituent pitches (see above, Ex. 6.3a) conceals their identity as a single harmonic mass.[22] A more melodic evasion of precise outlines comes in the heterophonic part-writing of the Traveller's "Marvels unfold" shape (see Ex.

Ex. 6.6: Aschenbach on the boat to Venice, Scene 2

6.8a–b). The simultaneous variation of a basic melodic impulse (central to Britten's scores by the 1970s) transcends traditional concepts of single-line melody. The Traveller's announcement of the germinal "Marvels" cell lacks pristine melodic identity. Outlines are clouded by the interplay of the voice pitches, moving <D–C–E–D♯>, with bassoon and horn parts loosely drawing out aspects of its contour. The intertwining melodic tentacles paint the distorted undergrowth-images ("trees distorted as a dream") of Aschenbach's vision. As the aria concludes, the Traveller's voice-part shrouds the Marvels shape still further by new permutations of pitch order

Ex. 6.7: The youths' song and Aschenbach's chromatic response

Ex. 6.8: (a) Evasion of precise melodic outlines: heterophonic part-writing in the Traveller's anouncement of the "Marvels" cell, Scene 1; (b) Further melodic transformation of the Marvels cell, concluding the Traveller's aria

(Ex. 6.8b), and by ungainly leaps. Contour is lost in shifts of register, yet the underlying pc cell remains intact. Three-fold repetition of the closing words, like some magical charm, brings Aschenbach back to waking consciousness, and a return to everyday perceptual habits is audible in the return to traditional melodic recitative ("Gone, he's gone").

Beyond the heterophonic blurring of melodic outline in the "Marvels" vision, the scene as a whole deepens its subjectivity effects by an unfolding tonal argument, elaborating the interplay of inner, emotional experience and outer, objective reality. By control of long-range motion between pitch centers, the journey from Munich to Venice is given an audibly tonal form. Few listeners can miss the aural thrill of arrival in Venice, announced to begin with by a D-major tonic (resolving the troublesome C♯/G♮ dyad of the "Serenissima" song at last). The boat trip, we noted, is dominated by an F♯ tonic, itself "new" in relation to the hesitant E and C tonics of the preceding scene. The entire sequence reveals a pairing of mediant motions, the Venetian D superseding F♯ just as Aschenbach's E previously gave way to the Traveller's C:

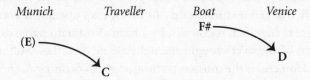

The parallelism is loose, in that each key center exerts its presence in a distinctive way. The E tonic of Scene 1, I suggested before, is a fleeting and elusive goal, while the Traveller's C focus is a vestigial frame to an aria whose inner workings are octatonic and mobile. The more stable and diatonic presences here thus belong not to the inner realm of Aschenbach's nervous, hallucinating mind, but to the more solid reality of the boat and the sight of Venice itself. These brighter, major-mode assertions, though, do not entirely eclipse the memory of the initial E–C nexus. Its tonal-dramatic role, at this point in the opera, is hidden and aurally problematic – keys are glimpsed but withheld – but the interactions of these two pitch centers prefigure the turning points in the drama to come.

(b) Facade and interior: harmonic and textural revelations in Scenes 3–4

Scenes 1–2 convey Aschenbach's subjectivity as explicitly sensory, an active perception defined in opposition to the vibrancy and strangeness of outer reality. In Scenes 3 and 4, the construction of an operatic self takes a specifically orchestral form, marked by emphasis on starkly polarized textural layers, and by fragmenting of the music's linear flow. In stratified musical textures, Britten's Venetian idiom comes closest to articulating a characteristic doubleness in Mann's tale. That "sharp extrovert front, behind which the mysterious mental processes seethe" of which Piper writes (1989: 20) well evokes the dramatic connotations of the opera's willful shifts of orchestral texture, moments at which the contrast of surface and depth – a facade and what lies behind – are suddenly revealed. The score's layered constructions, rife with inner tensions, embody an exploration of mental activity, in that they are redolent of post-Freudian models of the subject as divided against itself. A theater of subjective action comes into being, aurally, in the simultaneity of schematic musical oppositions. By the basic aural contrast of upper and lower registers, for instance, musical utterance connotes an internalized discourse, beyond the regular "change-of-speaker" rhythms of public, dialogic interaction. The opera's polarized textures form the sounding topography of Aschenbach's consciousness.

Aschenbach's articulate vocal presence is situated within this dramatically charged textural realm. In the opera's opening seconds, as his solo voice is engulfed, registrally, by a haze of ostinato patterns, one *hears* the form of the overwrought mental state he describes. Still more elaborate and forceful is the musico-textural scenario defining Aschenbach's arrival in Venice itself (in the orchestral "Overture" to Scene 3). It is an action fraught with signs of conscious perception driven by unexposed forces.

The orchestral "Overture" has the scenic task of showing Aschenbach's first views of the old city, but there is inevitably a buried symbolic level of action, too. A surprising pregnancy of utterance is immediately evident in the way that the opening Barcarolle phrase (Ex. 6.9a) swerves quickly away from a gently bobbing figure (varying the earlier "Serenissima" call). With sinister urgency (and an *accelerando* motion), the phrase arrives at a grotesquely dilated form, its three component melodic strands precariously situated over a gaping registral expanse. In the brass fanfares that follow, registral coherence is restored, only to be abruptly curtailed by the five o'clock chime of San Marco, at once thrillingly realistic timbrally, and yet, in context, deeply forbidding (Ex. 6.9b). It is a fissured moment – here are two imposing "views" of the city, related but antinomic. This is the "ambiguous Venice" Aschenbach hymns a few moments later, the duplicitous city where, in prophetic words, "passion confuses the senses." The soundscape is antiphonal – an authentically Venetian *coro spezzato* gesture – but riven by schematic oppositions. Warm harmonic consonances (brass, in sixths) are answered by cruder-sounding dissonances (bells and

Ex. 6.9: The arrival in Venice: "double-faced" harmonic gestures in the Overture to Scene 3

(a)

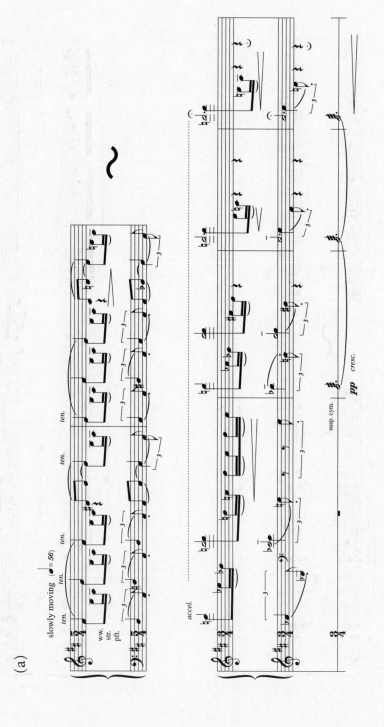

Ex. 6.9 (cont.)

(b)

(c)

winds, in parallel elevenths). After the liquid but still coherent two-part counterpoint of the Barcarolle, these Venetian phrases are alien polyphonies. Neither is contrapuntal in the familiar note-against-note sense: by heterophony, the brass elaborate a single chant incipit; the parallel bell-lines evoke organum. The juxtaposed phrases bristle with harmonic contradictions, too, in the friction of a major-mode collection with a Dorian fragment (with F and G♯ finals, respectively). The gesture is double-faced.

The Overture's sound blocks confront one another in a dense interlock – Aschenbach's view of the fast-approaching skyline from the moving boat shifts constantly – saturating the listener with an unprecedented fullness of purely instrumental sound. The opulence is an imposing opening to the paragraph, yet it is the final dying-away (Ex. 6.9c) that bears the most expressive weight. A nervous "unraveling" gesture, drawing out the decay of the last bell-tone, quickly changes the mood and at the same time evokes very specific events – the unruly woodwind trills are a memory of Aschenbach's hallucination in Munich. The link is brief, startling: a chink in the facade opens up, and we glimpse the puzzling resemblance of the magnificence before us to that earlier, fantastic scene. In the abrupt dissolve – as Aschenbach reappears in a gondola bound for the Lido – a question is left hanging: what links these Venetian facades to the "knotted bamboo grove" of his earlier vision?

Operatic drama thrives on a precise control of pace, and mechanisms of rhythmic accelerando and rallentando, as well as the very abrupt form of the dissolve, contribute to the mystery of Aschenbach's arrival. But there is no chance for reflection on these puzzlingly ambivalent vistas – the action pushes on, with the writer, to the Lido. Yet even here, as the familiar Barcarolle figure returns (Ex. 6.9d), something is amiss in the mood-shift. A darkening has occurred. The previous warm D-major theme is replaced by a lugubrious reincarnation of the same texture (letters *a* and *d*, Ex. 6.9 above). Neither music is diatonic in any simple sense, but the chromaticism of Example 6.9a merely adorns a stable tonal frame (the initial outer-voice tenth, D–F♯). False relations on the musical surface (the discrepant mediant, F♮, in m. 1) hardly challenge the security of D as tonic. The second, more shadowy Barcarolle (Ex. 6.9d) comes in the Overture's wake, as it were. Here, the outer-voice eleventh (C♯/♯F, last measure) is an echo of the bells, one whose tonal definition is eroded (by persistent C♮'s) from within. This is the alter ego of the Overture, a twisted image whose distortion is felt in relation to an F♯ melodic reference, common to both musics.[23]

The shifts of mood in this scene are rapid, and create a more fragmented impression than elsewhere in the opera, where transitions are remarkably fluid. The Overture's antiphonal interplay of blocks disrupts the music's linear flow by its locked tensions. As Aschenbach reaches the Lido, though, the music's vertical fragmentation – a separating-out of the musical space into polarized layers of sound – signals a new strangeness of atmosphere. In his "Mysterious gondola" aria, the hollowness comes from extremes of register. Over the Stygian depths of divisi lower strings hovers the glinting brightness of a solo harp, with oboe and piccolo support (Ex. 6.10, at a). In this tonally stratified world, we are less *in* A minor – the key presence asserted by the bass stratum – than "over" it: the harp filigree, like the voice, floats free of lower-register moorings, without firmly defining any alternate tonic. The aria, as in Mann's novella, conveys Aschenbach's rather pedestrian symbolic interpretation of his trip with the rogue-gondolier as a "last silent voyage" across the Styx. This layered orchestral sound, however arresting as a local source of atmosphere, makes its most startling effects in Scene 4, after the gondola ride itself is over.

Flashing back to the "Gondola" aria, Scene 4 places Aschenbach in a strange temporal netherworld. As the Manager offers effusive and vapid greetings, Aschenbach's thoughts remain with the mysterious gondolier (Ex. 6.10b). The scene cuts now between the tedious present (the Manager's perfunctory chorale-phrases) and the strangeness of the recent past (the returning A-minor chords in the orchestral bass). Precisely because the musics are so highly contrasted in registral and harmonic form, an implied simultaneity results. The Manager's chorale never strays from the middle register; the residue of the gondola music remains fixed on the thick sound of close-position bass pitches. But behind the overt contrast there is an ominous second-order coherence. Aschenbach's first A-minor triad answers the Manager's A major, as if in mechanical response while lost in thought. But this touch is enough to link the Manager and the Gondolier as one and the same figure, a point confirmed when the upper-register harp figure of the gondola trip returns (as the Manager reassures Aschenbach of his "happy chance" at riding for nothing). The music at this moment at one level enacts Aschenbach's impatient response to the Manager; at another, it reveals to the audience an uncanny thread of super-natural continuity. Both revelations are possible by a complexity of musical texture familiar throughout Aschenbach's journey to Venice. At every point along the way, moreover, that "complexity" – a musical reima-gining of the layerings of speaking presence in Mann's prose – places Aschenbach's subjective perception at the center of the drama.

Ex. 6.10: (a) A hollow texture of polarized tonal strata in Scene 3; (b) flashback to the gondola ride upon reaching the hotel, Scene 4

3. "The charming Tadzio": Aschenbach's sonic gaze

> But of beauty, I repeat again that we saw her there shining in company with
> the celestial forms; and coming to earth we find her here too, shining in
> clearness through the clearest aperture of sense. For sight is the keenest of
> our bodily senses; though not by that is wisdom seen, for her loveliness
> would have been transporting if there had been a visible image of her, and
> this is true of the loveliness of the other ideas as well. But beauty only has this
> portion, that she is at once the loveliest and also the most apparent.
>
> Plato, *Phaedrus* 250D

Aschenbach's ironic, detached relation to his surroundings is from the first
expressed, in the novella, by scenes of vision. His earliest encounter in the
Munich graveyard is disturbing, even before the hallucination, because of
the way he meets a challenge to his own "inquisitive and tactless" gaze:

> he became suddenly conscious that the stranger was returning it, and indeed
> so directly, with such hostility, such plain intent to force the withdrawal of
> the other's eyes, that Aschenbach felt an unpleasant twinge.   (5)

In Venice, seeing Tadzio a second time at the hotel, Aschenbach, as he compares him to a sculpted deity, again underestimates the power of his own
gaze:

> the head was poised like a flower, in incomparable loveliness. It was the head
> of Eros, with the yellowish bloom of Parian marble . . . "Good, oh, very good
> indeed!" thought Aschenbach, assuming the patronizing air of the
> connoisseur to hide, as artists will, their ravishment over a masterpiece. (29)

Moments earlier, the narrator remarks prophetically on the artist's
"wanton and treacherous proneness to side with the beauty that breaks
hearts" (26); as Aschenbach gazes on Tadzio's statuesque features, his self-
deceit is likened to the connoisseur's hidden "ravishment." By chapter 4,
Aschenbach's visual sense, watching for Tadzio on the Lido beach, is
suffused by an interweaving of Platonic quotations and mythic allusions.
His gaze is now that of the Platonic lover, recognizing in Tadzio a divine
form – "he told himself that what he saw was beauty's very essence; form as
divine thought" (44) – but prone to the dangers mentioned in the
Phaedrus, of one who, in a corrupt and purely sensual response, "rushes on
to enjoy and beget" (*Phaedrus* 251). Aschenbach's and Tadzio's relations,
the narrator remarks, are strange and uneasy, since they "know each other
only with their eyes" (50).

For the novella's optical discourse to survive in an operatic form, music
must find an auditory equivalent for the workings of Aschenbach's perception. On stage, the significance of mere physical glances cannot, for a

viewing audience, retain the symbolic weight it has in prose for the reader, unless the music itself "glances" somehow. The operatic problem is solved by making Tadzio and his family silent dancers, existing only on a separate mimetic level, isolated in Aschenbach's eyes from the opera's other public actions, all sung. The remoteness is also musical, since each dance is accompanied in a percussion-rich gamelan idiom, drawing on Balinese models.[24] The balletic episodes are seen on stage only by Aschenbach; their exotic form and sonority, a score note confirms, begins and ends with his gaze:

> the composer's basic intention . . . was, through the use of appropriately stylized movement, to suggest the "other" and different world of action inhabited by Tadzio, his family and friends, especially as seen through Aschenbach's eyes.[25]

Associating gamelan scoring in *Death in Venice* with the exotic, unreachable figure of Tadzio, Britten returns to a dramatic trope familiar in the earlier operas. Both Quint and Oberon are marked out by their exotic, gamelanesque music as threatening figures, boy lovers whose operatic depiction of homoerotic desire, Philip Brett argues, might well have sounded a composite expression of "fear, shame, and defiance" to mid-twentieth-century ears (1994b: 250). It would be simplistic, though, to localize Aschenbach's still-unconscious erotic desires in Act 1 solely in his gamelan-accompanied views of Tadzio.[26] The drum sounds erupting to herald the Traveller's Munich appearance and the incessant throbbings of the tom-toms throughout the "Marvels" vision are both facets of what draws him to Venice.[27] The gamelan music accompanying Tadzio's dancing is hardly the opera's first or even – given the opening *Tristan* allusions – its most direct symbol of erotic desire. Nor is the gamelan music identified simply with one character, as with the musics "belonging" to Quint or Oberon. The *Venice* gamelan belongs to Tadzio only "as seen through Aschenbach's eyes." Operatically, Tadzio is all object, without subjective presence. The gamelan, a symbol of sensory perception, is another manifestation of Aschenbach's perceiving self. In what I term the opera's sonic gaze, one hears an exotic musical idiom attuned, in its mesmerizing harmonic stasis, to the physical fixity of Aschenbach's sight of the boy. (In an abstract sense, too, the sonic gaze evokes orientalist discourse, in privileging an observer's *vision* over the reciprocal interaction of oral encounter.)[28] The sonic gaze, one might say, is a rather unusual form of musical utterance – less the articulation of feeling or thought than of sensory perception. The presence of an object in Aschenbach's field of vision is made audible; "the charming Tadzio" has operatic reality as the product of the observing subject.[29] The sonic gaze returns discussion to the opera's delineation of subjective experience at distinct, but mutually significant, levels of action.

Aschenbach's first sight of Tadzio (Ex. 6.11) dramatizes very directly the distinction between his perception as sheer sensory experience – a musical "now" – and the reflective, evaluative turning of his intellect. Seeing and thinking are, more clearly than before, presented on two entirely different levels of action. First, there is the sight of Tadzio, who fairly leaps out of the musical grayness of the hotel-guests' ensemble. Suddenly, everything *gleams* – the timbre of the vibraphone theme itself, and the iridescent cluster-chords beneath. The freezing of the musical action here is a cessation of harmonic motion, and a clarification of the penumbra of dense chromatic cluster-sounds, into one glittering tonally suggestive form. The modally ambiguous chord below the theme (G♯,A,C♯,D) is a resting-point for Aschenbach's gaze, its "bright perfection" – two interlocking perfect fourths – giving way, with the entrance of Tadzio's mother, to a second pedal point, the final-pitch, A, a dim after-glow of the brightness of harmonies Tadzio's presence evokes. Once Tadzio has gone, Aschenbach, as if released from hypnosis, reverts to the rational mood (and dry timbres) of his piano recitatives. Where Mann's narrative weaves aesthetic questions subtly into Aschenbach's perception, the opera at this point opposes reason and intoxication by the schematic division of the recitative plane from the orchestral, percussion-dominated moment of vision. Aschenbach himself, in the recitative, voices the book narrator's cautionary remark about "a wanton and treacherous proneness to side with beauty," yet he remains oblivious, in what follows, to his own vulnerability to a "wanton" erotic desire for the boy.

On the beach, in Scene 5, Aschenbach's thoughts continue in recitative – "the voice of his literary sanity" (Myfanwy Piper [1989: 18]) – but are abruptly curtailed by Tadzio's appearance, distracting the writer. The scene is dominated by Aschenbach's visual perception, but his gaze is mingled too with his straining to hear distant sounds (those of an off-stage chorus). Calls of the name "Tadzio" – blurred by heterophony and by a confusion of vowel-sounds – shade into the soundscape of the beach, with its panoramic views, evoked always by the sound of orchestral strings, and with the gamelan percussion music of the children.[30] As in the Scene 2 boat trip, a contrast between the outer landscape and closer focus on one aspect of it, Aschenbach's view of the children, is made aurally clear. Each element of Aschenbach's Scene 5 vision is distinct, yet plays a part in an unfolding musical continuity. This interplay is clear motivically, for instance, when his melodic vocal phrase ("My temples throb, I cannot work") recurs

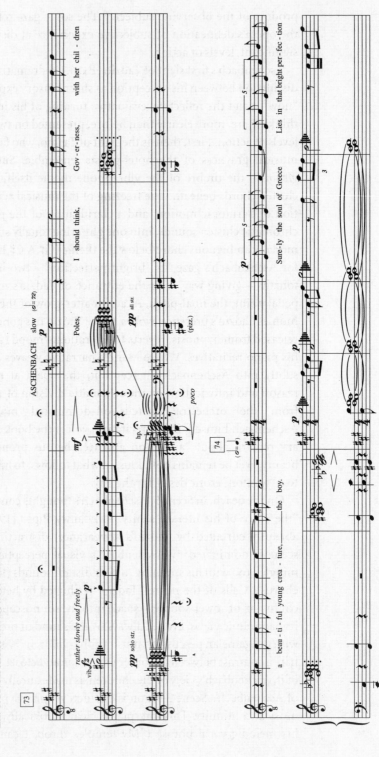

Ex. 6.11: Aschenbach notices Tadzio

immediately as a percussion melody in the children's games, then returns once more to the singer, refreshed after buying fruit from the Strawberry Seller ("what can be better than this?"). The music of the games grows from the observer's mood – the gamelan is thematically linked to Aschenbach's gaze, even as it is isolated, timbrally, from the larger scene's orchestral palette. We hear the games, and the harmonically plangent Strawberry Seller's cry, itself overlaid on the children's music, as filtered through the writer's senses.

The gamelan music is exotic not only in its sharp percussive attacks and metallic timbres. Beyond the contrast of orientalist percussion timbres with "European" string and woodwind groupings, the fundamentally static modal-harmonic identity of the gamelan is sharply distinct from the harmonic restlessness of the full-orchestral music. All elements of the scene (see Ex. 6.12) offer a harmonic richness of stratified layerings, and in the opening view of the beach (a) the bass line is active. The first game (b) is far more static, its proto-Balinese display of revolving ostinati fixed over a B pedal, doubling a low gong stroke. When the upper line is restated by the Strawberry Seller herself (c), its new harmonic "direction" is the result of a wandering bass line (the astringent inner-voice harmonies compress into one central register the pitches polarized in [b] as competing layers).

If Aschenbach is "alienated" (as Piper has said) from the object of his gaze by the "melancholy gaiety" of the gamelan, this reflects his typically restless and chromatic musical persona.[31] But the alienation here is that of writerly contemplation, an ironic detachment from the scene *as he construes it*, rather than from the more objective operatic reality implicit in the conventions of a "phenomenal performance" audible to others on stage. Aschenbach's alienation from the gamelan dances, then, is of a different mimetic order than the adults' musico-dramatic isolation from Miles and Flora in the *Screw*, listening in on the "Lavender's Blue" rhyme (see Chapter 4 above). In *Venice*, the children, including Tadzio, are captive of the writer's gaze alone. Aschenbach's "detached and solitary way," his eschewal of social exchange with the guests, is of his own making, for he has chosen – as he admits in a recitative – to live "not words, but beauty, to exist in it, and of it."

The music catches Aschenbach's growing absorption in Tadzio himself. The children's Balinese idiom employs only mallet-percussion, its special brightness based likewise on the characteristic intervals in a synthetic modal collection (see the second passage in Ex. 6.12, c). Tadzio's thematic presence, though still Balinese in sound and inspiration, is consistently more blended, less exclusively percussion-oriented, than the beach games, and employs a very different tonal palette.[32] His vibraphone theme first

Ex. 6.12: (a) Aschenbach's view of the beach, Scene 5; (b) stratified pitch oppositions in the first children's game; (c) The children's melody restated by the Strawberry Seller (earlier pitch oppositions compressed into a single register). The synthetic pitch collection of the second beach game; (d) Return of Tadzio's theme, end of Scene 5; (e) Tadzio's theme reharmonized

(a)

(b)

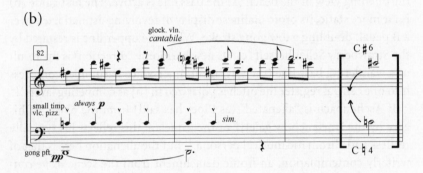

(c)

Ex. 6.12 (*cont.*)

(d)

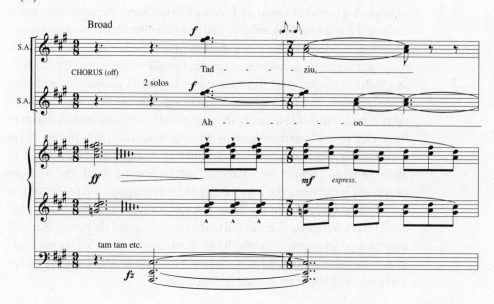

(e)

appears here against a heterophonic clarinet line, joined by bassoon as Aschenbach comments on the boy's "dark side." At the end of the beach scene, the same theme twice returns. The first return (Ex. 6.12d) comes in an imposing gamelan *kebiar*-style ensemble outburst, its pentatonic mode enhanced (G♮ is a new ingredient) and grounded firmly on a stable A tonic. The range evident in these two statements – a bold tutti, then a softer, transfiguring A-major counterstatement for solo vibraphone (Ex. 6.12e) – sets Tadzio's music apart from the other children's games. Aschenbach's gaze rests most intently on "Eros his very self," the score implies. Tadzio's calm A-major music is actually the first simple *root-position* triadicism of the entire opera (warmed here by the major-seventh, G♯, in the vibraphone). The A-major tonic is as sustained as Aschenbach's bids for an E-major tonic in Scene 1 were fleeting; within Scene 5 itself, the A-major climax is a response to the wandering triadic aspirations (on G, A♭, and A♮ roots) of the scene's opening. Triadic purity – a sign of Aschenbach's contented state, watching – acts as foil to the more crowded chromaticism, still over an A pedal point, with which the scene dissolves. As Tadzio smilingly joins his mother's party, he moves beyond the field of Aschenbach's gaze, a move to which the score is acutely responsive.

4. "One moment of reality": the love vow as focal utterance

Aschenbach's climactic expression of love for Tadzio stands apart from the operatic selfhood of earlier in Act 1. Where earlier scenes reveal a subjectivity largely through the experiential channels of sensory perception, the love vow itself aspires briefly to public utterance. When Aschenbach sings "I love you" (Ex. 6.13c), he attempts, for perhaps the only moment in the opera, to move beyond a relationship of gazes. As listeners, we must believe in the sincerity of that attempt, if the chaotic loss of selfhood of Act 2 is to have meaning. Tadzio himself is already beyond earshot, but the vow remains an arresting shift – a turn away from the psychological "inner speech" of earlier scenes (words as the semiotic material of consciousness) to the possibility of addressing another.[33] Abandoning delusionary fantasies ("I must speak to him, we will become friends"), Aschenbach speaks directly: "I love you." The announcement of erotic feelings – voiced for and *to* Tadzio – is one of those intense, heightened utterances so idiomatic to opera as a dramatic medium. The "I love you" formula is, Aschenbach later remarks, hackneyed and inadequate, and yet the words sound urgent and passionate; as the score says, he is "realizing the truth at last." Such force of utterance comes about by a

Ex. 6.13: The love vow in context, end of Scene 7

(a)

Ex. 6.13 (*cont.*)

(b)

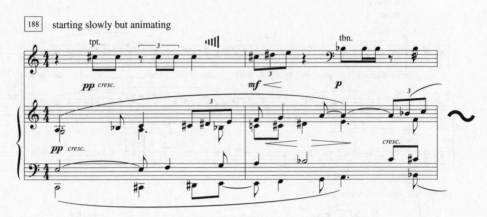

(c)   (realizing the truth at last.)

dense confluence of returning themes, and as the culmination of the scene's wider harmonic and rhythmic energies.

"I love you" flows out of the essay-writing aria ("When thought becomes feeling") as a climactic speech act breaking free of both the distorted reality of earlier orchestral music and the detachment of Aschenbach's piano recitatives. "Love" is more than a belated revelation of forces latent since the opera's *Tristan*-saturated opening; the vow is a dramatic ictus, acting like Grimes's "God have mercy" cry, as a pivot. From here onwards, the opera turns on its dark side to the protagonist's outright destruction (in Mann, too, "I love you" is significantly placed to close the penultimate chapter). As in *Grimes*, the moment of epiphany defines itself in thematic revelation and tonal closure, signaling "arrival" in several domains at once. A further *Grimes*-like touch is rhetorical: after its announcement, the new theme undergoes emphatic orchestral elaboration, set off from the main dramatic action, but positioned so as to magnify the image of a focal utterance. In *Grimes*, the process occurs in the passacaglia; in *Venice*, Aschenbach's "I love you" is taken up immediately in the opera's longest wordless passage of orchestral music, a Mahlerian string adagio beginning Act 2.[34]

To get at how the love vow makes its great effect is to speak of opera's precise control over the pace, density, and flow of dramatic events.[35] Opera's "arrivals" – its moments of revelation – work in ways not open to spoken drama or literary narrative. A sense of sudden epiphany can be rooted in more dense overlay of reference than is possible in the less polyphonic world of the play, or the linear sequence of literary narration. All this is true of the love vow as a verbal utterance preceded by a crowding-in of motivic references from various points in the earlier action (see Ex. 6.13a). Aschenbach's fear that "the heat of the sun must have made me ill" coincides with orchestral murmurings of the Marvels theme of his Scene 1 visions. The Marvels shape reasserts itself now at several different pitch levels, in counterpoint with a new vocal idea ("so longing passes back and forth"), with the stage entrance of Tadzio's mother (to her familiar theme), and, finally, with a return to Tadzio's coy smile-music (first heard in Scene 5). The first three motives here are all chromatic, malleable in tonal implications, interwoven, in this case, with a bass-line ascent that strives for the E tonic first mooted in Scene 1 at "I, Aschenbach." The thematic process, in other words, coincides with a harmonic one, as Aschenbach's E tonic is brought into a functional (quasi-dominant) relationship with Tadzio's A tonic.

Tonal considerations aside, the intensity of the musical drama to the moment of Tadzio's smile depends both on the rapid accumulation and contrapuntal overlay of motives, and on discursive contrasts. Leitmotivic utterance has a range of articulations, for Aschenbach's vocal presentation of the new "Longing" theme coincides with insistent reiteration of the more compact Marvels shape, and between its initial statement and its return, Tadzio's mother appears. One hears a texted vocal theme conveying the protagonist's inner feelings ("longing"), a contrasting orchestral theme identifying a stage character (Tadzio's mother), and the return of a theme (Marvels) without direct links to those on stage at this point. The return of the Marvels shape is among the first signs of an orchestral utterance not tied to the consciousness of any single character.[36] (Whether the orchestra is ever a "commenting" narrator-like presence is a question I return to below, discussing Act 2.)

The packed accumulation of returning themes does not exhaust itself with Tadzio's smile. What follows – an accelerating orchestral crescendo (Ex. 6.13b–c) that ascends in register to Aschenbach's final vocal outburst – is itself recapitulatory, a vast expansion of earlier desire-music. The great emotional distance between the inarticulate desires of Scene 1 and the present moment of realization is audible in a harmonic transformation from diatonic to octatonic modality.[37] Motivic return is embedded in this orchestral crescendo, too; its intensity is not simply a matter of "ascent" in various parameters. Thus the flickering brass soli echo the nervous ostinati of Aschenbach's unease in Munich. This first definitive utterance of an "I" attempting to reach a "you" is woven of two thematic strands, string and wind musics, both associated directly with Aschenbach in his private and public identity ("my mind beats on" . . . "I, Aschenbach"), yet initially presented as autonomous musical acts. Here, they fuse in the orchestra, while Aschenbach's vocal line at Example 6.13c takes the form of a response to the rising-third impulse of Tadzio's smile.

With its quivering melodic shocks, the orchestral ascent transforms the languor of the earlier desire-music into a newly visceral, animated gesture. Given the sluggish, quietly dazed atmosphere of the drone opening Act 2, the connotations of "I love you" as erotic climax are as much somatic as spiritual. The massive release of tension, though, is grounded not only in the motivic argument parsed above; the love vow resolves harmonic and rhythmic tensions rife throughout the preceding scene.

"I love you" appears, harmonically speaking, as a firm arrival on triadic E major, closing a scene commanded by hypnotic A tonics personifying first Apollo, and then – as Aschenbach writes – a literary vision of Tadzio himself. The entire Games of Apollo ballet is framed by that freezing of all harmonic activity familiar from Aschenbach's sonic gaze

Ex. 6.14: Tonal stasis in Apollo's first appearance, Scene 7

at the beach. As the "spell-bound man" visualizes the children's games as enactments of Hellenic myths (Phoebus driving a chariot, and so on), a world "gilded with mythical significance" closes around him (Mann 49). In the opera, we hear this in the way that Scene 7 settles on the plateau-like A tonic in Apollo's vocal appearances (Ex. 6.14), and throughout the writing aria.

When Aschenbach awakes from his reveries and writes his hymnic essay under Tadzio's inspiration, the music fuses the love-object (the static Tadzio-chord grounding each vocal phrase in Ex. 6.15a) with the rhythmic bursts of Apollo. These fibrillating signals break out of the metric balance of the dance rhythms of the ballet. Aschenbach writes in Apollo's rhythms, yet as his own excitement mounts, they tumble out uncontrollably. The aroused lover approaches the boy, but cannot speak (Ex. 6.15b). Apollo's oracular warning ("Love that beauty causes is frenzy, god-inspired") is confirmed in a shooting-forth of coiled rhythmic impulses, devoid of metric control.

The whole sequence – from the Games to the failed approach to Tadzio – prepares the closing love vow. After the mounting rhythmic frenzy, the unbroken welling-up of the orchestral crescendo and Aschenbach's final vocal phrase amount to a physically charged gesture of release. His new intoxication crystallizes in vibrating gestures that resonate all the way back to the opera's opening. The love vow is a focal utterance, "one moment of reality" deepened by sense impressions of all that has gone before. The visceral power of the gesture, equally, prefigures the Dionysiac chaos that in Act 2 will spell the dissolution of Aschenbach's former operatic self.

Ex. 6.15: (a) Aschenbach writes in Apolline rhythms, anchored by Tadzio harmonies; (b) more frenzied rhythms at Tadzio's approach, Scene 7

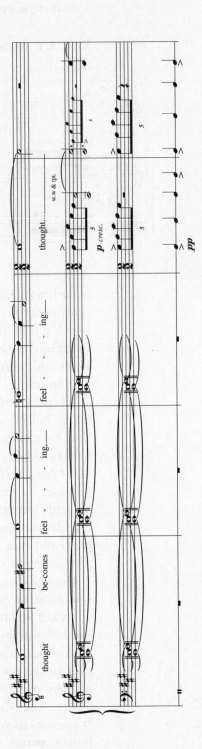

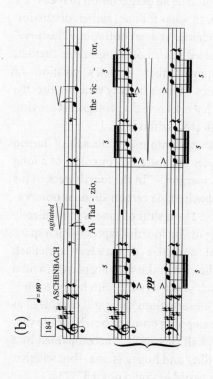

5. "Bliss of madness": the shattered operatic self in Act 2

> . . . it was only his Apollinian consciousness which, like a veil, hid this
> Dionysian world from his vision.   Nietzsche, *The Birth of Tragedy*, ch. 2

Aschenbach himself, as thinking, watching, and experiencing subject is central to the music of Act 1; everything we hear in the orchestra from the distorted realism of the boat journey all the way to the final love vow, speaks directly of the writer as a center of consciousness – music, in this context, denotes hidden mental activity. This ultra-subjective mode, I have claimed, is heard in moments of pronounced orchestral layering: when the texture is sharply polarized, the depth of psychic reality as we familiarly conceptualize it is palpable.[38] Similarly, the opera's stark shifts, from orchestral to percussion-orchestral colors, as well as to the self-conscious "detached" reality of the piano recitatives, are all different manifestations of Aschenbach's experiencing consciousness. All of this will change in Act 2, and if the demise of the recitatives is one sign of Aschenbach's failing "self-possession" (his phrase), it is by no means the only one. The shattered operatic self of Act 2, I will argue, is evident in further techniques of thematic and textural distortion. But it would be an exaggeration to speak of a complete eclipse of operatic presence. In what follows, rather, discussion will turn on the opera's revelation of character as a continuous "history," an identity perpetuated in the ever-varied return of recognizable themes, textures, and colors. I do not suggest that Britten's creation of Aschenbach's operatic self recapitulates Mann's literary scheme directly, yet there are obvious parallels, for both works reveal a protagonist moving ever further from the possibility of reflective selfhood.

In Mann's novella, Aschenbach's descent into manic pursuit of Tadzio and finally, to a choleric death, occupies the sustained intensity of a long final chapter. From its matter-of-fact opening – "In the fourth week of his stay on the Lido, Gustave von Aschenbach made certain singular observations touching the world about him" (52) – a shift of tone is immediately felt, away from the mythic detail of the idyllic fourth chapter (which spans several weeks' events) to a more realistic narrative (of just a few days). Each episode – feverish pursuit of Tadzio, the visit of the strolling players, a final physical collapse – deepens Aschenbach's loss of touch with his surroundings, "driven by his mania" (52). The "observations" he is still capable of as the chapter opens are soon to vanish; stepping onto the beach for the very last time, his giddy feelings are only "half physical . . . accompanied by a swiftly mounting dread, a sense of futility and hopelessness – but whether this referred to himself or to the outer world he could not tell" (73).

In its literary form, Aschenbach's decline comes to the reader by manipulation of narrative viewpoint. From a narrator closely identified with Aschenbach's own thoughts and moods, the novella moves, in the fifth chapter, to a voice of growing detachment, evident in discursive comments. The whole sordid path of his decay is given a pseudo-classical frame by the narrator, emulating the protagonist's former habits of thought, even while articulating his overall loss of "reason":

> ... it would be untrue to say he suffered. Mind and heart were drunk with passion, his footsteps guided by the daemonic power whose pastime it is to trample on human reason and dignity. (55)

The narratorial habit of distancing Aschenbach by descriptive periphrasis (the "spell-bound man"; "the fond fool"; 49, 54)[39] becomes more pronounced in the final chapter, where he is most frequently *der Einsame* – "the solitary one"[40] – and Tadzio "his idol," "his charmer," or, again reverting to a mythic register, "instrument of a mocking deity" (52, 54, 66). Such formulae dissociate narrator and protagonist, a strategy reaching its harsh extreme in the scornful depiction of Aschenbach, collapsed at the well – "There he sat, the master; this was he who had found a way to reconcile art and honours" (71) – the sarcasm a parody of the account of Aschenbach's public career earlier in the story.[41]

Britten's operatic *Death in Venice* offers a significant shift of emphasis in its treatment of Aschenbach's demise. Colin Graham sums this up in saying that "Mann's story is sadistic in its treatment and observation of Aschenbach's plight whereas Britten's is compassionate."[42] Examining directly the scenes in which Aschenbach's failing control is first revealed – Scenes 9–10, "The Pursuit" and "The Strolling Players" – it will be possible to develop a more fine-grained view of this operatic compassion. As will emerge, Britten's score eschews the kind of orchestral narrative that constitutes a judging voice detached from Aschenbach's own. Mann's sadism is restricted mostly, in Britten, to the scene of the Strolling Players, where irony results from a phenomenal performance, rather than a separation between Aschenbach's vocal persona and the supporting pit orchestra. In the absence of a judging rhetoric, the question remains as to how the opera shows the *collapse* of its subject – a dismantling of the operatic self – without the discursive resources of literary narration. Here, I argue, attention must focus on intrinsically operatic means, notably a special density of thematic reference and recall, and on other dimensions of the musical idiom – its great textural fluidity, and ever-shifting possibilities of harmonic inflection.

(a) The pursuit (Scene 9)

The dramatic force of the pursuit scene is in the first place a question of form. The passacaglia scheme centering on a returning bass pattern is an effective symbol of mounting obsession (just as the Screw theme's varied returns symbolize a sinister, all-controlling mechanism at Bly). In Aschenbach's case, though, far more than the obsessive quality of thematic repetition is at work; what we witness too is the struggle of passionate utterance set within an ostensibly strict frame. A dialectic underlies the psychological truth of the passacaglia,[43] a relentlessly churning amalgam of the free and the strict. The path traced is harmonically fixed in the short term, yet unpredictably mobile over longer stretches of musical time (Ex. 6.16 summarizes). Roving but circular in form, the theme is rooted to a framing E pedal. From E, the scene moves with Aschenbach to four new pitch levels, each group of statements corresponding to one locale among his peregrinations around Venice (the café, San Marco, and so on). Each transposition brings a faster tempo; when a G tonic arrives, moreover, the urgency of this feverish chase is stepped up by truncating the theme itself.

The precise gestural form of the passacaglia theme is personal to Aschenbach. Beyond the motivated, actional level of its incessant quarter-note tread, leitmotivic reference identifies not one, but two themes. Both recall the rapid succession at the climactic ending of Act 1 – the "longing" theme as a melody supported by a bass line that elaborates the climactic "I love you" vow (both motives return now at their initial pitch-level, E). By the interwoven density of its dual reference, the thematic complex is (in Erich Auerbach's phrase) "fraught with background" (12) – its surface beckons to a further level of meaning. What began in separate vocal utterances now reaches a new, fused, state. As the passacaglia begins, the rapid pace of events in performance, and the density of the voice-and-orchestra texture, veils conscious awareness of these thematic origins; the connection is confirmed only in retrospect, at that later point in the chase when Aschenbach, exhausted, lingers silently outside Tadzio's bedroom, and the two themes unravel in an instrumental fantasy. The drone here immediately links this moment to an earlier one – the Act 2 Prologue – and so by the magic of leitmotivic association, the semantic pregnancy of the passacaglia itself is manifest.

A more distant context informs the shape of the passacaglia theme – that of the Wagnerian allusions of the opera's opening. No actual *Tristan* chords are heard, but their dissonant framework of unresolved sevenths is reproduced at the pitch levels of Wagner's famous Prelude (Ex. 6.17).

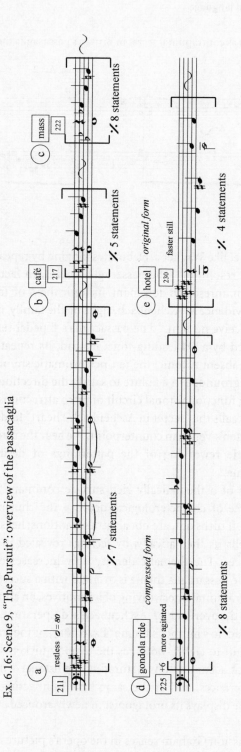

Ex. 6.16: Scene 9, "The Pursuit": overview of the passacaglia

Ex. 6.17: *Tristan* as contrapuntal secret in Britten's passacaglia theme

Britten's theme, like Wagner's, elaborates longing by repeatedly withholding harmonic resolution. The passacaglia begins, in fact, as a perpetual hovering on an unresolved dominant, its tonic the A of Tadzio's mode, so forcefully in evidence as Aschenbach, sighting the family, madly proclaims "they must receive no hint." The passacaglia's E pedal remains tentative, never tonicized by a D♯ leading-tone; instead, its repeated ascent to G♯ aspires to the absent A tonic: the ten-pc chromaticism of the passacaglia theme is thus grounded in a failure to satisfy the directional tendencies of an underlying functional-tonal circuit of pitch attractions. What Mann at several points calls the "secret in Aschenbach's heart" finds sounding realization in Britten's Venetian counterpoint. We hear the traces of a thematic secret, a subtle reworking of the patternings of desire that animate Wagner's drama.

The details of a thematically rich surface command attention as an operatic source of characterological depth – the churnings of Aschenbach's desires, it turns out, are not arbitrary motions; he is "driven on," the passacaglia tells us thematically, by feelings revealed in his own earlier vocal utterances. The thematic density only increases once the pursuit begins, and the passacaglia theme is overlaid with a succession of melodic ideas. By contrapuntal interweaving of leitmotives, an audience is exposed to the semantic overload of Aschenbach's desperation. In the blurred shimmer of Tadzio's mother's theme (Ex. 6.18a), or the frantic rhythms of the sudden shift to eighth-notes, as the tempo quickens (Ex. 6.18b), one hears effects of accumulation. Saturating the listener with multiple back and cross-references, and at the same time reinflecting their harmonic basis, the score displays its protagonist in newly aroused and chaotic states of being.

The compassion Graham senses in the opera's picture of Aschenbach is found in the total identification of the orchestral thematic discourse with

Ex. 6.18 Textural-thematic density in the passacaglia: (a) Tadzio's mother's theme; (b) the "I love you" vow returns at the orchestral tutti

(a)

(b)

his inner turmoil. The pursuit scene is every bit as subjective as earlier scenes; like them, it uses the orchestra to support and amplify Aschenbach's vocal presence. This absorption of the orchestra by the protagonist is evident in actual doubling, when he adds his own words ("yet am I driven on," repeated in a hypnotic and dizzying build-up) to the Desire theme spinning in the orchestra, and later, in vocal echoes of the frantic tutti outburst (Ex. 6.18b). There can be no question, at such moments, of a detached orchestral voice. This impression is confirmed, too, by those thematic aspects of the scene independent of the passacaglia itself. When Aschenbach's boarding of a gondola is accompanied by the Serenissima motive, rescored for gamelan percussion, it is clear, as Mervyn Cooke says, that "Venice for him now means only one thing – Tadzio" (1987: 214 n. 11). When the violin tune in the café orchestra's waltz plays scraps of melody that audibly transform themselves into Tadzio's vibraphone theme (in a glittering solo, R214), the orchestral texture – even when ostensibly functioning as realistic street-music – turns out to be yet another version of Aschenbach's obsession. The "self" and the "outer world" (to recall the opposition of Mann's own text) are indistinguishable. Inner and outer realms are one.

(b) The Strolling Players (Scene 10)

To argue that Aschenbach's operatic self is an all-encompassing thematic presence, dominating the orchestral texture even at moments where the music has a "realistic" scenic significance (the sound of café music, say), is not to ignore the opera's clear delineation of inner and outer experience. Rather, it is to confirm how for Aschenbach, outer-world experience is colored by the deeper reality of passion. The café orchestra plays, but the sounds we hear, however "accurate" as café music, are still mediated – the product of Aschenbach's perceptions. The opposition between what Carolyn Abbate (1991) terms "noumenal" and "phenomenal" performance in opera – music heard only by an audience, and music heard on stage too – is at such times a fluid one. Yet it remains relevant to those episodes in the pursuit scene where real-world phenomenal performances occur (the café-orchestra, the sung blessing at San Marco). At such points, the incursion of "real" sounds into the chaos of the pursuit either confirms just how circumscribed by obsession are Aschenbach's perceptions of the surrounding world – as café and Tadzio musics mingle, for instance – or else signals a momentary release from the tumult of the subjective – as at San Marco, where the modal "Kyrie" chant sounds distant from the chromatic wanderings of the main passacaglia music.

The Strolling Players' scene provides a more extended release from Aschenbach's perceptions, for it is mostly taken up with pit orchestral music giving the illusion of emanating from the stage scene, "on the terrace outside the hotel." The popularism of the Players' ditties mixes banal dance accompaniments with brash, unblended timbres to mimic the strumming of open guitar strings (a harp) and wheezing accordion sounds (woodwinds). The orchestral realism, though deftly stylized, is divorced from Aschenbach's consciousness, and yet the opera avoids treating the orchestra as a voice condemning its protagonist. The songs all slyly refer to Aschenbach's pathetic situation ("does a young man want to give an old woman kisses?") but their stage-music realism ensures that audiences hear them at face value – as the live music Aschenbach hears too. The scene draws analogies, but stops short of judgment. However savage the climax of the laughing-song – as violent, in its way, as a work like Henze's *El Cimarrón*, (heard at Aldeburgh in 1970) – the threat to Aschenbach is oblique; his own "ridiculous" infatuation remains invisible to the other guests. We witness in the Players' scene a carefully staged burlesque of Aschenbach, but the opera – unlike the novella – avoids humiliating its protagonist by narrative intervention.

The Players' scene is almost entirely a phenomenal performance. The exceptions are those moments when orchestral Marvels-shapes cluster menacingly during Aschenbach's brief exchange with the Leader of the Players. Leitmotivic reference identifies the plague threat (the topic of Aschenbach's questions) with the tropical vision back in Munich, and in the scurrying postlude, scales identify the Leader with the Traveller of Act 1. There is a shift of discursive level here: Aschenbach's subjectivity is interrupted by thematic shapes that bear leitmotivic meaning for an audience; we broach the uncanny-mythic level of Aschenbach's story. In doing so, we sense an inevitability to events. Aschenbach's loss of dignity stands "explained" – or rather, left unexplained – as a thing fated. With an undertow of the fantastic, Dorrit Cohn notes, Mann's story subverts the authority of any single narratorial perspective (192–93). In Britten's operatic *Death in Venice*, too, the uncanny figure of the Traveller and his alter egos, and his associated Marvels shape, are conspicuously identified with the plague as an unstoppable physical fact, yet remain otherwise enigmatic. When the Marvels theme appears, the orchestra stands apart from Aschenbach himself and the opera's core of subjective experience. But such gestures remain at the level of omens, not judgments.

6. "I go now": parting utterance

> Opera is a highly artificial art form in which nothing corresponds to the facts
> as we know them and the music has to answer for the credibility of the
> oddest and most exceptional states of mind.   Henze (1998: 32–33)

Aschenbach's last words of recitative – his final rational, self-possessed utterance, one might say – are a surrendering to fate, and to a coming departure: "Let the gods do what they will with me." In the opera's closing scenes (the return to the Hotel Barber, the last visit to Venice and to the deserted Lido beach) his much-prized "self-possession" recedes as the time of departure nears. As the Barber holds up his mirror, the image Aschenbach sees staring back is a vulgar counterfeit. The opera's abandonment of contemplative recitatives is itself an abandonment of the possibility of self-reflection, a final severing of ties to an earlier singing self. Aschenbach, as the face in the Barber's mirror, resembles the made-up fop, while it is the Barber who, admiring his "masterpiece," assumes now the writerly tones of a connoisseur. As Aschenbach consigns himself to the role of one of his own early heroes, "passive in the face of fate," one is reminded that all images of self – philosophical, literary, operatic – are reflections, the traces of an implicit doubleness. Division, as Irving Howe puts it, is both "premise and price of consciousness," for "what knows the awareness of self if not the self?"[44]

Aschenbach's tragedy, in its parting phase, unfolds as a retreat from self-knowledge. But his death, even in its denial of the possibility of a reflexive experience of selfhood, is authentically an operatic death. The very manner and force of its disintegrative momentum are a kind of self-definition, rather than merely an eclipse.[45] To hear the drama as a straight-forward destruction of what was once coherent is to over-simplify. Aschenbach, for all his cosmetic garb, is no Pentheus; he is not torn to shreds in one frenzy of destruction. In Britten's inflected operatic retelling of the *Bacchae* myth, moreover, it is Tadzio who, in Aschenbach's night-mare, becomes the sacrifice, a symbolic action accomplished in musico-thematic terms (the amalgamation of his theme with the twisting Marvels shape).[46] The dream, no doubt, allows us and Aschenbach to understand by analogy – to recognize in Tadzio the lure of a Dionysiac power that will soon destroy the writer himself. But my point, again, is that his departure is accomplished by a distortion of the operatic self, not by its extinction. Our perceptions of Aschenbach, in fact, are *deepened* by this distortion. Characterological depth arises in the very moment of his physical and mental decay – and the decay itself is perceptible through a tracing of per-sonal identity in the return of operatic themes.

It is this "historical," time-bound aspect of Aschenbach's operatic self that we are most aware of in the final few scenes. The parting utterance, here, is none other than the familiar semantic work of leitmotivic return. The famous writer may have lost all self-reflective faculties, but an audi-ence remains attuned to the subtle or blatant contrasts between a present thematic utterance and an operatic past. As the themes we identify with (or better, *as*) Aschenbach return in atrophied, dying forms, their cumula-tive meanings accrue. The Aschenbach of the closing scenes – manic, exhausted, out of control – is no less vividly present than at any other point in the opera. Unlike Vere, he does not retreat behind an orchestral mask as crisis strikes. Unhinged and "powerless in the demon's grip" (68), Aschenbach's operatic self does not fall silent, but endures with a literally feverish intensity.

Musical symbols of distortion and atrophy are part of the more volatile operatic presence who steps out of the Barber's chair and into a gondola for a last trip to Venice (Scene 16). The familiar Barcarolle travel music, remade now in a heavier brass-dominated scoring, and with a more weighty rhythmic undertow, possesses a new menace. Aschenbach's sung

Ex. 6.19: The Tadzio chord and Pursuit theme, distorted, Scene 16

TADZIO chord,
transposed

words at this point are all borrowed, memories of the youths' and the fop's crude ditties on the boat to Venice. An unfamiliar roughness comes to the fore: Tadzio's identifying vibraphone chord, for instance, once a pristine modal force field within which Aschenbach's own contemplation was bound (cf. Ex. 6.11, above), is now sullied in his tonally confused mumblings. As the Poles appear, and one last round of pursuit begins, the boy's chord is itself subject to harsh distortion. In the uncharacteristically violent attack of ensemble percussion (rather than in the limpid solo vibraphone), roving transpositions of Tadzio's chord (Ex. 6.19) are an aural shock, the loss of a previous ideal defined by its absolute tonal fixity (even in the Dionysiac nightmare, Tadzio's theme retains its A tonic).

The new vehemence in Aschenbach's pursuit is evident too in the equally frantic manipulations attending the returning passacaglia theme (the other element in Ex. 6.19). Gone are the urgent but obsessive strivings of its earlier form; Aschenbach here is lost in a frenzied wandering. The canonic mirror process is strict (upper voices invert the lower pair) but sounds "free," so aimless are the individual lines. The bass line too has lost its anchoring adherence to a single pedal pitch, the focus of a circular melodic contour. Dissonance, in this newly chromatic harmonic-contrapuntal setting, is harsher, and more persistently thwarts an intervallic "desire" for resolution.[47] The two components of the texture – the Tadzio chords and the canon – follow separate, unpredictable, transposition schemes; only with a return to Tadzio's original A-mode, as Aschenbach catches the boy's full gaze ("he saw me, and did not betray me") does the "chaos and sickness" show signs of abating.

Ex. 6.20: The empty orchestral space of Scene 16

Aschenbach, at this moment, loses sight of Tadzio. The unraveling of the orchestral canon at this point is a reminder that his state, however distracted, is still revealed in a musical "translation" of his sensory perception. The "out-of-normal-focus" quality in Act 1 relies, we saw, on a set of textural choices – a heterophonic, blurred polyphony, the surface-depth effects of stratified registral spaces, and the static harmonies of gamelan-inspired percussion sonorities. Comparable (though never identical) textural arguments attend the distinctive milieu late in Act 2. A pronounced feature in this distorted soundscape is that of the "emptied-out" orchestral space, evacuated to its outer extremes. Aschenbach's final encounter with the Strawberry Seller embodies a migration to registral limits, and a striking reduction to solo colors (Ex. 6.20). The polarized division of the registral space here goes beyond an earlier topography of heights and depths (the latter prominent in the Travel Bureau scene, with its febrile bass clarinet). The Strawberry Seller's music, as phenomenal song, presents a sounding image of the outside world. But it is an image in which the filter of Aschenbach's listening perception distorts more wildly than in the Players' songs.

The Strawberry Seller intrudes on the pursuit, and her song is framed registrally by its chaotic unravelling of imitative lines, though the rhythmic lethargy opening Example 6.20 is equally a sign of Aschenbach's physical exhaustion. The remote, exotic quality of this passage results from a precarious tonal balance, articulated in the schematic registral discourse (the tonal aspect of Britten's idiom being inextricably linked to considerations of texture). Widely separated upper- and lower-register pedals (on B and G) frame a gnomic, yet warm dominant-seventh chord. Distortion here – as with the Pursuit theme, is perceived against the backdrop of an accrued, leitmotivic history: we remember the Strawberry Seller of Scene 5, and we hear how desolate she sounds now, compared with then.

A comparable tonal indeterminacy governs the Manager's dialogue with the Porter in the hotel lobby (Ex. 6.21a), though in this case, the mood is very different. We cannot ascribe a loss of tonal focus to Aschenbach's perceiving presence: this is the one scene in which, prophetically, he is initially absent from the stage. The Manager's Act 1 chorales (cf. Ex. 6.10), as empty of tonal meaning as his greetings were vacuous, return here to create the scene's odd conjunction of the desolate and the pompous. An F♯-minor home tonic hovers just out of aural reach, its triadic function masked in the upper-stratum brass chords by an intrusive fourth pitch (D), and in the lower stratum by modal complications. Aschenbach's final exit to the deserted beach (Ex. 6.21b) presents a similar aural "distance." Loss of actual pitch definition here reflects the idiosyncratic scoring: two solo double basses, in tingling parallel seconds.

The tonal desolation of this soundscape provides the backdrop, in the opera's closing moments, for its two final oases of tonal clarity. In the "Phaedrus" dialogue by the well, all that was chaotic and undisciplined in the pursuit music is brought under control. The dialogue, I noted earlier, is stripped of the harsh narratorial judgment of Mann's narrative; in the opera, nothing compromises its lucid calm, as a moment of truth, a protagonist's anagnorisis,[48] albeit couched in philosophical abstraction. In a score that opens with a confusion of ostinati pulsations and places such prominence on the blurring of part-writing distinctions via heterophony, the "Phaedrus" aria startles one with its simple, note-against-note counterpoint in two voices (Ex. 6.22). Gone, suddenly, is the exhausted non-alignment of shadowy voices, and the mismatch of inversion gone awry (as in the final pursuit music). Inversion here underpins an exquisite and sharply etched logic – the aria sounds as a philosophical dialogue, played out in lines that, while not devoid of chromatic difficulties, restrict themselves to plain triadic shapes.

This new tonic of C major, transfigured by an added sixth, A, echoes a Mahlerian sign of departure.[49] Beyond this, though, it elaborates, within *Death in Venice* itself, the tonal origin of Aschenbach's focal "I love you"

Ex. 6.21: (a) Tonal indeterminacy at the opening of the final scene; (b) loss of pitch clarity; (c) valedictory cadences to Aschenbach's E-major tonic

(a)

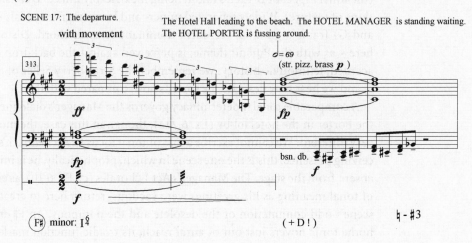

(b)

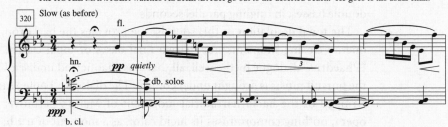

(c)

Ex. 6.22: The return of textural and tonal simplicity in the "Phaedrus" aria

utterance, which had concluded Act 1 with a decisive tonicization of a luminous E tonic, approached (in quasi-plagal manner) from the different brightness of a C added-sixth chord. Aschenbach's new state, in the "Phaedrus" dialogue, reflects his loss of a tonal selfhood. When, moments before, his "I, Aschenbach" fanfares trail off indeterminately, we hear an inability to secure, even in self-assertion, the shards of a tonal identity rooted on E. It is here that the lambent natural harmonics of the "Phaedrus" chords steal in magically, at the new, transcendent level of C. Beyond this point, indeed, E major belongs not to Aschenbach himself, but to the Manager. His obsequious patter, even at its most duplicitously ominous ("no doubt the Signore will be leaving us soon") controls the stable E-major tonic that eludes Aschenbach himself. Only in the valedictory form of cadences – musico-rhetorical symbols for death as an end – is there tonal rest (c, Ex. 6.21).[50]

For Aschenbach, a more lasting tonal security is found only at the very moment of his death, in the calm ecstasy of an orchestral epilogue. Here is apotheosis as the retreat beyond human perception, to the numinous. The earlier discourse of registral extremity is here transfigured, with Tadzio's modal theme hovering in coexistence with the melody of Aschenbach's Act 1 "Eros" aria, the two lines grounded by a timeless drone, oscillating endlessly between the salient boundary-pitches of Tadzio's mode (only after the Act 1 love vow do we earlier hear such a drone). Here, finally, is Aschenbach's tonal and thematic union with his beloved. As apotheosis, this is one final, expansive gesture of thematic return. The melody, in this case, evades the atrophy that surrounded Aschenbach's closing vocal moments. What we hear instead is an utterance revoiced at the distanced level of myth. That which was vibrant and passionate is now, in its much-extended, slow-motion incarnation, ecstatic. The theme here stands apart from Aschenbach's physical body, slumped before us on the stage – less an utterance than a memory. The orchestral voicing of Aschenbach's apostrophe to Tadzio, as speech, hovers at the boundaries of the ineffable. Through the instrumental return of the "Eros" melody, the drama recedes beyond the articulate. In this, the most commanding of the opera's parting utterances, eloquence resides beyond the word, and finally, in a prolonged dying-away motion, the orchestral voice recedes to an aural vanishing-point, beyond hearing.

Notes

1 Introduction: Britten's musical language

1 The *Oxford English Dictionary* traces "utter," as an adjective, to a comparative form of the Old English root *út* (out); as a verb, "utter" resembles the Dutch *uiteren* and the German *äussern* (to announce, declare, bring forth).

2 Boys 236; Britten 1944: 4; Schafer 118; Stein 1953b: 150; Britten's comment in a newspaper article published on the occasion of his fiftieth birthday refers in similarly broad terms to a quality of musical utterance: "I haven't yet achieved the simplicity I should like in my music" (1963: 9).

3 Sackville-West 1944: 115; Britten's piano textures, in the *Michelangelo Sonnets*, are simple, he notes (73); cf. Erwin Stein's comments on the economy of Britten's *Grimes* orchestration (1953a: 116).

4 Both Sackville-West, in his 1944 *Horizon* article, and Goddard, in a 1946 portrait, draw attention to an alleged "insensitivity to prosody as such" (Sackville-West 116, n. 1) in Britten's verse settings. The related topic of speech rhythms is taken up in White's 1948 monograph, with examples from *Grimes* of both conversational parlando and more stylized prolongation of syllable lengths in the kind of "high-handed treatment of words" Britten himself advocated as the opera composer's prerogative in dramatic scenes (Britten 1983: 149). Stein (1953b) explores the issue of text setting as an outgrowth of Britten's English-language setting in *Budd* and *Grimes*. Sackville-West mentions Britten's skill with word painting, an "aptitude for finding phrases that delineate the visible world," no doubt with the experience of collaborating on the 1943 radio feature *The Rescue* fresh in his mind (1944: 117).

5 For a typically acute defense of operatic dramaturgy against devotees of theatrical models, see Dahlhaus 1989; influential studies of narrative in opera are Abbate 1991 and 1996; Hyer suggests the value of Abbate's narrative categories to Baroque opera; Feldman explores *opera seria* dramaturgy via anthropological accounts of ritual; an important metacritical view of the Wagnerian leitmotive is Grey 1996; among recent accounts of operatic subjectivity, see Žižek (for psychoanalytic insights) and Tomlinson (a transhistorical essay). Valuable perspectives on narrative and genre-based meanings in non-texted music include Hatten and Street.

6 An exception is Kaminsky's recent study of the promise in *Don Giovanni*, drawing on Austinian speech-act theory; for an exploration of what speech-act theory might hold for untexted instrumental works, see also London. Observing the challenge, in recent linguistic thought, to notions of language

as a vehicle of stable reference, David J. Levin remarks that "we can no longer simply juxtapose music's ability to emote with language's ability to concretize and refer" (Levin 9).

7 Cook's wide-ranging survey (1998: 98–129) discerns three models of musical multimedia, while noting that the very concept of "a perceived interaction of different media" (music and film, for example) tends toward models of contest between constituent media with the ability to assert autonomy of utterance (106).

8 For a sense of the interplay between early and mid-twentieth-century linguistic philosophy and anthropology, see Tambiah 1985a, a study focused around the place of words in "magical" rite. Both the anthropological and the linguistic focus on an *operational* view of language – as formulated most famously in Austin's classic account of the speech-act (Austin 1975) – can be viewed, Tambiah notes, as a reaction against the "mentalistic" emphasis of an earlier generation of linguistic theories (Sapir, for example); Tambiah 1985a: 30.

9 Saussure gives very little attention to the "ancillary and more or less accidental" character of individual speech acts (14). Saussure's view of utterance (*parole*), Bakhtin complains, supposes a "completely free combination of forms of language" yet disregards the normative forms (speech genres) that utterance takes in actual usage (1986: 81). Tambiah contrasts the Saussurian focus on semiotic meaning with anthropological concern for speech as "part of concerted activity" with "words . . . equivalents to actions" (1985a: 30). My sketch of Saussure is necessarily brief; for a fuller account of the *langue/parole* binarism see Culler 1986: 39–45 and, in the context of later linguists' taxonomies, Barthes: 13–34, and Harris 1987: 14–36.

10 Quoting from "The problem of speech genres" (Bakhtin 1986: 99, 63). Bakhtin critiques the limitations of the structural linguistic restriction of utterance to the notion of an active speaker and a passive listener, ignoring "the active role of the *other* in the process of speech communication" (70). pp. 67–71. Bakhtin's critique is directed at diagrammatic models such as Saussure's depiction of the "*circuit de parole*" (*Course*, Introduction, Ch. 3, §2; Saussure 11–12).

11 The ancient Greek term for a verse line was *musiké*, a concept that "could not be separated into music and poetry as two tangibly distinct components"; Georgiades 6. More broadly, Dahlhaus observes, "the category 'music' . . . is an abstraction made only in certain cultures" (1998: 241).

12 Bernhard's comments, in their focus on words as the signs for objective "things," here recall the Port-Royal grammarians' division of mental phenomena along grammatical lines, into "objects" of thought, and "operations" – such as judgment or proposition, as in the copula "is." See Harris and Taylor 95–109.

13 A related distinction here is that between a musical response to words that is

essentially lexical – governed by single words – and one based on the semantic content and overall "mood" of larger utterances; see on this point Stacey 12. The heightened importance of painting "feeling" in eighteenth-century musical expression is evident, for example, in J. G. Walther's definition of the *Stilo Drammatico oder Recitativo* as "*ein, die Gemueths-Bewegungen auszudrucken, geschickter Styl*" – a style suited to expressing emotions (literally: movements of feelings); Walther 584, s.v. "Stylus"; and see the recitative examples in Fux's *Gradus* §274 (Fux 1992: 237-41).

14 Harris 1960: 14, a definition quoted by Lyons in his 1968 introduction to structural linguistics (172).

15 First editions of the score specify that the solo voice is a soprano (Sophie Wyss gave the première and second performance). The 1964 miniature score, on its title page, however, is designated "for high voice" (while the score for each song calls for a soprano). Although the work was revived, in 1950, by Peter Pears, who sings in a 1961 studio recording conducted by Britten, it is worth recalling that its composition antedates the composer's relationship with the tenor, for whose voice most of the later vocal works were composed.

16 See his program note for the 1936 première, reprinted in Mitchell–Reed 1991: 444–45.

17 Mitchell (1981) reads *Our Hunting Fathers* as an allegory of the worsening political situation in Europe during the mid-1930s.

18 On the interplay of utterance types – metricated vs. unmetricated speech, for example – in Britten's film work, see Philip Reed's well-documented account of Britten's part in the 1935 GPO film unit production, *Coal Face* (Reed 1999). The film score shares at least two techniques with *Our Hunting Fathers*: a "judicious repetition of certain words for enhanced effect" (69), and the prominent calling-out of a sequence of names – those of returning miners, in the film; in "Dance of Death," those of hunting dogs. Considering the close of "Rats away!", one notes that Britten's interweaving of the "Rats!" cry with the doxology is a touch not found in the original poetic text.

19 Writing to a friend in June 1936, Britten confirms the satirical impulse behind the prayer setting: "It has always puzzled me to think what the rats['] opinion must be of God . . . when being poisoned in the name of the Lord. Consequently you can imagine the setting isn't exactly reverent" (Mitchell–Reed 1991: 429). Parody of Anglican chant is prominent in *Grimes* Act 1, Scene 2; the Act 3 "Threnody" for Albert in *Albert Herring*; and in the children's taunting of the Governess in *The Turn of the Screw*, Act 2, Scene 2.

20 On intentionality in both human and animal utterance, see Wishart 239–62.

21 Reprinted in Mitchell–Reed 1991: 444.

22 The dramatic point is less vivid when the soloist is a tenor rather than a soprano.

23 The final solo appearance here, the alto saxophone, might be interpreted as the figure of Messalina herself, and one notes the parallel between this wailing saxophone solo and the lamentations of the first movement of the

Sinfonia da Requiem, and the personification implicit in the saxophone solos of the 1944 radio drama *The Rescue* (where the alto saxophone represents Penelope) and in Act 1 of *Billy Budd* (where it represents the flogged Novice).

24 Jakobson's schematic representation of six factors of the speech event is reproduced from Jakobson 353. Each of these factors is characterized also by an associated function, depending on the degree of emphasis it accrues in a given speech event. A pronounced focus on the addresser (as in exclamations, say), instances a set toward the "emotive" function; a focus on context is "referential," and so on.

25 The violence of the "whurret!" cry is clear especially when the solo singer's individual cries are taken up as the basis for massed orchestral *glissandi* at the song's climax. The passage, in this case, from a single speaker's sporting call (a falconer's to his bird) to a collective utterance whose aggression is far more pronounced, itself embodies the song's darker resonances for a 1930s audience willing to respond to Britten's and Auden's pacifist convictions. ("Whurret!" itself derives from the verb *whirr*, associated specifically with the fluttering of the partridge's wings as the bird is covered by the hunter's nets; *OED*, s.v. "whirr, whir.")

26 I will discuss the dramaturgy of the *Budd* "interview" in Chapter 3. The *Grimes* passacaglia, as the opera's more or less central pivot, is far more than a scenic convenience. When Grimes's boy apprentice falls from the cliff, we hear the terrible death-cry, and later, as Act 2 ends, a plaintive solo viola theme – *his* theme. The dead boy's "return," as a ghostly memory of the viola theme beginning the passacaglia (where it counterpoints Peter's reiterated Prayer motive) offers an uncanny stroke, for the "instrumental" boy speaks more eloquently than does his vocal twin through a single cry of (inarticulate) terror.

27 On the story/discourse binarism in narratology, see Culler 1981: 169–87. In Benveniste's analyses (217–30) various linguistic indicators (pronouns, demonstratives, and other forms of deixis) mark "the instance of discourse," at which "language is actualized in speech" (217). For exploration of music's discursive shifts via contrasts of stylistic register, topical identity, and by foregrounding disruption as a mode of transition between units in a sequence, see Hatten 1994.

28 Musical conceptions of "voice," as Moreno argues, are often restricted to a material, sonic activity distanced, in logocentric epistemology, from some prior order of meaning ("presence," "thought," "interiority"), of which voice is deferred manifestation ("sign," "expression"). In *Lachrymae*, as I will argue, clear-cut distinctions between instrumental and vocal signs of presence are blurred in a discourse of historic quotation.

29 Nor are the discourse techniques of language to be considered as universals: as Vološinov argues, Russian literature relies much less markedly on indirect discourse than do French and German literatures. The specific issue of

music's potential for narrative shifts of discourse – *vis-à-vis* those of the novel – is taken up in Chapter 3 below, in my reading of *Billy Budd*.

30 Britten's admiration of the work is well known. After hearing the 1936 Barcelona première, he heard the work twice more in concert in London (May 1, December 9), in the meantime buying a full score; Mitchell–Reed 1991: 424–26. The conflated themes opening *Lachrymae* recall Berg's canonic overlapping of first and second phrases of "Es ist genug" (Violin concerto, finale, at m. 134); Berg's score too (at m. 175) stresses multiple transpositions of a single motivic fragment.

31 For a literary parallel, see the discussion of interference between an author's and a character's speech acts in indirect narrative discourse in Vološinov,135–37.

32 In Ex. 1.8, as throughout the music examples in this book, the presence of a functional tonic pitch is marked by a circled pc letter below the score.

33 The intermingling of an ongoing, indirect discourse of variation with a second, more direct quotation brings to mind Henze's *Tristan*, where pervasive Wagnerian allusions are interrupted by one direct quotation of Brahms's First Symphony.

34 Another model of musical quotation for Britten may have been Debussy's *En blanc et noir*, again with a Bach chorale (a work he would perform at the 1958 and 1967 Aldeburgh Festivals).

35 Subjectivity in language, Benveniste notes, is expressed in personal pronouns: "*I* refers to the act of individual discourse in which it is pronounced, and by this it designates the speaker" (226). As Ricoeur notes, the *I* anchors the utterer to the utterance, but it is an empty referent, a shifter, migrating between utterers (1992: 44–52). Cone, who gives searching attention to problems of musical utterance, uses the term "persona" to denote distinct viewpoints articulated by voice and accompanying parts in polyphonic texted music.

36 I return to this point in Chapters 3 and 4 below, discussing *Billy Budd* and *The Turn of the Screw*.

37 Kerman (1966: 191–222) notes the folksong-like emphasis, in balanced phrase designs and drone harmonies, of the late quartets.

38 Dowland's "Lacrimae" pavan was itself an instrumental work – a lute solo – before acquiring the text "Flow my tears" in the *Second Book* (1600), where the song bears the subtitle "Lacrime" (the only such subtitle in this collection), marking borrowing of the famous precursor. In the 1604 *Lacrimae, or Seaven Teares* collection, Dowland arranged the pavan and uses its incipit migrating throughout the other six pavans of the collection. Britten's variation theme, "If my complaints," also appears in the 1604 collection, as "Captain Digornies Galliard." For details, see Poulton 125–33.

39 Describing the reversal by which Bach's chorale seems to grow from Berg's concerto, Joseph Straus invokes Harold Bloom's term *apophrades*, for a strategy by which a poet grapples with a precursor text by a reversal of

historic chronology (Straus 141). Britten's interest in such historical reversals is manifest not only in *Lachrymae*, but informs also the 1963 *Nocturnal after John Dowland* for guitar, again cast as a reverse-variation cycle.

40 *Noye's Fludde*, loosely an opera, is more strictly *sui generis*. The vocal score announces "The Chester Miracle Play set to music," a designation omitted in the full score (Boosey and Hawkes 18487). *Noye* originated as a project commissioned for television and specifically for school-age viewers; Carpenter 381.

41 Bakhtin 1986: 100; the next two citations are from pp. 75 and 73 of the same source. Bakhtin's emphasis on context for utterance is not entirely alien to musical writers, though it must be admitted that the seventeenth-century treatises of Burmeister and Christoph Bernhard concentrate largely on typologies of units of discourse and brief reference to figures that make ideas in the text vivid. For a notion of context, however, one thinks of Heinichen's early eighteenth-century discussion of the *loci topici* – see Buelow – as specific affective states suggested by the position of an aria in a plot sequence, and of Mattheson's mention of the rhetoricians' *locus circumstantiorum*.

42 Austin 6–7; Benveniste, along with Austin, began discussing "verbs that . . . denote an individual act of social import" (229) in work of the mid-1950s. I will return to Austinian speech-act theory as part of the analysis of naming in *Peter Grimes* in Chapter 2.

43 For a theoretical view of the role of such pitch discrepancies in Britten's textures, particularly where there is a polarity of registrally distant strata, see Rupprecht 1996.

44 "Unison is a common feature of ritual," the anthropologist Roy Rappaport observes (213), echoing a commonplace of anthropological theory; see also Tambiah 1985b: 123–24.

45 More strictly, this closing hymn, as Patricia Howard (1969: 156) notes, is itself a transhistorical object, uniting Tallis's sixteenth-century tune – broadly contemporary with the words of the Chester *Noye* text – with Addison's eighteenth-century text.

46 Rappaport 212; I return to anthropological perspectives on ritual in Chapter 5 below, on the *War Requiem* and *Curlew River*.

47 Blyth 66, a comment borne out in a striking remark of Britten's, in a 1969 interview with Donald Mitchell: "I feel as close to Dowland . . . as I do to my youngest contemporary" (Britten 1984: 95).

48 Britten's experiments with including an audience in the performance at some turning point during a dramatic narrative began with the traditional hymns incorporated in *Saint Nicolas* (1949) and, in a more secular vein, the original audience songs of *The Little Sweep* (1949).

49 Whittall 1995: 293; Palmer 1984b: 81–83.

50 Britten's much earlier 1935 setting of the poem (published by Faber Music, 1994) lacks the dark chorale-like texture of the later setting that stands as the centerpiece of the *Songs and Proverbs* cycle. Still, it is intriguing to note that

both songs are for baritone, and share a proclivity for chromatic lower-voice
motions by parallel fifths.

2 *Peter Grimes*: the force of operatic utterance

1 Letter to Elizabeth Mayer, 19 July 1944 (Mitchell–Reed 1991: 1211).

2 Wilson, "An account of 'Peter Grimes'" (1947), cited Brett 1983: 162.

3 The phrase "tremendous tension" is from Britten's comments, in a 1963
interview, on the relevance of his wartime experience as a pacifist to the
genesis of the *Grimes* scenario (Schafer 116). For interpretation of Grimes as
a sexual outsider, see for example Kennedy 123–24; Headington 4, 34–35;
Hindley 1992a; Brett 1993: 264 and 1996: 71–78.

4 Brett 1983: 195–96. Brett (1983: 47–87) charts revisions to the libretto from
early scenarios to the substantial reworking of Slater's mad-scene text. Brett's
interpretation of the sketch evidence is supported in Britten's complaint
about Grimes's character in a 1943 letter to Erwin Stein, some months after
completing an early draft of the libretto with Montagu Slater: "At the
moment he is just a pathological case – no reasons & not many symptoms!
He's got to be changed alot" (Mitchell–Reed 1991: 1130).

5 Garvie, in Brett 1983: 173; Frank Howe (*The Times*, 8 June 1945);
Mitchell–Reed 1991: 1253 (pp. 1253–65 collate several early notices).

6 Elsewhere, Brett calls the psychological process of internalization in *Grimes*
"a simple one resulting directly from social pressure and not from some
subtle Freudian operation of the subconscious" (1987: 357), a claim refined
more recently: "Britten . . . recognized [in *Grimes*] that oppression is not
simply an economic matter along Marxist lines but a multidimensional
phenomenon in which the oppressed in one situation is the oppressor in
another" (1993: 263).

7 Austin: 99–100. Austin's treatise is the foundational text of speech-act theory.
For a crisp summary of its main argument, see Rabinowitz 347–49.

8 Austin's inquiry initially proposes a contrast between explicit performatives
(promises or bets, for example), that are self-referential, purely linguistic
conventions, and so-called "constatives," statements with value as true or
false descriptions of reality. Austin abandons these categories in favor of the
concept of illocutionary force.

9 Searle 1979: 29. I adopt Searle's taxonomy of illocutionary point here, rather
than Austin's own provisional grouping. Vanderveken further refines Searle's
categories, in analyzing shades of illocutionary force among English verbs
within each of Searle's five classes of "point."

10 This and the next quotation cited from Brett 1983: 51–52. Britten and Pears
had formulated a basic scenario early in 1942 before the decision to approach
Slater as librettist. Brett 1983 documents the opera's progress from draft
scenario to final score; on the libretto's genesis, see also Brett 1996.

11 Nor, to my mind, does Donald Mitchell exaggerate in calling the opera "*one*

continuous trial, in which almost every human relationship and all the principal 'dramatic' events . . . are conditioned and musically shaped by the overriding ideas of accusation, interrogation and retribution" (1996: 153; emphasis in the original), or in viewing the technique of the *Grimes* Prologue as paradigmatic for many other of Britten's operatic dialogues.

12 In its rapid abandonment of a home diatonic pitch-collection (B♭ major) by successively added chromatic pitches, the *Grimes* opening recalls a technique prominent in Britten's earlier, more diatonic idiom; see Mark 1994: 294–96.

13 The tonal basis of Britten's music is amenable to proto-Schenkerian linear analyses – such as Ex. 2. 3 – of structural harmonies, contrapuntally prolonged and embellished by foreground diminutions, though Britten analysis has not often drawn on these theoretical resources. For valuable exceptions, see Travis, and Mark 1994 and 1995. An analytic challenge to Schenkerian paradigms, as Rupprecht 1996 argues, is the importance of chromatic oppositions ("discrepancies") among focal pitches, each associated with well-formed prolongational layers ("tonal strata") in distinct regions of registral space.

14 The tonal non-sequitur of Peter's D^7 oath-chord only highlights "the truth" as a key phrase, to which he returns at scene's end, to start the love-duet with Ellen.

15 As Halliwell (1987: 94) notes, modern ideas of character reflect the psychological bias of the novel, whereas staged tragedies depend, in Aristotle's view, on a reciprocal relation between a figure's motivations and the cumulative result of specific actions.

16 As Brett (1983: 183) hears, Peter's melodic line is often situated as a plaintive seventh degree within some local harmony, while the lawyer favors square tonic-note assertions.

17 Recounting the voyage itself, Peter steers the dialogue yet further from Swallow's starting-point, to B minor, only returning to the court's home tonic to recount the intrusion of unwanted Borough officials ("somebody brought the parson").

18 Mukarovsky, cited Pfister 128.

19 Central to Kaminsky's analysis of speech acts in Mozart's *Don Giovanni* is the contrast between sincere constative utterance and the Don's relentlessly "performative" issuing of promises that work as speech acts even in the absence of his sincerity. While Kaminsky's study draws inspiration primarily from Austin's foundational hypothesis of a constative/performative opposition in utterance (Austin 1–10), the present study of *Grimes* will work mostly with Austin's notion of "illocutionary" force (introduced on pp. 98–108) as a taxonomy of a wide range of performative utterances.

20 On links between opera and Renaissance concepts of the subject, see Tomlinson; on the 'monodic self' of early opera, see Chua 29–40.

21 On this point, see Lindenberger 34–36.

22 Britten's work, in 1936–37, with Montagu Slater (his future *Grimes* librettist)

and with Auden must count prominently among influences on the choral writing of *Grimes*. Cf. Britten's admiring diary entry – "real beauty in the choruses" – after seeing Auden–Isherwood's *The Dog Beneath the Skin* (cited Mitchell 1981: 87), a play containing remarkably close interaction of the Chorus (often divided into semi-choruses) and actors. In 1937, Britten would write music for the same authors' *The Ascent of F6*; for the Left Theatre, in 1936, he wrote scores for Slater's *Easter 1916* and *Stay Down Miner* – choruses from both are included in Slater's 1946 *Grimes* publication (Slater 1946a).

23 Rhythmically, as Patricia Howard (1969: 10) points out, Ellen's line quells the agitation by opening out the chorus's dotted rhythms and Hobson's earlier triplets into her more even succession.

24 In Britten's rejected sketch for this moment (see Banks 1996, I: 16v, 17r-v) the orchestral ostinato on Hobson's rhythm is lacking, and "you who help will share the blame" is set to the even descending scale that Ellen herself will introduce at "Let her among you" in the final version. By comparison with this sketch, the final version offers both greater focus on the issue of Hobson's cart, and a starker interruptive effect for Ellen as she defies the chorus.

25 Hence I do not accept Austin's exclusion of fictional discourse of drama or poetry as "parasitic upon its normal use" (22) and somehow "hollow" of performative force. As Maclean argues, the staged speech act could itself be viewed as a distinct illocutionary category.

26 Austin's sixth lecture (67–82) notes the role of such intonational factors and other "accompaniments of the utterance" as indicators of its precise force – "'how . . . it is to be taken'" (73).

27 I consider the Prayer theme a "new" idea on rhetorical, rather than strictly intervallic grounds. Peter Evans's observations of its earlier prefigurings – in the "Old Joe" theme of Act 1, in the string theme of the Sunday Morning interlude, and in the opera's frequent Lydian-mode formulae (117, 120) – suggest exactly why the Prayer enters the scene with such an air of inevitability.

28 On the relations of such operatic rituals – the interplay of divine powers and human appeals for clemency – to an Enlightenment discourse of subjectivity, see Žižek.

29 Hindley 1992a: 147. In Hindley's view (149), the prayer's positive connotations are confirmed by the modal reversal brought about through emphatic cadence to B♭ major. Arguing for a specifically homosexual reading of the opera's outsider allegory, Hindley notes the "desexualization" of the libretto documented by Brett, but sees Ellen's Act 1 allusion to the New Testament adultery story ("let her among you") and the chorus's Act 3 denunciation of Grimes's pride ("who holds himself apart, lets his pride rise") as coded references to a homosexual Grimes.

30 It is significant, for instance, that Grimes's prayer is not delivered using what

Austin would term an "explicit performative" formulation ("*I pray that* God have mercy upon me!" for example). In its avoidance of such markers of illocutionary precision, Grimes's prayer maintains a relative ambiguity of force; on this point, see esp. Austin's lecture 6 (67–82).

31 A phrase appearing for instance in a courtroom scene by the Victorian author Charlotte M. Yonge, in her novel *The Trial*, ch. xiv (181). Britten's opera is set "towards 1830."

32 In one sketch, Ellen's "we've failed" is conflated with the choral "Amen," while Peter's "God have mercy" theme is still a wordless cry (transcribed in Brett 1983: 77). In the composition sketch (p. 61r: reproduced in Brett 1983: ii), the choral "Amen" assumes its familiar position, *after* Peter strikes Ellen, and before he utters the prayer, worded "To Hell then, And God have mercy upon me!" For more detailed comment on these sketches, see Brett 1983: 75–78.

33 The link between these two prayer cadences is also timbral: the crucial pedal point, in both scenes, is heard in the orchestral horns. Peter Evans (111) notes that each V pedal serves as leading-tone to more local tonicizations (of G♭ Lydian, at "Peter, tell me one thing" in Act 2, and of a less triadically secure G tonic, at "In the black moment," in Act 3).

34 For Butler's arguments about hate speech and subject formation, see, respectively, Butler 1997a and 1997b.

35 The tonally arranged release that comes later in this scene, by successively falling transpositions of a single melodic phrase – as the posse march off to Peter's hut – is a schematic reversing of this earlier ascent. Compare the graphic "falling" motion in *The Turn of the Screw*, Act 2, at the Governess's decision to leave Bly.

36 *The Borough*, Letter XXII, lines 73–78 (Crabbe 566). The libretto's only other direct Crabbe quotations are in the framing Worksong chorus (Act 1, Scene 1 and Act 3, Epilogue).

37 Boles's words in Act 2 are in fact a return to his charge in the Act 1 pub scene: "his exercise is not with men but killing boys."

38 Butler 1997a: 31–33. Althusser, famously, compares ideology to a policeman hailing a passerby, who then turns around in response. I return to these questions below, considering the Act 3 mad scene.

39 Britten, remarking on a 1950 performance, catches the terms of the debate surrounding Peter's "character":

> This young singer has a voice of just the right timbre. It was not too heavy, which makes the character simply a sadist, nor was it too lyric, which makes it a boring opera about a sentimental poet *manqué*; but it had, as it should, the elements of both. (Cited in Blyth 14–15)

40 1960 interview with Lord Harewood, cited Mitchell–Reed 1991: 1043; Britten's interest in tying specific musical forms to a given social situation is evident too in the sing-song children's rhymes with which Albert is mocked in *Albert Herring*.

41 Only Balstrode uses the name "Grimes" in Peter's defense, in a single call to "let him be." By redundant, non-sensical repeating of the semantically vague "exercise" taunt, the chorus flouts a common convention of verbal exchange, a flouting paralleled in thematic terms by the scene's ostinato technique. For the analogy between verbal and musical discourses, from the linguistic perspective of what Paul Grice terms "quantity" of utterance, see London 59.

42 Among musical signs of a "chasm . . . between himself and the external world" (76), White cites Peter's tonally and rhythmically disruptive entry in the Act 1 "Old Joe" round.

43 Especially mysterious in agency is the inversion of the solo viola theme that follows the boy's death ending Act 2. The association of the ghostly theme with the deceased child is relatively unambiguous; what the orchestral presentation leaves open is the question of who is responsible.

44 Peter's "hearing" of the orchestral accompaniment, at this moment in the hut, occurs as the off-stage sounds of the nearing posse press ever more urgently on the scene. His consciousness of the Borough – and of Hobson's drum – is apparent at the moment at which his voice blends with their rough chant ("here's the way we go to sea").

45 Overturning an aside in Austin's treatise (Austin 22), Derrida treats citation as a property of *all* linguistic performances. For an overview of Derrida's position and those of his critics, see Rabinowitz.

46 *The Borough*, "Letter XXII. The Poor of the Borough: Peter Grimes," prefatory caption, and lines 256, 288–89, 327, 363–64 (Crabbe I: 564–74). Crabbe's prefatory quotations from *Richard III* and *Macbeth* alert the reader to Peter's end.

47 See Brett (1983: 78–80); Slater himself prints these "neurotic" passages in both the 1945 article (Slater 1946b: 24) – along with several other quotations of texts that were revised by the time of the première – and in his published poem (1946a: 43). Such textual disparities argue that these lines were cut by Britten after the libretto had been drafted, while composing the score, and that composer and librettist had contrasting images of Grimes's character.

48 Britten's fascination with an acoustically vivid drama is evident in the 1943 *Serenade*, where a natural-harmonic horn Prologue returns, in an off-stage repeat, as an Epilogue; timbral-dynamic "distance" frames the immediacy of the inner song cycle. Comparable aural imagination underlies the finale of *Curlew River*; see Chapter 5 below.

49 Peter bursts on stage after the Act 2 passacaglia to a comparably Mahlerian harmonic motion (♭VI over the F tonic); violent Galop rhythms perhaps reflect the composer's admiration for Shostakovich's *Lady Macbeth*. For brilliant reflections on the return of the "Ländler" topos at the scene's fearsome climax, see Mitchell 1996: 135–51.

50 "Hawking for the Partridge," in *Our Hunting Fathers*, offers a precedent, in Britten's oeuvre, for a violent "Dance of Death" climax springing out of the calling of proper names. Mitchell 1999 traces the prevalence of the "Dance of

Death" topic in Britten's music of the thirties and beyond.

51 The links of this gesture to Britten's early encounters with Balinese music are noted in Matthews (122), and further documented in Cooke 1998: 34–36.

52 For comparable instrumental collages of vocal themes restated in solo orchestral form, see the Act 2 prologue to *The Turn of the Screw*, and the Act 2 trial in *Billy Budd* (examined in Chapter 3 below). The operatic technique is carried over to purely instrumental drama in String Quartet No. 3, whose "Recitative" quotes Aschenbach's music from *Death in Venice*.

53 On the resignifying of injurious speech, see Butler 1997a: 13–14. Peter's Act 3 curses clearly employ the "to hell then" wording rejected in earlier drafts of the Act 2 Prayer (see Brett 1983: 76).

54 Britten's and Slater's radio and film soundtrack experience contributes here to the patterning of voices (Slater, in the poem, marks the relative volume of voices, and contrasts of single and group voices). The contrasts are vivid in Pears's unpublished 1948 mono recording for Columbia, produced by Lawrance Collingwood (issued in 1993 on EMI 7647272).

55 Similar confusions mark his disruption of the pub song in Act 1 ("when *I* . . . when *he* had gone fishing").

56 Britten's "do you hear them. . . ?" is thus a line retained from Slater's original text whose address is transformed in the final mad scene, spoken by a more distracted Peter.

Ronald Duncan's 1968 account of Britten's revisions to the *Grimes* mad scene, in which he takes credit for the idea of a textual collage of quotations ("I sketched out a last scene, deliberately echoing phrases from arias and numbers in the earlier part of the opera so as to force Ben to take the opportunity of recalling phrases of the music . . . He fell in with this pressure." (1968: 35 and repr. in 1981: 39) is challenged by extant sketch evidence. Textual reprises are prominent already in Slater's poem (cf. his refrain-like allusion to the Act 1 "young prentice come" line), and Britten, attempting to set Slater, uses *thematic* reprise for "I'll marry Ellen" (Brett 1983: 83–84 transcribes this sketch). See also Brett 1996: 69–71.

57 In Act 1, the "harbour" aria follows Peter's A-minor account to Balstrode of the first boy's death. "Home among fishing nets" in the first is balanced by the A-major vision of peaceful "harbour" in the second.

58 The softer cries, as Whittall (1990a: 100) remarks, are "'out of character' for the vengeful chorus," but evoke Peter's memories of Ellen. On the image network surrounding the keyword "home," see esp. Keller's unpublished 1946 "psychoanalytic note" on the opera (1995: 16–24).

59 Slater 1946b: 25; Slater, in the *Grimes* poem, omits this line from Ellen's dialogue with Balstrode over the boy's embroidered jersey (Act 3, Scene 1).

60 Peter's hearing is center-stage earlier, in the Act 2 hut scene, where his fantasies are intruded upon by the drumming sounds of the approaching posse. I return to the question of operatic "hearing" in readings of *Billy Budd*, *Turn of the Screw* and *Curlew River* in Chapters 3, 4, and 5 below.

61 Later in the same essay, Althusser extends the analysis of interpellation with reference to a Christian discourse of religious calling.

62 For Butler's far more detailed account of subject as grammatical and ideological construct, see esp. 1997b: 1–30, 106–31.

63 These lines were initially more vague; in one draft setting, Ellen sings "Peter you can restore yourself, a fisherman," identifying him by trade (cited P. Reed 1996a: 98).

3 Motive and narrative in *Billy Budd*

1 The mist image appears in the penultimate paragraph of the trial-scene chapter, in a metaphoric conflation of themes of moral obscurity and hasty judgment:

> Forty years after a battle it is easy for a noncombatant to reason about how it ought to have been fought. It is another thing personally and under fire to have to direct the fighting while involved in the obscuring smoke of it. . . . The greater the fog the more it imperils the steamer, and speed is put on though at the hazard of running somebody down. (114; ch. 21)

Page and chapter reference is to Melville, *Billy Budd, Sailor (An inside narrative)*, ed. Hayford and Sealts (Melville 1962); subsequent citations appear in the main text.

2 On the centric and modal opposition of B♭ major and B minor see esp. Stein 1972, P. Evans and Whittall 1990b. Brett 1984 links such oppositions to the moral ambiguity symbolized by the mist; Cooke (in Cooke–Reed) traces a wider scheme of semitonal oppositions with precise symbolic connotations. Rupprecht 1996 analyzes the role of textural strata in articulating tonal uncertainty in the Prologue.

3 On the registral detail of the Prologue and on the concept of intervallic "discrepancy" in Britten's music, see Rupprecht 1996: 320–31.

4 Britten, 1960 radio interview, cited Cooke–Reed 29.

5 Britten exploits a comparable dramatic tension in staged dramas and concert works: in both *Our Hunting Fathers* and *The Turn of the Screw*, an opening recitative introduces salient thematic events without revealing their precise reference.

6 As when a plain B-minor triad (setting the word "truth") appears amid more chromatic wanderings, or when the "imperfection" (in theme 4) is figured in a trill disturbing a pure F♯-major triad.

7 Theme 4 returns as Billy's stammer, 5 in Billy's devotion to Vere at the end of Act 1, Scene 1 (at "I'll follow you, all I can," echoed in the subsequent cabin scene); I examine theme 6's numerous associations below. Themes 1, 2, and 3a – heard before Vere appears – recur only in the Epilogue. For Wagner's notion of *Ahnung*, see esp. *Opera and Drama*, III.vi (trans. Ellis 1995a: 336). As Grey points out, Wagner's "foreshadowing" technique is of less practical

import in his works than the correlate "reminiscence," where modifications of rhythm, harmony, etc., hold expressive significance in relation to an earlier, definitive motive statement (1992: 239). On the "enigmatic introit" of the novel, see Genette (190).

8   *Opera and Drama* III.v, trans. Ellis (1995a: 329); Wagner 1888, vol. iv: 184–85. I have modified Ellis's English slightly, dropping his occasional capitals ("Feeling") and his pseudo-Germanic reference to music in the feminine ("*she* can materialize . . .").

9   I resort to visual diagrams mindful of Barthes's caution that the inherent ambiguity of signifier and signified (as much relations as items or terms) makes any graphic representation of signification clumsy; on the varying formulations of the signifier/signified pair, see Barthes 48–50.

10 The motive is played after Siegmund sings "*den Vater fand ich nicht*," for Cone (39) an instance of the accompaniment complementing the viewpoint presented by the vocal line; like the literary "omniscient" narrator, it reveals facts unknown to those on stage. For Swain (48), the music states "Wotan is the father."

11 On this point, see Grey 1995: 314–17.

12 Wagner discusses the centrality of stage action to the definition of motives in *Opera and Drama* III.v; for the question Why?, see also "Zukunftsmusik" (1995b: 320, 336–37).

13 Cited Szondi xiii.

14 Ian Bent stresses the purely empirical function of the name as a mere "device for recognition," noting in Wolzogen's guides the cautious attitude to the name bestowed – "a *Storm Figure* – it could equally well be called 'Galloping motif'" – and the way in which Wolzogen uses one name to refer to a cluster of related motive forms. For Bent, such nomenclaturism is problematic: "the motif so named in no sense 'represents' its associated image: the Sword motif in the *Ring* does not 'stand for' the sword; instead, motif, image or event, and poetic word coalesce" (90). The notion that musical leitmotives are named only by a proto-metaphoric shift recalls Nietzsche's claims (in "On Truth and Falsity in their Ultramoral Sense") for a fundamental metaphoricity to language itself, with all verbal concepts being tropes or metaphors calcified by long use.

15 The analogy between this move and the special use of language Austin terms "performative" is not lost on Goffman (40–82); see also Maclean 25–26.

16 On the arbitrary linguistic sign, see Saussure and Barthes 50–51. The contrast between verbal and musical signification might also be construed with reference to the Romantics' distinction between *allegory* ("instantaneous passage through the signifying face of the sign toward knowledge of what is signified"; Todorov 1982: 201) and *symbol* (in which the "face retains its proper value, its opacity"; *ibid.*). Saussure (68) mentions symbols as signs that "show at least a vestige of natural connexion between the signal and its signification" (the scale of justice, for example), though, as

Todorov observes, the symbol is ultimately excluded from Saussure's account of the linguistic sign (1982: 255–70).

17 The quoted phrase is from Emslie (52), who offers a detailed reading of the opera's fascination with symbolic uncertainties.

18 Model (a) exhibits contrasting motions between levels: the first shift is "metalinguistic," making a first-order sign into a higher-level signified; in the second "connotative" shift, a first-order sign becomes a signifier at a higher level (Barthes 89–94). While words and music of the Stammer are closely associated in the opera's Prologue, Billy's staged stammering in Act 1, Scene 1 exemplifies a more stratified model, in which musical and verbal signifiers (theme 4, then the officers' comment, "he stammers") operate independently.

19 "Not only do these melodic moments appear mutually explanatory, and thus at-one, but also the motives of feeling or show embodied in them . . . reveal themselves to the *feeling* as mutually conditioned, as at-one by their generic nature." *Opera and Drama* III.vi, trans. Ellis 1995a: 348; Wagner 1888, vol. iv: 202.

20 Dahlhaus, echoing Goethe, speaks of a division between "emotional" and "allegorical" motives, while cautioning that it is not always possible to draw a sharp distinction (1979: 61–62). Kerman (1968: 495–96) discriminates Verdi's "identifying" themes – associated with characters – from "recalling" themes that evoke a dramatic situation.

21 Kerman 1968: 502; in *Otello*, Kerman notes, the theme bridging Acts 2 and 3 records the workings of Otello's jealousy between the acts, while a purely orchestral "Bacio" theme frames the drama as a whole.

22 Rapid sequential manipulations of the Mutiny theme in the Act 1 worksong articulate long-range tonal unrest commensurate with the idea of "mutiny"; similarly, in Act 2, Claggart's direct accusations of Billy constitute a concealed variant of the Mutiny theme, with the chain-transposition process a still more direct embodiment of mounting chaos as the drama approaches its peripeteia.

23 The word "mutiny" itself, in Act 1, Scene 2, is set to a melodic shape redolent of Vere's Prologue (esp. the vocal line at "guided others rightly but I have been lost on the infinite sea"), and – more directly – the crew's exclamations of "the French" (R57). It is the phrase "Spithead, the Nore, the floating republic" that actually carries the rising-fifth Mutiny theme (at R67, and reiterated a few measures later). Billy's "Rights o' Man" cry is reported to Vere at the same pitch level (before R71).

24 "*auf das Gefühl einen bestimmten . . . Eindruck . . . hervorbringen*" (Wagner 1888, vol. iv: 185)

25 Peirce 135, emphasis added. This psychological emphasis is present too in Saussure's definition of the linguistic sign: "not a link between a thing and a name, but between a concept and a sound pattern . . . a two-sided psychological entity" (66). Mental cognition, for Peirce, is always part of a

chain, and signification is never static; amplifying his working general definition of the sign, he writes: "It addresses somebody, that is, creates in the mind of that person an equivalent sign, or perhaps a more developed sign. . . . the *interpretant* of the first sign" (135; Peirce's italics). On Saussure and Peirce in a musical context, see Nattiez 6.

26 Billy's adoption of the Mutiny motive for his "Rights o' Man" cry (at R33) may not reflect his own hearing of the chorus, but their wordless imitation at this point does suggest that *they*, at least, *hear him*, and it is this musical affinity between Billy and the chorus that immediately draws the officers' attention to Billy as a mutiny threat.

27 Taruskin challenges Abbate's claim that operatic characters are deaf to what she terms "noumenal" orchestral music, while in "phenomenal song," they become momentarily aware of the orchestra as sound, noting that the ambient world of the orchestral music is "not meant for them, but for us . . . stage characters do not merely hear [the noumenal orchestral music]; they live it" (194, 196). But a character's sensitivity to orchestral motives varies according to stylistic and dramatic contexts; for useful debate on this point, see Kivy and Rosen. For Kerman, Verdi's *identifying* themes are directed simply to an audience (as a "sonorous . . . extension of . . . physical or psychological presence"), whereas *recalling* themes "link one stage of the drama to another," and thus play a more complex role (1968: 495–96).

28 Billy's innocence is precisely that which prevents him moving beyond surface appearances – "To deal in double meanings and insinuations of any sort was quite foreign to his nature" (49; ch. 1). Such comments assume great importance in Johnson's deconstructive reading of the Melville.

29 A more subtle link between Vere's Prologue entrance and Claggart's in Act 1, Scene 1 is the mutation of martial dotted rhythms (theme 3a) into the more fierce lurching motions of the string ostinato (Ex. 3.4, fig. 20 ff.).

30 The term SLIDE, as a description of transformation that preserves the third of a triad, while changing its mode and root, is David Lewin's (1987: 178, 228). Riemann cites a Schubert example for such a *Gegenterzwechsel* ("exchange of opposing thirds"), a dualistic description foregrounding the exchange of major and minor thirds about a static axis pitch (in Riemann 126, for example). In the following discussion, triad qualities are referred to by abbreviations for major (+) and minor (−) modes, following the pc letter – G+ and G♯− denote single G-major and G♯-minor triads, respectively; in music examples, triads are shown in brackets – [G+], [G♯−].

31 The G♯–G♮ root motion marked in Example 3.4 reiterates a similar SLIDE from the G+ horn sennets that announce Claggart's appearance on deck to the G♯− preceding his first vocal utterance (shown in the first measure of Example 3.4).

32 Mitchell (Mitchell–Reed 1998: 15) cites *Don Carlo* as a model for Claggart; on other Verdian models, and on Britten's conscious reference to Verdi while

writing *Budd*, see P. Reed (1993a: 59). Britten's early knowledge of Wagner's music (documented in Mark 1995) serves him well in the Wagnerian parodies of a 1939 radio score, *The Sword in the Stone*.

33 The relationship in Example 3.6 between the voice's fourths-theme and the lower-register dyads is stratified and heterophonic: it encompasses both an obvious dissociation, and a veiled imitative unity (the T3 move is common to both strata).

34 I return to the difficult issue of a singer's awareness or obliviousness to the orchestra in my reading of the Act 2 trial scene.

35 Vere's silence in Billy's trial is a major reworking of his role in Melville, where (ch. 22) he is eloquent on the need for a drumhead court to ignore Claggart's motivations and restrict deliberations to the consequences of Billy's actions. As Forster later wrote, he and Eric Crozier in their libretto had "ventured to tidy up Vere":

> How odiously Vere comes out in the trial scene! At first he stays in the witness box, as he should, then he constitutes himself both counsel for the prosecution and judge, and never stops lecturing the court until the boy is sentenced to death. (1951: 6, 5)

Earlier, in a 1949 letter, Forster mentions "the rescuing of Vere from his creator" (cited Cooke – Reed 55); in the 1960 radio talk, he finds "we all felt that Melville was disgracing Vere," and Crozier speaks of "humaniz[ing]" the Captain (cited *ibid.*, 29).

36 See D. Mitchell (1993: 122–34).

37 A temporary rift between Britten and Forster over Claggart's Act 1 "Credo" (see P. Reed 1993a: 60–61) might with hindsight be judged a symptom of divergent responses to Melville by composer and librettist. As Brett (1984) notes, the libretto's emphasis on Vere's quest for an ultimately mysterious "salvation" is redolent of the moral universe of Forster's own fiction.

38 > Die zu genau unterscheidbaren, und ihren Inhalt vollkommen verwirklichenden melodischen Momenten gewordenen Hauptmotive der dramatischen Handlung bilden sich in ihrer beziehungsvollen, stets wohlbedingten – dem Reime ähnlichen – Wiederkehr zu einer einheitlichen künstlerischen Form, die sich nicht nur über engere Theile des Drama's, sondern über das ganze Drama selbst als ein bindender Zusammenhang erstreckt . . .
>
> (1888, vol. 4: 202. Trans. Ellis 1995a: 348)

39 Compare Cone's observation that "opera, although it appears superficially to be a purely dramatic form, is . . . a mixture of the narrative and the dramatic . . . . the composer's persona comments directly, through the orchestra, on that portion of its message that is mediated through the characters" (21). For comparisons of opera and the novel, see Adorno 1994, Conrad, and Lindenberger; examining operatic narrative, Michael Halliwell argues that "characters, as part of a musical narrative act, have little autonomy, but . . . assert their independence particularly strongly during those moments when the presence of the performer is most apparent" (136).

40 In Jakobson's terms (see Chapter 1), aggression translates itself here into repeated emphasis on the *contact* factor of the speech event, a physical channel of communication between accuser and accused. As in *Grimes*, naming enacts subordination.

41 In speaking of narrative *tempo*, Genette himself invokes musical analogies (94).

42 Genette's term *anachrony* refers to disturbance of the temporal order of events in the "story" by the syntagmatic ordering of their succession in the "narrative" (35). Anachronies include analepsis (reaching back from the narrative present) and prolepsis (advance notice of some future event). Genette notes too the determination of *reach* (how far back or forward), the degree to which pro- or analepses are to a point within or beyond the main narrative, and whether or not the return from these second-level narratives to the main narrative is marked or unmarked. Another distinction relevant here is that between single and multiple recurrences of one story event (in this case, the moment of accusation as recalled by orchestral leitmotive).

43 The phrase "access to consciousness" is familiar to theorists of literary narrative (see Martin 130–51 for an overview). As Abbate notes, it is a commonplace of opera reception to find that "musical gestures . . . somehow represent or equal specific actions or psychological states in the accompanying staged drama" (1991: 20). I return to the issue of point of view below.

44 Chatman (135) makes a similar point in comparing the simultaneity of exposition possible in filmic narrative with the necessarily sequential exposition of detail (personal appearance, setting of a landscape) in literary narration.

45 On literary theories of plot, see Culler 1981: 169–87 and Martin 107–11; Abbate (1991: 47–56) critiques attempts to adapt such concepts to untexted instrumental music. Stories do not exist independently of some discursive presentation – they are heuristic fictions by which one interprets the way a storyteller is imparting events.

46 Surveying the local tonal scheme for Claggart's face-to-face accusations against Billy, one finds a sequence of rapid shifts: G bass: six measures; B: seven measures; A: six measures.

47 Vere's speeches to Claggart, for example, are at Allegro (♩126); Claggart's accusations, and Billy's stammer bear the much slower indication Lento (but lack a metronome mark); both include sixteenth-note subdivision of the main beat. The trial begins Grave, ♩58. Britten's 1967 studio recording takes just over seven minutes from Claggart's cabin entrance to the end of the officer's reactions, ten and a half from Vere's call for a trial to his "acceptance" aria.

48 My diagram simplifies by omitting the framing presence of an S4 (the historical personage of Herman Melville, writing in 1851) and R4 (the flesh-and-blood paperback reader Rupprecht, in 1999).

49 Analyzing the conventions of the "theatrical frame," ethnographer Erving Goffman notes that an audience is "filled-in . . . covertly, so the fiction can be sustained that it has indeed entered into a world not its own" (142). Conventions compensating for the lack of narrative intervention in drama include "a more than normal amount of interrogation, self-confession, and confidence giving" (143).

50 Thus the orchestral Siegfried-motive ending *Walküre* is uttered by "the voice of a narrator, who, in a proleptic move, conveys information about a future event: that Siegfried will rescue Brünnhilde. This voice . . . *looks back* upon the *Ring* as if all action in it were already past" (Abbate 1991: 169).

51 See Prince, s.v. "point of view" for a comparative synopsis of literary theories.

52 Literary point of view is only metaphorically a matter of sight: "Textual perspective," Gebauer–Wulf note, "must be distinguished from [that] of pictorial representation; the former does not function as a peephole, is not limited to a specific representational extract conveyed by the succession of events, and is not characterized by a vanishing point" (242).

53 I ignore here such secondary factors as the position of individual seats within the house, and the "narrative" heightening of stage space by lighting design (a relatively recent phenomenon in opera production).

54 The mixed timbre of the Mist-chains (winds, strings pizzicato) and the octave-shadowing of the Light phrases (brass) assert a distance from the soloistic scoring in the surrounding sections. The central contrapuntal section of the interlude expands, in "thick"-sounding orchestral doublings, on a theme heard earlier (before R49) in voice and solo piccolo.

55 Rehm 51–61 explores the interactions of lyric and dramatic speech in Greek tragedy.

56 Genette's detailed analysis resists *précis*; for a kind of overview, see his closing comments on "functions of the narrator" (255–59).

57 "Zukunftsmusik," trans. Ellis (Wagner 1995b: 338).

58 As Kerman (1999: 50) notes, the solo/accompaniment trope is worn-out, and can often be replaced by more vivid metaphorical characterizations of musical agency (mentor/acolyte, master/servant, etc.).

59 Genette (246) cites a story by Borges in which the narrator-hero adopts first the stance of a victim, then of an informer, previously referred to solely in the third person. On the disintegration of character in twentieth-century fiction, see Carroll; on the turn against psychological notions of dramatic character, see Fuchs.

60 Chapter 21 of the Hayford–Sealts text corresponds closely to Plomer's Chapter 18, except that Plomer's text begins two paragraphs later.

61 As with the *Grimes* foghorn, and the boat engines in Aschenbach's trip to Venice, a real-world sound permeates the scene to larger symbolic effect.

62 Comparable "wedge" gestures emerge in the Prologue (see Cadence 1, Ex. 3.1b); retrospectively, they work as signs of the trial as a cardinal event in the older Vere's hazy memories. As Hindley (1994: 120) observes, the trumpet

signal is problematically conflated in the Prologue and Epilogue with melodic signs of Claggart and Billy respectively in a way not heard in the main action.

63 On Greimas's distinction between actant and actor, see Prince 1–3. Freud's concept of overdetermination emerges early in his long chapter on the dream-work: "Each of the elements of the dream's content turns out to have been 'overdetermined' [*überdeterminiert*] – to have been represented in the dream-thoughts many times over" (1965: 318; 1991: 290).

64 The dismissal of a key center as an act of violent suppression is equally evident in the "Down all hands!" order quelling the mutinous chorus later in Act 2, following the execution. As in the *Grimes* Prologue, it is a B♭ tonic that exerts the oppressing force.

65 Mitchell suggests that "each chord or perhaps group of chords within the total arch represents a stage in the development of the encounter between Vere and Billy" (1993: 122).

66 Plomer's edition reads ". . . the rarer qualities of *one* nature" (Melville 1946: 101, emphasis added).

67 Closing Act 3 in the four-act 1951 score, the interview-chords precede an interval in the performance (between Acts 3 and 4); in the 1960 revision, they precede the scene change to Billy below deck awaiting execution. In either case, the orchestra plays to the empty stage visible to the audience, rather than before a curtain marking an extra-dramatic scene change.

68 Or to Britten's music; comparable chains of triads (often in close-position voicings) encircling a tonic are prominent in the 1942 *Hymn to St. Cecilia* and the "Sonnet" of the 1943 *Serenade*.

69 Cf. Keller's (1981) reflections on the listener's varying level of awareness of thematic references during a performance.

70 The F-minor tonic prolonged in Vere's "verdict" aria and the F-major tonic of Scene 3 act as a frame confirming the functionality of F tonics *within* the interview itself. After the first I–V succession at chords 12– 13 from F− to C+ (F minor: I–V, in other words), F+ is tonicized in repeated F+/C+ (I–V) half-cadence pairs (at chords 18–19, 22–23, 27–28, 30–31). Chords 32 and 34 are a final half-cadence motion (the D+ challenge of chord 33 is a local interpolation); Hindley's claim that "the overall tonality of the interview chords moves from F major to C major" (1994: 110) remains unconvincing.

71 Both are "loud" and "high" in context, and approached by tritone bass motion from a preceding low-register C+ (V) chord (such a tritone leap could be avoided, in the interview's system, by writing an F♯− triad in § position).

72 I must refrain here from detailed comment on the less affirmative chordal syntax of the subsequent interview-chord flashbacks in Scene 3 and in the Epilogue; for a provocative reading of these passages as a retreat from harmonic "decisiveness," see Whittall 1990b.

73 Only four chords (2, 5, 6, and 14) in the interview blend timbres. Spacing also argues against Claggart's influence: while individual chords (14, for example) arrange polarized registers around a hollow center, none sounds the "fifthless" voicing of Act 1 (since interview chords are all complete triads).

74 Gesturally, the lower-register triplet ascents in Example 3.19 add a further level of reminiscence: to the sequential ascents of Claggart's trial-scene accusations.

75 Christian Metz, cited Genette 33.

76 Themes that return in the opening ritornello (Ex. 3.14) provide the material for the later ritornelli marking Billy's exit (Ex. 3.15) and the officers' exit. In the body of the trial (Vere's testimony and Billy's cross-examination), fresh thematic returns (Claggart's death, Billy's stammer, and so on) are interwoven with additional, more compact restatements of the Claggart themes more fully exposed in the three ritornelli.

77 As Lyons (305–06) notes, the English-language concepts of past and present are not the only discursive formulations of mood.

4 *The Turn of the Screw*: innocent performance

1 Cited in Piper (1989: 10); for further brief excerpts from the 1954 correspondence between librettist and composer, see Carpenter, 335–37.

2 James, *The Turn of the Screw*, 147–48; further page and chapter references will appear in the main text; I quote James's revised 1908 text, in volume 12 of the New York edition.

3 *What Maisie Knew*, pp. 96–97; ch. 12.

4 *What Maisie Knew*, p. 42; ch. 2.

5 Britten and Piper, after initial hesitation, settled on James's own title for the opera; on one earlier possibility (*The Tower and The Lake*), see Britten 1977.

6 For a reading of James's text as a problematizing of psychic notions of interior and exterior, see Felman. Piper's words (Act 2, Scene 1) echo James's reference, in the New York Preface, to "my young woman engaged in her labyrinth" (xviii).

7 For an introduction to the questioning of the Governess's reliability as a narrator, a topic prominent in the novel's earlier reception, see Lustig xv.

8 Overdetermination, in Freud's description of the dream-work, refers to a combination of multiple meanings within a single image (Freud 1965: 181–82); see also the account of speaking presence in the *Billy Budd* trial scene (in Chapter 3, above).

9 The intervallic complementarity of the Screw and Thread themes was first described in P. Evans 214.

10 Wilson 115; as he goes on to observe, James, in the New York edition, groups the *Screw* not with his other ghost stories, but with *The Aspern Papers* and *The Liar*, both studies of protagonists driven to extremes of pathological

behavior (120). On the ferocity of the critical debate surrounding the *Screw*, between proponents of a heroic and a hysterical Governess, see Felman, esp. 142–49.

11 See Donald Mitchell's liner note to the 1955 recording (London XLL 1207/8) conducted by Britten.

12 On the origins of Wagnerian leitmotive-criticism, see esp. Grey 1996.

13   The actual title phrase never occurs in the opera . . . and the theme may be interpreted as representing Quint, since in the last scene where the Governess presses Miles to utter Quint's name, the theme appears in the bass in the orchestra, first eight notes, then ten, then eleven, and finally as he cries "Peter Quint, you devil," the twelfth.

(*The Guardian*, 15 September 1954, 5; cited Howard 1985: 133)

14 Recalling the story/discourse opposition of structural narratology, the Screw theme is discursive. One might even suggest that this narrative aspect is implicit at the start of the Prologue: "It is a curious story," sung to two adjacent fifths <G–D, E–A>, prefigures the distinctive pattern (and the pitch level) of the Screw theme on A, soon to appear.

15 And cf. Schoenberg's observation (244) that "when Richard Wagner introduced his *Leitmotiv* – for the same purpose as that for which I introduced my Basic Set – he may have said: 'Let there be unity.'"

16 On the negative connotations of Britten's twelve-note ideas, see the discussion below (chapter 6) of Aschenbach's exhaustion at the opening of *Death in Venice.*

17 Cited Carpenter, 335. Britten had completed Act 1 by early May. A visit to Myfanwy Piper's house at Fawley on May 16th enabled work on Act 2: how to open Scene 2 (the children's mock-processional had yet to be suggested), and the addition of the Governess's letter writing scene; J. Evans 1985a: 65.

18 The dotted rhythms of the first Screw theme announcement recall those of the French overture. In early performances of the opera (including the Venice première), and in the MS score itself, the Prologue's stage appearance was heralded by three "Introductory Knocks," following a European theatrical convention; J. Evans 1985a: 66.

19 Mellers 1984b: 146. Mitchell, in the 1955 note, hears the solo piano Prologue as "expos[ing] in musical terms the contrast between the world of reality (*The Prologue*) and the fantastic world of Bly." By late in Act 2 (in Variations 13 and 14) the piano will re-emerge from the ensemble as a concertante soloist, this time as a direct extension of Miles's stage presence.

20 Britten's preference for a chamber-orchestral scoring of course reflected practicalities, including the presence of an unbroken boy's voice among the solo roles, and the costs of touring-opera production.

21 "Über die Anwendung der Musik auf das Drama" (Wagner 1888, vol. 10: 185), trans. cited from Grey 1996: 189.

22 *The Guardian*, 15 September 1954, p. 5; cited in Howard 1985: 133.

23 Peter Evans's neutral x and y labels – for Screw and Thread themes – have the advantage of stressing this complementarity, and they avoid reductive dramatic associations.

24 *Collier's Weekly*, the first in the January 27 1898 issue, the last on April 16; the original serial text is also divided into five "parts" (removed in the revised text); for the chapter and part divisions, see Kimbrough's edition.

25 Britten's Verdian interest in monotonal modal contrast as a dramaturgic resource is not, however, limited to stage contexts, but also governs the large-scale architecture of concert scores such as the *Sinfonia da Requiem* (D minor, D minor, D major) and the Second Quartet (C major–minor–major).

26 Critics of the chamber-orchestral scoring underestimate the importance of this timbral balancing to the dramaturgy of individual moments; cf. Howard 1985: 134–35. The interplay of unaccompanied voices and solo instrumental lines is a feature that sets the *Screw* apart, in scoring, from the other chamber operas.

27 Only a few lines later, though, the Governess's account draws attention to its own subjectivity:

> I gave him time to reappear. I call it time, but how long was it? I can't speak to the purpose to-day of the duration of these things. That kind of measure must have left me: they couldn't have lasted as they actually appeared to me to last. (185; ch.4)

28 As Howard notes, the instrumental shake transforms the Governess's "who is it?" figure, as an echo of the previous scene, as if "the governess now sees the children through vision . . . distorted by her experiences before the tower" (1985: 37), though whether she actually *sees* at this moment is unclear, since she is off stage. Either way, Howard's interpretation depends on a transformation of the book's literary/visual discourse into an operatic form that is sonic/auditory.

29 The major-to-minor direction of the Act 1 mode shifts is sometimes reversed in Act 2, as in Scene 3, at the moment of Miss Jessel's disappearance.

30 Cited in Carpenter 334. Miles, in James, says "When I'm bad I *am* bad" (234).

31 Letter of 6 November 1954, cited Carpenter 361.

32 See on this point Mellers 1984b: 149.

33 On the role of the "open secret" of Britten's sexual identity in his public career of the mid-century, and the influence of the dynamics of the closet on critical reception of the operas, see Brett 1994a.

34 The much-publicized imprisonment of a homosexual member of the British aristocracy, in 1954, was a reminder of the possibility of becoming a scapegoat. Carpenter 335 reports that Britten himself was interviewed by Scotland Yard in early 1954, though no criminal charges were pursued.

35 Cf. Britten's comment in a letter to Piper on the "sexy" connotations of Mrs Grose's ambiguous line "when Quint was free with ev'ryone, with little Master Miles" and the London *Times*'s "improper question" "Why did he choose this subject"? (cited Howard 1985: 136).

36 On Britten's informal "adoption" of Ronald Duncan's son Roger in the mid-fifties, see Duncan 1981: 132–33 and Carpenter 367.

37 "If I tell . . . an event that I have just lived, insofar as I *am telling* (orally or in writing) this event, I find myself already outside of the time-space where the event occurred. To identify oneself absolutely with oneself, to identify one's 'I' with the 'I' that I tell as [is as] impossible as to lift oneself up by one's hair." Bakhtin, cited in Todorov 1984: 52; original emphasis. Carpenter's valuable documentary survey of Britten's career is marred by reductively biographical interpretations of individual works.

38 Sommerville 168. In both *Grimes* and *The Little Sweep*, the historical setting is the early nineteenth-century.

39 Operatic children are more commonly limited to cameo musical entrances, as in *Carmen*, Act 1, or (a work Britten admired) at the close of Berg's *Wozzeck*. Britten's treble part for Miles is itself an innovation and there was the intriguing possibility of Flora's part also being sung by a child; see Piper in Blyth 33 and Carpenter's report (334) of Britten's consulting George Malcolm in early 1954 about children to play Miles and Flora; elsewhere, Piper's recollections (Howard 1985: 129) suggest that the possibility of writing Flora for a girl's voice was never a serious one.

40 The childlike aspect of Britten's *Screw* also reflects the composer's admiration for Mahler (whose Fourth, as Adorno [1992: 55] observes, "shuffles nonexistent children's songs together").

41 See for instance the tune's shrill reprise as an instrumental descant to the climactic ensemble of Act 2, Scene 1 (in Mrs. Herring's shop), rounding out the scene and offering the three kids' ironizing comment on Albert's trapped status as May King.

42 See her recollections of this and other musical games in Mitchell 1983: 30.

43 Imogen Holst draws attention to the "insatiable appetite for repetition" of childrens'-choirs (1972: 279); as Michel Poizat observes, the angelic connotations of high voices are common to several cultures (128).

44 Palmer 1985: 109–10; exploring the opera's inversion of the "'natural' musical order of things" further, Palmer notes that the relative timbral darkness of Miss Jessel's music in contrast to Quint's brightness inverts culturally based gender stereotypes.

45 For the details of Freud's account, see Erikson 215–16. Erikson notes that play, for adults, is most readily construed in relation to work, with consequent theoretical emphasis on children's play as mere expending of surplus energy (214).

46 As, for instance, in Jonathan Miller's 1979 English National Opera staging; cf. Howard 1985: 37. Still, Britten's and Piper's direction, that "Flora and Miles ride in on a Hobby Horse," is neither more nor less overtly sexual than the games of younger children, where, as Erikson describes, "others [other children] are treated as things, are inspected, run into, or forced to 'be horsie'" (221).

47 Claims to the contrary – e.g. "there is never any doubt that the two children and the Governess see Quint and Miss Jessel, as do we as audience" (Mellers 1984b: 146) – misrepresent Britten and Piper at this point.

48 Hail Mary becoming "Haley, maley"; or "Hotchy, Potchy" for the Latin mass phrase *hoc est corpus*. See Charles Francis Potter, "counting-out rimes," in Leach I: 255.

49 On the interplay of phenomenal song with surrounding operatic plot events, see esp. Abbate's account of Cherubino's Act 1 "uncovering" in Mozart's *Figaro* (1991: 68).

50 The uncertainty surrounding Mignon's sexual status (girl or woman) is a recurrent trope in the numerous representations of her in later nineteenth-century culture, as surveyed in Steedman, 21–42.

51 The cantilena of the *Grimes* passacaglia, returning inverted after the boy falls to his death, is not the earliest example of Britten personifying the viola; the second of the *Two Portraits* of 1930, subtitled "E. B. B.," is a self-portrait in which Britten's own string instrument, the viola, takes the leading role.

52 Piper 1989: 10. Piper also mentions drawing the song's words "from an old-fashioned Latin grammar that an aunt of mine produced."

53 Reading this song as an expression of Quint's power over Miles, it is hard to believe (as Hindley 1990 claims) that this power is benevolent, Quint's idea of "friendship" notwithstanding.

54 In the last few measures, an A bass is qualified by the hanging G♮ seventh concluding the Governess's "Malo" phrases: any real sense of functionality between the E-major (V) and A-major triads here (at R138 and 139) is broken up by the concluding rocking back and forth from tonic to supertonic. On sketch evidence of Britten's unusual last-minute hesitancies about the form of the ending, see Mitchell 1963.

55 On Schoenberg's mistrust of strict symmetry, see Morgan 46.

56 The prominence of the thematic argument of the variations is only heightened for a listening audience by the absence of any staged action (since each scene change occurs with lights down). In *Death in Venice*, Britten creates a similarly uncanny effect by melodic return for each of Mann's various death-figures (Fop, Hotel Manager, Barber *et al.*).

57 This continuity is confirmed by Mrs. Grose's direct thematic recall (at "A good lady, I'll be bound") of her Scene 2 phrase at the opening of Scene 3; no other consecutive scenes are melodically linked in this way.

58 This framing strategy forms a precedent for using plainsong melodies as thematic sources in the church parables, as if to represent a controlling numinous power beyond the newer music of the main action.

59 Howard 1985: 81–82; given this recognition of the theme's lack of univocal significance as a "mechanical" sign of character, Howard's comment on the Thread theme – "[It] can be called the 'catalyst' theme because it is continually associated with the governess's coming to Bly and the impact this has on the events of the story" (82) – appears needlessly reductive.

60 The "who is it?" figure was likewise central to one rejected version of the climax to the Act 2 finale (in the build-up to Miles's last words, "Peter Quint, you devil!"), as Mitchell 1963 reveals.

61 For accounts of the early psychoanalytic criticisms of James's *Turn of the Screw*, see Felman and Lustig; Renner considers the Governess's and Quint's conformity to Victorian clinical stereotypes.

62 Howard hears the scene differently, noting Quint's trichordal presence in Miles's harp-accompanied responses to the Governess as evidence either that Miles is thinking of the ghost, or that the Governess imputes as much to the boy's evasive words (1985: 88).

63 Cited Kimbrough 210; Oliver Elton, in 1907, is among the first critics to ask if the ghosts are "facts, or delusions of the young governess who tells the story" (cited Kimbrough 176); James himself, in the Preface, speaks of readers divining her "nature . . . in watching it reflect her anxieties and inductions" (xix), without otherwise casting doubt on the status of her perceptions.

64 Even here though, the ghosts' visible presence on stage *without* the Governess ("nowhere," as the score says) could equally attest to the reality of their existence apart from her imagination. In the opera, as in the book, we may agree with Lustig in finding that "identical signs can support quite opposite readings" (xxii).

65 Most impressively in the 1961 film directed by Jack Clayton, *The Innocents*, starring Deborah Kerr. As I write (February 2000), the American PBS television channel is broadcasting an adaptation billed as the "classic tale of a repressed governess and the terrifying things within us all."

66 As Hindley (1995) has argued, Britten's operas are a "parable art" in which private issues of sexual identity could be explored in symbolic terms in a public forum.

67 Freud's copy of Iwan Bloch's *Beiträge zur Aetiologie der Psychopathia Sexualis*, quoted in Masson (127).

68 The Victorian discourse of "anti-sensualism," as Michael Mason shows, was common to both religious conservative and libertarian feminist causes throughout the nineteenth century. A code that preached the continence of passion, and an ethic of restraint, was founded on Enlightenment hymning of the rational, specifically on the idea that sexual drives are subject to cultural control, advanced in texts such as Rousseau's *Émile* (1762) and Priestley's *Considerations for the use of young men* (1776). The British physician Beddoes, in his *Hygeia* of 1802, advocated restraint from youthful masturbation, advice connected with a belief that sexual drives should remain dormant (unaroused by information) before their natural biological onset; M. Mason 14. On the relevance of anti-sensualist discourse to James's and Britten's *Turn of the Screw*, see Brett 1992.

69 "Two Loves," *The Chameleon* 1 (1894), cited in Sedgwick, 203, 74, with specific reference to John Marcher's "secret" in James's story, "The Beast in

the Jungle." The characteristic "blanks" of James's *The Turn of the Screw* are also to be read against the backdrop of the nineteenth-century Anglo-American novel's reticence in depicting sexual passion, in stark contrast to French counterparts; for James's views on the situation, see his reviews of Zola, Maupassant, and others, in Miller: 129–50.

70 In cinematic versions of the story, too – to say nothing of bona fide "horror"-genre offerings – the first incursions of the supernatural are always specifically musical moments. In Clayton's *The Innocents*, the ghosts' presence is most palpable in a plaintive song, first heard in a child's singing voice, and returning in the mechanical rendition of a music-box. Visual effects too – lighting shifts, slow-motion action, layering of images – rely on musical support to create their departure from the "everyday."

5 Rituals: the *War Requiem* and *Curlew River*

1 Britten 1964a: 11, 18, the first remark illustrated with reference to Beethoven's Ninth, the second linked to a critical view of the role of technology ("the loudspeaker") in the cultural dissemination of music.

2 Tambiah 1985b: 126; Rappaport 179–83.

3 For a brief report of Britten's involvement in a 1938 recital, by Ezra Pound, of one of his *Nō*-play translations, to musical accompaniment, see Cooke 1998: 24–25. For Ronald Duncan's recollections of plans for an oratorio entitled *Mea culpa*, conceived as a response to the 1945 atomic bombing of Hiroshima and Nagasaki, and, in 1948, for a requiem in honor of Gandhi, see Duncan 1981: 55–56. Duncan also reports Britten's interest, around 1952, in *Nō* drama (Duncan 1981: 112–13). For chronological details in the following discussion of the *Requiem* and *Curlew River*, I rely on the more extensive documentary accounts in Reed (1996b) and Cooke (1998) respectively.

4 Cooke 1998: 115–18; Plomer, who had worked in Japan, later recalled that he had described a *Nō* play to Britten in 1955, "and imitat[ed] some of the gestures used by the actors" (cited Cooke 1998: 116).

5 Cited Cooke 1998: 139. Plomer showed a first complete libretto draft to Britten in November 1958, and the two met again over Christmas; Cooke 138–42 analyses their early correspondence on the subject. Plomer's text was based on an authorized English translation (Japanese Classics Translation Committee 1955).

6 Copland's 1936 "play opera" *The Second Hurricane* uses choruses of parents and students, and unbroken solo voices, to tell its story of civility and respect among a group of children facing a violent storm. Copland himself played Britten the work during a 1938 visit to Snape; writing to Copland *en route* to Canada, in May 1939, Britten expresses admiration for the work; its subsequent influence on the operetta *Paul Bunyan* is noted by Copland himself in a much later comment (see Gishford, 71–73). As Mitchell and

Reed (1991: 635) note, Copland's likely model for the work would have been Kurt Weill's 1930 *Der Jasager* (using a Brecht text based on a *Nō* source). Weill himself continued to contribute to the genre in his 1948 adaptation of the radio play *Down in the Valley* as an opera for colleges.

7 On the Mass as "sacred drama," and the medieval tradition of allegorical interpretation of each physical gesture of its celebration, see Hardison, and esp. Young 79–111 (a text Britten himself knew; see n. 19).

8 Britten's 1942 declaration to the Conscientious Objectors' Tribunal, for instance, affirms a belief in God, but not in Christ's divinity (Mitchell–Reed 1991: 1046). On Britten's pacifism as a context for the *War Requiem*, see Cooke 1996: 1–19.

9 See Britten's statements on the work's "anti-war" idea, quoted in the *New York Sun* (27 April 1940), cited Mitchell–Reed 1991: 705–06.

10 On the *Sinfonia*'s "Dies Irae" movement in relation to "Totentanz" movements from *Our Hunting Fathers* to *Grimes*, see Mitchell 1999: 199–204.

11 "[T]here was no question in any case of a pastiche from the ancient Japanese," Britten's program note remarks (1964b).

12 In the April 1959 letter to Plomer, describing his reasons for staging *Curlew River* in a local Suffolk church, Britten cites both practical reasons, and "artistic ones includ[ing] placing of orchestra, long entrances, beauty of sound (if in Orford Church) & contact with audience"; cited Cooke 1998: 142.

13 Reed (1996b: 21–22) dates the Coventry committee's awareness of Britten's plans to early December 1958, though later correspondence from the cathedral still mentions only a setting of the Ordinary. See the letter from Reverend Canon J. W. Poole to Britten (15 February 1959), cited in Strader 5.

14 "Preface," liner notes, with Britten's 1963 recording, Decca Set 252/3.

15 Bakhtin's word "heteroglossia" (*raznorechie*, literally "different-speech-ness") suggests that language encompasses an interplay of "specific points of view on the world" (Bakhtin 1981: 291). This is an apt characterizaton of the situation among juxtaposed Latin and English speakers in Britten's *War Requiem* text. For a recent application of such thinking in a musical setting, see esp. Korsyn 1999.

16 Compare the opposition of trebles with a soprano soloist in the two poems of "The Driving Boy" in the *Spring Symphony*.

17 The composition process began with Britten's handwritten selecting and copying out of both *Missa* and Owen texts side by side in facing notebook pages, supplying his own English translations of the liturgical Latin (at the center). Bracket and arrow notations pinpoint the arrangements of portions of text; for a reproduction of one page, and description of Britten's cuts to Owen's words, see Reed 1996b: 32–36. I will say more in Section 2 below on Bakhtin's concept of "speech genre."

18 For the full texts of the "Dies irae" and its sources, see Robertson 1968: 15–19.

19 See Cooke's investigation (1998: 160–65) of Britten's familiarity with Young's 1933 study (the earliest *Quem queritis* tropes are examined in I: 201–22), and his viewing of the 1960 King's Lynn performance of the Beauvais *Play of Daniel*, revived and staged by Noah Greenberg. Young I: 178–97 offers an overview of the tropes as "literary embellishments of the liturgy."

20 St Gall, Stiftsbibl., MS 484, cited and reproduced in Young I: 201, 203;

> [Question:] Whom seek ye in the sepulchre, O Christians? [Response:] Jesus of Nazareth, who was crucified, O Angels. He is not here; he has risen as he foretold. Go and announce that he has risen from the sepulchre. *I rose again and I am still with thee.*

The third sentence ("He is not here"), though lacking a rubric in this MS, may well have been delivered by the angelic speaker; in later MSS, variant rubrics imply different distributions of trope and liturgical texts among speakers; Young I: 202–09.

21 "*Immer und immer wieder wird zum Bewußtsein gebracht, daß hier gesungen wird*" (86). My thanks to Charles M. Atkinson for drawing my attention to this source.

22 "*Alt und Neu sind gleichgesetzt, beide sind gegenwärtig*"; Stäblein 89. According to Stäblein, trope poets do not present themselves as self-consciously "new" in relation to the biblical text they introduce; sequences, on the other hand, as self-contained interpolations, are more separate in mood from the surrounding liturgy.

23 Owen texts, here and throughout this chapter, are quoted as they appear in the *War Requiem* score. Britten himself worked from a copy of a 1931 edition by Edmund Blunden; Reed 1996b: 28.

24 "Cross-fade" refers to a link between two scenes established by a shared sonic feature in cinematic (or radio) soundtracks. Britten's interest in the technique is evident in Act 2, Scene 1 of *Grimes*, as Edward Sackville-West points out in his published 1946 comments on the opera (1946: 41).

25 In the music of Ex. 5.2, the presence of diatonic D minor is restricted to a single region of a multi-layered texture. For further analysis of Britten's tonally stratified textures, see Rupprecht 1996.

26 On the opposition between a gravitational bass function and its abandonment, in many twentieth-century scores, for a symmetrical tonal environment, see Harvey.

27 Cf. Britten's 1961 article, "On Writing English Opera," with its plea for vernacular translations of opera, and Britten's own practice of including translations in the original editions of his texted publications with Faber Music after 1964.

28 Spence himself organized the design around the idea that "the new Cathedral should grow from the old and be incomplete without it" (134). Construction of the new walls was well under way by 1959, when Britten inspected the site. Britten's refers to "the Coventry piece" in a 1961 letter (cited Carpenter

408–09). On Britten's and Spence's statements at Coventry as public symbols of reconciliation and forgiveness, see J. Herbert.

29 Britten's libretto omits Stanzas 11 and 14 of the "Dies irae," and the whole Communion text "Lux aeterna." The "Agnus Dei" includes one telling addition, of the single phrase "dona nobis pacem" (from the Ordinary, rather than the Requiem Mass) to the tenor soloist's part – the only moment when either male soloist sings in Latin.

30 Jungmann I: 171; on the choice of archaic language for ritual utterance, see Tambiah 1985a: 22–30.

31 Rappaport 175. See also Tambiah 1985a for an examination of the differing ratio of actions to words in various rituals.

32 Even the "Dies irae," as Robertson remarks, softens brash first-person singular verbs, in its final "Lacrimosa" segment, to a prayer including all souls of the departed (1968: 20). The Sequence is possibly by Thomas of Celano, but the "Lacrimosa" is the work of a second, unidentified, writer. The only other sign of first-person presence in the Mass itself is the Introit ("exaudi orationem meam"); the thrice-repeated line "Libera me" belongs to the Absolution.

33 Even the Ordinary of the Mass embodies a tension between events presented in a world beyond time and the "historical" staging of events enacted around the altar (Hardison 55).

34 See Kermode 12–17.

35 See Bakhtin 1986 passim; the question of relations among whole utterances is addressed at pp. 72–73.

36 The "Dies irae" is rich in parallels to Verdi's setting: among many features, Boyd (5) notes Verdi's illuminating chord change (from B♭ to G-major triads) at the "Amen" as a model for Britten's surprising F-major close, and the large-scale recapitulation of "Dies irae" material in G minor in both settings.

37 In a 1969 interview, Britten acknowledges Verdi as a conscious model while composing, but seems to regard audible similarities between his score and the precursor as evidence of an insufficiently "absorbed" influence (1984a: 96).

38 Excepting the bracketed word repetitions, and the contraction in line 3 of "whispering" (for declamatory reasons), Britten's setting is faithful to Owen's poetic text.

39 Henze 1982: 255.

40 Lines 1–7 and 9–13 of Owen's poem may be traced directly to the language of Genesis 22: 3–13 in the King James translation. In lines 7–8, building on the biblical account ("and bound Isaac his son," Genesis: verse 9), Owen introduces images of modern trench-warfare: "Then Abram bound the youth with belts and straps, / And builded parapets and trenches there."

41 The tenor is heard singing Isaac's direct speech but the shift of singing voices is "early," so that he also sings part of the narrative.

42 As Cooke (1996: 68) observes, the angelic C major here, with Lydian F♯s, follows many other Britten scores in associating C major with innocence, and – one might add – in pairing C- and E-major triads as luminous diatonic presences in more chromatic and hostile surroundings.

43 The boys' "Hostias" entry derives from their opening antiphony, as Roseberry shows in perceptive comments on the movement's harmonic scheme (1995: 259).

44 Both Roseberry (1995) and Cooke (1996), accounting for irony in the "Offertorium," lay great emphasis on its intertextual links to Canticle 2.

45 The intertextual shifts (whether recognized or not) dramatize direct speech within the trope, first Isaac's and then the supernatural voice of the angel. The change of speaker, in each case, commands more attention than the link to a precursor text.

46 While the *Requiem*'s stepwise "quam olim Abrahae" figure evokes the Canticle's diatonic scalar lines, intertextual references do not stop there. The Canticle, in its closing "Amen," draws on a famous protestant hymn ("Old One Hundredth") with little sense of distortion in relation to the main musical context (see Palmer 1984b: 81–82). Full quotation of the same hymn in *Saint Nicolas*, as Whittall likewise observes, is "absorbed" without parody or distortion (1995: 296) into the work's structure.

47 Words from the January 1963 Kingsway Hall recording sessions, issued as "Rehearsing *War Requiem*"; 1962 letter, cited Robertson 1962: 310.

48 Early liturgical usage admits the *Kyrie eleison* formula – "a word or two to express our beggary" (Jungmann I: 339) – both in litaneic response to longer prayers, and as an independent prayer inserted into the *Missa* following the Introit (*idem* 333–46).

49 The concentration, in "Strange meeting," on a scenic representation of Hell, as Kerr observes, reflects both a poetic tradition beginning with Dante, and Owen's Evangelical religious background.

50 Goffman's "ceremonial" can be equated with other writers' use of the term "ritual" to describe physical events of heightened gestural formality. In both cases, the master trope is of ritual as "a distinct and autonomous set of activities" (Bell 70), rather than as simply an aspect of all human behavior; on terminological difficulties common to the field of ritual studies, see Bell 69–70.

51 See on this point Tambiah 1985a: 18.

52 For a fuller account of Britten's stay in Japan during the 1956 Asian tour, see Cooke 1998: 112–29.

53 "New Year's message to the people of Japan, 3 December 1957," cited Cooke 1998: 120. For the diary entries of Britten's traveling companions during the Asian trip, see esp. Hesse (describing the *Nō* performances on pp. 60–61), and excerpts in Reed 1995b and Cooke 1998.

54 On Britten's evasive approach to conventional genres, see Ashby, surveying the four works bearing the title symphony. The composer was equally adept

at reviving defunct genres, as in the neo-Baroque "Canticles" from Purcell, or the extended strophic form of the medieval *Ballad of Little Musgrave and Lady Barnard*.

55 Britten 1964b.

56 The introduction to Pollard's *English Miracle Plays* (8th edition, 1927), from which Britten created his *Noye* libretto (annotating the text directly in sketching the division into recitative, ensembles, *et al.*; Cooke 1998: 161), includes much information about the origins and performance practices of both traditions.

57 "Introductory Note," *Noye's Fludde*, miniature score (London: Boosey and Hawkes, 1958).

58 Cooke 1998: 160–65. Cooke also describes the composer's work for an unrealized nativity play for Pimlico school, derived from the Chester cycle (of which sketches and a 1974 libretto typescript survive). The geography of the *Curlew River* story must accommodate the sense of travel, as Colin Graham's Production Notes show: "During the journey the boat turns in the middle of the river so that the raised circle [on the main stage] becomes the far shore on arrival" (Graham 1983: 144). Graham had directed *Noye*.

59 Plomer 297.

60 See Young for a detailed commentary on the physical form of the Mass as action (I: 15–43); the dramatic qualities of the Mass are assessed by both Young (I: 79–111) and Hardison.

61 Waley 15; the term *yūgen* occurs often in the writings of Seami Motokiyo (AD 1363–1444), among the founders of *Nō*; Waley 21.

62 Britten's predilection for heterophonic part-writing occurs as early as the 1937 "Bridge" Variations (see P. Evans 469); D. Mitchell 1984 was among the first to draw attention to the pervasiveness of this facet of the composer's style. The specifically Japanese traces in Britten's score, as Cooke (1998) shows in detail, suggest the orchestral interplay of the "elegant" *Togaku* repertory, or the voice and shamisen songs he heard in *Kabuki* performances, rather than the simpler musical style of *Nō* itself.

63 As Cooke notes, Britten never actually uses the flute and drums as an isolated duet scoring in *Curlew River*, "and so the most distinctive *Nō* sonority is therefore lost" (1998: 167).

64 Commenting on the numerous technical terms distinguishing shoeless foot stamps, Waley (32) quotes Seami:

> In the play *Sano no Funabashi*, at . . . "The willows green, the flowers, crimson," the real beat comes on "flowers" and one should stamp twice there, but if an additional stamp is inserted at the *-ri* of *midori* ("green") the effect is pleasing.

65 On this point, see, for example, Rappaport 206.

66 The organ part, as Cooke has shown, draws closely on a Japanese musical source beyond the *Nō* itself, the cluster-harmonies of the *shō* mouth organ of the court orchestra *Togaku* repertory; see Cooke 1998: 183–84.

67 Such as the "multiple soliloquy" (note 99) relation Graham demands between vocal imitations of the Madwoman's "Birds of the Fenland" song, in which all voices copy her melody, while speaking words applicable to their own situations. See also Production Notes 148, 160, 210.

68 A point captured in Seami's couplet, "Life is a lying dream, he only wakes / Who casts the World aside"; trans. in Waley 64. On various twentieth-century European responses to *Nō*, including Britten's and Plomer's, see esp. Albright 68–100.

69 The synthesis of Ferryman and River musics, as Peter Evans observes, reflects a shared motivic source for the superficially contrasted ideas in the intervals of the "Te lucis" frame-chant (472).

70 Komparu, *The Noh Theater* (1983), 37, cited Cooke 1998: 137. Such figures are a familiar type in *Nō* drama, as the preface to the English translation of *Sumidagawa* used by Britten and Plomer confirms: "bereaved mothers . . . are represented as abnormally sensitive and peculiarly susceptible to their surroundings, and fall into fits of poetic exaltation which expresses itself by frenzied gestures"; Japanese Classics Translation Committee 145.

71 A quite specific aspect of this process is the score's suggestions of parodistic mockery when the chorus appropriates the Madwoman's characteristic melodic shapes.

72 The Madwoman/chorus interaction is further evident here by a rising sequence of starting pitches, first in her music (viola, by minor thirds: G – B♭ – C♯), then in the song itself (by major thirds, C – E – G♯; R28–30).

73 The Madwoman's entrance, in the terms of *Nō* dramatic theory, corresponds to the beginning of the second, intensifying (*ha*) motion of the entire play. For a more detailed exposition of formal parallels between *Curlew River* and *Sumidagawa*, see Cooke 1998: 135–36 and 172–73, and Malm.

74 Cooke (1998: 155) notes a parallel between Britten's desired church acoustic and the resonance cavities of the *Nō* stage.

75 The flute E♭s (R34.2) switch to the complementary whole-tone hexachord; beginning in the next measure, pitches mingle more freely, preparing the bold contrast of unison Cs at "my only child was lost."

76 The performative focus in recent theories of ritual is well summarized in Tambiah's working definition of the term:

> Ritual is a culturally constructed system of symbolic communication. It is constituted of patterned and ordered sequences of words and acts, often expressed in multiple media, whose content and arrangement are characterized in varying degree by formality (conventionality), stereotypy (rigidity), condensation (fusion), and redundancy (repetition). (1985b: 128)

77 Letter to Plomer, 15 February 1964, cited in Cooke 1998: 148.

78 Prayer scenes in conventional opera (in *Otello* and *Wozzeck*, say), are frequently interludes "away" from the main action, rather than climactic scenes in their own right.

79 Britten was still toying with the negative image of the Madwoman clawing at the tomb as late as rehearsals for the 1964 première, where he finalized the Spirit's music (see Oliver Knussen's recollections in Carpenter 438). The present cathartic ending replaces a passage of more rapid, nervous music that was to have accompanied the Madwoman's attempts to grab the passing ghost. As Cooke reveals in his documentary study of the opera's genesis (1998: 142–53), the idea of moving from a relatively strict adherence to the Buddhist *Sumidagawa* towards an overtly Christian reworking of the tale was Britten's.

80 The English prayers are Plomer's own invention, substituting for the Buddhist formulations of *Sumidagawa*. For details of the libretto's relationship to the source text's wording, see Cooke 1998: 137–53.

81 The "Custodes Hominum" chant was Britten's "big new idea," while at work on setting Plomer's libretto, as his letter to Plomer (15 February 1964) confirms (cited Cooke 1998: 148–49), and he asks Plomer for an English translation. Typescript translations of the chant survive, but were not used (Cooke 1998: 149).

82 Carefully chosen harmonic patterns enact the transformation. Thus the Spirit's voice is first heard as the *Custodes* chant moves from its initial D to an A tonic, and the boy's shape is witnessed from the "distance" (in relation to A) of a focal E♭ ("See, there is his shape!"). The circling healing motion is leitmotivic – a return to the "clear as a sky" song of the Madwoman's first appearance – and built around circular harmonic substitutions that traverse the distance between the Spirit's E♭ and the A counterpole of the earlier chant (reached briefly at R95), within a chromatic cluster context.

83 The somber ending of *Sumidagawa*, with the Madwoman left with her grief without a miraculous healing, is, the Japanese Classics committee notes (145), unusual among "mad-woman" pieces, which more typically end with the finding of a lost one and restoration to sanity.

84 Van Gennep's formulation of the *rite de passage* is taken up, more recently, in Victor Turner's investigation of Western theatrical convention from the perspective of his earlier studies of ritual as a cultural production (see Turner).

6 Subjectivity and perception in *Death in Venice*

1 Mann 1958: 304.

2 The opera's first critics, on the other hand, may have made the opposite mistake – of effacing the work's erotic dimension while grabbing, in Philip Brett's words, "at the straw of allegory" (1993: 280). For probing interpretations of Britten's oeuvre as marked by the reticence of the mid-twentieth-century homosexual "closet" see esp. Brett 1994a and 1994b; on discursive and political formations structuring modern sexual identity, see esp. Sedgwick.

3 Sedgwick 29. Lloyd Whitesell makes a similar point, specifically in relation to Britten's oeuvre, in noting that "the 'eros' of these operas is recessive, only tenuously physical, sublimated into other channels" (Whitesell 475).

4 On this facet of the narrative technique in *Death in Venice*, see esp. T. J. Reed 1974 and Cohn.

5 Žižek makes the former point at the outset of a psychoanalytically inflected reading of operatic subjectivity (178); for Tomlinson (5), opera's picture of sensate perception invariably borders on a metaphysical, supersensible reality.

6 Mann, in his 1936 lecture on Freud, defines a bond between psychoanalysis and literature precisely in terms of their shared "understanding of disease, or, more precisely, of disease as an instrument of knowledge" (1958: 306).

7 Freud, 1963a: 85. Later in the same essay, instinct is defined as "a border land concept between the mental and the physical," a concept one might conceive of as "the mental representative of the stimuli emanating from within the organism and penetrating to the mind" (87). Freud expresses such dynamic processes with the German word "*Trieb*" (drive), separating a psychological concept of instinct from zoological ideas of hereditary behavior (for which he retains the term "*Instinkt*").

8 On Freudian theories of the sexual subject as inflected by the later models of Lacan and Foucault, see de Lauretis.

9 Thomas Mann, *Death in Venice*, trans. H. T. Lowe-Porter (New York: Vintage Books, 1954), 3; further page references appear in the main text. Britten's annotated working copy of this translation (in its 1929 Adelphi Library edition) and of T. J. Reed's 1971 German edition, both survive. Myfanwy Piper, Britten's librettist, characterizes her own German as "almost non-existent" (Piper 1989: 21), so we may assume Lowe-Porter's text, rather than Mann's German, as a central reference for both composer and librettist in crafting the opera. (Kenneth Burke's 1925 translation was never available in England.)

10 As Peter Evans (526) notes, the inversion of the vocal line beginning at "taxing, tiring" is constructed to closely resemble a retrograde form of the initial "my mind" phrase, but the inversion here (and later, at R7) is melodically strict – I_8 of the first vocal phrase.

11 The *Dream*'s dusk-music uses major triads on twelve different roots, but Britten often associates total chromaticism with a specific kind of sinister, twisting melodic idiom: the initial horn melody in "O Rose" from the 1943 *Serenade* traces an all-chromatic descent from G♯, clearly tonicizing E at the end of the phrase, and repeating only two pcs. In the "King of the West" dance (*The Prince of the Pagodas*, 1956), twelve-tone prime and inversion phrases parody the pointillism of post-Webernian serialism. "A Poison Tree" (*Songs and Proverbs of William Blake*, 1965) is the only song to state a row as a main theme. The characteristic contours and balancing of contours of Aschenbach's opening twelve-tone melody return in the

"Duets" of the Third String Quartet (1975), an early sign of the work's links to the opera.

12 Britten often partitions all-chromatic melodies in an uneven 7:5 pc grouping, as in the "Nurslings of immortality" phrase of the 1958 *Nocturne* (where individual pcs are repeated), or in the "Poison Tree" theme in the Blake songs (where each pc is stated only once; see Ex. 1.13 above). The melodic row of Aschenbach's "my mind" phrase is no less asymmetric, each of its three sub-phrases linked to its neighbor by repeated boundary pitches, giving an overall 4:3:5 grouping of pcs. Only with the complementary whole-tone hexachords of the mortuary texts ("they enter into the house of the Lord") does *Death in Venice* reveal a symmetrical aggregate partition, unfolding by a rigid mirroring of prime and inversion phrases.

13 The *Tristan* quotation is readily audible, yet goes unmentioned in published commentary until Travis. Britten's Wagnerian musical allusion parallels Mann's literary homage to Venice as a city "where musicians were moved to accords so weirdly lulling and lascivious" (56).

14 T. J. Reed traces Mann's phrase ("*eine seltsame Ausweitung seines Innern*") to a comment on Dionysiac orgies by Erwin Rohde, noting also that tigers drew Dionysus's chariot (1971: 159). Piper, who recalls finding Reed's edition useful during the libretto's composition, would surely have known such details (see Piper 1989: 20). Reed later wrote a programme note for the opera's 1973 première (repr. D. Mitchell 1987: 163–67).

15 Analyzing the ironic in Mann's literary tone, T. J. Reed notes that the symbols of the opening scene are presented by a narrator close to the protagonist's thoughts: "[D]eclining to disagree openly with the character's thoughts, the narrator leaves them exposed to the reader's scepticism, subtly engendering doubt without seeming to do so" (1971: 13).

16 Cf. Edward Cone's account of voice-accompaniment relations in Lieder, esp. of Schubert's accompaniments as "symbolically suggest[ing] both the impingement of the outer world on the individual represented by the vocal persona, and the subconscious reaction of the individual to this impingement" (35–36); a comparable hearing of *Lied* textures informs Lewin 1982.

17 Donald Mitchell (1987: 4–8) has recalled Britten's very explicit delineation of these three levels of action (in a 1971 conversation at the time of the opera's planning). At that stage, Britten conceived of production in the round with the percussion orchestra visible on stage. A prefatory note in the vocal score describes the recitatives as "interior monologues . . . declamatory in style, rather than lyrical."

18 Britten at one stage "would have liked to have these passages spoken," Piper notes of the recitatives (1989: 18). Their rhythmically free pitch notation was modeled on that of the Evangelist roles in the Schütz Passions, as sung by Peter Pears during the period of the opera's composition (see J. Evans 1985b:

31–33). Mann's text itself includes a proto-operatic shift from prose to the heightened speech of Homeric hexameter at certain moments.

19 See Mitchell 1987: 4; in the 1990 Glyndebourne Touring Opera production, Robert Tear writes down his thoughts, underlining the improvisatory feel of the recitatives.

20 The cutting of the first recitative in the 1973 recording (conducted by Steuart Bedford) is marked, in the subsequent 1974 published vocal score, as optional. The cut gets Aschenbach on his way to Venice more quickly, but we lose the shift of levels introduced between the opening nervous music, the "rational" decision to travel, and the strangeness of the following Scene 2 journey. Britten himself worried (in a letter to Piper, February 1972) that the first recitative "reduces the dramatic tension"(cited D. Mitchell 1987: 12). Mitchell (1987: 10–16) reports in detail on the composer's concerns about the pace of Act 1.

21 The asterisked chords here – (0156) and (0157) in Forte's list – are pitch-specific premonitions of later Tadzio harmony.

22 Another dilatory factor at the opera's opening is the trilling of the fourth "*Tristan*"-pitch (D♯) in the trombone (Ex. 6.1, m.5). The "blurring" extends to textural relations: the way in which the voice itself, initially prominent, is steadily engulfed by the rapidly growing registral expanse of the mechanical ostinati.

23 The "generative motion" of Britten's harmony, Whittall finds, often "takes place *within* the tonic triad, rather than between tonic and dominant triads" (1980: 33). Thus the F♯/D mediant–tonic dyad is common to both forms of the Barcarolle (*a* and *d* in Ex. 6.9), but in the latter case the tonic-dyad is recontextualized by the force of the new C♯ bass pitch (even as a D-major key signature is restored).

24 Britten at first considered placing the percussion orchestra on stage (the plan he mentioned to Mitchell in 1971; see note 17). An early typed scenario, Cooke reports, has "marginal directions for ballets with off-stage orchestra and chorus" (1998: 231). In the final opera, the initial location of the chorus in the Scene 7 Games of Apollo is unspecified; at the conclusion, a stage direction refers to "hotel guests retreat[ing] to the distance (still singing)." Some productions treat the "Voice of Apollo" as a visible stage personage (though in the 1973 recording, he is separated from the main action – rather starkly – by contrasts in recording level and ambience).

25 Vocal score, "performance and production notes"; Piper later revealed her dissatisfaction with the classical balletic style Ashton used for the children's games. "I had imagined a much more modern style of dancing ... Colin Graham and I both thought in terms of a certain roughness or coltishness, [but] Britten did not feel safe enough to venture into a type of performance that he knew nothing about and could not visualize" (Piper 1994).

26 For a critique of Brett's readings of the gamelan as an erotic symbol see Cooke (1998: 248; 1999: 186).

27 On this point, see Palmer 1987: 131–32.

28 For probing comments on Edward Said's notion of "orientalism," see esp. Clifford.

29 Desire and the gaze are of course inextricably linked in Lacan's elaboration of the Freudian subject.

30 Aschenbach's sonic gaze, as an emphatically perceptual activity evoked in gamelanesque textures, is of a different mimetic order than the orchestral "View"motive (timbrally identified by massed strings) first introduced by the Manager at the Hotel in Scene 4, and reappearing, in varied form, in the orchestral music of Scene 5. On the View motive in its association with the sea as a Platonic symbol of infinity, see Hindley 1992b.

31 "The type of melancholy gaiety in the Balinese sound is in total contrast to the rather Germanic character of Aschenbach's self-absorption and underlines his feeling of alienation": Piper, cited in Cooke 1998: 231.

32 For details of the relations between Britten's *Venice*-gamelan and his first-hand experience of Balinese gamelan (as documented in his sketchbooks), see Cooke 1987 and 1998: 220–44. Tadzio's characterizing vibraphone theme, in timbre and improvisatory mood, resembles the solos of Balinese *trompong* (Cooke 1987: 119).

33 My formulation here draws on the social account of language familiar in writings of the Bakhtin circle; on "inner speech," see Vološinov 14.

34 This division of the opera into two acts was Britten's final compositional decision (Strode 36–37). In the theater, this musical continuity ensures that audiences experience the opening of Act 2 as a resumption of the temporal flow broken by the Act 1 curtain.

35 On operatic pacing in relation to the possibility of orchestral narration, see my discussion, in Chapter 3 above, of the *Billy Budd* trial scene.

36 Earlier, in Scene 5, the blowing of the Sirocco is given in menacing wind trills (first heard at R107.3) traceable to the Marvels shape, but such utterances are tied directly to Aschenbach's singing presence ("while this Sirocco blows"), and so do not assume the discursive force of a narrative comment. In Scene 1, the Marvels theme was more directly a product of Aschenbach's consciousness (his vision); here in Scene 7 his thoughts are elsewhere.

37 The crescendo unfolds Collection III, inflected by F♮s. The same octatonic/diatonic opposition is revisited in connection with the C-rooted Love-motive quotation in the finale of Quartet No. 3, immediately preceding the E-major passacaglia.

38 Characteristic of Freud's models of the psychic apparatus, throughout his career, are layered arrangements of mental surfaces, with memory a pattern of paths traced on and between strata; see Derrida 1978. As an account of "the inner life" (Langer), Freud's topography appears no less metaphoric than Britten's polyphonic arrangement of motives among simultaneously sounding registral layers.

39 "*den Berückten*"; "*der Betörte*" (Mann 1983: 56, 60).

40 Lowe-Porter sometimes renders such phrases with an English possessive, as in "our solitary" (57); her reference to "the solitary" (on p. 63) is too loose a substitute for Mann's phrase, "*der Starrsinnige*" (1983: 70) – the obstinate one.

41 T. J. Reed (1971: 178, n. 205) notes the suspicious crudity of such narrative attacks on Aschenbach, a point taken up by Dorrit Cohn, who reads, in the gulf between Mann's textual narrator and the more compassionate viewpoint articulated by the book as a whole, a deliberate authorial strategy (*passim*, esp. 187–91, on the "There he sat" speech).

42 Colin Graham, "A personal note for today" (1992), reprinted in the New York Metropolitan Opera *Playbill*, 18 February 1994.

43 The contrast here is with the scenes of debauch in the later two church parables, less convincing, so Robin Holloway argues, because their "sinfulness" is rendered only "with monkish distaste" (222) as a negative example, within the didactic framework of the parable genre.

44 Howe 249. The concept of personal identity, Ricoeur notes, is bound up with this doubling. To Hume's complaint:

> When I enter most intimately into what I call *myself*, I always stumble on some particular perception or other, of heat or cold, light or shade . . . I can never catch *myself* at any time without a perception, and can never observe anything but the perception.

Ricoeur notes that with the question Who perceives? "the self returns just when the same slips away" (1992: 128).

45 "Let the Gods do what they will with me" is also a vocal statement of the Vision theme associated earlier with Aschenbach's experience of a Platonic concept of the immeasurable, a vision that fades in Act 2; the argument is traced in detail by Hindley 1992b.

46 Piper recalls consulting Euripides's *Bacchae* text while writing her libretto (1989: 20). Direct traces of this source are found in Dionysus's words during Aschenbach's nightmare ("beat the drums," etc.), close in wording to Mann's version (67–68).

47 One index of this is contrapuntal: the pursuit-music of both Scene 9 (Ex. 6.16 above) and Scene 16 (Ex. 6. 19) moves by parallel motion. But while the former is minor-seventh driven, dyad verticals in the later scene are major sevenths. Another obvious contrast between the two passages is formal: the far broader dimensions of each transpositionally discrete passage in Scene 9 create thematic repetitions that sound almost hypnotic; the argument of Scene 16 is, by comparison, vastly telescoped.

48 I borrow the term from Cohn, who in her acute reading of Mann's scene, compares it to "the expression of that lethal knowledge the hero of Greek tragedy reaches when he stands on the verge of death" (191).

49   Musical allusion to Mahler's "Der Abschied" is echoed verbally in Britten and Piper's English title for the opera's next (and last) scene, "The Departure."

50   On the interplay of E, C and A tonics throughout the opera, see Roseberry 1987. On the pairing of C- and E-major tonalities in the Third Quartet as an intertextual link to the opera, see Rupprecht 1999.

Bibliography

Abbate, Carolyn. 1991. *Unsung Voices: opera and musical narrative in the nineteenth century.* Princeton: Princeton University Press.

1996. "Immortal voices, mortal forms." In Craig Ayrey and Mark Everist, eds., *Analytical Strategies and Musical Interpretation: essays on nineteenth- and twentieth-century music.* Cambridge: Cambridge University Press: 288–300.

Adorno, Theodor W. 1992. *Mahler: a musical physiognomy.* 1960; trans. Edmund Jephcott. Chicago: University of Chicago Press.

1994. "Bourgeois opera." Trans. David J. Levin, in Levin: 25–43.

Agawu, Kofi. 1999. "The challenge of semiotics." In Cook and Everist: 138–60.

Albright, Daniel. 2000. *Untwisting the Serpent: modernism in music, literature, and other arts.* Chicago: University of Chicago Press.

Althusser, Louis. 1994. "Ideology and ideological state apparatuses (notes towards an investigation)" [1970]. Repr. in Slavoj Žižek, ed., *Mapping Ideology.* London: Verso: 100–140.

Ashby, Arved. 1999. "Britten as symphonist." In Cooke 1999: 217–32.

Auden, W. H. 1950. *The Enchafèd Flood: Or the Romantic Iconography of the Sea.* New York: Random House.

1989. "Notes on music and opera." In *The Dyer's Hand*; 1962; repr. New York: Vintage: 465–74.

Auden, W. H., and Christopher Isherwood. 1938. *The Dog Beneath the Skin, or Where is Francis?* London: Faber.

Auerbach, Erich. 1953. *Mimesis: the representation of reality in Western literature.* 1946; trans. Willard R. Trask. Princeton: Princeton University Press.

Austin, J. L. 1975. *How to do Things with Words.* 1962. Ed. J. O. Urmson and Marina Sbisà. 2nd ed. Cambridge, Mass.: Harvard University Press.

Ayrey, Craig. 1994. "Debussy's significant connections: metaphor and metonymy in analytic method." In Anthony Pople, ed., *Theory, Analysis and Meaning in Music.* Cambridge: Cambridge University Press: 127–51.

Bakhtin, M. M. 1981. *The Dialogic Imagination: four essays.* Ed. Michael Holquist, trans. Caryl Emerson and Michael Holquist. Austin: University of Texas Press.

1986. "The problem of speech genres." In *Speech Genres and Other Late Essays*, trans. Michael Holquist and Caryl Emerson. Austin: University of Texas Press: 60–102.

Banks, Paul, ed. 1996. *The Making of "Peter Grimes": I: Facsimile of the composition sketch; II: Notes and Commentaries.* Woodbridge: The Britten Estate Ltd/The Boydell Press (vol. 2 repr. separately, 2000).

Barthes, Roland. 1973. *Elements of Semiology*. 1964. Trans. Annette Lavers and Colin Smith. New York: Hill and Wang.

Beidler, Peter G., ed. 1995. *Henry James: The Turn of the Screw*. New York and Boston: Bedford Books of St. Martin's Press.

Bell, Catherine. 1992. *Ritual Theory, Ritual Practice*. New York: Oxford University Press.

Benjamin, Walter. 1969. "What is epic theater?" (1939). In *Illuminations*. Trans. Harry Zohn, ed. Hannah Arendt. New York: Schocken Books: 147–54.

Bent, Ian, ed. 1994. *Music Analysis in the Nineteenth Century. II: Hermeneutic Approaches*. Cambridge: Cambridge University Press.

Benveniste, Émile. 1971. *Problems in General Linguistics*. Trans. Mary Meek. Coral Cables, Fla: Miami University Press.

Bernhard, Christoph. 1973. "The treatises of Christoph Bernhard." Trans. Walter Hilse. *The Music Forum* 3, ed. William J. Mitchell and Felix Salzer. New York: Columbia University Press: 1–196.

Blyth, Alan. 1981. *Remembering Britten*. London: Hutchinson.

Boyd, Malcolm. 1968. "Britten, Verdi, and the Requiem." *Tempo* 86: 2–6.

Boys, Henry. 1938. "The younger English composers: V. Benjamin Britten." *The Monthly Musical Record* 68 (October): 234–37.

Brandon, S. G. F. 1973. "Ritual in religion." *Dictionary of the History of Ideas*. 4 vols., ed. Philip Wiener. New York: Charles Scribner's Sons; 4: 99–105.

Brett, Philip, ed. 1983. *Peter Grimes*. Cambridge: Cambridge University Press.

Brett, Philip. 1984. "Salvation at sea: *Billy Budd*." 1978; rev. version in Palmer 1984: 133–43.

    1987. "Grimes and Lucretia." In Nigel Fortune, ed., *Music and Theatre: essays in honour of Winton Dean*. Cambridge: Cambridge University Press: 353–65.

    1992. "Britten's bad boys: male relations in *The Turn of the Screw*." *repercussions* 1: 5–25.

    1993. "Britten's dream." In Ruth A. Solie, ed., *Musicology and Difference: gender and sexuality in music scholarship*. Berkeley: University of California Press: 259–80.

    1994a. "Musicality, essentialism, and the closet." In Brett *et al.* 1994: 9–26.

    1994b. "Eros and orientalism in Britten's operas." In Brett *et al.* 1994: 235–56.

    1996. "'Peter Grimes': the growth of the libretto." In Banks 1996: 2: 53–78.

Brett, Philip, Elizabeth Wood and Gary C. Thomas, eds. 1994. *Queering the Pitch: the new gay and lesbian musicology*. New York: Routledge.

Britten, Benjamin. 1944. "Conversation with Benjamin Britten." *Tempo* 6 (February): 4–5.

    1955. Liner note to London CM 9146 recording, *Simple Symphony*, dir. Goossens.

    1961. "On writing English opera." *Opera* 12/1 (January): 7–8.

    1963. "Britten looking back." *The Sunday Telegraph* (17 November): 9.

    1964a. *On Receiving the First Aspen Award: a speech by Benjamin Britten*. London: Faber.

1964b. "*Curlew River.*" Note in the 1964 Aldeburgh Festival Programme Book.

1977. "Three letters to Anthony Gishford." *Tempo* 120 (March): 7–9.

1983. "Introduction." [1945]. In Crozier, ed., *Peter Grimes:* 7–8; repr. Brett 1983: 148–49.

1984. "Mapreading: Benjamin Britten in conversation with Donald Mitchell." In Palmer 1984a: 87–96.

Brown, Hilda Meldrum. 1991. *Leitmotiv and drama: Wagner, Brecht, and the limits of "Epic" theatre.* Oxford: Clarendon Press.

Buelow, George J. 1966. "The *Loci Topici* and affect in late Baroque music: Heinichen's practical demonstration." *The Music Review* 27: 161–76.

Burmeister, Joachim. 1993. *Musical Poetics.* [Rostock, 1606]. Trans. Benito V. Rivera. New Haven: Yale University Press.

Butler, Judith. 1993. *Bodies that Matter: on the discursive limits of "sex."* New York: Routledge.

1997a. *Excitable Speech: a politics of the performative.* New York: Routledge.

1997b. *The Psychic Life of Power: theories in subjection.* Stanford: Stanford University Press.

Carpenter, Humphrey. 1992. *Benjamin Britten: a biography.* London: Faber.

Carroll, David. 1982."The (dis)placement of the eye ('I'): point of view, voice, and the forms of fiction." *The Subject in Question: the languages of theory and the strategies of fiction.* Chicago: University of Chicago Press: 51–87.

Chaikin, Joseph. 1991. *The Presence of the Actor.* 1972. Repr. New York: Theatre Communications Group.

Chatman, Seymour. 1981. "What novels do that films can't (and vice versa)." In W. J. T. Mitchell 1981: 117–36.

Chua, Daniel K. L. 1999. *Absolute Music and the Construction of Meaning.* Cambridge: Cambridge University Press.

Clifford, James. 1988. "On *Orientalism.*" Repr. in Clifford, *The Predicament of Culture: twentieth-century ethnography, literature, and art.* Cambridge, Mass.: Harvard University Press: 255–76.

Cohn, Dorrit. 1994. "The second author of *Death in Venice.*" Repr. in Clayton Koelb, ed. Thomas Mann: *Death in Venice.* New York: Norton: 178–95.

Cone, Edward T. 1974. *The Composer's Voice.* Berkeley: University of California Press.

Conrad, Peter. 1977. *Romantic Opera and Literary Form.* Berkeley: University of California Press.

Cook, Nicholas. 1998. *Analysing Musical Multimedia.* Oxford: Clarendon Press.

Cook, Nicholas, and Mark Everist, eds. 1999. *Rethinking Music.* Oxford: Oxford University Press.

Cooke, Mervyn. 1987. "Britten and the gamelan: Balinese influences in 'Death in Venice.'" In D. Mitchell 1987: 115–28.

1996. *Benjamin Britten: War Requiem.* Cambridge: Cambridge University Press.

1998. *Britten and the Far East: Asian influences in the music of Benjamin Britten.* Woodbridge: The Boydell Press/Britten–Pears Library.

Cooke, Mervyn, ed. 1999. *The Cambridge Companion to Benjamin Britten.* Cambridge: Cambridge University Press.

Cooke, Mervyn, and Philip Reed. 1993. *Benjamin Britten: Billy Budd.* Cambridge: Cambridge University Press.

Copland, Aaron. 1963. "A visit to Snape." In Gishford: 71–73.

Crabbe, George. 1988. *The Borough,* "Letter XXII. The Poor of the Borough: Peter Grimes." In *The Complete Poetical Works.* 3 vols. Ed. Norma Dalrymple-Champneys and Arthur Pollard. Oxford: Clarendon Press, 1: 564–74.

Crozier, Eric, ed. 1946. *Benjamin Britten: Peter Grimes.* Sadler's Wells Opera Books No. 3. London: John Lane. (First published 1945).

Culler, Jonathan. 1981. *The Pursuit of Signs.* Ithaca: Cornell University Press.
1986. *Ferdinand de Saussure.* 1976; rev. ed. Ithaca: Cornell University Press.
1997. "Performative language." In *Literary Theory: a very short introduction.* New York: Oxford University Press: 95–109.

Dahlhaus, Carl. 1979. *Richard Wagner's Music Dramas.* 1971. Trans. Mary Whittall. Cambridge: Cambridge University Press.
1989. "What is a musical drama?" Trans. Mary Whittall. *Cambridge Opera Journal* 1: 95–111.
1998. "Music – or musics?" Trans. in Oliver Strunk, ed. *Source Readings in Music History,* rev. Leo Treitler, *7: The Twentieth Century,* ed. Robert P. Morgan. New York: Norton: 239–44.

de Lauretis, Teresa. 1998. "The stubborn drive." *Critical Inquiry* 24: 851–77.

Derrida, Jacques. 1978. "Freud and the scene of writing" [1966]. Trans. Alan Bass. In *Writing and Difference.* Chicago: University of Chicago Press: 196–231.
1982. "Signature event context" [1971]. In *Margins of Philosophy,* trans. Alan Bass. Chicago: University of Chicago Press: 307–30.
1988. "Limited Inc abc . . ." [1977]. Trans. Samuel Weber, repr. in Derrida, *Limited Inc.* Evanston, Ill.: Northwestern University Press: 29–110.

Ducrot, Oswald, and Tzvetan Todorov. 1979. *Encyclopedic Dictionary of the Sciences of Language.* Trans. Catherine Porter. Baltimore: Johns Hopkins University Press.

Duncan, Ronald. 1968. *How to make enemies.* London: Rupert Hart-Davis Ltd.
1981. *Working With Britten: a personal memoir.* Bidford: The Rebel Press.

Eagleton, Terry. 1991. *Ideology: an introduction.* London: Verso.

Emslie, Barry. 1992. "*Billy Budd* and the fear of words." *Cambridge Opera Journal* 4: 43–59.

Erikson, Erik H. 1963. *Childhood and Society.* 1950. 2nd ed. New York: Norton.

Euripides. 1968. *The Bacchae.* Trans. William Arrowsmith. In *Euripides V,* ed. D. Grene and Richard Lattimore. 1959. Repr. New York: Washington Square Press.

Evans, John. 1985a. "The Sketches: chronology and analysis." In Howard 1985: 63–71.
1985b. "On the recitatives in 'Death in Venice'." In Marion Thorpe, ed., *Peter*

Pears: a tribute on his 75th birthday. London: Faber Music/The Britten Estate: 31–33.

Evans, Peter. 1989. *The Music of Benjamin Britten*. 1979. Rev. ed. London: J. M. Dent and Sons.

Feldman, Martha. 1995. "Magic mirrors and the *seria* stage: thoughts toward a ritual view." *Journal of the American Musicological Society* 48: 423–84.

Felman, Shoshana. 1985. "Henry James: madness and the risks of practice (turning the screw of interpretation)" [1977]. Repr. in *Writing and Madness*. Ithaca: Cornell University Press: 141–247.

Forster, E. M. 1951. "Letter from E. M. Forster." *The Griffin* 1 (September): 4–6.

1955. *Aspects of the Novel*. 1927. San Diego and New York: Harcourt Brace Jovanovich.

1983. "George Crabbe and Peter Grimes" [1948]. Repr. in Brett 1983: 7–21.

Forte, Allen. 1973. *The Structure of Atonal Music*. New Haven: Yale University Press.

Freud, Sigmund. 1963a. "Instincts and their vicissitudes" [1915]. Trans. Cecil M. Baines in *General Psychological Theory: papers on metapsychology*, ed. Philip Rieff. New York: Collier Books: 83–103.

1963b. "The uncanny" [1919]. Trans. Alix Strachey. In *Studies in Parapsychology*, ed. Philip Rieff. New York: Collier Books: 19–60.

1965. *The Interpretation of Dreams*. Trans. James Strachey. New York: Avon Books.

1991. *Die Traumdeutung*. 1900. *Gesammelte Werke*, vols. 2–3, 1942. Repr. (afterword by Hermann Beland). Frankfurt: Fischer Taschenbuch Verlag.

Fuchs, Elinor. 1996. *The Death of Character: perspectives on theater after Modernism*. Bloomington: Indiana University Press.

Fux, Johann Joseph. 1992. "*Gradus ad Parnassum* (1725): concluding chapters." Trans. and introduced by Susan Wollenberg. *Music Analysis* 11: 209–43.

Garvie, Peter. 1983. "Plausible darkness: 'Peter Grimes' after a quarter of a century" (1972). Repr. in Brett 1983: 172–79.

Gebauer, Gunter, and Christoph Wulf. 1995. *Mimesis: culture – art – society*. Trans. Don Reneau. Berkeley: University of California Press.

Genette, Gérard. 1980. *Narrative Discourse: an essay in method*. 1972. Trans. Jane E. Lewin. Ithaca: Cornell University Press.

Georgiades, Thrasybulos. 1982. *Music and Language: the rise of Western music as exemplified in settings of the mass*. 2nd ed., 1974. Trans. Marie Louise Göllner. Cambridge: Cambridge University Press.

Gishford, Anthony, ed. 1963. *Tribute to Benjamin Britten on his Fiftieth Birthday*. London: Faber.

Glyndebourne Touring Opera. 1990. *Death in Venice*, directed by Stephen Lawless and Martha Clarke, conducted by Graeme Jenkins. Directed for video by Robin Lough. BBC TV/RM Arts.

Goddard, Scott. 1946. "Benjamin Britten. b. 1913." In A. L. Bacharach, ed., *British Music of Our Time*. Harmondsworth: Pelican: 209–18.

Goffman, Erving. 1986. *Frame Analysis: an essay on the organization of experience.* [1974]. Boston: Northeastern University Press.

Gomme, Alice B., and Cecil Sharp, eds. 1976. *Children's Singing Games.* London: Novello, 1909–12. Repr. New York: Arno Press.

Graham, Colin. 1983. "Production notes and remarks on the style of performing *Curlew River*." 1965. Repr. as an appendix to *Curlew River*, full score. Faber Music Limited: 141–60.

      1989. "Staging first productions 3." In Herbert 1989: 46–58.

      1994. "A personal note for today" (1992). Note reprinted in the New York Metropolitan Opera *Playbill*, 18 February 1994.

Grey, Thomas S. 1992. "A Wagnerian glossary." In Barry Millington, ed., *A Wagner Compendium.* New York: Schirmer: 230–43.

      1995. *Wagner's Musical Prose: texts and contexts.* Cambridge: Cambridge University Press.

      1996. "… *wie ein rother Faden:* on the origins of 'leitmotif' as critical construct and musical practice." In Ian Bent, ed. *Music Theory in the Age of Romanticism.* Cambridge: Cambridge University Press: 187–210.

Grotowski, Jerzy. 1968. *Towards a Poor Theatre.* New York: Simon and Schuster Inc.

Halliwell, Michael. 1999. "Narrative elements in opera." In Walter Bernhart *et al.*, eds. *Word and Music Studies 1: defining the field.* Amsterdam and Atlanta, Ga.: Editions Rodopi: 135–53.

Halliwell, Stephen. 1987. *The "Poetics" of Aristotle: translation and commentary.* Chapel Hill: University of North Carolina Press.

Hardison, O. B., Jr. 1965. "The Mass as sacred drama." In *Christian Rite and Christian Drama in the Middle Ages.* Baltimore: The Johns Hopkins Press: 35–79.

Harewood, [George,] Earl of. 1981. "Benjamin Britten, 1943–76." In *The Tongs and the Bones: The Memoirs of Lord Harewood.* London: Weidenfeld and Nicolson: 129–49.

Harris, Roy. 1987. *Reading Saussure: a critical commentary on the "Cours de linguistique générale."* La Salle, Ill.: Open Court.

Harris, Roy, and Talbot J. Taylor. 1997. *Landmarks in Linguistic Thought I: the Western tradition from Socrates to Saussure.* 2nd ed., New York: Routledge.

Harris, Zellig S. 1960. *Structural Linguistics* [1951]. Repr. Chicago: University of Chicago Press.

Harvey, Jonathan. 1984. "Reflection after composition." *Contemporary Music Review* 1: 83–86.

Hatten, Robert S. 1994. *Musical Meaning in Beethoven: markedness, correlation, and interpretation.* Bloomington: Indiana University Press.

Hawkes, Terence. 1977. *Structuralism and Semiotics.* Berkeley: University of California Press.

Headington, Christopher. 1981. *Britten.* London: Eyre Methuen.

Heidegger, Martin. 1968. *What is called Thinking?* Trans. J. Glenn Gray. New York: Harper and Row.

Henze, Hans Werner. 1982. *Music and Politics: collected writings 1953–81*. Trans. Peter Labanyi. London: Faber and Faber.

1998. *Bohemian Fifths: an autobiography*. Trans. Stewart Spencer. London: Faber.

Herbert, David, ed. 1989. *The Operas of Benjamin Britten*. 1979. Repr. New York: New Amsterdam Books.

Herbert, James D. 1999. "Bad faith at Coventry: Spence's Cathedral and Britten's *War Requiem*." *Critical Inquiry* 25: 535–65.

Hesse, Prince Ludwig of. 1963. "*Ausflug Ost 1956* (excerpts from a travel diary)." In Gishford: 56–65.

Hindley, Clifford. 1990. "Why does Miles die? A study of Britten's *The Turn of the Screw*." *Musical Quarterly* 74: 1–17.

1992a. "Homosexual self-affirmation and self-oppression in two Britten operas." *Musical Quarterly* 76: 143–68.

1992b. "Platonic elements in Britten's *Death in Venice*." *Music and Letters* 73: 407–29.

1994. "Britten's *Billy Budd*: the 'interview chords' again." *Musical Quarterly* 78: 99–126.

1995. "Britten's Parable Art: a gay reading." *History Workshop Journal* 40: 64–90.

Holloway, Robin. 1984. "The church parables (ii): limits and renewals." In Palmer 1984a: 215–26.

Holst, Imogen. 1962. *Tune*. London: Faber.

1972. "Britten and the young." In Mitchell–Keller: 276–86.

1980. *Britten*. [1966]. 3rd ed. London: Faber and Faber.

Howard, Patricia. 1969. *The Operas of Benjamin Britten: an introduction*. New York: Frederick A. Praeger.

Howard, Patricia, ed. 1985. *Benjamin Britten: The Turn of the Screw*. Cambridge: Cambridge University Press.

Howe, Irving. 1992. "The self in literature." In George Levine, ed., *Constructions of the Self*. New Brunswick: Rutgers University Press: 249–67.

Hyer, Brian. 1994. "'Sighing branches': prosopopoeia in Rameau's *Pygmalion*." *Music Analysis* 13: 1–50.

Jakobson, Roman. 1960. "Closing statement: linguistics and poetics." In Thomas A. Sebeok, ed., *Style and Language*. Cambridge, Mass.: MIT Press: 350–77.

James, Henry. 1908. *The Turn of the Screw*. New York: Charles Scribner's Sons. New York Edition, vol. 12: 147–309.

1985. *What Maisie Knew* [1897]. Repr. Harmondsworth: Penguin Books.

Japanese Classics Translation Committee. 1955. "*Sumidagawa: The Sumida River*." In *Japanese Noh Drama*. Tokyo: Nippon Gakujutsu Shinkokai; Rutland, Vermont: Charles E. Tuttle: 145–59.

Johnson, Barbara. 1979. "Melville's fist: the execution of *Billy Budd*." *Studies in Romanticism* 18: 567–99.

Jones, Vivien. 1985. "Henry James's 'The Turn of the Screw.'" In Howard 1985: 1–22.

Jungmann, Joseph A. 1951, 1955. *The Mass of the Roman Rite: its origins and development (Missarum Sollemnia)*. 1949. Trans. Francis A. Brunner. 2 vols. New York: Benziger Brothers.

Kaminsky, Peter. 1996. "How to do things with words and music: towards an analysis of selected ensembles in Mozart's *Don Giovanni*." *Theory and Practice* 21: 55–78.

Keller, Hans. 1981. "Britten: thematic relations and the 'mad' interlude's 5th motive." *Music Survey* 4 (October 1951): 332–34. Repr. in ed. Donald Mitchell and Keller, *Music Survey, New Series: 1949–1952*. London: Faber.

1983. "'Peter Grimes': the story, the music not excluded" [1952]. Repr. in Brett 1983: 105–20.

1995. *Three Psychoanalytic Notes on "Peter Grimes"* [1946]. Ed. Christopher Wintle. Aldeburgh, Suffolk: Britten–Pears Library / King's College London: Institute of Advanced Musical Studies.

Kennedy, Michael. 1981. *Britten*. London: Dent.

Kerman, Joseph. 1966. *The Beethoven Quartets*. New York: Norton.

1968. "Verdi's use of recurring themes." In Harold Powers, ed., *Studies in Music History: essays for Oliver Strunk*. Princeton: Princeton University Press: 495–510.

1988. *Opera as Drama* [1956]. Rev. ed. Berkeley: University of California Press.

1999. *Concerto Conversations*. Cambridge, Mass.: Harvard University Press.

Kermode, Frank. 1967. *The Sense of an Ending: studies in the theory of fiction*. London: Oxford University Press.

Kerr, Douglas. 1993. *Wilfred Owen's Voices: language and community*. Oxford: Clarendon Press.

Kimbrough, Robert, ed. 1966. *Henry James: The Turn of the Screw*. Norton Critical Edition. New York: W. W. Norton.

Kincaid, James R. 1992. *Child-Loving: the erotic child and Victorian culture*. New York: Routledge.

Kivy, Peter. 1991. "Opera talk: a philosophical 'phantasie.'" *Cambridge Opera Journal* 3: 63–77.

Korsyn, Kevin. 1999. "Beyond privileged contexts: intertextuality, influence, and dialogue." In Cook and Everist: 55–72.

Kramer, Lawrence. 1995. "Musical narratology: a theoretical outline." *Classical music and postmodern knowledge*. Berkeley: University of California Press: 98–121.

1992. Review of Abbate 1991. *Nineteenth-Century Music* 15: 235–39.

Langer, Suzanne K. 1957. *Philosophy in a New Key: a study in the symbolism of reason, rite, and art*. 1942; 3rd ed. Cambridge, Mass.: Harvard University Press.

Leach, Marie, ed. 1972. *Standard Dictionary of Folklore, Mythology and Legend.* 2 vols. New York: Funk and Wagnall (first published 1950).

Levin, David J., ed. 1994. *Opera Through Other Eyes.* Stanford: Stanford University Press.

Lewin, David. 1982. "*Auf dem Flusse:* image and background in a Schubert song." *Nineteenth-Century Music* 6: 47–59.

1987. *Generalized Musical Intervals and Transformations.* New Haven: Yale University Press.

Lindenberger, Herbert. 1984. *Opera: the extravagant art.* Ithaca: Cornell University Press.

London, Justin. 1996. "Musical and linguistic speech acts." *Journal of Aesthetics and Art Criticism* 54: 49–64.

Lustig, T. J. 1992. "Introduction" to Henry James, *The Turn of the Screw and Other Stories.* Oxford: Oxford University Press: vii–xxxiii.

Lyons, John. 1968. *Introduction to Theoretical Linguistics.* Cambridge: Cambridge University Press.

Maclean, Marie. 1988. *Narrative as Performance: the Baudelairean experiment.* London: Routledge.

Malm, William P. 1986. "The Noh play *Sumidagawa* and Benjamin Britten's *Curlew River:* one story in two musical worlds." *Six Hidden Views of Japanese Music.* Berkeley: University of California Press: 151–97.

Mann, Thomas. 1954. *Death in Venice and Seven Other Stories.* Trans. H. T. Lowe-Porter [1930]. New York: Vintage Books.

1958. "Freud and the future" [1936]. Trans. in *Essays.* New York: Vintage Books: 303–24.

1983. *Der Tod in Venedig. Neuen Rundschau* (1912). Reprinted in T. J. Reed 1983: 7–82.

Mark, Christopher. 1994. "Britten and the circle of fifths." *Journal of the Royal Musical Association* 119: 268–97.

1995. *Early Benjamin Britten: a study of stylistic and technical evolution.* New York and London: Garland.

Martin, Wallace. 1986. *Recent Theories of Narrative.* Ithaca: Cornell University Press.

Mason, Colin. 1985. Review of *The Turn of the Screw. The Guardian* (Manchester, 15 September 1954): 5. Partial reprint in Howard 1985: 133–34, 136.

Mason, Michael. 1994. *The Making of Victorian Sexual Attitudes.* Oxford: Oxford University Press.

Masson, Jeffrey Moussaieff. 1992. *The Assault on Truth: Freud's suppression of the seduction theory.* New York: HarperCollins.

Mattheson, Johann. 1981. *Johann Mattheson's "Der vollkommene Kapellmeister": a revised translation with critical commentary.* Trans. Ernest C. Harriss. Ann Arbor, Mich.: UMI Research Press.

Matthews, David. 1983. "Act II, Scene 1: an examination of the music." In Brett 1983: 121–47.

Mellers, Wilfrid. 1984a. "Through *Noye's Fludde*." 1968. Repr. in Palmer 1984a: 153–60.

—— 1984b. "Turning the Screw." In Palmer 1984a: 144–52.

Melville, Herman. 1946. *Billy Budd, Foretopman.* Ed. with intro. by William Plomer. London: John Lehmann.

—— 1962. *Billy Budd, Sailor (An Inside Narrative).* Ed. Harrison Hayford and Merton M. Sealts, Jr. Chicago: University of Chicago Press, 1962.

Miller, James E. 1972. *Theory of Fiction: Henry James.* Lincoln, Nebr.: University of Nebraska Press.

Milner, Anthony. 1984. "The choral music." In Palmer 1984a: 329–45.

Mitchell, Donald. 1955. Liner note to London XLL 1207/8, recording of *The Turn of the Screw*, cond. Britten.

—— 1963. "Britten's revisionary practice: practical and creative." *Tempo* 66–67: 15–22.

—— 1981. *Britten and Auden in the Thirties: the year 1936.* London: Faber, 1981.

—— 1983. "Montagu Slater (1902–56): who was he?" In Brett 1983: 22–46.

—— 1984. "What do we know about Britten now?" In Palmer 1984a: 21–45.

—— 1993. "A *Billy Budd* notebook (1979–1991)." In Cooke and Reed: 111–34.

—— 1994. "The screw keeps on turning." Liner note to Collins Classics 70302, recording of *The Turn of the Screw*, dir. Bedford.

—— 1996. "'Peter Grimes': fifty years on." In Banks 2: 125–65.

—— 1999. "Violent climates." In Cooke 1999: 188–216.

Mitchell, Donald, ed. 1987. *Benjamin Britten: Death in Venice.* Cambridge: Cambridge University Press.

Mitchell, Donald, and Hans Keller, eds. 1972. *Benjamin Britten: a commentary on his works from a group of specialists.* 1952. Repr. Westport, Conn.: Greenwood Press.

Mitchell, Donald, and Philip Reed, eds. 1991. *Letters from a Life: the selected letters and diaries of Benjamin Britten.* Vol. 1: 1923–1939; Vol. 2: 1939–1945. London: Faber.

Mitchell, Donald, and Philip Reed. 1998. "Four acts and two acts: architecture and irony." Booklet with the recording of the 1951 *Billy Budd*, dir. Nagano, pp. 11–16. Erato 3984–21631–2.

Mitchell, W. J. T., ed. 1981. *On Narrative.* Chicago: University of Chicago Press.

Moreno, Jairo. 1999. "Body 'n' Soul?: voice and movement in Keith Jarrett's pianism." *Musical Quarterly* 83: 75–92.

Morgan, Robert P. 1998. "Symmetrical form and common-practice tonality." *Music Theory Spectrum* 20: 1–47.

Nattiez, Jean-Jacques. 1990. *Music and Discourse: toward a semiology of music.* Trans. Carolyn Abbate. Princeton: Princeton University Press.

Nietzsche, Friedrich 1967. *The Birth of Tragedy and The Case of Wagner.* Trans. Walter Kaufmann. New York: Vintage Books.

—— 1968. *The Will to Power.* Trans. Walter Kaufmann and R. J. Hollingdale, ed. Kaufmann. New York: Vintage Books.

Oxford English Dictionary. 1971. Oxford: Oxford University Press.

Palmer, Christopher, ed. 1984a. *The Britten Companion*. London: Faber.

  1984b. "The ceremony of innocence." In Palmer 1984a: 68–83.

  1985. "The colour of the music." In Howard 1985: 101–25.

  1987. "Britten's Venice orchestra." In D. Mitchell 1987: 129–53.

Pears, Peter. 1972. "The vocal music." In Mitchell and Keller: 59–73.

Peirce, Charles Sanders. 1932. *Collected Papers*, Vol. 2 (Elements of Logic), ed. Charles Hartshorne and Paul Weiss. Cambridge, Mass.: Harvard University Press.

Pfister, Manfred. 1988. *The Theory and Analysis of Drama* [1977]. Trans. John Halliday. Cambridge: Cambridge University Press.

Piper, Myfawny. 1989. "Writing for Britten." In Herbert 1989: 8–21.

  1994. "Creating words for Aschenbach" [1992]. Repr. in New York Metropolitan Opera *Stagebill* (18 February), n. p.

Plato. 1993. *Symposium and Phaedrus*. Trans. Benjamin Jowett. New York: Dover Publications.

Plomer, William. 1989. "Foreword" to *The Burning Fiery Furnace*. In Herbert 1989: 297.

Poizat, Michel. 1992. *The Angel's Cry*. Trans. A. Denner. Ithaca: Cornell University Press.

Pollard, Alfred W. 1927. *English Miracle Plays, Moralities and Interludes: specimens of the Pre-Elizabethan Drama*. Oxford: Clarendon Press, 1890. 8th ed., revised.

Potter, Charles Francis. 1972. "Counting-out rimes." In Leach: 1: 255.

Poulton, Diana. 1972. *John Dowland*. London: Faber.

Prince, Gerald. 1987. *A Dictionary of Narratology*. Lincoln, Nebr.: University of Nebraska Press.

Propp, Vladimir. 1968. *Morphology of the Folktale*. Trans. Laurence Scott. 2nd ed. Austin: University of Texas Press.

Psomiades, Kathy Alexis. 1997. *Beauty's Body: femininity and representation in British aestheticism*. Stanford: Stanford University Press.

Rabinowitz, Peter. 1995. "Speech act theory and literary studies." In Raman Selden, ed. *Cambridge History of Literary Criticism, Vol. 8: From formalism to post-structuralism*. Cambridge: Cambridge University Press: 347–74.

Rank, Otto. 1993. "Narcissism and the double." Repr. in Emanuel Berman, ed., *Essential Papers on Literature and Psychoanalysis*. New York: New York University Press: 122–38.

Rappaport, Roy A. 1979. "The obvious aspects of ritual" [1974]. Rev. in *Ecology, Meaning, and Religion*. Richmond: North Atlantic Books: 173–221.

Reed, Philip. 1993a. "From first thoughts to first night: a *Billy Budd* chronology." In Cooke and Reed: 42–73

  1993b. "The 1960 revisions: a two-act *Billy Budd*." In Cooke and Reed: 74–84.

  1996a. "Finding the right notes." In Banks: 2: 79–115.

  1996b. "The *War Requiem* in progress." In Cooke 1996: 20–48.

  1999. "Britten in the cinema: *Coal Face*." In Cooke 1999: 54–77.

Reed, Philip, ed. 1995a. *On Mahler and Britten: essays in honour of Donald Mitchell on his seventieth birthday*. Woodbridge, Suffolk: The Boydell Press/The Britten–Pears Library.

　1995b. *The Travel Diaries of Peter Pears, 1936–1978*. Woodbridge: The Boydell Press.

Reed, T. J. 1974. "The Art of Ambivalence." In Reed, *Thomas Mann: the uses of tradition*. Oxford: Clarendon Press: 144–78.

Reed, T. J., ed. 1971. *Thomas Mann: Der Tod in Venedig*. London: Oxford University Press.

　1983. *Thomas Mann: Der Tod in Venedig: Text, Materialien, Kommentar mit den bisher unveröffentlichten Arbeitsnotizen Thomas Manns*. München: Carl Hanser Verlag.

"Rehearsing *War Requiem*." 1999. 1963 recording by John Culshaw, issued with Decca /London CD 414 383–2.

Rehm, Rush. 1992. "The Greek chorus." *Greek Tragic Theatre*. New York: Routledge: 51–61.

Renner, Stanley. 1995. "'Red hair, very red, close curling': sexual hysteria, physiognomical bogeymen, and the 'ghost' in *The Turn of the Screw*." In Beidler: 223–41.

Ricoeur, Paul. 1984, 1985. *Time and Narrative*. Vols. 1–2. Trans. Kathleen McLaughlin and David Pellauer. Chicago: University of Chicago Press.

　1992. *Oneself as Another*. Trans. Kathleen Blamey. Chicago: University of Chicago Press.

Riemann, Hugo. 1921. *Handbuch der Harmonielehre*. 1880. 8th and 9th ed. Leipzig: Breitkopf und Härtel.

Rimmon-Kenan, Shlomith. 1990. *Narrative Fiction: contemporary poetics*. London: Routledge.

Robbins, Bruce. 1995. " 'They don't much count, do they?': the unfinished history of *The Turn of the Screw*." In Beidler: 283–96.

Robertson, Alec. 1962. "Britten's *War Requiem*." *Musical Times* 103 (May): 308–10.

　1968. *Requiem: music of mourning and consolation*. New York: Frederick A. Praeger.

Roseberry, Eric. 1987. "Tonal ambiguity in *Death in Venice*: a symphonic view." In D. Mitchell 1987: 86–98.

　1995. "'Abraham and Isaac' revisited: reflections on a theme and its inversion." In P. Reed 1995a: 253–66.

Rosen, David. 1992. "Cone's and Kivy's 'world of opera.'" *Cambridge Opera Journal* 4: 61–74.

Rowe, John Carlos. 1984. "Psychoanalytic significances: the use and abuse of uncertainty in *The Turn of the Screw*." *The Theoretical Dimensions of Henry James*. Madison, Wisc.: University of Wisconsin Press: 119–46.

Rupprecht, Philip. 1996. "Tonal stratification and uncertainty in Britten's music." *Journal of Music Theory* 40: 311–46.

1999. "The chamber music." In Cooke 1999: 245–59.

Sackville-West, Edward. 1944. "Music: some aspects of the contemporary problem." *Horizon* 54 (June): 382–92; 55 (July): 68–73; 56 (August): 114–27.

1946. "The musical and dramatic structure." In Crozier: 27–55.

Sapir, Edward. 1949. *Language: an introduction to the study of speech.* 1921. New York: Harcourt, Brace and World.

Saussure, Ferdinand de. 1986. *Course in General Linguistics.* Trans. Roy Harris. La Salle, Ill.: Open Court.

Schafer, Murray. 1963. "X. Benjamin Britten." *British Composers in Interview.* London: Faber: 113–24.

Schoenberg, Arnold. 1975. "Composition with twelve tones (1)." In *Style and Idea,* ed. Leonard Stein, trans. Leo Black. London: Faber: 214–45.

Searle, John R. 1969. *Speech Acts: an essay in the philosophy of language.* Cambridge: Cambridge University Press.

1977. "Reiterating the differences: a reply to Derrida." *Glyph* 1: 198–208.

1979. "A taxonomy of illocutionary acts" [1975]. Repr. in Searle, *Expression and Meaning: studies in the theory of speech acts.* Cambridge: Cambridge University Press: 1–29.

Sedgwick, Eve Kosofsky. 1990. *Epistemology of the Closet.* Berkeley: University of California Press.

Slater, Montagu. 1946a. *Peter Grimes and other Poems.* London: John Lane/The Bodley Head.

1946b. "The story of the opera." In Crozier: 15–26.

Sommerville, C. John. 1982. "The high and low point in the history of childhood." *The Rise and Fall of Childhood.* Beverly Hills: Sage Publications: 160–78.

Spence, Basil. 1964. *Phoenix at Coventry: the building of a cathedral.* London: Fontana Books.

Stäblein, Bruno. 1963. "Zum Verständnis des 'klassischen' Tropus." *Acta Musicologica* 35: 84–95.

Stacey, Peter F. 1989. "Towards the analysis of the relationship of music and text in contemporary composition." In *Music and Text,* ed. Paul Driver and Rupert Christiansen. *Contemporary Music Review* 5: 9–27.

Steedman, Carolyn. 1995. *Strange Dislocations: childhood and the idea of human interiority, 1780–1930.* Cambridge, Mass.: Harvard University Press.

Stein, Erwin. 1953a. "Opera and Peter Grimes." *Tempo* 12 [September 1945: old series]. Repr. in Stein 1953c: 110–117.

1953b. "Britten seen against his English background." In Stein 1953c: 149–63.

1953c. *Orpheus in New Guises.* London: Rockliff.

1955. "*The Turn of the Screw* and its musical idiom." *Tempo* 34: 6–14.

1972. "*Billy Budd*" [1952]. In Mitchell and Keller: 198–210.

Strader, Nikola D. 1996. "The stylistic placement of *War Requiem* in Benjamin Britten's oeuvre." Ph.D. diss., Ohio State University.

Straus, Joseph N. 1990. *Remaking the Past: musical modernism and the influence of the tonal tradition.* Cambridge, Mass.: Harvard University Press.

Street, Alan. 1994. "The obbligato recitative: narrative and Schoenberg's Five Orchestral Pieces, Op. 16." In Anthony Pople, ed., *Theory, Analysis and Meaning in Music.* Cambridge: Cambridge University Press: 164–83.

Strode, Rosamunde. 1987. "A *Death in Venice* chronicle." In D. Mitchell 1987: 26–44.

Swain, Joseph P. 1997. *Musical Languages.* New York: Norton.

Szondi, Peter. 1987. *Theory of the Modern Drama* [1956]. Trans. M. Hays. Minneapolis: University of Minnesota Press.

Tambiah, Stanley. 1985a. "The magical power of words" [1968]. Repr. in Tambiah 1985c: 17–59.

1985b. "A performative approach to ritual" [1979]. Repr. in Tambiah 1985c: 123–66.

1985c. *Culture, Thought, and Social Action: An anthropological perspective.* Cambridge, Mass., and London: Harvard University Press.

Taruskin, Richard. 1992. Review of Abbate 1991. *Cambridge Opera Journal* 4: 187–97.

Todorov, Tzvetan. 1977. "The secret of narrative" [1969]. In *The Poetics of Prose.* Trans. Richard Howard. Ithaca: Cornell University Press: 143–78.

1982. *Theories of the Symbol.* Trans. C. Porter. Ithaca: Cornell University Press.

1984. *Mikhail Bakhtin: the dialogical principle.* Trans. Wlad Godzich. Minneapolis: University of Minnesota Press.

Tomlinson, Gary. 1999. *Metaphysical Song: an essay on opera.* Princeton: Princeton University Press.

Travis, Roy. 1987. "The recurrent figure in the Britten/Piper opera *Death in Venice.*" In *The Music Forum* 6/1. Ed. Felix Salzer and Carl Schachter. New York: Columbia University Press: 129–246.

Turner, Victor. 1982. *From Ritual to Theatre: the human seriousness of play.* New York: PAJ Publications.

Vanderveken, Daniel. 1990, 1991. *Meaning and Speech Acts.* 2 vols. Cambridge: Cambridge University Press.

Vološinov, V. N. 1986. *Marxism and the Philosophy of Language.* 1929. Trans. Ladislav Matejka and I. R. Titunik. Cambridge, Mass.: Harvard University Press.

Wagner, Richard. 1888. *Gesammelte Schriften und Dichtungen.* 10 vols. Leipzig: E. W. Fritzsch.

1995a. *Opera and Drama.* [1888, vols. 3–4]. Trans. William Ashton Ellis, 1900. Repr. Lincoln, Nebr.: University of Nebraska Press.

1995b. "Zukunftsmusik." [1888, vol. 7: 87–137]. Trans. William Ashton Ellis, 1900. Repr. in *Judaism in Music and Other Essays.* Lincoln, Nebr.: University of Nebraska Press: 293–345.

Waley, Arthur. 1957. *The Nō Plays of Japan.* New York: Grove Press.

Walther, J. G. 1953. *Musikalisches Lexicon oder musikalische Bibliothek.* 1732. Facsimile repr., ed. Richard Schaal. Kassel: Bärenreiter.

White, Eric Walter. 1948. *Benjamin Britten: a sketch of his life and works*. London: Boosey and Hawkes.

Whitesell, Lloyd M. 2000. Review of Cooke 1999. *Music and Letters* 81: 473–76.

Whittall, Arnold. 1963. "Tonal instability in Britten's *War Requiem*." *Music Review* 24: 201–04.

1980. "The study of Britten: triadic harmony and tonal structure." *Proceedings of the Royal Musical Association* 106: 27–41.

1990a. *The Music of Britten and Tippett: studies in themes and techniques*. 1982. Rev. edition. Cambridge: Cambridge University Press.

1990b. "'Twisted relations': method and meaning in Britten's *Billy Budd*." *Cambridge Opera Journal* 2: 145–71.

1995. "Along the knife-edge: the topic of transcendence in Britten's musical aesthetic." In P. Reed 1995a: 290–98.

Wilson, Edmund. 1960. "The ambiguity of Henry James" [1934]. Reprinted with revisions in Gerald Willen, ed., *A Casebook on Henry James's "The Turn of the Screw."* New York: Thomas Y. Crowell: 115–53.

Wishart, Trevor. 1996. *On Sonic Art*. 1985. New and rev. edition, ed. Simon Emmerson. Amsterdam: Harwood Academic Publishers.

Wittgenstein, Ludwig. 1963. *Philosophical Investigations*. Trans. G. E. M. Anscombe. Oxford: Blackwell.

Yonge, Charlotte M. 1996. *The Trial* [1862–4]. Gloucester: Alan Sutton.

Young, Karl. 1933. *The Drama of the Medieval Church*. 2 vols. Oxford: Clarendon Press.

Žižek, Slavoj. 1994. "'The wound is healed only by the sword that smote you': the operatic subject and its vicissitudes." In Levin: 177–214.

Index

352